Shavin

Shaving the Beasts

WILD HORSES AND RITUAL IN SPAIN

John Hartigan Jr.

University of Minnesota Press

Minneapolis

London

The University of Minnesota Press gratefully acknowledges the financial assistance provided for the publication of this book by the University of Texas at Austin.

All photographs are by the author.

Published by the University of Minnesota Press
111 Third Avenue South, Suite 290
Minneapolis, MN 55401-2520
http://www.upress.umn.edu

Printed in the United States of America on acid-free paper

The University of Minnesota is an equal-opportunity educator and employer.

27 26 25 24 23 22 21 20   10 9 8 7 6 5 4 3 2 1

Library of Congress Cataloging-in-Publication Data
Names: Hartigan, John, Jr., author.
Title: Shaving the beasts : wild horses and ritual in Spain / John Hartigan Jr.
Description: Minneapolis : University of Minnesota Press, 2020. | Includes bibliographical references and index.
Identifiers: LCCN 2020023677 (print) | ISBN 978-1-5179-0473-9 (hc) | ISBN 978-1-5179-0474-6 (pb)
Subjects: LCSH: Wild horses—Spain—Galicia (Region) | Wild horses—Control—Social aspects—Spain—Galicia (Region) | Galicia (Spain : Region)—Social life and customs.
Classification: LCC SF360.3.S7 H37 2020 (print) | DDC 636.1/30946—dc23
LC record available at https://lccn.loc.gov/2020023677

TO MY BROTHERS
Zay and Geo
who know horses.

Contents

Introduction

HORSE SOCIALITY

Roughly eleven thousand horses roam the mountainous terrain of Galicia, Spain, in the northwest corner of the Iberian Peninsula. They have inhabited these slopes for millennia and are one of the largest free-ranging populations in the world. Every summer in more than a dozen rural localities, many of these horses are rounded up in a ritual called *rapa das bestas,* or "shaving the beasts." The earliest historical accounts of this ritual date to the 1500s, but archeologists argue that this tradition extends from the Neolithic era, based on petroglyphs featuring horses being driven into small rock enclosures.[1] That is the heart of the *rapa*: wild horses, roaming communal lands in the mountains, are herded together and driven into *curros*—structures similar to rodeo corrals—where their manes and tails are systematically shaved. Their hair, which in the past had many folk uses, falls worthlessly to the ground.

Though they belong to *Equus ferus,* these animals are called *bestas* (beasts) or *burras* (asses), reflecting a widely held view that they are a degenerate mountain breed. They are intensely disparaged and not considered "real" horses in comparison with the glorified Andalusians and other Spanish breeds. Smaller in stature than most of their conspecifics, this population features a distinctive body type: they have relatively large bellies and short legs, some feature a distinctive gait, and a few sport a thick "mustache," which is probably an adaptation to the thorny gorse they feed on extensively.[2] These physical characteristics indicate that this population was certainly passed over by modern breeding regimes, starting with royal projects in the 1400s.[3] That is, rather than a degenerate strain, these are possibly a refuge population that survived when the last Ice Age decimated European horses. That would make them *Equus ferus atlanticus,* a distinct subspecies from *Equus ferus caballus,* the domesticated horse.[4]

FIGURE I.I. *On the Montes de Montouto range, above Sabucedo, Galicia, Spain. The peak on the right is O Peón.*

Their status as "wild" is complicated.[5] They survive in the mountains by forage alone and are subject to intense predation by wolves. Their interactions with humans are limited to *besteiros,* who organize and conduct the *rapa das bestas.* The label *besteiro* identifies them as "beast keepers," and some of the stigma attached to the horses adheres also to the humans who associate with them. Ownership of these animals—established through branding foals caught during the *rapas*—allows a person to claim subsequent offspring, which in turn might be sold. But there is little profit to be generated from such sales, and they often do not match recent costs imposed by the government for microchipping, registering, and insuring the horses. Many *besteiros*—mostly old men (60s and 70s), often with limited financial means—increasingly see ownership as an imperiled practice. For some, this precarious status makes preserving the tradition all the more important. Their efforts, though, are frequently pitted against wealthier villagers who see cattle as a more lucrative option and would like to have the horses removed entirely from communal parish lands. The Galician government, Xunta de Galicia, considers them a nuisance (due to rising insurance costs from car wrecks) and seems intent on regulating them out of existence.[6] The government's interests may be fueled by the increasing global notoriety of the *rapa das bestas,* but more on that in a moment.

The basic technique by which these animals are herded is centuries old.[7] People on foot and on horseback fan out in long lines that snake through woods, meadows, and tangled underbrush along mountainsides. With sticks in hand—sometimes well-worn and familiar canes, other times found and fashioned on the spot on the day of the event— they move forward, shouting and banging noise makers to roust the horses and drive them toward a catchment area. Historically, a similar technique was directed at wolves, who were then slaughtered at the culmination of the process. Deeper in time, this method is likely the means by which horses were first captured and domesticated.[8] I was incredulous, initially, that slow-footed humans could catch horses this way. But they scare easily as the raucous line moves through the brush, and horses are loath to try to break through the cordon that forms around them as lines converge, close, and then encircle clusters of the creatures. Partly this is from fear of the swinging sticks and noise, but it is also a reflection of their social instinct to band together—individuals typically do not break through on their own.

The encircled horses are then driven toward a large fenced pasture where they are penned and given time to settle down. It is a period of confusion for the horses: bands have fragmented and they may struggle to reassemble and, most poignantly, mares and foals, separated in the ordeal, desperately search for each other. Frantic whinnies and plaintive cries rend the air as horses churn about and people course through the herd. Mostly these are *besteiros* looking to identify and claim new foals. They push horses aside to get at the targeted beasts, causing a cascade effect as displaced horses crash into others, generating altercations. Though they try to avoid such contact, transgressions of social space are often unavoidable, inviting bites and kicks from annoyed conspecifics. Spectators who show up to see these equines also move freely among them. This is an attraction for people who come out for the day to watch the *rapa* unfold. The *curros* are frequently ringed with pop-up kitchens housed in huge tents boasting long tables and folding chairs, where families and groups of friends, such as riding clubs, feed on large plates of freshly cooked octopus or grilled pork ribs and chicken. These kitchens also feature well-stocked bars, fueling a festive atmosphere for the humans.

After lunch, the hard work of the *rapa* begins—shearing the horses. This starts by moving them into the *curro,* a much smaller, tightly confined space. These are traditionally stonewalled structures but some *rapas* now sport metal-fenced corrals. In any case, the next step is to extract the foals from among the adults. This process may take twenty minutes or longer, depending on the size of the herd. The larger *rapas* capture up to seven hundred horses, but most work with around two hundred or so. The earlier trauma of separation from the foals during the initial herding is revisited, only this time in far more frenzied fashion because the adult horses are compressed together now; this makes the humans relatively safe from rearing animals, while profoundly disturbing the horses' keen sense of social space and distance. Aggressions flow freely, at least initially, as kicks and bites swirl about. After the foals are removed, the shaving begins.

For the shearing—the source of the ritual's notoriety—techniques vary widely.[9] In the south of Galicia, near the border with Portugal, the practice is to remove horses one by one from the *curro* using a rope *cabestro* that dangles from a hook at the end of a long pole called a *vara.* The rope is knotted to form two loops—one slips over the horse's ears and the other closes on its mouth, making a halter. Then one person runs the horse out to the open pasture, where it is sheared and sprayed with an antiparasite treatment. At the end of this process, the horses are simply released singly to return to the range. Many bolt immediately from the grounds, heading up to the high country. Some mares may linger, hoping their foals will be released. For those with male offspring, that hope generally goes unfulfilled, since they are culled and sold for meat. This culling is more a matter of population control, to limit the size of herds, than a source of revenue. In the north and central areas of Galicia, in contrast, horses are mounted bareback and then shaved. The *rapa* near Viveiro, on the northern coast, features riders who jump onto the animals from the corral railings; they then take large metal hand-shears and methodically clip away at the mane from behind its neck. In Sabucedo, *aloitadores,* or "fighters,"[10] take running leaps onto the horses' backs from the ground; they ride the animal hard, driving it into the others, until it tires and then is tackled by several men, who

FIGURE I.2. Rapa das bestas *at the Curro de Torroña. The* cabestro *hangs from the end of the* vara.

pin it and hold it for the shearing. These horses, too, are then sprayed and microchipped, according to EU regulations.

In Sabucedo, a village of about three dozen people, this ritual is thoroughly elaborated and intensified.[11] Unlike the others, this *rapa* takes place over several days, typically on the first weekend in July. Also, Sabucedo attracts tourists; often over ten thousand people, who camp in fields and woods about the village.[12] The opening event is a mass for San Lorenzo, patron saint of Sabucedo, at 6 a.m. on Friday morning, after which locals and tourists alike (about a hundred people, initially; more join in over the course of the day) ascend the mountain in search of the bands. After a long morning of herding, followed by lunch in the field, the captured animals are driven down to the valley and then paraded through Sabucedo to the *peche,* an enclosure in a large hilltop pasture. Along the route, people crowd against or atop stone walls to watch the spectacle pass. Camera operators and film crews, many from other countries, dash about trying to capture vivid images of the procession. The narrow lane is also transformed with huge kitchens (each seating up to a hundred people) on one side and several carnival rides on the other. Vats of boiling water for the octopus and large charcoal grills for the other meats front the roadside, and narrow bar tops along the kitchen railings prop up increasingly drunk spectators.

From Saturday evening through Monday midmorning, the horses are run through the village and into the *curro*. Each day the process repeats. First the foals are removed from the *curro* and moved to a small stable. The horses left in the *curro* are, if possible, more frantic than their conspecifics in other *rapas*. Their ordeal is intensified by the riders who purposefully drive through the herd, frequently striking at their heads to disorient them. Being tackled to the ground, too, is a jarring shock. But perhaps most frightening for them is the swirl of horse violence that permeates the *curro*.[13] This is purposefully culti-vated by the humans, who ensure that as many stallions as possible are in the arena at any one time, because the stallions fight each other energetically, a hallmark of the spectacle. Promotional flyers, posters, and online images—many generated by spectators and curated by participants—feature thunderous clashes of two rearing males biting and kicking each other viciously. This is what people come to see. Be-sides the danger posed to the male combatants, who may draw blood, mares are also at risk; mostly from the bites and kicks of other mares as they writhe about trying to avoid the stallions, but from the males as well, who aggressively attempt to carve out social distance around themselves in the too-tight confines of the *curro*.

Rituals have long fascinated anthropologists, and the *rapa das bestas* offers up many intriguing aspects that warrant analysis. First, there is the variety of *rapas,* ranging from mostly workmanlike affairs in the south to the spectacle in Sabucedo. This variation reflects changing forms of labor and tourist economics in rural Spain. Second are the co-pious symbolic dimensions. Up through the 1960s, the shaved hair had many uses—as mattress stuffing, used in wall plaster, for rope-braiding, and as fiddle bow strings.[14] New synthetic materials replaced all these uses, but the *besteiros* still shave the manes and tails, believing this prac-tice is good for the horses. But shearing also seems to be a technique of domination and reassertions of mastery related to domestication. A third aspect of interest are the audiences, which are quite varied as well. Some are adult children or grandchildren who have moved to cities; the *rapa* is an annual event for which they return to the village. For tourists, the *rapa* is a dramatic spectacle, a "battle" of "man versus beast," as is oft invoked in Sabucedo. As "spirits of the mountains," the horses' forced presence in the *curro* and the narrow lanes of Sabucedo offer glimpses of the wildness of untamed spaces that loom high above the civilized terrain of highways and houses.

The human dimensions of this ritual will receive attention here, but the focus is on the horses' experience of the *rapa.* I pose and answer a simple question: what impact does this ritual have on the social structure of these horses?[15] The answers will draw from and have relevance for both ethnography and ethology. Though ethnographers have historically studied humans, there is a burgeoning interest in the array of nonhumans who are entangled in the lives and identities of people. Multispecies ethnography is making the case that a range of animals—mostly, but not exclusively, domesticates—are constituted as relational subjects in human domains.[16] At the same time, ethology, which analyzes animal sociality in an evolutionary framework, is opening up to thinking in cultural terms that recognize plasticity and contingencies in nonhuman social dynamics.[17] The potential for overlap between these two forms of fieldwork—one ensconced in the social sciences, the other in the natural sciences—has been the subject of philosophical speculations for some time.[18] But I proceed in a mostly methodological bent, by fusing observational techniques and orientation from both ethology and ethnography. Regarding the *rapa das bestas,* ethologists might be dubious that any significant insight can be gained from observing animals in such a stressful, unnatural setting. But my ethnographic approach to horses in Galicia will demonstrate how revealing this ritual can be regarding the pliability and responsiveness of horse sociality to unusual and disturbing circumstances.[19]

The stakes in regarding horses as ethnographic subjects can best be highlighted by contrasting this perspective with the dominant orientation of cultural anthropologists, as illustrated by Clifford Geertz's classic work, "Deep Play: Notes on the Balinese Cockfight."[20] This essay continues to be prominently featured in introductory courses because it succinctly and persuasively frames the proper subject of cultural analysis. Geertz observed cockfighting in Bali and paid close attention to the types of bets people placed on the outcomes. He discerned a "deep" structure whereby, as the wagers rose, increasing effort was expended to ensure the fighters would be as evenly matched as possible;

subsequently the outcome that catapulted one man to great wealth while financially ruining his opponent would be almost arbitrary. This drama, Geertz argues, is what drives the Balinese' obsession with cock-fighting. In this view, the cocks—and animals, generally—are reduced to representations of cultural values and ideals.

In characterizing this ritual, Geertz asserts that "it is only apparently cocks that are fighting there. Actually, it is men."[21] He argues that the Balinese ritual "is fundamentally a dramatization of status concerns," for which the cocks serve only as symbols: "Like any art form—for that, finally, is what we are dealing with—the cockfight renders ordinary, everyday experience comprehensible by presenting it in terms of acts and objects which have had their practical consequences removed and been reduced (or, if you prefer, raised) to the level of sheer appearances, where their meaning can be more powerfully articulated and more exactly perceived." In this analysis, the thrashing, writhing, dying cocks serve merely as a representational screen for human cultural concerns and obsessions.

This formulation depends upon a conception of culture as opposed to nature, of humanity as opposed to animality. "In identifying with his cock, the Balinese man is identifying not just with his ideal self, or even his penis, but also, and at the same time, with what he most fears, hates, and, ambivalence being what it is, is fascinated by—'The Powers of Darkness.' The connection of cocks and cockfighting with such powers, with the *animalistic demons* that threaten constantly to invade the small, cleared-off space in which the Balinese have so carefully built their lives and devour its inhabitants, is quite explicit." Geertz continues, "This crosswise doubleness of an event which, taken as a fact of nature, is rage untrammeled and, taken as a fact of culture, is form perfected, defines the cockfight as a sociological entity." In the domain of social facts, animals only have a role as "nature"—certainly an odd characterization for a *domesticated* species, such as chickens. Geertz's formulation, though, neatly highlights the challenge here: fully incorporating nonhumans in ethnographic accounts entails more than adding supplementary characters or subjects; it requires developing a postdualist conceptualization of culture, one that does not require an abstract notion of "nature" as its foil.[22]

The surge of research on animal cultures over the last decade offers a firm foundation for such a rethinking of cultural analysis in relation to nonhumans.[23] Starting with a focus on primates and a narrow concern with the beginning of hominin culture, ethologists have additionally found culture operating in copious socially learned traditions among a variety of taxa, from cetaceans to birds to fish.[24] Culture, in these approaches, is conceptualized as a shared system of group-specific behaviors, passed through generations by social learning. This succinct definition allows for ample applications across species, though it will likely strike many cultural anthropologists as a rather thin or flat rendition of the concept. Admittedly so, and in a way that highlights a second important contrast in my approach from classic ethnographic analyzes.

Geertz promoted "thick description," a text-based model of analysis in which the ethnographer reads the "texts" of others, over their shoulders, as it were: "an image, fiction, a model, a metaphor, the fight is a means of expression . . . in a medium of feather and blood" to display human social concerns.[25] This analytical approach directs attention from a superficial "text" to the "real" meanings hidden in its folds, and in so doing further inscribes nonhumans strictly as representational fodder: "to connect . . . the collision of roosters with the divisiveness of status is to invite a transfer of perceptions from the former to the latter." This is justified, Geertz assures us, because "like most of the rest of us, the Balinese are a great deal more interested in understanding men than they are in understanding cocks."[26]

In regarding horses as social subjects rather than representational screens, I have drawn upon the recent interest in "thin description" and "flat ontology" as alternative perspectives for social analysis. John L. Jackson (2013) depicts thin description as a means to reconstitute the ethnographic subject—not as an impenetrable subjectivity, knowable only through deep interpretive penetration, but as social entity constituted in a variety of shifting domains of expertise. Bruno Latour (2007) advocates "flattening" social analysis in order to widen the scope of entities (agents, actors, and subjects) that can be incorporated into reliable accounts of the world. My previous ethnography of botanical projects in Spain and Mexico deployed both of these perspectives and concluded with a provisional model for rendering plants as ethnographic subjects. In Galicia and with the *rapa das bestas,* I advance that approach to engaging and analyzing nonhuman social subjectivity. I am able to do so based on the considerable ethological research on horses, which, like botanical field description, is also relatively "thin" and "flat."

Like humans, horses in bands exist in a world of social encounters. Group life in horse societies is shaped by complex, long-term relationships, maintained over wide distances of time and space.[27] These relations result from bands interacting as they contend for limited resources, such as water and forage. Horses have good long-term memory and rely on a range of social skills to facilitate a dynamic cultural world, such as intervening in third-party interactions or engaging in postconflict consolation or reconciliation. As well, band-belonging may shift over time through fission-fusion dynamics, the same type of social organization seen in humans, chimpanzees, bonobos, and spider monkeys, along with elephants, hyenas, and many cetaceans.[28] So interband encounters may involve horses with some level of familiarity with each other. But relations are more complicated within bands; these unfold and develop through daily microinteractions during which status is asserted and contested, or the boundaries of the group are reproduced or challenged. Horses possess a keen sense of *social distance,* maneuvering to maintain proximity with conspecifics they favor or asserting and maintaining a remove from those they do not.[29] As well, dominance within bands manifests in the capacity of certain mares to claim space, typically through forcing others to move.

As social subjects, I observed how their relations and interactions on the range were impacted through the course of the *rapa das bestas* ritual in Sabucedo. Briefly, I found that the band structure of the horses—which is meticulously maintained and reproduced through a near-constant stream of performative and interpretive activity—initially collapses during the traumatic shock of the *rapa,* but then gradually reemerges before the ritual's conclusion. This finding is predicated upon my expertise as an ethnographer and what I was able to learn from ethologists' methods and modes of analysis. To pursue this project, I absorbed what I could from a range of experts, beginning with my own colleagues—biological anthropologists who study primate behavior in the field. From them I gained an understanding of how data on nonhumans in natural settings is produced and analyzed. Importantly, too, my colleagues educated me on the assumptions informing such research, all of which reflects a fundamental investment in evolutionary theory. But for the detailed and particular work of observing horses, I turned to a different set of experts in Spain.

In the summer of 2016, a year after I first observed the *rapa das bes-*

tas in Sabucedo, I participated in a field survey of horses on the Serra do Cando range, about thirty-five kilometers south of the village. This project was run by Laura Lagos of the University of Santiago and Victor Ros, an independent horse ethologist and trainer. Laura and Victor set up a program that offered training in the basic techniques of observing and recording horses in the field as part of an ongoing study of *garranos*, as this population is being designated in an emerging literature.[30] Laura started studying these animals after earlier work on wolves.[31] Victor, whose wide-ranging interest in horses has carried him around the world, was interested in this population partly for its antiquity but also its precarity.

After learning what I could of these techniques and imbibing what Laura and Victor imparted of their substantial knowledge, I headed out on my own to observe the horses above Sabucedo. My plan was simple: focus on several bands in the mountains, develop at least a schematic understanding of their social organization and band structure, then see whether or how it held up during the ordeal of the *rapa*. I had neither sufficient experience nor time to do this work in depth or in great detail, but the observations I generated were substantive enough that I could identify prominent mares in each band and track them through the chaos of being penned up with hundreds of other horses. The extent to which I succeeded is not because I became an expert ethologist; rather, this project worked because, as an ethnographer, I was already accomplished at social analysis. Because I understand how to observe and analyze social processes, I was able to recognize and think through patterns of social interactions among the horses.

In approaching horse sociality, I found it both easy and productive to apply basic techniques of interactional analysis. I drew these principally from the sociologist Erving Goffman, whose concepts such as "face," "civil inattention," and "footing" were readily observable in the bands in Galicia.[32] Goffman served as an apt resource for at least two reasons: he drew inspiration from ethology, and he harbored doubts about overemphasizing the role of language in analyzing human social interaction. On the first matter, James Chriss points out that "three of Goffman's most important concepts—presentation, claims, and ritual—can be considered appropriations from the corresponding ethological concepts of display, territory, and to a lesser extent, ritualization."[33] On the second, Goffman counseled that participant observation "is to not, of course, just listen to what they talk about, but to pick up on . . . their gestural, visual, bodily responses to what's going on around them."[34] In both regards, Goffman's style of microanalysis focused on observable behavior, such as spacing, gesture, posture, timing, and eye contact. With horses, I was able to apply this analytic because I found that they too have a concept of face. Goffman characterized "face-work" as partly about affirming others' self-presentation, but more often, he found, we do this by ignoring or looking away from little discrepancies or disruptions to a person's presentation of self—"civil inattention," Goffman said. Among the horses, I found copious forms of face-work; these were heightened during the violence of the *rapa,* when the rituals of everyday life collapsed in the chaos of the *curro.*[35]

Ethologists already know that the face is crucial to how horses socialize, as is also the case with most primates. But transposing *face* from social science to natural science opens up the potential to frame and analyze subjectivity across these domains, perhaps revamping social analysis in the process. Face, in horses, suggests that, as social subjects, they engage in ongoing interpretive work in understanding, reproducing, and contesting their relationships. Such interpretive subjects are assumed by ethnographers in relation to humans; for ethologists, positing subjectivity in nonhumans risks anthropomorphizing them. But the basis for transposing this concept is grounded in the physiological fact of fundamental commonalities in facial musculature in our two species. This is documented by the EquiFACS (Equine Facial Action Coding System) method for identifying and recording horse facial expression based on underlying mimetic musculature and muscle movement.[36] FACS was initially developed for use on humans, but it has since been applied to a number of primate and domesticated species, such as dogs and cats. In adapting it to horses, researchers found a surprising number of similarities with humans. These are mostly in the region around the lips, mouth, and nostrils. In developing this system, researchers recorded facial movements in various social contexts to facilitate thinking comparatively about social cognition across different taxa. Such similarities, sensorial and social, likely played a role in their domestication.

Like humans, horses are a highly visual species, with an ocular system adapted to discern predators across a wide savannah. They have the largest eyes of any land-based mammal. Their ocular musculature differs considerably from ours—horses have three eyelids and lack signaling features like eyebrows—but for nonprimate large mammals, they have considerable visual acuity (much better than dogs and cats, for instance). Horses also exhibit perceptual similarities to humans regarding curved shapes, vertical/horizontal lines, and diagonal lines.[37] Of course, their sensorium is much broader than ours. They also rely heavily on high-frequency hearing and an olfactory structure that allows for detailed chemosensing through their voluminous nostrils. Horses also depend upon their highly mobile, flexibles ears and their extremely complex and robust auricular muscles to "pay attention."[38] The important point amidst all these sensorial considerations, though, is that, like humans, horses also practice the *social gaze.*

The social gaze refers to the capacity for eyes to both transmit and receive social information.[39] With the gaze, we observe others and legibly offer up our interest and attention to them. As with humans, eye contact between horses is a conduit alternately for affection or aggression, and so it is intensely socially managed.[40] The first lesson I learned in horse ethology is that it is impolite to stare. Horses avoid staring at each other—as is similarly the case among many primates—and regard it as a source of concern or threat when we stare at them. These commonalities in the social gaze allowed me consistently to track horses' attention, because their facial features are so large and expressive. This did not give me unmediated access to a horse's subjective state, but it did allow me to observe how it might be thinking about another horse—because their expressions are meant to be legible to others, and because the effects of their gestures, affiliative or aggressive, visibly register with fellow band members.[41] When a mare asserted her status, the outcomes of that assertion were evident, not just to me but to other horses in the band, who respond in acknowledging (or at times challenging) that assertion.

As a basis for face-work, the social gaze, in horses and humans, links to an important concern in ethology with the cognitive capacities associated with facial recognition. This is a starting point for questions of how or whether nonhumans can be said to think. Ethologist Frans De Waal focuses on facial recognition both in contesting *anthropodenial* about our commonalities with nonhumans and expanding our capacity to recognize and analyze their thought processes. For too long, scientists assumed the cognitive capacity for recognizing individual

faces among a sea of conspecifics was limited to humans and our closest primate cousins. As De Waal recounts, "Face recognition, science
concluded, is a specialized cognitive skill of primates. But no sooner
had it done so than the first cognitive ripples arrived. Face recognition
has been found in crows, sheep, and even wasps."[42] Sheep actually use
"the same brain regions and neural circuits as humans, with some neu-
rons responding specifically to faces and not to other stimuli." De Waal
questions, "If face recognition has evolved in such disparate pockets of
the animal kingdom, one wonders how these capacities connect."

The answer involves two aspects of evolution that are fundamental
to ethology—homology and analogy. Homology identifies shared traits
from a common ancestor, such as the way we share so many of our social and mental capacities with other primates, or how the morphology of our hands derives from a common ancestor we share with birds.
Analogy indicates that similar capacities were arrived at independently,
like the way dolphins (as mammals) share similar shapes with fish (as
Chondrichthyes), or how whales and bats both developed echolocation.
De Waal explains, "The sensitivity to face in wasps and primates came
about independently, as a striking analogy, based on the need to recognize individual group mates." Horses' capacity for facial recognition is
analogous to our facility with faces, suggesting that the cognitive activity required in such an interactional orientation perhaps indicates parallel forms of social subjectivity. This possibility undergirds my interest in
applying ethnography to analyzing horse social structure. But doing so
requires tacking through an additional set of questions about thought
or cognition and how it might be observed or analyzed in other species.

De Waal recounts the various ways observed primate behavior seems
to indicate clear cognitive activity, such as in experiments around hidden food sources. These are enormously revealing of how chimpanzees,
for instance, calculate what their differentially ranked band mates may
or may not know about the location of tasty treats. Researchers track
gaze direction to tease out the social calculus concerning status and
position that informs how animals decided when and where or what is
safe to eat. Gaze direction, De Waal holds, may not lead to "mind reading," only "body reading." This stance is quite generative because our
human attunement "to the postures, gestures, and facial expressions
of others" is shared with many other social species, providing a foundation to observe similarities in social dynamics. "Animals do plenty of

perspective taking, from being aware of what others want to knowing what others know." For ethologists, this entails a mode of cognition, one linked generally to "environment"—that crucial register for natural selection. But as a cultural anthropologist, "perspective taking" sounds very much like "interpretation"—the process of sense-making that is informed by shifting contexts we refer to as "social."

Where environment or nature are fairly immutable and implacable in the face of species' never-ending challenge of "fitting" or adapting, interpretation directs attention to the changing, ritualistic ways that subjects are positioned at any one moment as part of a mutable social setting. For De Waal, "a species' cognition is tied to its evolutionary history and ecology." From my perspective, as a cultural anthropologist, it is sensible to consider that cognition also is shaped by emergent forms of sociality.[43] This entails shifting from environment as the context—one to which nonhuman sociality responds—to sociality as the modality and medium. Such an attention to social assessments as practiced by nonhumans is slowly coming into view for ethologists, as well.

De Waal acknowledges that "social challenges have been neglected for too long in discussions of cognitive evolution, which tend to focus on interactions with environment." In the *rapa das bestas,* horses face immense social challenges: not only does their band structure collapse, but they are set adrift in a swirl of aggression and violence as the conventions around *social space* and signaling collapse.[44] What do they do in this situation; how do they respond socially? This is an ethnographic question because the *rapa* is not a natural setting—this is not an environment to which their sense of sociality naturally responds, but rather a manmade spectacle—one that turns out to be deeply revealing of horses' capacity for sociality, which would go unnoticed or underappreciated in more naturalistic contexts. The answers that follow will also speak to the much larger question of the durability of sociality in relation to violence, especially in situations of intense crowding of conspecifics—a matter of pressing concern thanks to dire forms of habitat loss across the globe.

An additional point I take from De Waal is his insistence that, counter to the connotations we place around *wild,* "self-control is an age-old feature of animal societies," many of which possess considerable forms of restraint that mitigate against the use of violence. He writes, "being wild implies being undisciplined, crazy even, without holding

back," but those associations apply more aptly to humans breaking
from social constraints; in nonhuman realms, "social hierarchy" operates as "one giant behavioral regulator." Social animals simply cannot
disregard behavioral consequences of how their actions will be considered and responded to by others. De Waal reviews numerous instances
of self-restraint being practiced by nonhumans, particularly in terms
of "displacement activities"—a concept that dovetails with Goffman's
theories of face. As he sums it up:

> Animals just can't afford to blindly run after their impulses.
> Their emotional reactions always go through an appraisal
> of the situation and judgment of available options. That is
> why they have self-control. Furthermore, in order to avoid
> punishment and conflict, the members of groups need to
> adjust their desires, or at least their behaviors, to the will
> of those around them. Compromise is the name of the
> game. Given the long history of social life on earth, these
> adjustments are deeply ingrained and apply equally to
> humans and other social animals.[45]

Such an investment in restraint or comportment, I argue, involves interpretation of whether these capacities are being observed or breached
by conspecifics and group members—concerns that are then doubled
or paralleled in attention to boundaries and matters of belonging or exclusion. Which brings up an additional concept I am transposing from
social analysis—*boundary work.*[46]

Social groups are constituted through the near-constant activity of
delineating the boundaries of their shared identity. For humans, this
involves a great deal of ideological work in relation to representations,
typically on a national scale and involving diacritics of class, race, and
gender. But as with much else we do, as Goffman noted, this activity
is also realized and articulated in microinteractions between individuals who are face-to-face. Boundaries are the products of interactions
between individuals that cumulatively position social subjects within
a group set over and against other groups, as with different bands on
the range. The value of this transposition is evident in the contrast
between how ethologists think about "personal space" and how ethnographers focus on "social space."[47] George Waring, in *Horse Behavior,*

writes, "horses typically prefer to have their own personal space. They exhibit this by maintaining an individual distance between one animal and another."[48] As with all staples of ethology, this can be observed and quantified as part of the species' ethogram—a catalog of discrete and distinct behaviors rendered as objectively observable as possible. This behavioral inventory reflects the natural science framework that grounds ethology, which focuses on the individual as the principal unit of analysis.

In contrast, in boundary work, "social space" is a *relational unit of analysis*—one that cannot be discretely delimited because the participants in it are altering or reproducing varied positions within an ever-mutable social context. I observed horses sorting out perceptions and performances of distance and closeness in social terms. Goffman characterized "social distance" as an effort to draw nearer those of similar or higher rank, while remaining at a remove from lower ranking individuals. The boundary work of horses sorts out social distance and proximity simultaneously within and between groups, playing out in the fission-fusion dynamics that are characteristic of this species. The transposition of these concepts of face and boundary work provide the basis for the version of social analysis I bring to bear in analyzing the horses' experience of the *rapa das bestas* in Sabucedo.

If animals have culture, then they warrant ethnographic attention. Ethnography was developed on humans, but given that nonhuman social species manifest cultural dynamics, they too can stand as ethnographic subjects.[49] The entry points, in this case, are the manifold forms of social signaling that comprise everyday life for horses in bands. In this project, through the course of the *rapa* I was able to see how conventional this signaling is.[50] On the range, affiliation and aggression are expressed through subtle gestures that signify an intent or an assertion about a relationship. In the *curro,* during the most disorienting moments, such gestures abruptly give way to acts of violence. The question of violence in relation to sociality is a deep one.[51] Hopefully I can shed some light on it here. But I'll mainly emphasize now that this matter of conventionality suggests ways to expand considerably the social analysis of horse behavior. In particular, I track how forms of politeness, operating "in the wild," collapse in the face of unnatural social circumstances imposed by humans.[52]

My analysis of horse sociality rests upon a great deal of ethological knowledge about this subject, which will be introduced in chapter 1 and elaborated on throughout the book. As an ethnographer reading and engaging with this knowledge base, I was struck by its capacity to document the intense sociality of horses yet render it in largely reductive, functionalist terms. So, "free-ranging horses are always occupied, alert, and interactive with herd mates as they together seek shelter, groom, rest and protect one another"; yet all this activity is somehow reducible to determinations of dominance?[53] Dubious gendered assumptions are also plentiful, evident in the continued anthropomorphic characterization of bands as "harems"; though that designation has been criticized for years, both for its sexism and for fundamentally misconstruing the sexual-social dynamics of groups of horses.[54] The reigning concept in horse ethology is "harem maintenance" or, more neutrally, "female defense polygyny"—the idea that the stallion's role is to protect his reproductive partners. But in many instances reported below, stallions are not engaged in or evidently concerned with protecting mares, who, it should be noted, are quite capable of protecting themselves from overly aggressive, assertive stallions or against attack by predators. In the *rapa,* stallions are concerned principally with fighting each other; mares become entirely ancillary to them. Mares are even subject to attacks from the males, but most of the aggression they face is from each other. Along these lines, perhaps my most significant finding is that mares do most of the work of maintaining social order, contrary to continued ethological assertions about the centrality of stallions.[55]

Much of the following account is developed through my learning ethnographically to navigate the horse ethogram—a compendium of naturalistic, discretely quantifiable behaviors. When I reference these for the first time in the following text, the word will be bolded. But as an ethnographer I am prone to seeing behaviors as fluid responses to particular contexts and relationships. Where ethologists record "displays" of dominance, I see it as "performed"—that is, conventionally expressed by and for socially situated subjects (interpretive/relational) rather than a brute assertion of physical capacity.[56] While these are distinct analytical frames, they are also easily overlapping subjects. At the conceptual level, there is much movement around "dominance," but at the level of description and analysis, it continues to be operationalized and analyzed in fairly static terms. Ethnography is a means of attending to and analyzing the plethora of instances and interactions that escape even a rigorous quantitative approach, rendering "dominance" or "submission" as achieved or assumed states in what are ongoing and often uncertain social negotiations of relationships and identity. There is far more to consider about the science of horse ethology than I can sketch here. I will address and elaborate on the range of interesting debates about how to meld ethnography and ethology— in the conclusion. First I turn to my account of learning horse ethology and applying it in the field in an ethnographic framework.

Chapter 1 recounts my experiences learning ethological methods of observation from Laura Lagos and Victor Ros. Chapter 2 covers my experiences applying these techniques on my own, in the high country above Sabucedo. Chapter 3 focuses entirely on the *rapa,* as I recount how the bands I observed experienced this profoundly disturbing ritual. The format is a day-by-day account of how I learned to observe horses and analyze their sociality; within each chapter, subsections cover each day in detail. Chapter 1 is set on the Serra do Cando range, where we surveyed and learned about horse ethology. Victor conducts these field schools in Spain and Venezuela. Laura Lagos was working independently since completing her dissertation research. They both presented lectures—Laura, on *garranos,* while Victor's ranged widely over ethology as a science (historically and currently) and the study of horse behavior generally. We all shared an interest in sociality, though I soon realized we conceptualized it in rather different modalities. There were two additional participants: Rachel, a British college student, and Simona, an Israeli horse enthusiast.

Chapter 1 opens as we start our first day in the field, leaving our base in a lodge just outside of the village of O Verdugo, getting ready to spend our day on the mountain surveying *garranos* and practicing ethological observation. This chapter will introduce the fundamentals of horse ethology and highlight a range of substantive theoretical and philosophical issues raised by horse sociality.

Into the Field

TECHNIQUES OF OBSERVATION

DAY I

We begin by squeezing all five of us into the confines of Laura's white two-door Nissan Terrano and start up the valley. Our gear—jackets and poles, binoculars and cameras, backpacks and blankets and such—clutters about the cramped rear, poking and prodding into hips, shins, and booted feet. Laura steers the Terrano out onto the narrow stone bridge over Rio Verdugo, then turns left, heading north. The drive takes about twenty minutes as we wind past isolated farmhouses and through one small cluster of homes nestled around the junction of two narrow roads. Eucalyptus groves rise around the curves and crevices below us. Some of the farms are overgrown and a few houses look abandoned. I ask Laura how much they might cost. She guesses about €70,000, but that's only for the roughly two hundred meters of land on which they sit; and it's quite a challenge to establish ownership. For some, it can't be determined, which unintentionally aids conservation in the area. I realize it's hardly accidental that horses, like other emergent "wild" populations, range freely in regions depopulated by humans.[1]

Laura says there's a common saying in Galicia, that there's a Galician or Galego on the moon. She has to explain that the odd phrase refers to the substantial out-migration of people from the province, whom you can find so thoroughly scattered across the world that they even end up in outer space. There are a few instances of people buying up summer homes and an increasing tourist trade based on redeveloped farmhouses, but the property laws are complex—for instance, you have to establish that you have a working chimney: "*chiminea con fuego.*" The subject of fire leads her to mention they have a big fire problem in the area: young men burn the fields, sometimes to improve grazing but also for jobs, to extinguish them. She sums it up: "We have a fire economy."

Laura pulls the Terrano off the main road and onto a rutted gravel track that passes by an electrical transfer station and a cemetery before angling up the mountain. The track is used by crews who service the windmills that spire across the peaks and ridges ahead of us. In addition to being communal parish lands, this stretch of the Serra do Cando is also designated as a wind park, Parque Eólico A Cañiza. Time slows as the vehicle jostles and inches along the road. Laura tells us now to be on the lookout for horses, but from the back I can't see much. Victor and Laura, in front, scan opposite sides of the road. After roughly five minutes, we have the first spotting—there's motion on the next slope over, a gray horse running laterally below what appears to be a small group on the edge of the crest. Laura stops and out we clamor.

Uncorked from the cramped vehicle, there is much to take in, starting with the terrain, which is dominated by gorse (*Ulex europaeus*), a sharp low-clumping shrub, quite rugged, with harsh points at the apices of its evergreen blades. This thick growth is interspersed with patches of winter heather (*Erica carnea*), perky with lavender pink racemes dangling from its whorls of needlelike leaves. Taking off from the road to get a better view means negotiating a jagged-rimmed route through this dense brush, ideally by climbing up and then jumping to and from many of the large granite outcrops scattered about the slope. The stone is lavishly daubed with colonies of lichen in varying hews of gray, white, and burgundy. Open patches of grass peak through the blanket of gorse and heather; these have been heavily grazed and they make a fractured quilt. Though the gorse annoys, it's lovely as a patchwork smattering of bright yellow flowers against its light green foliage.

Gingerly I navigate the landscape, listening to Victor and Laura speculate on what they see about a kilometer away: two horses running—stallions, they guess—one is checking the other's ascent along the crest line. Perhaps the one trying to gain the heights is a roving bachelor looking to hive off a mare or two. There's likely a band nearby but not much will be clear or certain until we get much closer, which means stuffing back into the Terrano. My dangling camera, binoculars, and pouch make climbing in and out of the back cumbersome, so I vow to shed some gear at the next stop, which comes along directly.

Before we have gotten far Laura spots another band just ahead, which was obscured by a ridgeline where we first stopped. We halt and spill out. This band, though about two hundred meters away, is visible enough to be counted, so we launch our first effort at tallying horses. Laura starts to count, while the rest of us spread out and take up viewing positions. I assumed this task was straightforward until I tried it. First, I'm at a loss to get the horses clearly in sight; I've not really used binoculars before, so there's the trick of adjusting the focus and setting up the right depth of field. Laura counts aloud as she scans but this is a tentative effort, since some of the herd seems to be just out of sight, over the distant high ridge across which the group is moving. More critically, we're not close enough to establish sex or even accurately gauge the age-grades. Foals are easy enough (there are two) but the yearlings and two-year-olds are more challenging to distinguish from adults at this distance. She settles initially for a head count: nine horses. But we'll need to be more precise as the survey progresses.

Before leaving, Laura points out an old stone road just under our feet. The contours are faint, most legible in the edge work that delineates a fairly straight path moving opportunistically over exposed plates of granite. She jokes that this is "low energy infrastructure"—in contrast to the track we're using, created by bulldozers—used actively by wolves as they circuit these mountains. Laura hewed to these when she was surveying wolf populations because they contain important information—wolf fecal droppings. There's even a pile of stallion droppings, which Victor identifies because it's slightly mounded—another male has gestured at boundary work by unloading his feces onto those of the first. While mares defecate freely, for stallions defecation is often conventional—they create "stud piles" of accumulated feces and often competitively layer theirs atop those of other males. Wolves and horses, males and females, all consult fecal droppings as they circulate. "It's like reading the morning newspaper," Victor remarks.

We stroll the old road briefly, looking for another angle on the band above. While we're walking, Victor prompts me for my definition of culture. As an anthropologist, my mind instantly swirls with thoughts from the century-long effort to delineate this key concept. But I've also been thinking extensively about a version of this concept that might apply to species broadly. So I offer up a succinct reply: "Culture is socially learned local patterns of behavior." This covers the basics—place-based dynamics that are transmitted intergenerationally. Victor considers that for a moment, then says that he thinks of culture in terms of "food preferences," elaborating that the choices any species makes about what they like to eat probably involves a range of local variations. Though his rendition seems rather slight and narrow, I appreciate Victor's interest in the topic. But I'm not sure of the concept's import to him. Over the days that follow, Victor rails frequently against abstract characterization of "the horse" as an ethological object. "People like to say the horse is this or that. No, the horse is however his environment is going to ask him to be. So in each environment he has to tackle different problems and might do so in slightly differently ways." Victor's use of culture recognizes lots of variation in a species, while many fellow ethologists fixate on generalized characterizations of preferences and inclination.

In contrast to culture as local variation, Victor brings up the tick, a classic example for ethologists developed by Jakob von Uexküll. "Ticks have only three or four instructions," he says. They hang from branches or bushes until they detect the smell of butyric acid, a component of animal sweat. At that moment, they release their hold, switching off the butyric acid detector and activating a tactile sensor that causes them to land on an animal, whence they commence to feed. The tick represents one pole on a continuum of behaviors, from the simplest and most instinctual to those that entail **social learning** and imitation. Horses are on the latter end: while they have some fixed behaviors, aspects of what they do reflect their responses to and interpretations of social dynamics in particular settings.

Back in the Terrano, skittling farther up and along the ridge, we reach the next band in about five minutes; two horses are standing along the flank of a knob that crowns a low peak, just above us as the grade of the road dips down the other side. But Laura surmises that several more might be just out of sight. A lone windmill looms overhead at the top point, and three others are stacked along the rest of this road spur. In the distance, looking south, dozens more windmills spool out like mechanical spikes on a devilish backbone. And sure enough, there's another collection of horses farther below along the track to the south. They hardly seem to notice us, though they're roughly fifty meters away. I'm mesmerized by these animals immediately and work fumblingly with camera and binoculars, not sure yet of how or what to observe or record.

FIGURE 1.1. *The stallion is on the left; the dark palomino is on the right.*

Victor instructs us on how we are to operate as a team. Our purpose is twofold. In terms of the field school, the aim is to learn ethological techniques for observing horses. But we are also helping Laura conduct a census of these bands, from which she'll develop a study of the effects of wolf predation. "So we need to count these horses," Victor explains, "but we also have to identify them, so we can follow whether they stay in this band or maybe move to another." Simple enough, I thought. But both these aims are more complicated than I imagined, starting with the basics of identification.

I had crammed for this undertaking by consulting with my brother, who's a working cowboy in southern Arizona. With his tutoring, I could recognize the basic color templates. Black and brown were easy enough, with "flaxen" denoting a blonde mane on a chestnut-colored body; but gray breaks into several categories, such as "dappled" (with small white spots), "flea-bitten" (with small black or brown spots), "steel" (a very dark gray), and "light" (looking quite white but with dark patches around the nose and ears). My brother also prepared me for the confusion that was about to engulf us, deriving from the considerable variety of more nuanced color-terms and the lack of consensus on what they reference. When Victor charged us to describe the horses in front of us, we differed immediately over terms like "bay" (reddish-brown coat with a black mane and black markings in the legs and ear edges), "dun" (a golden or chestnut coat with dark legs and a dark dorsal stripe), and "buckskin" (similar to dun but lacking its dorsal stripe). For that matter, what looks black is generally characterized as "dark brown" instead. I struggled to distinguish "grullo" (light brown bordering on tan with burnt patches of black around its extremities) from "seal-brown" (a near-black coat that shades to brown along the flank and shoulders, looking "brown" in bright sunlight). And the difference between "palomino," "sorrel," and "flaxen" eluded me for a while. But colors were just the beginning.

As more of the band comes into view before us, Victor points out there are two bays and challenges us to tell them apart. The options are many but mostly break into two categories: leg and facial markings. Legs might feature white bands of differing lengths called "cornets," narrow white rings just above the hooves; "socks," where the white marking extends over about a quarter of the lower leg; while "stockings" reach up to the knee or hock. Faces might boast "blazes," "stars," or "stripes," denoting different lengths or patches of concentrated white coloration in the face. Then, too, manes differ—some extend farther along the neck on one side than the other, or may be longer or shorter overall. Victor explains this while I try to shift my vision from one horse to another, but quickly I am completely lost. Because the horses are in gradual motion, grazing through deep clumps of gorse, I catch only glimpses of legs and faces, then am unsure of what I saw on which of these two parallel bays. The features Victor lists seem kaleidoscopic, shifting configurations that fall temporarily into alignment, then just as quickly shift again. The exercise is also reminiscent of looking through a microscope at some uncertain sample on a slide. As I have troubles with the lens adjusters on the binoculars, I have an unfixed sense of what it is I'm looking at with the horses.

Laura, meanwhile, is trying to get an accurate tally, even though we can't get closer without startling the animals, and some of them are obscured by dips and rises in the terrain. She asks us each to generate a count—collectively, after several calibrations, we come up with at least six adults and three foals. There are two bays and perhaps a third but that one maybe is just brown or grullo, then a flea-bit gray, with small flecks of dark color on a coat so light it looks white. Rachel and Victor debate whether another one is palomino (typically a golden coat offset by a blonde mane) or a dark chestnut with a flaxen mane. They provisionally settle on "dark palomino" over "flaxen." The next task Laura sets us is to find the stallion. She follows a standard approach of identifying bands by the stallion, and this becomes a fixture of all our subsequent efforts to survey these horses. The surest way to identify the stallion is to scan for its penis.

You might think an organ of that size would be easy to locate. But if the horses are close together, it's mostly hidden from view; or it might be retracted enough to be difficult to see even in a full silhouette, or even mistaken for a teat on a bulging udder. Considering the mild awkwardness of a group of people searching for a stallion's penis, I take to calling it the "indicator" when asking whether it had been spotted yet. This time, we quickly make out the stallion—a black horse toward the end of the band, downslope from us, with a large "star" or white blotch on his forehead.

The problem with this approach to identifying bands, Laura points out, is that when she returns to this range next summer, the stallion might be gone, driven out by a rival. How will she be certain that it's the same band? Fixating on the stallion is sensible and economical, in terms of time, because he typically is a singular presence in what might be a large collection of horses. Also, these males engage in ostensible acts of **herding** to keep a band well-bounded. Behaviorally, this involves lowering their heads sweepingly along the ground, menacing at biting vulnerable fetlocks or "ankles." But this fixation also reflects gendered assumptions in horse ethology, as in the notion that stallions keep females in a "harem," which they protect through acts of "harem maintenance" by blocking mares from leaving with other stallions. But Laura notes that these bands might be cohesive prior to and long after the tenure of any particular stallion, largely because the mares' social ties are substantial, as an outgrowth of kinship as well as affiliation. Yet identifying mares might not be any more certain, as one or more might hive off from a band; Laura sees this occurring when one has lost a foal to wolf attack, and it's also quite frequent with young females.

One way around this might be to identify a dominant mare at the center of the social group, but as we'll see, this also is a complicated and analytically fraught matter. Dominance raises all kinds of issues for Victor, because it links to "aggression" or "violence" and smacks of essentializing. Victor disparages the concept for the way it reductively treats the matter of horse belonging and sociality; also for the way trainers make use of it in promoting "natural horsemanship" techniques he finds abhorrent. There is a tendency, in the literature but especially in horse discourse, to assume everything turns on establishing the order of dominance in any context. Trainers will try to assert dominance over a horse, while ethologists might assume the social order entirely revolves around the dominant male. But in bands, rank is often flexible, as in many human societies, with individuals rising and falling as status is differently asserted or evaluated by others, over the course of a lifetime or even just a day.

For that matter, there might be several prominent mares, each one vying with the others in contests that might play out over weeks or even months. The outcome of any one contest over dominance may yet shift in the future, making it dicey to select any one prominent horse to be the identifier. More challenging still, these determinations take a great deal of time. Dominance is a relationship, so you need to map many of these interactions over the course of days or weeks to come up with any reliable assessment. And time is something we lack in our survey. There are too many horses yet to tally. Considerations about uniquely describing individual horses in relation to band-belonging complicates the basic methods of the census, which are designed to generate population-level data.

But this is what interests me most—social relations—to which I quickly shift my attention, giving up on distinguishing between the bays as I notice an interaction unfolding. Rather suddenly, in what strikes me initially as an idyllic scene, the light gray mare directs a bite at another's foal, a male who has drifted too close to where she is nibbling on the short grass. The foal scampers away and slowly moves toward his mother maybe fifteen meters distant, who seems to take no notice of this encounter.[2] It's over almost instantly but the scene sticks with me because I realize I've just witnessed my first assertion of *social distancing* among horses. Quite like humans and perhaps most social mammals, horses have a keen sense of how close they want others to be. The gradations and variations of this basic sensibility may be infinite, with personality and individuality also being significant factors. Perhaps even this may vary by locality, with some bands preferring more proximate or distant positioning. But as with this foal I just watched, the nuances must be learned at an early age, with both mares and stallions asserting social space by punishing transgressions of these invisible boundaries and lines.

Meanwhile, we're compelled to revise the count. Initially, we count five mares—two bays, the gray, a palomino, and a brown—and three foals. But noticing that they sporadically look back down the slope, it becomes clear there are at least two trailing mares, each with foals, obscured by the brush. Laura points out that the band is moving; perhaps they had been stilled by our arrival, waiting to see what we were doing, but are continuing in motion now. She guesses most of these foals are about two to three weeks old, though one was born just days ago. "They were born at a good time," Laura says approvingly, heightening their chances of surviving wolf attacks. The mares slowly pass from bunched to spread out off toward the east, while the stallion stays fairly stationary. Victor says when the foals are this young the mothers will **wait** for them to catch up, but soon they'll transition and it will be the foals' task to keep up with the mares.

Watching their gradual progression, it dawns on me that in the ten minutes we've been standing here the dark palomino mare has moved from the rear of this loose formation, by the stallion, to emerge in the forefront of the pack, having passed the other mares who were grazing more slowly along the slow ascent. I suggest aloud that perhaps now she's leading them. But Victor, in a quick, tart rejoinder, asks me to explain what I mean by "leading." His pique and provocations turn out to be an excellent barometer of what are loaded or contested concepts and terms in horse ethology. Victor is perturbed by the insinuation that what we are seeing is an enactment of leadership. He has a problem with the way studies of leadership are formulated—typically in artificial experimental settings with tame horses. He railed particularly against work by Konstanze Krueger. But Victor also had just been complimenting the stallion, remarking that he was a good one because he was waiting for the other mares. Contrarily, he offered, "maybe those two mares were just bothered by some grasshoppers"; or, he added, "they might just be following a tasty track of grass." Who knows? Anything but directed movement.

FIGURE I.2. *Is the palomino mare (on the right) leading?*

I take several things from this exchange. First, a sense of the contentious aspects of characterizing horses—from their actions to their
dispositions—over whether intention can be discerned or established.
Second, a recognition that the sources of contention stem from the
difficulty of studying horses in adequate settings or finding the time to
do so and generate high quality, large quantity data. But more subtly,
Victor's use of the word "just" sticks with me. I heard him and others
use it with frequency, marking a disregard for or rejection of an interpretation of the horses' behavior that went beyond the individual
animal, particularly in suggesting social dynamics. I recognized it because "just" works similarly when I offer anthropological or cultural
interpretations: if I suggest a film is popular for the way it dramatizes
tropes of neoliberalism, my students are quick to protest that really
they *just* like the movie.

However the movement of this band might be characterized, in another six minutes the stallion, seemingly bringing up the rear, passes
above us and up the slope toward a small, marshy pool. We follow,
ascending to the leveled circle around the windmill. This location is
ringed by a low wood-rail fence and is designated as a *mirador,* a view-
point with a small picnic area for visitors. I have a hard time imagining

that many would venture up the twisty route we took to this point. But the view is tremendous and I catch glimpses of the Atlantic through gaps in the low-lying fog hugging the coast below us, some thirty kilometers away. Really I'm mostly seeing *rias,* fjordlike inlets that spring up from the narrow openings where a river meets the sea. The three *rias* in sight are the Vigo, Pontevedra, and Azora. The track snakes off below us in several directions, each leading farther along the range to more far-flung windmills.

Caught up in the scenery, I miss what's happening with the horses. In an eight-minute span which Victor tracks closely, the dark palomino and gray mares—the latter closely followed by her male foal—pass around the pond, prompting the stallion to race ahead and check their movement forward, turning them back toward the rest of the band; an instance of herding or boundary work to which I was initially oblivious. Then Victor poses a question about what the stallion is doing now. As I tune back in, all the horses seem to be grazing. But the direction of the stallion's munching leads away from the dark palomino and gray mares, passing a bay with a large "blaze" (a wide white stripe down the forehead to the muzzle), who seems to be offset from the others and has no foal. With most of the horses chewing contentedly at the short blades in the glade, why is he reversing course, going back in the direction they came? "What is the stallion doing?" Victor's prompt is aimed at the ethological challenge posed by the action of any individual animal: Are they playing a social role or acting individually? Is this a reflection of instinct or of personality? Is this a goal-driven purpose or *just* a series of unmotivated behaviors? "Leading" implies there is a group, as does "dominance" and "rank." The pitfalls arise as soon as you try to narrate actions, because the irrepressible question is "Why?" Why would the stallion be heading in the opposite direction from the band? Why does anyone do anything?

Victor says we'll wait to see what happens. "Be a piece of gorse," he advises—be still as the plants so as not to interfere with the horse behaviors. He is meticulous and dogged in maintaining this stance throughout the field school, because without doing so "we can't consider these behaviors to be natural," as the ethos for ethology holds. But also, "disrupting them is not fair to the horses." So the minutes pass and we wait and watch. It turns out there is yet another bay mare behind and below us, obscured by a rock outcrop. She has a large "star" (a marking more wide than vertical) that narrows and descends into a sinuous stripe dropping to her nose. Beside her is a sleeping foal, as we realize once it rises. Meanwhile, the stallion has shifted from a seemingly nonchalant, aimless drift to a more focused movement toward this lone mare. "He's getting worried about her," Victor suggests; catching himself, though, he qualifies this remark by adding, "This is just my language."

Still, before long Victor is unable to resist: "What a good stallion," he coos, when the male advances more decidedly toward the bay. His admiration for the stallion wells up further when the male sniffs the mare's fresh droppings and begins to **flehmen**.[3] This complex behavior, with head elevated and neck extended, draws aromas into the vomeronasal organ to be assessed and interpreted; ears rotate to the side and the upper lip curls back, temporarily closing the nostrils, holding particles inside, while air and fluids pass over the teeth. This is a means of recognizing whether a mare is in estrus, but horses of any age or sex may do it when they come in contact with a new smell or taste. Though I wondered if this mare's rearward positioning had something to do with her relationship to the other females, I was more intrigued to see this important complex behavior unfolding a mere few meters from me. I was riveted: this is an important behavior with horses.

With the flehmen complete and the stallion still midway between the lone bay mare and the rest of the band, Laura suggests it's time we get moving. We've been at this location for just over an hour, and there are many horses yet to survey. Our count here is eight mares (one gray, one dark palomino, four bays, and two browns), five foals, and one black stallion; we decide to call them the Mirador band. As we leave, the stallion has also turned back to the rest of the band without reaching the distant mare. Perhaps whatever he smelled dissuaded him from attending to her more closely.

As we drive north, Victor opines further on his critique of "leadership," railing that "too much is posited from too little information." But before he can say much more, we pass a tiny stone structure, a little chapel made from massive stone blocks and roofed with well-maintained semicylindrical ceramic tiles. Its back wall, facing the lane, is less than ten meters across, and a tiny bell is hung below a stone crucifix at the roof's apex over the front door. Laura explains that this is the Capela Santa Mariña and that it is the destination for a local annual

FIGURE I.3. *The flehmen.*

pilgrimage, but is otherwise unused. It stands at a crossroads where another service track slouches west. Ahead of us, some distance from the road, we spot a fourth band down in a deep dell on the west side, so we stop and pile out.

This one is challenging to count because there are so many horses—close to twenty—and they're obscured by a clutch of well-weathered Scotch pines. We work with Laura to tally the animals, checking our numbers as they variously move in and out of view behind trees, some eighty meters away and much lower than the road. We count ten mares, one yearling, and six foals. Once we settle on a figure, Victor suggests another observational tack. "Let's try a free-write." Telling us to spread out to get different perspectives, he further instructs, "Look at what's happening; write what you see. Be imaginative; don't be constrained. We need it to break dogma," he intones; "later we can pare it down to an interpretation." Specifically, he says, don't just write "grazing," the activity that accounts for up to 80 percent of a free-ranging horse's waking hours.

With this directive to free-write, I panic. Strangely so, since I've written six books. But writing is often anxiety inducing, and I cringe at

having to share it with the group later. Also, in this situation I'm completely lacking a technical vocabulary or even a clear understanding
of what's happening here. Yet this is an interesting moment: first, because I start thinking about how the transition between "description"
and "interpretation" works in ethology; second, because Victor's charge
resonates with an emergent stance in cultural anthropology, as rep-
resented by my colleague Kathleen Stewart, who similarly encourages
ethnographers to eschew "ossified" social concepts in favor of a flow-
ing, impressionistic prose.[4] I almost hear her voice as Victor states, "We
need to break down categories." Amused at these mirrored bearings, I
decide to try, but still, I'm stressed.

Striding twenty meters back to the south, I get a vantage point on
a boulder just off the lane with a clearer line of sight into the dell. It's
all struggle at first—adjusting the depth of field on the binoculars, confused about what to do with my notebook, and trying to figure out what
to focus on among the semiobscured animals. I feel transported back to
when I first learned ethnography from Stewart: observe everything you
can; write it all down! The conundrum, of course, is doing the latter
crimps your capacity for the former. So I opt for observation foremost
and soon settle on something: there's a seal-brown horse (almost black
in this dull light) rubbing the left side of her face against a short broken
branch that's just at head level. Engrossed in watching her face work
back and forth methodically, I'm somewhat startled when a bay mare
with a foal come up behind her; they'd been just outside the narrowed
visual field of my binoculars. The seal-brown mare walks ahead a few
meters and starts to nibble at the scraggly grass, while up from behind
the bay takes her place and similarly strokes her face against the branch.
I can't tell if the bay's presence had hurried the brown mare or if the bay
had been patiently waiting until the brown finished.

I'm caught up in the challenge of deciding when an activity or interaction begins and ends when Victor approaches and asks, "What are
you seeing?" I recount all this briefly. "Ah good," he says, "that's **local
enhancement**." He doesn't say more, so I'm left to flesh out the concept.
Making use of some particular environmental feature, I guess. Later he
elaborates: this action involves not just an initial act by an animal, such
as scratching itself on a branch, but also that the act transmits to a
conspecific who then imitates or reproduces the behavior. Victor says
little about the social dimension of this, though it immediately strikes

me as intriguing. One animal observes another and then replicates its actions; this is an aspect of the interlocking observational dynamics that constitute the sociality of a group.

But much more is going on socially in the dell than this particular imitative moment. Victor points out that the stallion is engaged in actively herding another black mare and her foal; as she tries to leave the group he blocks her path and nudges her back to the others. Enthused to see another interaction unfolding, we decide to linger to understand what's happening. After fifteen minutes of watching, the pattern becomes apparent: each time the black mare approaches other mares they make kick-gestures or threaten bites. One—a darkly dappled gray—is particularly persistent in directing aggression toward this mare. The behavior is quite systematic and sharp; the mares have decided she doesn't belong, despite the stallion's efforts to keep her penned in the band. Victor speculates that the stallion might have hived her off from another band recently and she has yet to be accepted. But all is not agonistic here; during this stretch of observation Victor points to an instance of **allogrooming**. Two facing mares—a seal-brown and a roan (white splotches across a brown coat)—are using their teeth to dig at each other's shoulders, maybe scratching a hard-to-reach place or perhaps driving off annoying pests. Laura says that one is younger, probably two years old, so this is likely a mother–daughter pairing. Victor ventriloquizes, "It's like, 'mommy, mommy . . .'" I think that, rather than being an instance of anthropomorphizing, against which he is continually on guard, this may be a voicing of one mammal reading another.

Laura is anxious to move on to do more surveying but we're losing the light. She's hoping we can at least make it past Portalén, a mostly natural configuration of granite rock with a large lintel stone balanced by ancient humans over a gap, forming a portal to the other world, so legend says. It's only a kilometer farther to the north. As we ready to leave, I notice that the aggressive gray has angled off and started to climb out of the dell; she's trailed by three other mares. I suggest that maybe this is an indicator that she is the dominant mare in this band, since her rejection of the seal-brown mare seems to be quite consequential—the others appear to follow her lead. Victor counters, though, suggesting that "maybe she's *just* a bitch."

Over the next hour we scout two more bands along the road, tallying eighteen in one (ten mares, one subadult, six foals) and nineteen (eleven mares, five subadults, two foals) in the last.[5] But with the light failing and Portalén not yet in view, we have to wind back out the service lane to the main road. As we descend, Laura and Victor fall into expert discourse; this is the first time they're working together so they are still sounding out what and who each one knows. They talk about the International Wild Equid Conference in 2012 in Vienna, a gathering of scientists, managers, and wildlife professionals actively working on issues of equid conservation and management throughout the world. The conference was important in unifying the field of study they're participating in now. Its proceedings are encapsulated in the book *Wild Equids: Ecology, Management, and Conservation* (2016), to which Laura contributed a chapter. But I lose track as they start rattling off individual researchers they both know and referencing the different horse populations for this particular taxa and its line of research: Victor frequently mentions New Forest ponies and Exmoor ponies, both found in Britain, as well as mustangs in the Great Basin Desert of Nevada. What I do notice is their capacity for para-ethnography: they observe how disciplinary "tribes" emerge almost totemistically, bearing features of their respective taxa, both across the equid order and animal ethology more broadly. I'm not surprised to hear Victor identify as "a wolf man" at heart, as he considers wolf ethologist David Mech a hero. This is partly drawn in contrast to those who work mostly with dogs. I think of this as analogous to model organisms for biologists, where choice of species matters a great deal. Though it's also apparent that, across these distinctions, ethologists also work at transspecies analysis to study behavioral items that crosscut various species (highly conserved behaviors, perhaps).

We arrive back at the main road and turn south for the lodge. As she drives, Laura laments with frustration how people don't realize the horses are up here: "People live below; we need to get them up here." They have mistaken ideas about the horse, or they don't even care they exist up here.

DAY 2

The next day, a Sunday, we leave off from surveying bands in Serra do Cando and drive southwest, through Vigo and Baiona on the coast, then up the flanks of Serra da Groba to observe a *rapa das bestas*. We take this hour and a half trip for several reasons. Principally, Laura argues that the viability of these wild horses in Galicia depends entirely on the continuation of this ritual practice of "shearing the beasts." Without it, this population would grow such that they would pose an even greater nuisance to the government than they are now; increased accidents on the road and spiraling insurance costs would fuel incipient efforts to cull these herds entirely. As well, the *besteiros*—the humans who round up and shave these horses—are the only constituency who can make an argument that these animals can be maintained on the open range. Unfortunately, their situation is as precarious as that of the *bestas*—they are aging out in a depopulated countryside; of limited economic means, they face high costs from government regulation for claiming ownership of any mare or foal, and the practical, economic uses of these horses have vanished, along with traditions of farm labor and the various practices of using horse hair. These twined forms of endangerment, linking beast and *besteiros*, are further heightened by the growing notoriety of the *rapas* and the developing efforts by animal activists to ban these entirely.

This second reason poses a question that interests Victor. Can the *rapas* be conducted in a humane manner that protects the welfare of these horses? Victor consulted for the *rapa das bestas* association in Sabucedo four years ago, just after PETA began drawing international attention to the brutality horses endure in the ritual. He is interested to see how the *rapas* in Serra da Groba might differ in terms of how the animals are treated. We're attending the second of three held in the spring, this one at the Curro de Torroña, not far from Baiona. Both he and Laura speculate on the necessity for these rituals to reorient toward heritage tourism. Case in point, they are expecting a crowd of about two thousand people today. The problem is this: the tourism angle principally draws urban dwellers who are unfamiliar with and easily appalled by farm labor; they are disposed to see violence in the routine techniques of maneuvering and managing a large, powerful animal.

The third reason is the one that animates my project. I talked at length with Laura and Victor about my goal to analyze the *rapa das bestas* in Sabucedo in terms of its impact on the horses' social structure. This aim raises a host of theoretical, philosophical, and methodological issues within and between our respective disciplinary orientations, starting with fundamental questions: What is sociality? What is society or social structure? Are horses "natural" subjects? Victor and I variously tangle with these over the course of this long day, because we have distinct definitions of sociality. His features a functional perspective on evolutionary advantages of species-typical behavior; mine attends to the local spatial dynamics of sorting out belonging within a group.[6] But principally my concern here is more limited and largely ethological. I want to learn from both of them how to develop observational tactics for analyzing what happens to the horses socially once they've been driven down from the range and into the temporary captivity of the *rapa*. I ask them to work with me on figuring out what to look for interactionally among the horses, and where to look to discern patterns that might indicate something reflecting their band structures. They each are clear with me that, without prior observations on the range, what we observe today will be tenuous and limited. But they readily understand my aims and are exceptional guides to thinking through the behaviors of these penned animals.

We arrive just as the *besteiros* are driving the horses, about seven hundred in all, from the mountain into a large fenced enclosure. The narrow track down to the pasture from the road is crammed with small cars and hordes of people who've come out for the day to see the horses. Farther back in the woods—a mix of mostly eucalyptus and a few pines—several large trailers are parked that carried the horses of riding clubs up to the *rapa*. Soon dozens of saddled horses are tethered to trees along the high ground, making for an odd juxtaposition with the hundreds of wild ones penned up just below. Around the *curro*—a stone-walled enclosure, built in the early 1900s—about two dozen popup kitchens and food trucks are arrayed, and people are settling in, dinning on *churrasco* (charbroiled ribs), *pulpo* (squid), or stewed veal; a few imbibing beer and liquor from the well-stocked bars.

Fortunately, we have an excellent guide through the chaos. Laura has done extensive surveying of horses on this range, and she has written about this version of the *rapa* ritual in some detail. As we work through the scene, she points out "Terri" Modesto Domínguez Roda, the *rapa* association president, and promises to introduce us later when the action with the horses settles down. Like each of us, Laura wants to start with the horses right away, and they are easy to locate. We hear them well before they come into view. Horses have an impressive vocal capacity and a wide array of acoustical expressions. Voiced sounds include whinnies, squeals, nickers, and groans. Unvoiced ones comprise snorts, blows, mouth smacking, and soundings with their hooves. Squeals are emitted typically in aggressive interactions or as defensive threats or warnings, as when a mare rejects a stallion's sexual advances; they are short, sharp, and succinct. Nickers are low-pitched, broad-band vocalizations used to announce or respond to a horse's presence; stallions may emit them indicating sexual interest, and mares use them to warn foals of potential danger or to convey concern. Whinnies or neighs begin with a high pitch, then drop to the lower frequency of a nicker, eyes and ears pitch directionally, indicating attention, nostrils dilate, the mouth opens and closes; sonically they have distinct phases: an introduction, climax, and end. These are broadly communicative, conveying individual identity and location, and also degrees of emotional arousal (calm versus excited) and valence (negative or positive).[7] At times inquisitive or informational, they certainly are used when horses are separated, and in this moment the air is reverberating with whinnies.

The enclosure is a broad, fenced pasture, pockmarked with loose stone and peppered with tall pines. Laura guides us past the spectators draped along the four-foot-high welded wire fence and through one of the narrow openings that are too tight for mammals larger than humans to twist through. Once inside, we operate pretty much as we've done on the mountain—take up a position and start observing. But the scene is frenetic and we have little basis for generating any systematic data here. For me, the situation is simpler. I'm looking for affiliative behavior indicative of sociality, loosely curious about its frequency in this decidedly unnatural setting, anticipating how to do this methodically when I'll be on my own in Sabucedo in a couple of weeks. But my first ethological lesson in the Curro de Torroña is in observing signs of stress in the horses, something mostly absent during our observations on the open range. Laura calls my attention to a bay mare nearby—her dung is runny and yellowish. "That's not normal. She's stressed," Laura says. Then she points to the mouth of another mare, how it's drawn back sharply at the upper corner of the lips, and a ball-shape bulges below her chin: "That tightness is another sign of stress." I cast about for a discernible "normal" behavior and point to a pair that seem to be allogrooming. Laura agrees but adds, "That's calming, calming. She's like, 'don't worry, don't worry.'"

I ask Laura, "Are there things that you can see happening right now

socially?" She considers the question and replies, "Since I have not identified individuals, I don't know if these two"—a dark brown mare with
a broad blaze and a bay mare dashing past in tandem—"are in the same
band or not. I don't know. Maybe she's looking for a foal, or something.
What you see most frequently here is mares looking for the foals, or
foals looking for the mares." Indeed, the churn of horses mainly featured frantic mothers and missing offspring. This dynamic was goaded
further by the *besteiros* working through the crowd, targeting foals to be
branded; separating and tackling them, then spray painting a number
onto their left rear flanks. But even in this frenzy, Laura pointed out a
characteristic species behavior: as an anxious mare approaches, foals
uniformly snap their mouths deferentially. **Snapping** involves moving
the lower jaw up and down, as in chewing or sucking, with the mouth
open and lips drawn back, and head and neck extended. These are
unusual encounters, where neither participant is certain of the other.
The little colts, only days old, are mostly recognizable to their mothers through olfactory cues, but during the herding process their scents
are muddled and obscured. Yet the colts have already learned how to
respond properly to an adult who has yet to make clear whether they
are menacing or nurturing. Snapping reflects the conventions of social
interactions even at this most disordered moment.

Laura continued guiding my vision through the dense flow of motion and anxiety as I scanned for signs of adults bonding with each
other. In front of us were two bay mares. The larger one, with a small
star with as much shaded-in brown as white, had found her foal, a male,
and was licking his neck anxiously. Victor said, "She's consoling the
foal," who was nervously circling his mother, causing the mare to swirl
oddly about. The smaller bay, with a long, jagged blaze and four socks,
sniffed at passing lone foals, still searching for hers. But she seemed to
prefer standing with the other mare rather than go dashing about the
enclosure. I watched the larger mare with the small star extend her
nose to the face and shoulders of the smaller mare a couple of times,
when she took a break from attending to her foal. Over the next three
minutes, five adults and one subadult collected right behind the large
bay, so I asked Laura if she thought they might belong to the same band.
"I think they just found a calm place. They are attracted to calmness in a
situation like this." Underscoring her point, I realized that the adults in
back had pushed in close because a group of *besteiros* were approaching.

As the horses in back press forward, the big bay delivers a swift **kick** at the closest encroaching animal, who spins around and returns the gesture. As this unfolds, the smaller bay with the blaze moves to avoid the blow from the other mare, tucking her head briefly under the big bay's neck. They seemed quite familiar. But as the horses behind churn more, they both have to move forward and spiral around others nearby. In all the shifting, the smaller bay twisted in between the larger one and her foal; then ended up directly behind her. The big bay mare kicks at her, first with her right rear, then with both legs, sending the blazed bay reeling away. In less than a minute, though, the blazed bay returns to her, cautiously. This round of kicks was one of at least two dozen launched around us as horses pressed too close, shoved forward by *besteiros* or shifting out of the way of threats posed by other mares.

I remark to Laura that all the aggression we are seeing is coming from the mares. From what I had imbibed of horse ethology, I expected it would mostly be coming from stallions. "Yes," she replies, "the mares are trying to protect the foals." Laura explained that even if horses are in the same band, they will use aggression to guard their foals. "Now these two," she says, pointing to the pair of bays, who had ended up side by side again, "that smaller one is trying to be close. They are probably related. I think the bigger one is the mother of this bay with the crooked blaze." But the mother is worried first about the foal. "Really, in this stressed situation," Laura elaborated, "I don't think she can distinguish . . ." Victor chimes in that for the yearlings in this setting, since their social status is already vulnerable or uncertain, "when they're scared, they'll go find the mother. But that's all they need, just to find her again." In this case, the smaller mare is an adult, and she was quickly back alongside the larger bay with the brown-shaded star. "She could be a band mate," Victor allowed, "but it looks more like the big mare is the mother of both."

As we spoke, another trio of horses jaunted up, just as the ones previously in back were pushed along by a *besteiro*. The larger of these three, a bay with a broad blaze ending in a thick "snip" (a light colored marking usually found between the nostrils), was smelling extensively at the butt of the bay with the jagged blaze, who was eyeing a black two-year-old with a foal encroaching from her right. A surge of horses from the left pushed the trio in back closer. Laura opined that the middle one, who had been sniffing, was likely the mother of the one to her left.

The bay to her right, who looked to be about the same age (she thought they were both quite young) was maybe a bandmate or a sibling of the mother in the middle. Laura then adds that, in her experience, when the horses are left alone in an enclosure like this, they do start to re-establish their band structures. She suggests watching the duration of the smelling when they encounter each other, because scent recognition plays such a large role in relationships. The longer and deeper the mares investigate each other's scent, the more likely they already have a relationship. Victor notes that the positioning of the head, close against the flank or rear, could also be indicative of social ties; he then lauds the sensitivity and range of the equine nose.

But the larger question of sociality proved a sticking point for Victor. When I prompted him, "What's going on socially with the horses?" he replied tartly, "There's four foals that just lost their mother," pointing in front of us. "That's not social at all." I understood his stance but pursued the question further. At one point he rejected the notion that we would see anything social today; affiliative gestures would be re-duced to individuals relieving stress and alleviating fear. "In general," he pronounced, "they're going to look for another horse that's calm; they want to be close to it; that doesn't mean it's social." I replied that being close to another is fundamentally a social interaction and noted that some of the horses were trying to stay close together amidst the swirl of animals and *besteiros.* But Victor equates sociality only with band struc-ture. "Bands have a reason to exist. They serve a function," in terms of survival. "That's not what we're going to see here today." Absent a functioning band structure, he could not see sociality. When I pointed to one of the foals snapping, performing a social convention of submis-sion, he was dismissive: "That's not submission, that's just plain fear." But as we focused on my question further, he began to reframe what he knows in ways that meshed better with our overlapping interests.

It helped when I narrowed this down to questions of familiarity. Pointing to three adults closely wedged together, I asked if he thought they were familiar with each other. "Yes, I do, because what they are showing now is clear affiliative behavior." I take this as my baseline. Two of them were standing with their faces pressed together facing the same direction, the third's face also alongside the middle horse's but looking out the other way. The one standing on the far left shifted and pushed between the other two, but they all fell into lockstep with her and stopped when she did, faces all touching, sniffing at another mare who'd been standing there as long as they'd been nearby. To clarify, I asked him if it was the positioning of their heads that was indicative.

Yes, he confirmed, but also that they were so actively smelling each other. "And the horse in front of them, do they know her?" "I don't know," he replied, "they're investigating. But they could. It is a kind of social contact. But it's not really social. It's more of an aggregation," a loose collection of individuals. Again, he proved resistant to characterizing behavior as social outside of a naturalistic, functional frame. "For me, sociality starts when there's an interchange, not just an approximation. When one approximates another and the other responds positively, affiliatively, then we can talk about sociality." I respond that aggression is certainly social too, and that it depended upon social conventions and signaling to keep from becoming outright violence. But he demurred, "not necessarily." We were back to tripping over different disciplinary orientations. Victor's version of the concept of sociality, I realize, hews closely to that of the "social contract." Bands, he says, are something they choose freely; here, they are forced together. Hence, this could not count as "social" for him.

But I forego delving into a deeper theoretical debate, because Victor then rattles off the different forms of familiarity we might be seeing here. As other pairs and trios pass by, he suggests they could know each other in a variety of ways. Perhaps they were siblings from a natal band; maybe they were friends or preferred partners in a previous band. "Remember, horses have fission-fusion"; members of bands may come and go. He points, saying, "See that mare? She probably has the same mother as that one. Look at that marking. So the yearling is probably one of theirs as well." He regarded these instances of bonding favorably. "Eventually, if left alone, they should group together." But whether that would occur before the shearing began was unclear.

As we continued our observations Victor told me about his discomfort with "aggression" as a category, and how it had been studied. In free-roaming horses, he said that rates of aggressive acts were something like 1.3 per hour. But if you have penned horses with limited feed buckets, the rate soars to something like 47 aggressions an hour, dropping down to just 15 when they are offered more food options. So aggression, in this regard, is something both artificial and "unnatural" in terms of their sociality on the range. I understood his point but said that for me what's interesting is how they respond socially in such "unnatu-ral" settings—what forms of social interaction arise when they contend with artificial forms of management. Victor appreciated the question but the more pressing concern for him here was just how aggressive and violent the humans were being toward the horses. The *besteiros* passed through wielding stout sticks, sometimes walking canes, some with long poles. They used these mostly to scare the horses into moving but sometimes struck them instead. As he watched, steadily angering, Victor shifted from the observer role to considering how to document "the horrible things we're seeing."

Before he got much farther with this line of thought, a dark bay stallion strode up and started smelling one of the mares. His mane was long and matted on the right side but absent on the left. I asked Victor if he was looking for the mares from his band. As the mare quickly darted away, he replied, "No. He's just looking for mares in heat." Before she was even out of sight, the stallion started energetically sniffing a nearby two-year-old. "See, he's already moved on." "So that's not based on prior familiarity?" I ask. "Not necessarily; it could be. But look." The mare twisted her head around and snorted. "She's warning him" that she's not interested in sex. The message apparently doesn't take, since the stallion persists in snuffling his nostrils toward her groin until she darts forward and away. "See," Victor added, "in a band, that wouldn't have happened." The stallion would have picked up the signals sooner and would also likely have smelled her dung and had a better knowl-edge of her sexual status. But the stallion pursues her further. That's when it becomes noticeable that a bay mare is following him; I hardly noticed her at first, but Victor said she arrived with the stallion. When the two-year-old female finally kicks at his face, the stallion rolls away from her and the bay follows him. As the stallion and bay mare turn about they lock necks briefly, then connect nose to nose. I asked Vic-tor if that might indicate familiarity. "Possibly. Keep in mind, horses have dispersal. They could be brother and sister and grew up together." When she suddenly flehmens—which I didn't realize mares could do—Victor remarks, "Well she is really following him around, so there must be something between them. What it is, I don't know."

Though the stallion grew more irritable, delivering kicks at two different passing mares, the bay stuck close to him throughout, and he sporadically smelled her knowingly; not driving her away as he was doing with the others. Soon they were lost from view in the ebb and flow of mares and lone foals. But twenty minutes later they reappeared, now accompanied by a very dark bay mare with a foal. These four hewed closely together, walking in synch, until they separated briefly as a *besteiro* approached and the stallion angled off to the right. When the stallion returned he was clearly skittish; a stone dislodged by his right foot sent him leaping high in the air, launching a back kick with both legs. As he settled down again he stuck close to the two mares, especially as two passing groups of mares—a pair and a trio—trekked through in search of their offspring. I asked Victor about this configuration and he allowed that, "yes, that's likely the band stallion and these are his mares," adding that we would need to check back with them later to be sure. I appreciated seeing an example of a band structure beginning to reemerge.

More examples were to follow. In the background, Victor points to a cluster of five horses: two mares we'd been observing are joined by two more and one foal, also suggesting a band beginning to recoalesce. "That's good, it's another little piece of the puzzle. But the puzzle is not complete." Fortunately, the action with the *besteiros* is settling down, as they have largely moved to another portion of the enclosure in search of unclaimed foals. Laura points to several mares with their rear legs crooked, at rest, indicating they are calming, although Victor calls

FIGURE 1.4. *A band reassembling? The dark bay stallion is on the left; the bay mare who followed him is on the right.*

attention to the pair closest to us, noting that one is still whinnying for her foal and quite nervous. "See, if she keeps up like that, the other one won't want to be around her." Anxiety and stress are contagious in horses. So, too, apparently, is calmness, and as the searching, prodding humans headed elsewhere, the horses sought out and tolerated greater degrees of closeness than we had seen earlier.

We've been in this spot for an hour and fifteen minutes, so we decide to circulate a bit. Working our way through the enclosure, Laura and Victor help me spot other instances of horses clumping together, reestablishing individual relationships and perhaps the first vestiges of bands reconstituting. These manifest in proximity but also in terms of duration. "What's important," Victor stresses, "is writing down how long they're together." Both aggression and affiliative gestures involve closeness, but they differ in duration: generally short and edgy with aggression, while affiliative gestures are longer and sustained. We wind our way among the captured animals, watching mouths slowly grow less tight and tense while heads come closer together, largely looking in the same direction. I was particularly intrigued to watch as **flared nostrils** grazed flanks, caressing as much as sniffing each other, a visible display of how crucial the sense of smell is to their social interactions.

We gradually shifted from circulating among the horses to mingling with people. As we did, Laura called attention to the size difference between the *garranos* and the horses from the riding clubs, which are considerably taller and larger, reflecting some five hundred years of directed breeding and development. As we strolled, Laura introduced us to various participants, particularly Terri and his brother José Manuel, making sure I explained my interests and project to them. They were quite welcoming and encouraging, suggesting that I return earlier next year in order to join in with the herding. I accepted happily, and did indeed participate the following summer (2017) at the *rapa* that occurs at Curro de Mougás. But we didn't talk long because it was time to eat. Most of the *besteiros* went home for lunch, though a few stayed to eat with friends in the kitchens. The one we chose boasted several tables full of boisterous lads. As we ate, Laura, ever inquisitive and personable, managed to strike up interesting conversations all around us.

A couple of hours later, just after 5 p.m., the *besteiros* get back to work and drive the animals from the enclosure down to the stone-walled *curro*. This maneuver requires the same technique they used to

FIGURE 1.5. *Social proximity, reestablishing individual relationships.*

gather the horses up on the mountain—forming a loose line and waving sticks. The *besteiros* get them all moving in one direction, funneling them down into the *curro* across a distance of about two hundred meters. Occasionally a couple of horses prove elusive and skitter around the food trucks and kitchens. But mostly the movement is fluid and

FIGURE 1.6. *Terri and José Manuel,* besteiros.

directed—until they start packing into the *curro* and the compression of animals becomes intense, as the dust surges up and the shouts of humans whirl with the frantic whinnies of the horses. One edge of the wall cuts into higher ground by the pasture, making a natural platform of sorts for spectators. It slowly fills with people—families with little kids, a variety of teenagers, and groups of adult friends and family—to watch the horses writhe.

The smell of seven hundred horses is intense. With the summer sun burning down and the animals surging in the dust below, the aroma saturates my nostrils and thunders in my lungs. In the *curro,* the closeness selectively chosen between familiars earlier now becomes a serious problem for every horse. Necks seesaw up and down, back and forth, in fleeting attempts to avoid the faces and rear ends of conspecifics. Kicks are thrown with increasing frequency; bite gestures flash to the left and right. Stallions **rear** and slash at each other, instilling fear in those around them.

The horses' frenzy is familiar to me from the *rapa* in Sabucedo. In each case, compression is the central principle—pushing the horses closer together makes them more manageable; they're less able to **strike** at humans and more concerned with the animals pressing them forward and backward. The notable contrast is that the *rapas* here in the Serra da Groba, near Baiona, are far more efficiently organized and executed. Where Sabucedo's now is mostly performed for tourists, here the *rapa* remains a form of agricultural labor. Victor noted that in these *curros* they extract the stallions first, to limit the amount of conflict. In

FIGURE 1.7. *Chaos in the* curro; *two stallions clashing.*

Sabucedo, they make sure there's a maximum number of these males in the arena; their violent battles are exactly what the tourists come to see.

This afternoon at the Curro de Torroña is not a spectacle. Several dozen *besteiros* wielding long *varas* loop a *cabestro* or rope halter over the mouth and ears of individual horses, extracting them from the *curro* one by one. Crews wait to hold the animals in place, shear their manes and tails, then spray them with a disinfectant before releasing them singly to return to the high country. Most flee immediately; only the mares who are missing a male foal linger near the grounds, looking for offspring who have already been extracted to be sold for meat. The work is dirty and grinding; the men are grime covered by the time the last horse is finished, about two hours later.

As we drive back to O Verdugo, Laura and Victor animatedly debate what we've just witnessed. Victor's paramount complaint is the rough treatment of the horses and the stress induced in them by this ritual. He focuses keenly on the moments of brutality when horses are subjected to blows with a stick or pole, which are also the concern of animal activists who condemn the *rapas.* This stems partly from the *garranos'* disparagement as *bestas*; "They wouldn't treat their horses that way," he asserts. Laura conversely see the bigger picture: "There's no way you could move this many animals through in any other way," with so few men working so many horses. She also underscores that these *besteiros* conduct three of these *rapas* across the range within a month, which is a massive undertaking. But her main point is that these herds have to be managed, or they will create such a nuisance—for the government and for landowners—that they will eventually be eradicated. Without the *rapas,* the horses would be unmanageable and then would not survive, a point with which Victor concurs. They both want these animals to remain roaming the mountains, and that requires the *rapas.*

DAY 3

We return to the mountain the next day to resume surveying and observing the bands. I'm surprised how much appears to have changed over the course of a day. First, the weather is bitter, with damp skies and biting wind. Standing long hours in the cold will be challenging today. But I'm surprised too at how different everything looks. As the color and strength of light is muted, the features of hills, ridges, and vales all seem oddly different—shallower perhaps or even altered in form and depth. We were through here only a day ago, and though the contours are surely unchanged, my ability to get my bearings is off kilter.

Grinding up the service track for twenty minutes, we see no signs of horses until we near the little Capela Santa Mariña. The chapel is situated at a spot where several of the bands cross in the course of the day's wanderings, and sure enough, the first group we see seems to have just left from there. They're on the right or east side of the road, slowly ascending across a hilltop about seventy meters away. Easing out of the Terrano, we start to fan out to get a better look, but Victor is quick to advise that this is the wrong approach. "It looks too much like hunting to them," he counsels. Instead, he says to proceed "single file, Indian style." As we fall into line, Victor expounds on the correct way to approach horses. "Always walk in a zigzag," which he then briefly pantomimes. A direct advance is threatening or appears like a challenge to horses. He also emphasizes, "Don't stare at them!" Horses are much like humans and many primates in regarding fixed eye contact as a form of aggression, conveying hostility or menace. "Look up and around in different directions as you approach," he says. "This makes you appear less threatening." I internalized this valuable advice, which served me superbly the rest of my time in the field.

Regardless of such cautions, the stallion gets a little spooked as we slowly advance in staggered fashion. He is easy to spot, on the periphery of this small band and a bit taller than the others. Laura says species dimorphism is common though not pronounced among *garranos*. As each of us gradually move, he skitters off on a parallel line to us, keeping his distance. The mares, in contrast, seem unperturbed and maintain their slow upslope graze. So we settle in to our survey tasks, quickly tallying one gray stallion and four mares—two grays, a palomino, and a bay—with three foals between them. "I like this band," Laura comments. I ask why and she answers, "because the foals were born at the proper time," pointing out that they are larger (and so, older) than the ones we saw our first day, making them even more likely to survive both wolf attacks and treacherous weather.

Eventually, the stallion returns to the bunched up mares, so we decide to try out more observational techniques. I opt for position mapping. Victor shows us how this data is logged on blank sheets of paper with little gender signs directionally arrayed across it, indicating how each horse is facing. Times are marked for each entry; Victor emphasizes that these should be recorded in short, frequent intervals, especially when nothing important or dramatic seems to be happening. His charts from previous studies are quite detailed, listing wind direction, weather, and the positions of resources such as water. But the core focus of this exercise is easy to approximate: tracking how pairs and triads move in timed sequence. This provides insights into relationships within the band as individuals affiliate with one another over the slow course of a steady graze. Trying my hand at position mapping jars me out of the descriptive orientation of the free-write and makes me think more tangibly about proximity and distance within a band.

I start by focusing on one of the gray mares and the bay, who are grazing side by side: every minute I jot down small parallel lines indicating their relative nearness. Within a few minutes I can see that grazing is much more than eating: it involves a trajectory, intended or not, that's typically aligned with or at least attuned to the movement of others. Ethologists characterize this as socially facilitated behavior. After four minutes, the gray "leads" out across the slope, eating steadily; the bay stays alongside her, roughly paralleling each step or shift. Soon I'm wondering about their relationship. Are they related or just friends (or "preferred partners," a less anthropomorphic characterization)?[8] After my eighth entry, the gray mare separates, moving farther to the north while the bay does not. This gap between them holds for three more minutes, until the gray's head rises up from feeding and she looks around, assesses her distance from the others. Then she turns and begins eating her way back to the bay, who soon is also joined by the palomino. Now they're a triad, shifting in an aligned manner that takes the three of them back near the other mares and foals over the next five minutes.

This was a simple trajectory or development, hardly the basis for speculation about horse behavior. Mostly it served as a means for me to practice both an observational attention and a mode of generating data. Performing it also allowed me to see why Victor regards leadership as suspect: the same observed movement may be principally an affiliative act between two or three animals rather than one directing the movement of the whole group. In addition, through this exercise I glimpsed how individual movement is informed by the composition of the band and its positioning. Socially, I could see them registering and responding to relative distance or proximity with other members, synchronizing their movements. That is, while engaged in a generic activity of species-being—eating—they were also participating in a social dynamic of aligning themselves with their companions. Another value of this exercise was that I began to see the basic social units of band life: mare pairs or triads, mares with foals and/or yearlings, and individual mares. Sure, the stallion here policed the outer boundaries, keeping the group from spreading out too far, but the social structure seemed predicated on the pattern of mare affiliations.

Another point Victor stresses in position mapping is that it's a way of dealing with the subjective aspect of the crucial question of distance. Clearly, proximity matters in social species—it can both generate and ameliorate conflicts. But what counts as close, too close, or not close enough among animals? The position map helped me recognize, first, that I needed some objective basis to gauge the distance between and among horses; second, that they too are engaged in a similar process of gauging social space, and their assessments might vary individually: one horse's sense of "close" might not match another's. For Victor, this prompts the "just" retort (*just* the quirks or happenstances of any number of elements); for me, this underscores that all of the horses are engaged in an interpretive and performative process of assessing social distance and proximity all through their waking lives.

Horses' interpretive capacities and sensibilities are formed through the process of social learning, which begins when they are just days old. And before long, this dynamic is on display among the several foals present in this small band. I take a break from position mapping when I notice that one of the male foals is quite . . . pushy, precocious, assertive, aggressive? Any adjective comes value laden, so I try to be cautious in characterizing personality types. But what catches my attention is that he's trying to nurse from one of the gray mares, whose own foal is sticking close to her left flank. At first, her foal makes an effort to keep this interloper away, but its gesture at kicking has no effect. As the male foal tries to squeeze out the gray's foal, the mare aims a sharp bite at him. This drives him off by a few meters, but she has to threaten him again before he gives up trying to nurse from her. Within three minutes, though, he's aiming for the palomino mare and the process repeats. This time though, the first gray mare, who has formed a triad with the palomino, **intervenes**, sending a nip in his direction, which is effective at driving him away. He's the offspring of the bay but does not seem interested in staying close to her. Instead, he angles back toward the other gray again, as all of the mares start moving away, up the slope and out of view—a development the stallion seems unconcerned about.

I realize then that I've let the position mapping exercise slip. It wasn't adequate to capture or help me focus on the more rapid interactional sequences of behavior involving the male foal and the subsequent direction the mares take farther to the east. But perhaps it had attuned me to the kind of policing of social distance I just observed. The foal was certainly "too close" to the other mares, and they made sure he knew that. Whether it altered his "personality" or behavior I surely can't say. But the mechanisms were clearly on display as an example of the social learning involved with proximity and distance that constitutes horse sociality. Meanwhile, the palomino is the last mare to follow the others, and the stallion still acts oblivious. I have lots of questions about instigation of movement here, but it's time for us to move on, as well.

We don't go far before we re-encounter the band by the chapel, still in the dell where, on the first day, the stallion had been so actively engaged with herding the outlying mare, who the others were driving away. But as we set up to do our observations, no one easily remembers which one is the stallion; partly because we saw dozens of horses that day and then we took one day off for the *rapa* near Baiona. But also, because we were just tallying numbers, none of us had written a physical description of his characteristic features. Again, we don't get closer than eighty meters because the band is far from the road. Several guesses as to which one is the stallion are made, but none confirmed. Victor and I angle around the outer reach of the dell to get a better line of sight on one possibility, in order to see his "indicator." But within moments the horse lies down in the grass, scuttling our hope of making a sex determination. With no chance of confirmation any time soon, Victor says, "that's very unusual behavior for a stallion," so perhaps it's not the one. While we're observing the scene, I excitedly notice that two mares are engaged in allogrooming. "Yes," Victor says, "but be precise. What is it you're seeing?" Are their heads parallel or their shoulders? Are they nibbling at necks or torsos? Are they using their tails?

Again, he's pushing me to open up a **fixed action pattern** with a more fine-grained attention to the physical interaction. Then there's the social aspect. Though I can't make the determination, it also matters whether these are siblings or mother–daughter pairs or favored partners among band associates. It is important that it's mares, and Victor encourages me to think about how this form of proximity looks different from what stallions do when they meet nose to nose, or when stallions approach mares. "Watch their feet," he says, "record how they're positioned," in order to get a sense of facing and stance. I give up on identifying the stallion and concentrate on writing a detailed description of how these two horses are physically engaged. Then Laura finally spots him—it's not the horse Victor and I thought. Rachel writes down his characteristic features: bay stallion with a large star that's offset to the left on his forehead, barely peeking out from under a thick black forelock; he has a triangular snip on his muzzle, just below his right nostril, with a full bushy mane on both sides of his neck.

Naming ethological subjects is a fraught matter, ripe with all manner of projections and potential for anthropomorphizing; but it also marks an important transition. Ethology shifted tremendously with the capacity of observers to reliably identify individual animal subjects; similarly, recognizing the complexity of sociality within species turns on the relative capacity for recognizing individuals among a host of conspecifics.[9] Long-term relationships and reciprocal gestures become both possible and foundational. We decide that since our time is short and we will likely see this band repeatedly—given its position on the range—we will name both the stallion and the band. Since they're so close to the chapel Laura suggests *capilla* for the band. With that association in mind, Victor proposes Monk as the bay stallion's name. We count ten mares, six foals, and one subadult (yearlings and some two-year-olds), for a total of eighteen horses in the newly christened Capilla band. That task complete, we head off to do more surveying.

Following a side lane that ambles eastward, we drive for only a couple of minutes when up ahead we see a band that's almost in the roadway, underneath a large windmill. Our slow approach seems to leave them unperturbed, so once parked, we're able to get quite close, moving unhurriedly in single file until it seems reasonable to spread out. The scene before us evokes a good deal of gushing about cuteness, because a pair of subadults are lying side by side, recumbent on folded forelegs, heads drowsily erect and angled toward us. Even Victor purrs, "This is a beautiful example of affiliative behavior," so I take several photos. We speculate on their relationship—siblings, perhaps, or age-mates?

Victor and Laura guess one is a yearling and the other a two-year-old, but based on their positioning so close together it's hard to be sure. Behind them a mare is dozing in similar fashion with a sleeping foal stretched out nearby. Two bay mares are napping standing up but another adult is also sprawled asleep on the ground, similar to the foal. Minutes later, when he rises, we learn that, yes, stallions, too, do sleep that way sometimes.

This band is spread out over forty meters. We tally eleven mares, nine subadults, and three foals. This is my first experience of encountering sleeping horses. I can see how their necks are all level or slightly drooped; none are grazing. Their heads face in various directions, none particularly alert. That changes as we inch closer—necklines start to rise gradually, and all are soon facing us. Then, slowly, one bay stirs and shifts; another moves a few feet forward; a foal startles awake and stands groggily. Soon they're mostly all looking at us, as we simply look back. Minutes pass after the stallion rises, and the mares fall into a grazing pattern that gradually leads them up through a large outcrop of boulders beyond the windmill. Because they're so close to the crossroad where we turned east, we decide on *Cruces* as the band's name. Lacking much more imagination for the naming process, the gray stallion who'd been sleeping as we pulled up also gets designated Cruces. Laura and Victor debate whether his coloring might be considered *grullo,* since he has a black dorsal stripe and darkly shaded coloring on his legs. But his mane is quite light colored and his flanks are clearly dappled (dark

FIGURE 1.8. *Affiliative behavior; a pair of subadults are lying side by side.*

rings around lighter colored hair), so we start with "dappled gray" as our identifier for him but alternately call him "Cruces."

It's time to move on again, though not far, it turns out, to where another band waits a quarter mile ahead. With the next cluster of horses grazing some forty meters off, I quickly spot the stallion. But Victor corrects me—that is a two-year-old, or subadult. The "indicator" is not sufficient; age matters. A few minutes later he makes quite a flehmen, indicating an interest in the sexual status of the females around him. Victor remarks that it won't be long before the stallion drives off this young male. Rachel locates the stallion, a dark chestnut with two socks in back, so impromptu she names him Calcetines. Simona decides it's time for coffee and gets out the gear, but I'm restless, wanting to keep moving to stay warm. So while the others work at detailing the individual horses, I decide to scout the opposite side of the road, toward the west, where a large pile of boulders eight to ten feet high promises an inviting perch to view the landscape ahead of us.

From atop the boulders I have an excellent vista of the terrain, which drops steeply, opening out into a wide triangular basin. I realize that now we are on the back side of a low peak that we had gradually traveled up since leaving the dell band behind. Facing south, I'm looking down a long *bajada* or descending slope, bulged in places by pitched portions of rock and earth. At the bottom is a spring, or *aguaje,* that catches the drainage from both the peak I'm on and a long, steeply sinking ridge about two hundred fifty meters to the west of my roost in the stones. The road bends around the basin, then rises again before dropping off to the south. The basin is well below the grade of the road, so whatever water falls there also winds up in this low point. Not surprisingly, a large number of horses are spread out across this ground.

The task of tallying them is daunting because they are so diffusely scattered. Easiest to spot is a black stallion and a clutch of mares loosely ringing the water source—five adults, no foals, which I suspect will interest Laura. More challenging by far are several horses strung out distantly along the flanks of the western ridge. I spend ten minutes patiently watching through my binoculars as they slip in and out of view along its crest. Since they all looked to be bays, I wasn't sure if I was double counting some. More confusingly, I wasn't sure if they were in the same band as the one with the black stallion, or if they were the lead elements of yet another band out of sight to the west. Further muddling the picture, atop a small knoll across the road, roughly three hundred meters away, another group of horses spreads out loosely—perhaps advancing toward the spring or maybe just leaving from there. I knew Laura would expect a tally, but the numbers kept shifting as I tried to keep track of all the movement.

Victor eventually joins me and we spend forty cold minutes getting a fix on how many horses are here and in what configuration. Yes, there is another band behind the west ridge, and they seem fairly fixed along its crest—perhaps availing themselves of the strong wind to keep the flies away. Yet as we start identifying individual horses in the basin below, we become quite perplexed, because beyond the black stallion's group we can see another cluster closer to the road that has three adult males. Victor says that multistallion bands are an interesting but contested topic in horse ethology, because it's not clear what they might reflect about dominance relationships, and also because of uncertainty over the temporal duration of such relations—is this configuration just a passing moment before "bachelor" stallions leave a band, or a more long-term arrangement? These larger questions will have to wait until we can observe the horses more closely, but first we have to meet up with Laura and the others.

Rejoining them by the car on the lower, east end of the ridge, we find an encounter between bands shaping up. While we were gone, Calcetines's band had ambled off, first to the east, loosely paralleling the track we drove up on, then turning back to a westerly heading, passing through a bowl-like depression, presumably aiming for the spring in the basin across the lane. As they climb up, facing the lane, the mares in front stop, seeing ahead the horses Victor and I had been observing. Calcetines, in the rear, starts forward briskly in what Victor characterizes as "decided walk." He passes a white yearling, who snaps as he nears, and her mother, also white, with a full mane on her left side but only a little on the right, near her ears. The mare doesn't advance; nor does another white mare close by, who has a dark mane (all on her right side) and a bit of a black muzzle. But several other mares do advance—two bays and one brown, each with foals, falling in behind Calcetines's stride. One of the foals is caught up in the excitement and matches him, while the three mares and two other foals fall in a few steps behind.

The closest group across the road on the west side is the multistallion band. One young male is grazing just off the west side of the track. What unfolds now is a highly stylized **ritual interaction** between males in different bands, which Victor narrates.[10] Calcetines makes an approach, crossing the road and heading straight for the young stallion with head elevated and **ears lowered** menacingly; one of the male foals has followed him, close behind. As Calcetines closes within two horse-lengths, the younger male **bolts** back toward the cluster of others. Quickly, another stallion from that band, a bay who seems senior or more established than the other two, strides forward. At a distance of about four horse-lengths, he commences the ritual interaction sequence. With an **arched neck threat**—neck tightly flexed, muzzle drawn to the chest—he **stomps** the earth once with his left foreleg, then feints a **lunge**, jutting forth several steps before turning to his left, parallel to Calcetines, who immediately pivots away. Then the bay turns away, too, both now looking askance with their rears facing each other at a distance. When Calcetines interests himself in a clump of grass near the road, breaking off the threat, the bay struts back to his bunch; then abruptly turns and repeats his lunge gesture. Calcetines reacts with a sharp **head toss**, his neck snapping back abruptly, though the threatening stallion is more than twenty meters distant. Almost instantly, though, Calcetines regains his footing and assumes a stance facing the bay—they **stare** at each other for a brief moment, until the bay turns back to the others.

Then Calcetines turns back the way he came in an **avoidance retreat**. Immediately, the mares and foals who tagged along retreat back to the rest of their band, clumped up a few meters to the east. But Calcetines pauses briefly before he drops off the road, bends his head to the right and stares over at the other stallion, who **stands** and returns the gesture, staring back at Calcetines. After ten seconds, though, Calcetines turns away again. Victor says that the other stallion's glare is enough to establish a line between the bands that Calcetines will not cross. He notes this outcome is unusual, since bands of horses generally settle on some form of turn taking around access to water. He wonders if it's something to do with competition between the three males in the multistallion band. In any case, they're more than Calcetines wants to contend with.

While Victor expounds on all this, I'm watching as Calcetines returns to the waiting mares, who have attentively observed the interaction. Now he encounters more problems. The horses who had followed him truck past the two white mares, who stand unmoving. Calcetines makes an effort to nudge them back along with the others, but they refuse to move. In fact, one has fixed her stare on him so intently that I have to consider that she, too, is glaring. Calcetines lowers his head and gestures at herding them in the opposite direction, but the staring white mare swivels quickly and aims a kick at his face. Calcetines springs out of reach and turns away, then makes one more gesture toward her, which is similarly repaid with a backward kick; then he trots slowly past them in the direction he'd been trying to coax them, away from the spring.

What just happened here? As I'm learning, in observing horses (and animal social interactions generally), long mundane periods are punctuated by brief outbursts of drama. The hour we spent in this location revealed several bands' activity in space: two largely static, one loosely in motion, and another (Calcetines's group) in directed movement. But condensing this into a narrative account is challenging because we couldn't know what happened before we showed up. Mostly, I'm struck by the aggressiveness of the white mare toward Calcetines and want to discuss it, but Victor is dismissive. Where I see a female directing aggressive blows at a stallion, he sees a mare perhaps under physical stress. "It's like she's just saying, 'I really need to use the toilet,'" in terms of needing to get to the spring. Though the mare's capacity for bellicosity does not interest him much, I find it striking that she hardly seems concerned about garnering or maintaining the stallion's "protection." Her kicks clearly show the physical ability to drive off a stallion. But if she had need of a stallion to clear the way to the spring, Calcetines clearly has failed. Given Victor's propensity to praise certain stallions, I'm curious why this one doesn't draw some negative assessment.

Before we get deep in debate over how to characterize what we've been observing, the weather turns against us and a driving rain begins pelting the range. Victor suggests it's a good time to return to the lodge so he can give us a lecture on the history of ethology and some evolutionary background on the horse. We pack it in for the morning and head back down from the high country. In the communal space of the kitchen and dining room, Victor sets up his laptop with a projector that flashes slides on the bare wall between two shaded windows. The photos are mostly from his other field schools, in Venezuela and near Piornal, Spain. The topics he covers are wide ranging but consistently orient around his points of contestation with ethological literature on horses and his own countervailing efforts to formulate new research focused on affiliative behaviors.

Victor's starting point is the immense amount of time horses spend together in close proximity nonaggressively. "You'll see that I'm throwing in affiliation all the time because it's something that has not been looked at much in horses. We know so much about horses, yet all we see is that they have dominance hierarchies; it's rubbish!" He cites studies of Shackleford Banks horses by Daniel Rubenstein, an ethologist at Princeton, and Joel Berger's foundational work with mustangs in the Great Basin of Nevada. In both cases, ethologists emphasized these animals' aggressive competition over scarce resources, such as forage and water. Victor counters that many ethologists are finding, across a range of taxa, that enhancing social bonds has important fitness consequences for individuals—particularly in avoiding being killed by predators or in locating resources. Drawing on personal conversations with Berger, Victor argues that the correlates between reproductive success and dominance have yet to be clearly demonstrated, and also notes that, in relying on observations of horses at a distance of one hundred fifty meters or more—as in the Great Basin study—playful behavior may be mistaken for acts of aggression.[11] "Cooperation in horses has largely been overlooked and the focus has been placed solely on a by-product of it—aggression and dominance hierarchies." That is, when spending so much time together, violence is bound to break out at some point, and because it's dramatic—as was the clash that morning—it draws more attention. Here Victor is channeling the thinking of the influential ethologist Konrad Lorenz (1903–1989).[12]

Using Calcetines and the other stallion's encounter by the watering hole, Victor questions whether we saw aggression on display at all. In his account:

> We don't know. So if he's walking decidedly but he's like yup, there's someone in the toilet, let's stop, I'm going to take my group over there. It doesn't imply whatsoever that the other band impeded anything, avoidance is important. So basically, if I have to caricature all of this and say, what I saw was a decided walk which is normally what you get when you're going towards water anyway. You have this stallion that starts okay guys let's go, boo boo boop, oh shit

there's someone in the toilet, let's go over there. He's like
phew, wonder what they're doing in there, god I got to pee,
uh oh, you know what, there's another toilet over there,
but that's being very anthropomorphic, permit me this
goofiness.

We all laugh, but I point out, incredulously, that it was not "a toilet" at
issue but a watering hole. Victor counters that we'd already seen several watering holes that morning, so it is not a scarce resource. He is
focused instead on how the interaction between the two stallions did
not result in combat, which Calcetines avoided by leaving. This is an
opening onto Victor's complicated stance on dominance. "I won't say
that it doesn't exist, that would be silly. But rather than 'dominance
hierarchies,' let's talk about 'dominance behaviors' instead." I get his
point. Instead of seeing dominance as a biologically determined genetic
predisposition of an individual, regard it as something context-specific
that's worked out between aging and growing horses in a variety of
settings, over the course of a day, a month, a year, and a lifetime. In this
regard, our thinking is closely aligned; I see social behavior as interpretive and performed, rather than "hardwired." Yet I also notice how
this characterization of Calcetines portrays him in largely valorized
terms—as avoiding conflict, even if the mares are dissatisfied—instead
of seeing him as a stallion who failed to gain access to the spring, which
seemed to be how the mares regarded him. But Victor's concerns are
not with my analysis so much as the challenges he faces both in promoting his views about affiliative behavior and in criticizing the overemphasis on dominance hierarchies.

Victor continued his lecture, covering contested concepts like
"leadership" in horses and the tricky matter of how to differentiate between dominance and aggression, then winding through how observationally to code affiliative behaviors. But gradually it dissolved into
a free-flowing conversation with Laura and myself over topics such as
the problems with horse ethologists' fixation on "female defensive polygyny." Laura pointed out that at the *rapa* yesterday the stallions did
not evince any interest in defending mares. As it grew late, I turned to
sift through the small library of ethological books Victor had brought
along for our use. I selected Berger's *Wild Horses of the Great Basin,* Sue
McDonnell's *The Equid Ethogram: A Practical Field Guide to Horse Be-*

havior, and *The Horse's Mind,* by Lucy Rees, another horse ethologist working in Spain. That night I worked with McDonnell's book to hone my note-taking on the day's activities. This paid off the next day as my observations grew more detailed.

DAY 4

Today we are joined by Julie Taylor of Epona.tv, an equestrian media outlet that covers a range of subjects, from training and sport to equine welfare, including behavior and psychology. Julie is here to interview Victor Ros for a series on horse ethology, and she wants to get footage of how he works in the field. We decide to pick a spot initially that will let us spend more time observing groups we've already tallied, resuming the surveying project later in the day. We are fortunate to have clear weather ahead. Morning breaks brightly and soon the sun-saturated rolling slopes are awash in a swirl of greens, yellows, and grays. Passing Capela Santa Mariña, we recognize the Capilla band off the road to the west, and ahead we see a band advancing slowly alongside the service track. We stop and spill out into the still-chilled air to observe them.

As the coffee thermos passes around, Victor reviews the various tools in the ethological repertoire at our disposal. "Choose which techniques you'll want to practice this morning and let's get started." As we take up a position along the road, the band ahead slowly continues its movement toward us. Rachel spots Cruces right away, the dappled gray stallion, so we check to confirm our tally for this band from yesterday, to see if perhaps a foal had gone missing, a subadult or mare might have hived off, or perhaps one had been added. Initially we only count eighteen (with two foals and two yearlings), so five are either hidden from view, lagging behind, or perhaps missing.

In my morning groggy state, this observational moment feels somewhat like dipping my head into another dimension, peaking into a different world. The horses have likely been moving at least since daybreak, and it's common for groups to travel during the night. Within each band, too, members have jostled and sorted themselves, opening and closing distances, reasserting or chipping away at social positioning with their bandmates. We are abruptly focusing in on all of this now, peering into the middle of so much activity. Our brusque reentry makes it easier to see movement without fixating on narrative. That distinction is not easy to articulate or maintain; one implies the other. But observationally, I suppose, positing the contrast aids in detaching from one mode of attention—causal, interconnected—to focus on another, that of flow and motion in its widest breadth.

The Capilla band we passed moments before is loosely arrayed behind and somewhat above us, as the road descends gradually from the chapel. Following the road straight ahead—instead of turning as we did when we first encountered the Cruces band—leads past Portalén, which we've yet to reach. Along the grassy shoulder of the road cut we stumble upon an excellent position to watch one band pass close by another. The Cruces band has paused in mid-meander up the slight grade, with the Capilla band ahead to their right. The dappled gray stallion, Cruces, is in the rear of this loose processional, sniffing up a bay mare who is bunched alongside three others. He's interested in sex and seems unconcerned about the lead elements of the band. From last night's reading of Berger's *Wild Horses of the Great Basin*, I recognize Cruces as engaged in "courtship" behavior, though other ethologists

FIGURE 1.9. *The Cruces band moving; Cruces, the stallion, is on the far right.*

would characterize his actions as a "pre-copulatory sequence," seeking to avoid anthropomorphizing.[13] Meanwhile, in front of the band is a gray mare, also dappled but with a brighter mane and tail than the stallion, and her face is quite light. Beside her is a foal, a yearling, and a bay mare. She's looking ahead, noticing that they've been seen by mares at the edge of the Capilla band thirty meters away.

Observing this exchange of looks, I begin to see how horses pay attention. Victor points out some of this—gradations in the level of their necks are quite telling. Standing with the head even with the shoulders marks the resting state where the horse is fairly inattentive. As the neck rises, the attention becomes more focused and directed.[14] Sharp, high, and stiff—this is full **alert**. In between are various levels of concentration on or consideration of a particular object or development. Speed matters too—sudden, jolting head movement versus slow and gradual. The lead gray mare's head is high but not alarmed, and the two yearlings standing beside her, along with her foal, are looking away from the other band in various directions.

After about four minutes, the gray mare moves ahead along the road. Behind her half a dozen mares fall into motion, following. As they drift forward, higher up the grade three outlying mares in the Capilla band, spaced well apart, sharpen their attention toward this development. Their gestures draw over their stallion, Monk, who takes up a position just beyond them. Now he stares, with elevated head, at the encroaching passel.[15] In two minutes of his focused attention, the yearlings and foal alongside the gray mare grow uncomfortable, pressing closer to her while she takes in these gazes. Then, gradually shifting her trajectory, the gray crosses over to the opposite side of the gravel road, and they follow her lead. This altered course, veering away instead of closer, registers legibly on the watching Capilla horses; gradually lowering their heads, they return to grazing. Monk eventually turns his back to the gray mare's procession, no longer interested or concerned.

While this boundary interaction unfolds, Cruces finally mounts and copulates with the bay mare whom he had engaged in foreplay. After they finish, Cruces begins to notice how spread out the mares have become. He slowly starts forward up the road. But I'm mostly fixated on a development with the lead gray mare. Whenever the four mares directly following her seem too close, she turns and **looks** at them, holding their attention: all four heads are raised and trained on her, ears pitched crisply forward, until she turns back to her grazing. What's transpiring here? After the gray turns away, the four stand with lowered heads, shifting their gazes, relaxing their ears, then they too resume their graze. I can't know with certainty, but they seem to regard the gray mare with deference, judging by the exchange of looks and the subsequent redirection of their gazes when she faces them. The gray mare turns away again and resumes her motion while the others stand looking about. Meanwhile, Cruces is advancing up the road, still some thirty meters behind her but getting closer to the Capilla band. As Cruces steps forward, the remaining mares and yearlings lurch into slow motion. All of this, once again, draws Monk's attention.

As Cruces approaches on the road, Monk reasserts his alert position, joined now by a male foal who stands close behind on his right side, while two other mares also focus on this motion. The other Capilla mares do not concern themselves with what's unfolding. Cruces positions himself in the middle of the road—facing away from Monk— while the rest of the band crosses over, climbing up in the direction of the lead mare. I notice Cruces avoids returning Monk's stare, nibbling instead along the road's edge as the band mares leisurely cross the road in sequence, some even looking in the opposite direction. None of the mares crossing the road look up at Monk. This control of gazes is probably crucial to how they are able to pass so closely without generating conflict. The work of boundary maintenance is in the stare, certainly, but also in how it is tolerated and not reciprocated or returned. Gradually, Monk reduces the angle of his neck, so he is less challenging or assertive. Meanwhile the gray mare has stopped and is looking back, observing the scene and watching the other mares pass her, then moving on ahead. This takes six minutes, until there's only Cruces and a foal in the road, with a yearling next to them above the grade.

Victor is riveted by what just unfolded, or rather what didn't unfold, and explains why. "Look at this. They're not being aggressive!" Much like Frans De Waal on self-control in nonhumans, Victor focuses on the many instances of restraint in stallions' repertoire of behavior. Agonistic interactions between stallions typically play out in ritualized displays, as we briefly glimpsed yesterday with Calcetines at the watering hole.[16]

FIGURE I.10. *Monk, upper left, and Cruces, center below, looking away.*

But here, with two bands within twenty-five meters of each other, the stallions are not making any direct contact. Cruces is studiously ignoring Monk. As they pass, a flaxen mare defecates on the road and Cruces smells it closely, so he is still engaged and attentive to bandmates. Within two minutes the Cruces band has passed fully up the opposite slope across the road. Victor again extols the importance of what we're observing. "See, there doesn't have to be aggression. These two stallions are handling the situation peacefully." My take is somewhat different. Cruces seems to be performing what Goffman termed civil inattention, or at least boundary work, in not reciprocating Monk's assertive stare. But there's a punctuation yet to this movement.

It takes seven minutes for the Cruces band to cross the road. During that time I watch, ever more distantly, the lead mare stares off the four other mares who, in single file and still tagging along in her wake, seem to have come too close to her. Left behind on the road are only Cruces and a young brown male foal, who is orienting himself to the Capilla band. Impetuously, the foal strides onto the crest of the gravel track and whinnies upward toward the other group. Monk ignores this, but the male foal beside him scoots out to the edge of their rise and glares back at this boldness. The two lock into a stare, heads at alert. Cruces is behind his youngster, watching what's unfolding—until the foal crosses over the center of the road; this prompts his father, striding past him, to redirect the foal back toward the rest of the band. Across the road, though, the other male foal advances. Monk has ignored all of this until now, his head low to the earth, grazing, but within seconds he too moves to the side of his foal, though his head and neck are not arched at alert—he is just watching.

Cruces, once his foal is reigned in, moves up the road, continuing past where the mares have turned off the road. Monk follows him in parallel for a few feet. For a moment the pairs are fixed in mirrored positions: foal-to-foal, stallion-to-stallion. Monk breaks the frozen moment by nudging his foal back toward the others. But he turns again, orienting toward Cruces, but with an interesting positioning. The two now are staring in the same direction, off to the west, the angles of their necks matching approximately—elevated but not alert. I would say they are gazing out to the ocean, which catches my eye in the distance, but there's likely something much closer than the horizon that they both observe in parallel, performing civil inattention in tandem. Behind Cruces, at a distance, his foal is alone on the road. Unconcerned, Cruces ambles west again before turning and climbing up the road cut and toward the band. Monk turns too and trots lightly to catch up with the mares who have drifted off to the northeast.

The unfolding movements fascinate me because I can see Victor's lesson extended. With the foals I recognize a moment of socialization around distance and boundaries, as notable as the nonaggressive exchange between two band stallions passing each other. The Cruces foal tried out an assertive challenge directed at the Capilla band. His counterpart responded, or at least registered the gesture. But the stallions intervened and redirected their charges, preserving a boundary between the groups and averting a direct encounter. The foals could be construed as following some "natural" urge to challenge another male, but both are socially constrained by their fathers, who evidence a keen sense of boundary work. It's just a moment, a brief exchange; who can tell what social lessons the young participants might draw. But clearly sociality, in terms of boundary work, was more consequential than natural instinct. It's also notable that the mares of both bands were engaged in boundary work as well—one set watching the other archly; the observed maintaining a kind of civil inattention rather than staring back.

Topping off all of this, I reflected that the gray mare was leading all of the morning's movement. The band dynamics were shaped by the mares' movements, their noticing or modes of attention, and the assertion of and acknowledgment of a boundary between the two groups. It was not territorial (place-based) as much as positional. There were no natural resources at stake; rather, an entirely conventional, largely unmaterial boundary maintained distance between the groups. Through this interaction the male foals were learning how to manage distance and proximity as well as testing its limits and intensity. They mimicked their fathers but also needed to be socialized in how to properly manage each situation to avoid conflict, which is what Goffman's concept of *face* is fundamentally about.

Meanwhile Monk has another problem rapidly emerging. Off to the north, maybe two hundred meters away, another band is advancing. They were initially parallel to the Cruces band but mostly obscured by a knot of Scotch pines. I count at least ten adults and four foals but can't identify the stallion. Monk's reaction to them is quite different.

This time he's very assertive, dashing from his position above the road, charging at the lead adults of the other band. Through repeated jousts he drives them back up the slope they were just descending. Since much of the action is obscured by trees or muted by distance, it's hard to be certain why Monk reacted this way. Victor speculates that perhaps he knew Cruces well, either from regularly crossing paths or perhaps they were from the same natal band. But the contrast highlights the distinctive interactions we have just observed. Before long, Monk returns to his band and begins moving them down into the dell, a process that takes about twenty minutes.

We decide to stay in this spot to see what else might happen, and it turns out to be a fortunate decision. Just after the Capilla band occupies the low ground around the spring amidst the pines, we notice two horses approaching from the east. They're both bays. One has a long, thick blaze that buckles in the middle, pitching to the left, and its mane

FIGURE 1.11. *Two bachelors, Star (left) and Blaze (right).*

is almost entirely on the right side; the other has a circular star and his mane is fullest on the left. Victor quickly notes that these are a pair of bachelors and are likely interested in the mares down in the dell. For hasty designations, we refer to them as Blaze and Star. When they see us, they stop at alert and size up the unusual situation.

They do so by gathering information, first about us, approaching our vehicles and sniffing them over, then moving along the roads where they smell piles of manure left by mares in the Cruces band. They seem uninterested or unimpressed and turn back toward the direction they came from, passing over a low hill and out of our line of sight. But they return within minutes from the back side of the knoll, in a direct line of sight with the Capilla band spread out in the dell. Monk has to check this out. He moves up gradually, while Star and Blaze watch his approach cautiously. Monk keeps his neck mostly bent toward the ground; he seems studiously nonchalant, in contrast to the arch-necked approach to Calcetines yesterday. He maintains this stance once he arrives; as Blaze extends his face toward him, Monk moves in between the two males, and Star starts **pawing** the ground with his right front hoof. Victor remarks that they are being surprisingly cordial, rather than falling into an aggressive ritual interactive sequence.[17] He speculates that Monk may know one or both of these encroaching males.

The three engage in **circling**, intensely smelling and jostling about assertively—the third stage of the ritualized sequence. Victor breaks down its component parts, as they twist and shift, positioning to smell genitalia and to press their massive shoulders against each other. This olfactory investigation then shifts caudally along the body, focusing on the neck, withers, flank, then back to the genitals and tail or perineal region. **Nasogenital investigation** is when the mutual examination is most heighted. Typically, this is followed by boisterous vocalizations (squeals, snorts) and threat gestures (kick, strike, or bite). What's key to the outcome—a violent clash or a more tempered exchange—is that these component parts vary in expression, either decreasing or increasing in intensity as an agonistic encounter grows more animated.

In this case, the intensity level, Victor observes, seems somewhat muted. Perhaps because it's three horses instead of a "duel," and he speculates that Monk and Blaze may know each other. Partly because when Blaze ends up by Monk's rear, as they twist about, this positioning to his vulnerable side does not make Monk respond aggressively; also, most of the physical wrestling is between Star and Monk. They sniff intensely, nose to nose or **nasonasal investigation**, but not yet with the arched necks of the alert stare. Blaze turns away and seems ready to go but Star stays, and so Monk physically confronts him; now both their necks tautly arch. This face-to-face exchange produces bellows from both stallions and their heads snap back. They then begin to **neck wrestle** until Blaze inserts himself between the other two stallions.

The sound of stallions shrieking is jarring and impressive—the pitch is high and quite shrill but the tone is broad and loud. They split apart after another round of bellows, then quickly close in together again, **weaving** side by side, sniffing and snorting. Blaze again aims to leave

FIGURE 1.12. *Blaze, with the right rear sock, is in front, Star in the middle, and Monk in the back.*

but Star stays and he and Monk tangle tightly. Their heads wrap around each other, up and down, sniffing and pressing. The power of assertion is evident in their taut, straining neck muscles. This slides into more genital sniffing, with Blaze now pressing in, too. Finally, Monk rears up and bellows, stomping down on the ground, and the bachelors scatter. He gives a light chase, but starts looking back at his band, turning his attention away from the interlopers, and instead of **following** them, Monk heads back toward the dell, first at a slow **trot**, then with a pronounced **prance** as he gets back into view of the mares. This interaction takes about three minutes.

Victor's take is that Monk has "escorted" the bachelors out of the threat zone, characterizing the action as much affiliative as aggressive. He points to initial affiliative gestures in the facial contact between Blaze and Monk as he first approached. Victor's assessment rests partially on the fact that the encounter did not result in open physical violence—**bites** and kicks—between the stallions. His interpretation is both underscored and complicated by what follows. Before Monk has entirely traversed the downward slope to his band in the dell, the bachelors return to the crossroads. This time they act different, addressing their attention to the mare dung along the cutaway for the lane. Star positions himself and drops his own feces atop a heap on the road—an assertive gesture of **fecal pile display**.[18] Monk maintains a sight-line while the two begin sniffing the droppings but doesn't move. That is until Star, sniffing another pile, lets loose with a flehmen. Suddenly, with surprising speed and drive, Monk charges up from the dell directly at the bachelors. This time the exchange is quite sharp, as he doles out bites and kicks to both bachelors, who scatter, this time for good. Returning to his band again, Monk's prance is even more pronounced, almost comical, but it's not clear that the mares have paid any attention to these clashing males. We've been in this spot for just about two hours.

Taking stock of the morning's interactions, we've observed three very different instances of boundary work involving this one stallion. In the first encounter, as the Cruces band slowly passed the Capilla band, Monk struck up a watchful pose but maintained himself at a respectful remove from both the lead gray mare and Cruces, who followed later. Cruces played an important role by avoiding eye contact with Monk, and the two maintained a courteous distance, largely through parallel positioning. This is in contrast to the direct confrontation between

Calcetines and the black stallion at the watering hole yesterday, and also the second encounter for Monk, with the encroaching band from the north. After the Cruces band passed, he dashed off to challenge them far more aggressively. The contrast between these reactions is perhaps prompted by a familiarity between the Cruces stallion and Monk. Familiarity was likely a factor in the third instance of boundary work, as well.

The arrival of the bachelors provided an excellent example not just of the ritual interactive sequence between competing males but also of the performative aspect of these actions and roles. The first stage of the interaction did not feature violence (actual bites or kicks) but mostly seemed to be negotiated ritually. In contrast, the second stage culminated in violence as Monk bit both bachelors. The difference lay in the symbolic gestures made by Star. When he defecated on the mares' fecal piles, he signaled an interest in them sexually; this message was loudly amplified when he performed an exaggerated flehmen. Notably, neither of the bachelors acted this way upon their initial approach, when they were unsure of the situation they were entering. But Star did so after he had engaged in a ritual exchange with Monk, compelling Monk to act aggressively to counter Star's assertion of an interest in the mares below. From what I've gleaned from Victor's lessons and from now having read horse ethology extensively, there is a pronounced tendency to characterize stallions as behaving in an instinctual manner. But from this series of exchanges I was able to glimpse that part of their action involves interpreting a situation, and this interpretation is likely influenced by existing relationships with other stallions and mares.

As the stallion dramas dissipated, Laura reminded us that we had much more terrain to cover and additional bands to survey. So we piled back into the vehicles and headed up the range, past Portalén, finally, heading north. We only go about a kilometer before spotting a small band off to the east—there's a flaxen stallion and three mares (a bay, dun, and gray) with one yearling and two foals. This is the tenth band we've recorded, and they fortunately are by a developed spring, one that's built up and channeled through a pipe, so we stop here, too. The day has grown hot and we're primed for a bracing drink of mountain water.

Back on the service road, we take another track off to the west and in quick succession spot four more bands strung along a two kilometer stretch. The eleventh band is more than two hundred meters distant, so we only tally its numbers: five mares, three subadults, and four foals; the flaxen stallion has a lush mane so Laura designates him Peluda because he's hairy. The twelfth band is close to the road so we stop. The stallion here is striking, certainly physically—his mane is long, dangling almost the length of his chest, with long bangs, as well—but also because two mares press close against him, one affixing to his ribs on the left, and the other wedging the side of her face against his. Someone suggests Compass for his name but I jokingly suggest Lovegod for his moniker. He has a scar on his right rear, perhaps from a wolf. Laura reminds us to watch for these in all the horses. He's quite active, as we watch him herding a couple of mares that had not strayed far. There are six foals here—most sleeping or grogging about—nine mares, and one yearling.

We decide it's time for lunch and settle in around a nearby windmill, the highest point in this stretch of rangeland, setting up on a series of low rocks ringing the turnoff, which serve as tables and seats. The air is so still that the blades above us rarely move while we eat. When they do, it's jarring—a sudden, leaden punctuation of a 'chop' sound, booming and reverberating like sprockets and gears inside a giant clock as its long hand shifts to mark a minute. As we munch on chorizo, cheese, bread, and apple slices, Victor notices a band on a rise off to the south, clustered around a rock outcropping. In among them is a mare with a chain locked around her neck—probably an escapee from a farm down below. He goes to watch them, taking his time by approaching obliquely and stopping for several minutes before shifting again. As he is so engaged, we notice yet another band off to the west, about a quarter mile away—a bay stallion with nine mares. Meanwhile, from behind us to the east, down in a broad ravine running parallel to the road we drove in on, a third group emerges, this one in full **trek**, with all the horses striding in directed movement. So around us we can see four bands, counting the group with Lovegod, which shifted as we ate and is now moving up and along a low ridge to the northwest.

Amidst all these developments, the band trekking up from the ravine notices Victor spying on the other band. It's almost amusing to see their attention register so legibly, their heads turning in synch as their churning climb slows. Even more interesting, this bunch is on a collision course with Lovegod's band coming along the ridge from where the ravine descends. The lead mares see this taking shape but don't seem perturbed; they're intersecting at an acute angle, each column partially obscured by high ground in between. Victor returns to watch what's unfolding and is entranced by the chestnut stallion with the band climbing up the ravine. "He's the most beautiful stallion," Victor mutters. "A wonderful presence." Xestedo we name him. Then the mare behind gives Xestedo a bite in the rump to push him forward toward the facing band. As he surges forward, Lovegod too dashes out on the broken ground between the two groups.

Their encounter is different than any of the earlier ones, because these stallions are more vocal, bellowing and screeching with ferocity. They run toward each other and meet on open ground between the bands. Xestedo is more aggressive, stomping fiercely as they lock together, then kicking with both his rear legs twice. But Lovegod doesn't back down and they engage in neck wrestling and genital sniffing. Then Xestedo peels back toward his band, but Lovegod mirrors him. The two now dash along an invisible line in a **parallel prance**.[19] There's nothing obvious in the terrain that marks this line except for the tracing of it by these two heated stallions. Victor labels it the thirty-eighth parallel, referring to the demilitarized zone between the two Koreas. "It's a no-man's land." A boundary is drawn between the bands, foreclosing movement in an intended or adopted direction. The challenge and counterchallenge plays out over a hundred meters until the stallions separate, returning to their bands. Strikingly, both bands now alter directions, each turning away from their previous direction and heading out in almost opposite paths.

The grand swath of all this movement unfolds over ten minutes and it's utterly mesmerizing. Partly it's the heat of the afternoon—the shimmer of light on a treeless plane produces a hypnotic feel. But it's also the coherence and pace of these bands, in a type of formation generated by copious instances of micropositioning within the band and an awareness of other bands in motion, as well as the promise and challenge of the terrain they're traversing. Perhaps mostly it's the thrill of recognizing the behavior pattern and watching it unfold, recognizing what's about to happen (the clash) but not knowing the outcome or the particular dynamics. I can see why ethologists are so fixated on formulating predictive models and analytics. That's a hallmark of natural science and what animates the thinking of ethologists.

We have a full afternoon yet ahead as we work the western flank of the Serra, slowly descending to the parish of Carballedo, where

Laura wants to show us something. After stopping to tally only the bands along our route—another four, bringing us to nineteen bands observed—we arrive outside the village of Paraños. Laura is taking us to see Foxo de Paraños, a restored wolf trap, so we can understand something more about the basic logic of the *rapa das bestas.* We pull over at a little glade, lush with warm grasses, then hike across an open field to file through a narrow passage in a long barbed wire fence. In this steeply sloped pasture, three domesticated horses watch us from a distance, mildly interested in our presence. Victor laments that they look bored, as we step along an overgrown footpath into a loose grove of oaks. Above and behind the trees rises a low ridge.

The stone structure we trek out to see is wedged into the rising earth and shaded by several trees that long ago sprang up in its shadows, too close to be cut by mowers. The front is like a squat round tower at the end of a long shallow ravine, about twelve feet tall in front; its rear, upslope side is maybe half the height. That side abuts a pair of parallel tall stone walls—also about twelve feet high at the lower end—which flange out, facing up the descending slope. From above, the logic of the design is easy to grasp—the steep slope is funneled into the round tower, where the walls' end creates an opening onto the pit formed by the tower. Laura explains how these worked—the humans fanned out in long sweeping lines across the high terrain, while some crouched behind blinds made of brush along the steep incline. Those in a line used torch and stick to drive the wolves out of hiding and funnel them down the ravine, where those behind the brush would leap out at the wolves, disorienting them and impelling them faster toward what they imagined would be escape—straight into the tall opening of the tower, into which they tumbled, a writhing mass where they were killed in turn. The same basic logic and operation of capture informs the *rapa.* We will see it again tomorrow afternoon in some petroglyphs recently uncovered by archaeologists that Laura knows.

That evening we drive to Sabucedo for dinner. Several years prior, Victor had consulted with members of the Asociación Rapa das Bestas collective (roughly sixty members) as they tried to respond to PETA protests over the event. He's interested in checking in with them and offers to introduce me around to people I hadn't met on my first visit to Sabucedo to observe the *rapa* in 2015. It takes about forty minutes to make the twenty-five kilometer drive, and we have fish fillets and french fries at the social club, the only public building in the village.

Later, Henrique Bazal, president of the association, stops by, accompanied by Pepe Paz, the previous president, Rubén Figueiras, or Fika, and Felipe Castro. Laura has lots of questions for them about the *rapa* and the horses. Then they have questions for her about the other *rapas* in the south around Baiona and in the north, near Vivero. That's the one that seems to concern them most, because the association up there has developed into a breeding organization and is promoting the *bestas* as a distinct breed: Pura Raza Gallega. We talk late into the night about traditions, bad publicity, and the future of these horses.

DAY 5

We're driving up to the range in Victor's car this morning. Laura has business in Vigo and made plans to meet us late that afternoon down by Baiona again, where a couple of her archaeological colleagues have unearthed some petroglyphs that depict a scene of horses being captured. As we roll along, Victor is cataloging his concerns about the vehicle, starting with a sporadic knocking under the hood, plus a series of mildly worrisome noises. On our right, the road edges across steep slopes of pastures broken by narrow, brushy ravines and low stone walls in various states of disregard. To the left, bright stalks of foxglove pop out from granite rock face, encircled by large mountain ferns. None of the mechanical noises he mentions put me on edge as much as his habit of hand-rolling a loose-leaf cigarette while guiding the steering wheel with his forearms. "I've had the car for ten years," he says, "so it's at an age when problems start accumulating." Victor reminisced back to when he bought it, explaining that he had just been diagnosed with cancer and, since he lived in a remote part of Catalonia, he would have to make numerous trips for medical treatment. So he wanted a reliable vehicle to get him back and forth. "What kind of cancer?" I asked him. "Skin," he barked, as if it was quite obvious, exclaiming, "You guys are so bloody polite, I'm missing half my nose!"

Indeed, one of the first things you notice about Victor is that the left tip of the end of his nose is a dull red reduction, as if it had been sliced off and healed poorly. That's about right: In his previous career as a naval engineer he suffered a chemical exposure while inspecting a cargo of diesel—some condensation from the previous shipment fell on his nose as he removed a cap on the container. The plastic surgery that followed the successful removal of the resulting cancerous growth was protracted and exhausting, so he opted to end that treatment before its full restorative capacity had been achieved.

Socially, though, what's interesting here is that, as Victor observed, each of us avoided mentioning it at all or even acknowledging the blemish. I pointedly avoided looking at it when we spoke, very carefully managing my gaze to assure that it never came close to landing on the damaged tissue above his nostrils. None of us asked him anything about it, either. I wasn't sure if it was a birth defect or from some form of violence, but I certainly wouldn't pry, both for his sake and mine, I felt, as this might only cause embarrassment. In a nutshell, this is the concept of *face* as characterized by sociologist Erving Goffman. There are many dimensions to this concept, which broadly addresses the presentation of self that humans engage in on a routine, daily basis. We present ourselves as acceptable people and everyone we encounter, directly or indirectly, variously responds to that presentation—normally acknowledging or even affirming it; occasionally challenging it by calling attention to some embarrassing, uncontrolled aspect of that self. Goffman calls the type of avoidance my colleagues and I engaged in by ignoring Victor's nose "civil inattention," and it's a lesson most of us learn early from parents who counsel "don't stare!" as someone passing exhibits some unusual aspect or perhaps has breached social etiquette.

Does this concept apply to horses? Is it a way of making sense of aspects of their social dynamics? I think so. Casting back to the Cruces band passing by the Capilla group at the *capela*, it's not a stretch to regard their studious avoidance of Monk's stare as a form of civil inattention. What Victor commended as admirable—the lack of aggression from such proximate stallions—likely hinged on the way the passing band performed inattentiveness to the assertive glare from Monk. The dappled gray stallion trained his gaze on the opposite side of the road, occasionally focusing it on the ground, feigning grazing. The mares, too, largely looked ahead or looked away. For that matter, Monk's glare contrasted sharply with that of the mares in that band—none of whom were paying any attention to the horses passing only a few meters away. They, too, were demonstrating inattention. This is how society hangs together, for humans and horses. If we did not practice such restraint, averting our eyes instead of staring at everyone we pass, then conflicts would abound. This rationale is evident in Victor's repeated guidance not to stare at the horses. Such little gestures are amplified massively, evidencing and constituting sociality.

Since we aren't working with Laura on surveying today, we decide to focus mostly on observational and recording techniques for generating field data. As we drive along, Victor recites various sampling techniques. One approach is focal-animal sampling, where all the behaviors of one animal are recorded over a certain period of time; a variation is instantaneous sampling, where this same animal's actions are chronicled at predetermined time intervals. Continuous sampling is more ambitious, documenting all the social interactions that occur during an observation, versus scan sampling, which opts to record what all the individuals in a group are doing at set intervals. I've been mostly focusing on recording occurrences of a specific behavior, allogrooming, which is as much a sequence as a distinct behavior, because it's interactional. This entails detailing when the act begins and ends, its duration, and who the participants are. From my brief work on this, I've begun to see the complexity of the interaction—who is involved, how these horses are positioned within the band, what happened just before and what interactions follow. Today I decide to shift my focus to something less "charismatic" or interesting and instead try observing

FIGURE I.13. *A tableau of social positioning. Juanito, the chestnut stallion, is in the foreground, just right of center, facing the opposite direction from the mares.*

and generating more mundane data. Victor suggests I keep working at position mapping.

We pass the Capilla and Cruces bands before we stop at a group we're not sure we've observed previously. Rachel wonders if this might be the Calcetines band but no one can spot the stallion initially. The uncertainty highlights our blindness to mares and recalls Laura's criticism of the overreliance on stallions to identify bands. We count twenty-five horses, including eight foals and four subadults. It's a large number, so we're not sure if this is a temporary mingling of horses or not. As we watch them graze, Victor again encourages us to break that down further by detailing all the activity we can observe. Sure enough, as the horses contentedly tear away at the dew-soaked grass cropping up between thickets of gorse, their upper and lower incisors slicing away at the blades, their mobile lips extending and retracting, their placid air sporadically ruptures. A foal drifts too close to a mare, or one chewing mouth has slowly progressed too close to another's. The stillness breaks—one horse nudges another away with a **bite threat** or **kick threat**, or maybe with a short head thrust in an aggressive gesture.

Implicit in such exchanges is status, which horses clearly observe and maintain. What counts as status, though, can vary and is hardly fixed or certain, especially as the composition of bands shifts across the seasons. The speculation is that mares achieve dominance through age, but perhaps alliances are important, as well.[20] Without yet identifying the stallion, it's easier to see how band composition builds out from mares and their offspring—foals, yearlings, then older daughters; perhaps siblings form pairs among the older mares. Some mares take to each other and become friends or "preferred partners," seen in how their grazing is proximate and in unison. But this proximity waxes and wanes—shifting to "too close" from "not close enough" very quickly, and judged differently from various individuals' perspectives. This is the interpretive work daily life requires. From this view, horse sociality is mare-dominated, though stallion drama draws the most attention. Characterizing groups as natal bands gets at this mare-centric dimension, in contrast to the distorting notion of harems. But I have no way of knowing who was born into this band or joined it later in life.

I start position mapping, jotting down the relative proximity of all the band members at two-minute intervals. Soon engrossed in the task, I settle on a scanning process, working from one end to the other of this span of twenty-five horses. I'm in the middle of jotting down positioning at the east end of the band when two mares stir it up back toward the middle. Who was that, which ones? I ask the others but everyone was looking in different directions or concentrating on something else. The after-effects linger—a seal-brown mare and her foal scamper away, but three bays are clustered close together behind her. Which one drove her off, and what might this reveal about status in the group? Only longer observations could make that determination. I would also need to combine my data with identifications of individual horses, which Rachel is working on. Her task proceeds slowly, too, because while types of marking are clear—stripes, blazes, stars on the face; socks, cornets, stocking on the lower legs—they are often not readily visible at any one moment. Leg markings are easily obscured by brush or rocks or tall grass; facial markings, too, can be obscured by overly long forelocks that may part for just a moment but then conceal once more what they had briefly revealed. This data-generation exercise opens a window onto the density of horse sociality while making clear the immense challenge entailed in recording it well.

Rachel spots the stallion—it's not Calcetines, the one who had the encounter with the multistallion band at the *aguaje.* This stallion is chestnut colored with a full blaze and cornets on each of his rear legs. Rachel suggests the name Juanito, but I didn't catch why. He was "hiding" on the back side in the middle of the band. His positioning prompts Simona to raise the matter of culture. In Piornal, during a previous field school with Victor, they observed stallions consistently in the rear of bands as they moved. Here in Serra do Cando, they are often positioned on the sides, or at least that's her impression so far. Victor allows there might be some cultural variation in how these males position themselves within the band, and this question leads to the contentious matter of whether a mare's status can be ascertained by her proximity to the stallion. We hardly give this question its due when Simona notes he's behaving oddly toward one of the foals. Victor crisply retorts, "I don't think he's behaving any way at all. He's just doing his job." I chalk it up as another instance of *just* being used to foreclose a more fulsome attention to social dynamics. But Victor adds that predictability is fun, and he's right about that—anticipating individual and group interactions, knowing what to watch for.

My attention ends up being drawn to who's on the periphery. This matter is generally nuanced—it could be a mare "leading," or one that is not accepted by the others. This involves something of a counterbalance to a stallion's efforts to mold the group: while he's keeping them from wandering too far, they're also potentially pushing out mares they don't like. Laura's basic stance is that mares want to stay together; this doesn't require special effort on the stallion's part, though herding is the behavior associated with their dominance. Here we notice a chestnut mare with a wide blaze and a sock on her left rear leg a good thirty meters from the others, grazing in the opposite direction they are heading. What's her story?

Perhaps she left another band, or maybe the stallion peeled her off from her natal group. Stallions' efforts to incorporate new members can be met with many challenges. But whether she stays turns on how she gets along with the other mares. Juanito meanders, grazing, in her direction, sniffs her dung, then pisses on her pile. A male yearling follows him, dangling an erection. Juanito does not go out to herd her back in; he angles off in an opposite direction. The male yearling does go toward her, very slowly.

We don't get to see how this culminates but the situation gets Victor talking about a two-year-old male from a herd he and Simona observed near Pironal, Spain, where Victor ran a previous field school. They called him Limpy, I think. That young male was expelled by the stallion "very violently," Victor says. I take note because he has been harping on how gentle stallions can be, stressing that they are the most playful members of bands, consistently engaging the foals and yearlings in social learning. This and the fact that open violence is avoided so often between males—gestured at, implied, or threatened, but not enacted—speaks to the depth of sociality. There are ritual forms and conventions by which distance can be asserted, maintained, and performed, or position and priority asserted and acceded to, so that violence isn't necessary and is rather limited. I make a note to check on the chestnut mare if we see this band again.

If the periphery matters so, perhaps the center does too, something that we might be able to consider in the larger schema of relative positioning among these animals. As Juanito and the male yearling are angling around the outlying chestnut mare, I notice a gray mare with a black mane and light colored coat in the midst of the band. She's notable in part because she's the only one looking back at us, seemingly taking stock of what we're up to and what threat we might potentially pose. She maintains this stance for about a minute, then she turns to her right and pulls alongside a bay that's been grazing just behind her.

They work at each other's backside vigorously, allogrooming, the gray perhaps a bit more than the bay. I think about the role this selective ritual act plays in cementing relations within a band, and I wonder what this interaction might reveal about the status of the gray, as initiator of the allogrooming. Again, too little data to draw on in too short a time, but I'm learning what to look for and beginning to see the performative aspects of what might be considered instinctual behavior.

We move on again, and along the road we happen upon what we've come to call the multistallion band, the one that engaged with Calcetines the other day. We're riveted because they're riveted, up on a ridge to the west of the road, at full attention, staring off into the distance. At first we think they are following the approach of two bay mares and one foal from lower on the ridge, or perhaps the technicians who are servicing the windmill just ahead to the south. It's certainly not us; the fact that we've stopped along the road has not drawn their attention at

FIGURE 1.14. *At the center, allogrooming, gray mare is on the right.*

all. After reconnoitering a little ways farther, we see it's another band of horses, across the road to the south. It's Calcetines's band, in roughly the same area we last saw them. He's again positioned right next to the two light gray mares, as if they're yet again "discussing" something. They're distant enough that it would be cumbersome to focus on them in detail, so I'm content to regard the legibility of the attention of these more proximate horses—so clear and durable. We locate three "indicators" among them, so the idea that this may be a multistallion band still holds, but Victor is unsure. So we decide to give them a closer look later when they're in a more favorable position for up-close observation.

As the morning slips on to noon, we decide to head in a new direction, following a service track we'd not been on yet. This involves passing down through a narrow, twisty stretch where the road hugs a shallow creek that drains the high ground above; then up to where a modest meadow nestles between a tall hill to the east and a low ridge opposite it, to the west. Piling out, we take up our various observation posts and quickly count thirteen horses: at least two gray mares and one buckskin (tan coat with black legs and mane), the rest are mostly bays;

there are three foals and one yearling; the stallion is a young-looking bay, somewhat small in stature. In the bustle of counting, it takes a few moments to notice that we're not the only observers. The two bachelors, Blaze and Star, who we'd been hoping to come across again, are approaching from the north along the road, through the grassy glade, closer to the ridge off to the west. So here's a second opportunity to watch them interact with a band stallion, and quite quickly we see contrasts with how Monk, the stallion with the Capilla band, interacted with these two on day four.

The first difference involves relative proximity. The bachelors advance until they are only about thirty-five meters away from this band; Monk had charged out to greet—or challenge—them at one hundred fifty meters. Where Monk had aggressively trotted up to the pair, this band stallion is only gradually approaching them, grazing as he goes. Without much show of assertiveness, he ambles up from the far or south side of the clustered mares, positioning himself between the bachelors and the mares. The males look at each other directly for just under a minute, with heads raised but not alert; then the band stallion lowers his to an even level and turns off to his left. He gestures at grazing as he moves toward them. Meanwhile, Blaze gives a quick grooming to his right rear, then eventually starts to graze.

At about twenty meters apart, the band stallion stops and strikes a parallel stance to the bachelors; all three are roughly facing west, but the bachelors' heads bend to the south, eyeing him and the mares, while the band stallion's head is down, avoiding direct eye contact. They are fixed like this for less than a minute when Blaze starts advancing, also with his head down in the lush grass, munching as he moves unhurriedly. The young band stallion mirrors this development and shifts toward the bachelors until he's about two horse-lengths from Blaze. Star remains somewhat behind his buddy, looking off to the west initially, then closing in back alongside Blaze. Now Blaze approaches the stallion but stops when they're five meters apart and turns parallel, while Star follows and pressures into Blaze's right, looking over his shoulder directly at the band stallion, who gradually turns his rump toward them while continuing to eat grass.

When I look back at the mares as this encounter develops, I'm surprised to find that they're paying little or no attention.[21] We're raptly focused but they are not. The buckskin and one of the grays are actually heading off toward the south, while most of the other mares just munch away; the yearling and one foal are sleeping. Before long, two of the bays start drifting westward, with a foal trailing. At no point do I see them demonstrate much interest in what might possibly be a dramatic contest among these males over who will belong to this band. They certainly show no evidence of feeling frightened or needing protection from these encroachers. Perhaps sensing the mares dispersing, the bay band stallion reorients his grazing toward them; or maybe he is turning away from direct conflict with Blaze, who now slowly follows in the band stallion's wake. This movement would take Blaze directly in among the mares. But as this is unfolding, Star abruptly turns toward the northwest, where a scent or a sight has caught his attention.

Following his gaze up the western ridge, I see what it is. A large bay stallion has appeared and is looking down on this scene. Victor mentions that he's seen several heads popping up from atop the heights, but this is the only horse that appears in full. This stallion has a thin stripe that morphs into a long, widening triangle of white that covers much of his muzzle between the nostrils. His mane on the left side has a big gap in the middle. The mares above soon lose interest and only

FIGURE 1.15. *Another observer, the older band stallion.*

this older band stallion remains in view, watching intently. The effect on the bachelors is galvanizing; both are suddenly at alert, with Star facing the stallion above, some two hundred meters distant, and Blaze leaning toward the proximate one. Notably, the nearby mares and foals are all facing away as they graze toward the south, drifting lower in the narrow vale, angling along the stream, without paying any obvious attention to what's unfolding.

As we wonder about this other band stallion—both older and larger than the one we focused on initially—he studies the scene below. After a minute he jaunts most of the way down the ridge and stops, still about one hundred fifty meters away. Then he breaks into a rapid trot, heading straight toward the bachelors, closing the distance in a matter of seconds. Blaze and Star start quick-stepping away, but they also have to avoid the younger stallion, who starts matching their steps. In a moment, the young one is parallel to and in contact with Star, while the older stallion pulls up next to Blaze. In doing so, he directs a double rear kick at the head of the younger band stallion. The young one reels and dashes away, while the older male turns his full attention to the bachelors. Star aims a kick at him but he's undeterred and closes in, arching his neck and sniffing Star's genitals; Star bends his head sharply back

FIGURE 1.16. *Blaze and Star, in trouble.*

toward this stallion. They lock *naso-naso,* with Blaze right alongside. Gradually the young stallion returns but is oblique to this exchange. The older one rears and shrieks, scattering the bachelors. Star turns toward the mares, but the young one intercepts him; Blaze heads toward the road and indirectly toward the east side of the band, but the older one cuts him off sharply. Now they all weave back and forth, Star trying to turn Blaze away at one point, the older band stallion cutting back and forth across any direction they take that might lead them closer to the mares, who have somewhat quickened their movement away from the clash but still seem largely uninterested.

The clash is sharpest between Star and the older stallion. Star is persistent in driving toward the mares, while the big band stallion doggedly and energetically keeps cutting him off. Soon the three of them—Star, Blaze, and the older stallion—end up off to the west, weaving in and out of the ritual sequence of conflict—parallel prancing, genital sniffing, and arched neck threats. At one point, all three are almost face-to-face. They navigate this sequence smoothly until Star flehmens. This sets the older one off; he shrieks and rears; the bachelors bolt in tandem along the road toward the south, well past the band and out onto the open plain. Rachel and I climb the hill to the east to follow the action, but I veer too far to the north, anticipating them looping all the way around. Instead, they continue the interaction mostly in a series of large loops to the south, which I can't follow. As all this unfolds, we try to figure out what it is we've just seen.

Why did this older stallion intervene as the bachelors approached the younger stallion's band? Victor reviewed the unusual features of this encounter. As is his wont, Victor took note of how the initial encounter did not seem aggressive, though it's questionable whether that would've held up for much longer as Blaze inexorably inched closer to the band. But the most striking aspect was the older stallion's intervention. His band was not directly threatened by the bachelors—they were largely out of sight on much higher ground; nor did it seem like he was aiming to move them down into the glade. As the older stallion chased the bachelors, the first band remained largely in place; he did nothing to displace the lower group. For that matter, during the twenty minutes we observed this protracted engagement, the older band stallion left his band potentially vulnerable as he passed well out of sight of the mares, giving repeated chase to the bachelors.

Victor speculated that perhaps he was "teaching" the younger stallion a lesson; maybe, given their proximity, the younger one was his offspring. Or perhaps the older stallion was annoyed by the puny defense this male barely seemed to muster against the encroaching bachelors. His first clear threat gesture, after all, was directed at the young band stallion, not the interlopers. Maybe there is a cultural convention over how band stallions should respond to such encroachment, and the older one intervened to maintain those local "rules." This would suggest that horses share some sense of forms of comportment or politeness—as with gaze management—that were being disrupted. Why would an interpretation based on the defense of conventions and rules apply here? The interaction really escalated when Star flehmened—a willful and symbolic gesture that provoked the older stallion to drive them from the scene. As Victor noted—ever attentive to the limitations of a reductive biological explanation (instinct, for instance)—the older stallion gained little in terms of "reproductive fitness" through this encounter and, moreover, put his band at risk through his protracted absence. Perhaps, then, he was offended at how poor to form the younger stallion was performing his role and decided to put on a demonstration for all concerned parties, or at least the males. In the end, it's unknowable. What we do have is a scene, a strange incident, that becomes an opening for speculative thinking—what's happening here?—rather than a basis for a knowledge claim. This is a difference between ethnography and ethology, I think.

Because we have to drive an hour or so yet to meet up with Laura at the archaeological site, we cannot wait for the vying stallions to return. Instead, we head back down the range, but squeeze in one quick stop when we spot the Mirador band—the group that had been the focus of our first extended observation. They're near the small pool where we last saw them as the group spread out, waiting on the trailing mare and her foal. The mare and foal are not in sight now, but they're not the only ones missing. Most of the mares and foals are already descending the distant side of the clearing, off to the west. I just catch a glimpse of the dark palomino mare (see Figures 1.1 and 1.2) that I thought was leading previously as she disappears over the edge, with the bays and their foals also moving that way. In the center is the black stallion with the small star. He makes a series of flehmens and urinates on a fresh pile of mare droppings. He's keenly focusing on a brown female who oddly seems to have two foals. Soon it's just him and her, the two foals, and a bay mare with a long blaze. I remember her from the first day, hanging back as the palomino and other mares walked past her toward the north. The rest have disappeared over the side. To the south, on a nearby hilltop, we can make out another band that seems headed this way. But there's no way to get closer without disrupting them—nor do we have time to survey a new band.

The brief scene we do observe is quite fascinating. The stallion is clearly aroused and is pursuing the brown mare, his erection waving in the breeze. It soon becomes apparent that the second foal is also a male; he too becomes erect and prances in parallel with the stallion as he circles the brown female, who is uninterested in all this attention. Meanwhile, the bay mare is moving in roughly parallel fashion to her. I wonder about the bay, why she hasn't gone with the others; whether she's just strongly attracted to the stallion; why she doesn't have a foal? Or perhaps the male foal is hers. We can only spend fifteen minutes here, so those questions are left dangling. The brown mare doggedly eludes the stallion's attention, but she's trailed closely by the foals. She walks toward the opposite side of the pool, and the foals start to get energetic. Soon they're both running in wide circles around the water. Meanwhile, the bay mare keeps finding ways to get close to the engorged stallion, who is showing her little or no interest. She's patient and we see her sniff repeatedly at his rear and genitals whenever they pass closely.

The stallion renews his push to have sex with the brown mare, but this only ends up driving her off down the distant slope toward the others. Now it's just the stallion and the bay. They graze in parallel, about a horse-length apart. He looks up occasionally to catch a glimpse of the brown down below. The bay positions herself behind him, sniffing his rear now and then. They're still in that position when we pack it in and head out to meet Laura at Outeiro dos Lameiros, where some of her archaeological colleagues will take us to see recently uncovered petroglyphs depicting horses being driven into a circular enclosure some three thousand years ago.

DAY 6

Our last day on the Serra arrived, and as befits a final day in the field, our culminating round of observations and surveying would leave us tantalized and wanting more. We had decided to concentrate on ethological techniques in the morning, leaving surveying for the afternoon. But as luck would have it, as we drove up the range and approached the *mirador*—our first extended observational setting—a band came into view we had not yet surveyed, the same one we glimpsed at the end of our field day yesterday. On a wide clearing around a towering windmill, just at the edge where the slope drops steeply to the west, four mares, two foals, and a yearling are standing. This clearing is at the foot of the hill upon which the *mirador* is perched, where two more windmills stand. No stallion is in view initially. One of the mares—all bays—steps several meters in our direction, stops, then stares fiercely at us for close to two minutes. Both her ears are clipped, probably by a *besteiro* some time ago. Another mare briefly parallels her gaze at us, then returns to eating. The foals here are quite active, zipping about in long looping circles around the older horses. But once their trajectory begins weaving closer to and between the more mature animals, one of the foals receives a lesson in social distance through a bite threat gesture from a yearling.

The stallion finally does appear: a seal-brown bay—black, I thought—that none of us recognize. He has a long forelock but if it shifts just right you can see a small dot of a star. The stallion stops at the lip of the clearing, sizes us up, and then returns to nibbling at the bright grass. Interestingly, over the next three minutes the mare with clipped ears approaches us, and she does so in exactly the zigzag manner Victor encouraged us to mimic: first several steps to her right, then forward

FIGURE 1.17. *Learning social distance through a bite threat gesture.*

again but crossing to her left, next advancing to her right again, bringing her closer to where we stood, all the while feigning interest in grass along the way. This movement is interspersed with head gestures toward the ground, though she didn't eat over the whole course of her forward trajectory.

Meanwhile, as the stallion steps up into the clearing we can see he is trailed by a domestic mare sporting a padlocked chain and bell around her neck, similar to the one we saw yesterday. Her presence prompts me to think about the contrasting notion of property in relation to these horses: unlike the wild mares, this mare was clearly marked as belonging in the world below the range, on a farm somewhere off the main road. Like the mare we saw yesterday, she wanted to be with this band but seemed unused to its mode of socializing. Upon noticing us, she walked past the other horses, avoiding the bay mare with a wide circuit, then strode in a straight line to stand in the track, also staring at us but perhaps expectantly rather than intently. In the background, several more horses climbed up over the edge—a gray mare with a foal and a black subadult with a large star; before long, one last mare followed, also with a foal, making a count of six mares, four foals, and two subadults.

As the domestic mare watches us, the others coalesce in a loose group around the stallion, about five horse-lengths from the domestic mare, who is mostly white but with a distinctive ring of brown coloring around her center. The clustered horses watch us attentively, all positioned behind the bay mare with clipped ears, who is grazing lightly. The stallion is smaller than her and looks quite young. Eventually the domestic mare turns back toward them, though by then the stallion has begun to step forward; the others, except for the bay mare, loosely following his trajectory. But the domestic mare steps into the stallion's path and stops, her body perpendicular to his but her head drawn somewhat awkwardly, parallel to his face. The stallion begins grooming her withers and back with his teeth. I start to record this as an instance of allogrooming when I realize she is hardly reciprocating. She makes some light gestures at stroking the left side of his face, but they're mild compared to his vigorous attention to her backside. I speculate that she was raised singly on a farm and didn't learn this affiliative practice or the sense of reciprocity it entails. As the core of the horses advance across the road, the bay mare comes up and interjects herself between the two, driving off the domestic mare, who ends up on the road again. She settles for sniffing a substantial fecal display pile, which registers the crossing point of several bands.

Sure enough, as all this unfolds another bunch of horses comes into view, descending from the hilltop—the Mirador band, in full trek. For a moment it looks like these two groups are bound to intersect like the two we watched yesterday, prompting the stallions into a ritual confrontation. But the Mirador group has an intermediate goal: to the northeast side of the hilltop there's a small pool in a narrow depression, punctuated by two small Scotch pines. As the first group treks off to the east—trailed by the dark bay stallion, who stops to add his drop- pings, topping off the fecal display in the middle of the road—the upper band strolls downward. Their movement is strikingly bifurcated. Lower down, on a well-established animal trail, most of the horses proceed, headed by the dark palomino mare that I had suggested was leading the group on day one. That seems still to be the case, though this time I notice that she's the only one without a foal, and that may have much to do with her pace relative to the others.

Meanwhile, their black stallion is descending along a steeper face of the slope above them to their right, trailed very closely by a bay mare with a wide blaze—the one who followed him as he pursued the seal- brown mare yesterday. Notably absent is the mare who had lingered so long behind as the others tried to move forward when we first observed them. What happened to her? Perhaps her foal died from a wolf attack or some accident and she had left the band, as Laura says they will do. Her positioning relative to the others had generated a good deal of speculation earlier—was it just the foal who kept her back or were the others shunning or avoiding her? If her foal had died from a wolf attack, was it because she was perhaps made more vulnerable by her mother's position relative to the others? We would never know for sure, but her absence opened up a host of broad questions about mare sociality.

The horses incline down the slope in two gradual lines, bound to converge: the dark palomino leading four mares—the gray, the seal- brown, and two bays—with four foals, each within a nose-length of each other, and a full deferential horse-length behind the palomino; the blazed bay is following close behind the black stallion. Twice the dark palomino stops and feigns grazing while looking ahead at the trajectory of the pair above her, but doesn't keep her head lowered long enough to tear at the grass.

As they near each other, she and the stallion start walking in parallel, about four body-lengths apart on the high ground above the pool. Interestingly, as the palomino mare keeps heading straight, overshooting the spring below, the black stallion proportionally veers to his right, avoiding her. For a moment these two lead horses edge toward converging with less than a full body-length between them, with the blazed mare still right on the stallion's rear. As he advances, the palomino matches his stride until the bay behind shifts to his right quickly, as if trying to go around in front of him to the spring. In an instant the palomino changes course to her left, trotting straight for the pool, as the bay cuts back behind the stallion, moving quickly toward the water, too.

The palomino arrives first and takes up a stance at the spring; the bay stops parallel to her, a horse-length to her right. But the others trot past quickly, only one stopping to drink below, where the pool unwinds into a slight stream. The bay quickly turns away from the water after only twenty seconds. The palomino remains in place through the rest of this observation. Moving first to a resource like water is an assertion of dominance, or at least prominence, among horses. This assertion by the palomino mare seemed to underscore what I thought I had seen in her movements on day one and today: if she was not leading them, the other females clearly showed her deference. Even if the palomino is not certainly dominant, she was performing or signaling dominance in relation to the resource of the spring, which is when dominance is situationally asserted or contested.

The status of the bay with the blaze is less clear. I wondered why she was following the stallion so tightly, apart from the other mares. Was she asserting some kind of prominence or perhaps just attracted to him, or was this an effect of being shunned by the mares? She certainly was assertive, matching the palomino's power gesture closely (though not actually drinking) and clearly commanding the attention of the stallion. Supposing he was the reason she was brought into the band, had that impacted his relations with the other mares? We certainly had too little time observing this group to even hazard much of a guess, but it was a good moment to give it more thought and attention.

Victor was mostly focused on the fact that, with the first group now passing only about thirty meters east of the pool, here was another instance of two proximate stallions who were not challenging each other. But the mares in the glade are more intriguing to me. While one bay and her foal drink at the stream, the other bay and the gray mare stride to the edge of the open grass and stop. The stallion follows and approaches the bay, sniffing her rear. She looks back at him for a moment, then moves away. Behind this cluster of five horses the blazed bay stands alone in the glade, at least ten body-lengths behind them, while the palomino continues her stance at the pool and the first band passes out of sight, north along the road. Slowly, the blazed bay shifts closer to the stallion, but as she does, the gray mare and her foal follow the other bay, moving out of the glade and up the next rise.

Meanwhile, I had lost sight of the seal-brown mare and her foal, who remained up above on the slope while the others descended. Now she descends too, also giving the palomino mare a wide berth. This gesture crystalized an impression that had been building for me—it's perhaps *social distance* as much as *access to resources* that highlight the status of a prominent mare. The palomino mare continues to be afforded deferential space as the rest shift about in relation to the stallion and the blazed bay. As the seal-brown mare moves down to the stream, the stallion approaches her, sniffing at her face, resuming his sexual interests from yesterday. Her foal snaps deferentially on her left side as he directs affections along her right, from face to flank to rear.

But she turns away and leaves him standing behind. The stallion watches her go. He bleats a plaintive whinny as his erection rises, but she doesn't look back, increasing the distance between them until she nears the two bays and their foals. Nearby, the gray mare's foal is nursing. She stands still while these horses eventually cross over the downward slope to the west. When the seal-brown mare finally follows, the stallion, the palomino, and the blazed bay remain in the glade, each distant from the other.

I want to stay longer to see if I can discern more about the social relationships in this band. But we have more groups ahead, so after twenty-five minutes in this spot we head northward. Before long we come across the band with Juanito, the other chestnut stallion (besides Calcetines; see Figure 1.13). They are on the move, slowly grazing, so we stop and sort through our notes on this group. A quick count shows that they are still at twenty-five: twelve mares, four subadults, and eight

FIGURE I.18. *The foal is snapping; the stallion is on the right.*

foals. As Rachel gets to work detailing particular mares' markings, I start in on behavior mapping, noting when dyads form and when they separate. My notes are timed for every three minutes: 9:48, two dyads; 9:51, two dyads and one triad, including a foal; 9:54, two dyads become a foursome, and the triad remains, and so on. As I record their interactions, I also take note of the mares I had focused on before.

The light gray with the black mane is again in the center of the bunch, walking flank-to-flank with Juanito. Just ahead of her is the bay mare she'd been allogrooming with previously. They remain close together as the band moves. And in front of them is the outlier chestnut mare, trailed again by the two-year-old male. Juanito is two body-lengths behind him and I wonder how that all might play out. But I return to recording dyads: 9:57, just one dyad, Juanito and the gray mare. Rachel notes that her mane is long on the left but short on the right; she's dappled, most thickly on her rear, and she has a small mustache with a dark muzzle. She records the chestnut mare's features too—long mane on the right, with just a nib behind her ear on the left side; two rear socks. Our ability to see and record the horses is improving.

Our next stop is the Capilla band, whose stallion is Monk, the large bushy-maned bay. The band is dispersed about in the dell, so we take this opportunity to get quite close to them. With all the attention we focused on Monk when he was vying with the bachelors and guardedly monitoring the movement of the Cruces band on the third day, we have paid scant attention to the mares. Initially, I recall little of our first day's observations with them, but remember watching a darkly dappled gray engage in local enhancement with a tree limb, followed by a bay who imitated her. She's easy to make out now, standing in the center of what seems to be a half-moon semicircle formed by the other mares. She's the one Victor suggested was "just a bitch." The outlier then—a black with a foal, who Monk was continually herding back into the group though the other mares threatened her—is still on the periphery, but a palomino, also with a foal, is at a bit of a remove from the others, too. I settle into behavior mapping again.

At 11:27 the palomino's foal lies down and I count two dyads—the darkly dappled gray and a bay with a star, then a seal-brown with a thin stripe and a bay with a thick forelock; 11:29, the dark gray separates from the bay; 11:32 she allogrooms with what appears to be a subadult whose coat is "roaning out"—white splotches are emerging in scattered fashion across her mostly brown flanks. This lasts for thirty seconds, then the roan walks away and the dark gray checks on her sleeping foal. After doing so, she rouses the foal drowsing next to hers, who startles awake and stumbles in search of her mother, the palomino. At 11:35 the dark gray and the bay with a star reform a dyad; 11:37 the starred bay lunges at the palomino, who rolls out of the way, the bay taking her grazing spot and separating from the dark gray. 11:38, no dyads. Meanwhile, Monk is pursuing sex with the outlier black mare, but she's not interested. The palomino is having a tough time: 11:40, one of the bays moves beside her, but five minutes later positions to kick her foal, who moves away from the threat gesture. 11:47: the dark gray and the starred bay, trailed by the palomino, make a move to leave the north side of the dell, but Monk breaks off and herds them back before they get far.

Over the next ten minutes the mares gradually shift and a collective movement or formation develops. The dark gray and starred bay form a core around which others start congealing; first the black without a foal, her ears cautiously lowered as she approaches the bay; then a seal-brown, the other bay, the roan and, very warily, the palomino. At 11:56, the black and the roan form a dyad as they start climbing up the rocky bowl to the west. I quickly map the position of the whole band: black mare, roaning subadult in front; two body-lengths behind them, the dark gray mare; right behind her is the starred bay, flanked by two seal-brown mares and two foals, who form a dyad; a body-length behind them is a palomino; behind her is a dark bay, looking back. On the floor of the dell are two sleeping foals, with one bay mare beside them; Monk is standing several horse-lengths from her, and the lone black mare and foal are maybe twenty meters from him. He seems to pay little heed as the mares form a procession that leads up out of the dell, passing from view.

It's an interesting progression. They graze the whole way, pausing occasionally. At one point the dark gray and her foal pull even with the two in front, while the others fan out ten meters behind them, loosely a body-length from each other. The palomino seems better integrated now, slowly working her way up front, where her foal forms a dyad with the dark gray's. Now the black is at full alert, staring ahead across the other side of the dell's rocky lip. The mares behind wait, no longer grazing but nibbling occasionally at shoots of gorse. I note that back in the dell, three foals remain; two crashed out entirely and the lone black's standing beside her. Only one bay remains behind, not far from Monk. I get a sense of what Victor meant when he said they slowly transition to expecting the foals to keep up with the mares. I see how this dynamic can lead to dissipation in a band's structure.

First the lead black, then the roan, the dark gray and her foal, a seal-brown mare, and then the palomino pass from view to the west. Monk is midway up the slope, grazing; the bays linger near the lip, waiting on their foals to waken. And the outlier black munches in the tall grass of the dell, distant from all, even her own sleeping foal.

Two realizations followed from this observational exercise. The first was that I could see the problem with "leading" as a concept—it leaves out the interactional dynamics that produce decisions to "follow." As these mares rose up from the dell, their interpersonal positioning gradually shifted into a collective movement, resulting in a **consensus** to advance on to the landscape ahead, which other bands appeared to occupy, even as they left their stallion behind. The second was that I felt ready to apply this type of observation in a more sustained manner on a couple of bands in the high country above Sabucedo, in advance of that *rapa*.

The day is slipping away and we've yet to survey new bands. We head off to have lunch at the spring, stopping only briefly with the Cruces band—led by the dappled gray stallion who smoothly passed by under Monk's watchful gaze on day four. We have to stop; they're right on the side of the road. The stallion and the mare are intensely allogrooming, working each other's right shoulders. Their interaction prompts me to think about how we've tried to gauge status among the mares, specifically in terms of positioning near the stallion. But maybe that's backward; maybe it's the stallion who seeks her out, rather than her him. If the dominant mare is central to social life, then most likely a stallion entering a band would need to be responsive to her. This mare is flanked by several of the horses I saw following her across the road as the boundary work developed between the two bands—a bay with her yearling and the palomino. These three stick close together—likely the bay is the mother and the palomino is just a year older than the gray yearling. While we're watching, the bay lets forth with a long flehmen, imitated directly by the yearling. With all the attention given to how stallions perform this behavior, I wondered why there seems to be little attention paid that mares do it too. I wonder how performing such a flehmen may relate to mare social interactions—is she gathering information on sexual status or a broader range of social information?—but there's little time left to observe further interactions.

After lunch we work quickly to survey as many bands as we can. Methodically, we reconnoiter the broad western basin out along the stretch of road that leads down to Carballedo. Again, this range is full of horses. We spot one band immediately, well south of the road, down in a broad, shallow ravine. The angle and distance makes observation difficult, and after ten minutes we have yet to spot the stallion. But Rachel records two distinctive mares: one dark palomino with four white socks, and a bay with a ring of white discoloration around her right eye. Ten adults in all, with five subadults and five foals. Then we pass a family band walking along the road—a dun stallion, one gray mare, her male yearling, and a foal. We pass one more family later that afternoon—a gray stallion, a reddish-brown and white mare (Barcino, Laura decides to name him), a similarly colored subadult, and one foal.

Such small bands typically result from a bachelor hiving off a single mare from a larger band.

But most of our afternoon is spent in one spot along the road from which we are able to observe several bands in motion. The range to our north is a series of low peaks, which drain down to the basin between us and them. In between, one long, low ridge rises gradually to a pair of hilltops off to the west, about five hundred meters from the road. Here we record our twenty-ninth, thirtieth, and thirty-first bands, bringing our total number of horses observed to 414, out of approximately seven hundred estimated to inhabit the Serra do Cando. Beyond the tally, though, what stands out for me about this spot is the opportunity to watch the movement of groups of horses across long distances. "Pageantry" is the word I settle on to describe it.

The sun is the hottest it has been all week, making the air shimmery and wavy. On the distant ridge we watch two bands: one with a bay stallion occupying the high ground; the other with a palomino stallion slowly working their way up the long grade from the east. Scattered loosely between them is a large herd of cattle spread over part of the ridge and into the swampy basin. The bay stallion watches the other band for several minutes, not making a move until the lead mare is within fifty meters; then he dashes out and engages the palomino vigorously, the two of them racing back and forth in parallel. Their shrieks are muted by the distance. I clock their exchange at two minutes. Victor again comments on how they are working this out without violence, but I'm thinking more about a point he raised earlier: that at such a distance, observing just through binoculars, it's almost a given you'll miss the subtleties of the interaction. I also think how by timing behaviors I've started to recognize many more fine-grained interactional nuances—like the alternating inclusive and exclusive gestures toward the palomino mare in the Capilla band over a matter of minutes.

While the palomino band is engaging the bay stallion's attention, I notice a lone bachelor down below starting up the slope from the southwest. His line of sight is blocked by an intervening knoll along the slope of the ridge; he seems oblivious to most of this, slowly eating, not moving in a directed manner. After much time, he passes over the rise and we can't see him. After waiting awhile, Victor and the others drive over to get a closer look. I walk a bit farther until I get a different angle on the scene but still can't locate the bachelor. But the palomino has, suddenly charging down the slope, stirring the bachelor from the brush. The contrast with his interactions with the bay stallion band is stark: the former stylized and showy, played out in parallel rather than the direct attack the palomino deploys now in pursuing the bachelor.

The palomino closes with the bachelor in less than twenty seconds, over a distance of maybe one hundred meters. The lone male reels and peels off to the south, with the palomino in pursuit, over rocky ground. Because the ridge is crusted with low hills and towering rock outcrops, I lose sight of them several times until they finally pour out onto the basin floor. Here they plow through the largest concentration of cattle and the bachelor rears up to give fight to the palomino. The engagement is brief and ferocious; the cows hurriedly scatter. But the bachelor breaks off the fight and scampers away off to the southeast. The palomino feints at several of the remaining cows as he returns. Each gesture has the similar effect of making the cow skitter out of his ascending path to rejoin his band. The stallion almost seemed to do this just to enjoy watching them scatter before him. Hard to say.

As the light begins to fade we pack it in and start heading back down. Along the way we see the multistallion band right along the road. Victor suggests we stop; he wants to try something. He alone gets out and stands a dozen meters from the car, with his hands in his pockets. He doesn't move toward the horses; just stands there, fumbling around with his packet of rolling tobacco. The older stallion, whom we had seen fend off Calcetines at the waterhole, grazes in the distance, but the two younger males are playing with each other, rising up and entwining their necks. Impressively, they grow curious about Victor and start working their way closer to him. This is Victor the trainer in his element, cultivating the horses' curiosity, luring them forward so he can take a better look at them. One approaches closely enough to sniff at Victor's outstretched hand, but the tobacco packet doesn't interest him. After they both return to their play, Victor comes back to the car and breaks the news—it's not a multistallion band: the two young males are geldings. So that's why they pose no threat to the older stallion. Like the two domestic mares we've seen, these two males also likely escaped from a farm down below and are now fitting in with a band on the range.

Just before we make the final descent, fittingly enough, we come across the very first group we observed on day one, when we saw the two stallions pacing along the rim. Here they are again: a light gray stallion with a white mane and five mares, still being trailed by a young chestnut stallion. Initially we were uncertain about the young male— had he possibly just been expelled by the band stallion? But as they cross the road before us, we can see that his interest in the mares seems quite keen, and he is pushing closer and closer to the gray stallion. Laura notes that likely, when she returns next year, this chestnut will have replaced the gray. I think once more of how it's a precarious matter to identify bands by the stallion alone.

That evening the proprietor of the guest house in O Verdugo, Daniel, provided us a farewell dinner of fish fillets and fried potatoes in the restaurant/bar. He topped it off with a *queimada,* a flaming alcohol punch made from *augardente* and flavored with herbs, lemon peels, coffee beans, cinnamon, and sugar. As we worked our way through this punch, two local young men came in for beers at the bar. Laura was curious about them, and she struck up a conversation after we finished the *queimada.* I was intrigued by how much they reminded me of similar men in rural West Virginia, where I first learned to do fieldwork. Still in work clothes, superficially they seemed surly, but I recognized a familiar mix of shame and pride. Laura melted them quickly into open socializing as she knowledgeably inquired about the horses.

Laura has talked with many *besteiros* during her survey work and was interested to know if these two men worked with them at all. Yes, answered the tall one, who spoke in a rapid mumble. But he and his friend were about the only young guys around to help the old *besteiros* deal with the foals each year. Laura asks whether there are local *rapas*; the other one answers that there used to be one nearby, in San Lorenzo de Estrada, but it was discontinued in the 1980s. Too many young people left for the cities; there were too few remaining to do the work. Laura worries aloud about what will happen to the horses—will the local cattle owners eventually drive them from the range? The two young men share her concern.

— 2 —

Bands

SOCIAL LIFE ON THE RANGE

DAY I

I arrive in Sabucedo one week before the *rapa* commences. The village is home to about three dozen people. No one is around in the social club when I stop by, so I head to Quireza, the next hamlet over, where I'll be staying in a guesthouse. After settling in, the first person I look for is Juan Carlos Bouzas—my guide in all things *rapa*-related. We met the previous year by chance when I was looking for lodging and stopped to ask him directions on the narrow coiling lane through Quireza. Juan wondered if I was a reporter or photographer coming to cover the *rapa*. "Close," I replied, explaining that I'm an anthropologist. We bonded quickly once we realized we had Detroit, Michigan, in common—my hometown and the place where he has been working for several years. Like many "young people"—a designation that seems to cover anyone here under sixty—Juan returns every summer to take part in the *rapa,* staying at his mother's house just up the lane. The young have left for jobs in the cities of Spain or abroad. The *rapa,* which historically was held earlier in the year, is now scheduled to coincide with summer vacations.

It's easy enough to find Juan; he's at the Saloon del Sheriff, one of three bars in the village. The Saloon is an old stone building that has accumulated several additions over the decades, including a second story of bedrooms. The barroom is below the grade of the road, so entering it feels like sinking down into earth. There I found Juan holding court just outside, amid a cluster of small tables ringed with red plastic chairs in front of the low, barred window of the Saloon. Juan is tall, with a lightly graying, closely cropped beard, dressed in a Team Suzuki motocross T-shirt and blue jeans. He likes sitting outside so he can smoke. Over several hours, he introduces me to a series of friends and cousins, most of whom are settling in for a late afternoon of chat and drinks. But others came and went, stopping in to say hello while running errands or making visits. Through the first few introductions Juan prompts me to explain my project; people listen politely but still seem to regard me as a "reporter," and they're not interested in talking to one or being asked to explain the *rapa.* Or maybe my ideas for doing a horse ethnography just aren't that interesting.

As these social conversations waxed and waned, Juan and I caught up on the past year and then dove into a subject he cares deeply about—the horses on the mountain behind us to the north. "They know we're coming," he told me. "This will be a difficult year." Juan seems perpetually to be anticipating that the horses will get shrewder and wilier each season, but he's also concerned with the quantity and quality of the horses they round up for the *rapa.* Last year he and others in Sabucedo were worried about having enough horses to make the event successful—they seem to grow more elusive and perhaps fewer in number. But as much as the horses, Juan worries over the people involved. "There's too much drama in Sabucedo," he says. As this *rapa* has garnered an international reputation—alternately favorable and unfavorable—he finds that the people involved become more difficult to deal with.

In Juan's telling, the reasons are varied. The first involves tangled lines of authority over who is running the show. He spools out a narrative of internecine rivalries between residents of Sabucedo and the surrounding hamlets, each with different claims and interests in the process of herding and shearing the horses. As the event grew famous, more people jockeyed to be the public face of the *rapa*—the ones who speak with reporters and get their pictures in the papers. Then there are competing sensibilities about how best to herd and drive the horses down the mountain—which techniques of trapping work best, for instance. But the crucial matter seems to be the declining number of *besteiros* and the rising number of outsiders who are drawn to the *rapa.* As the *besteiros* age or lose the financial ability to pay for heightened state requirements for veterinary treatment of the horses, they are replaced on the mountain by energetic but somewhat befuddled tourists and visitors looking to participate or the riding clubs that make a day of it, chasing horses across the range.

In the 2015 *rapa,* Juan and his companions had to cover fifteen miles tracking some sly bands, largely because groups on horseback had un-intentionally driven them farther away. "They don't understand, you can't chase these horses," he fumed. The advantage gained by mounted humans was squandered in a futile effort to run them down. "You have to trap them," he maintains, and that's a subject he delves into at length. The horses have to be surrounded, which is possible on foot—if the humans advance methodically. That's where the problems arise in Sabucedo. I tell Juan about the systematic way they work the *rapa* in Baiona, also mostly on foot, but he just laughs. "It's never that orga-nized here." From this perspective, it's not that the number of horses are declining; the humans are not doing as good a job of rounding them up. Before the start of last year's *rapa*, Juan and a bunch of his buddies trekked about ten miles west along the range to gather horses from an area where they are more concentrated and easily caught. This year they're doing the same, and he invites me along. I'm tempted but ex-plain that I'm most interested in studying the horses close by, so I can observe them on their home territory.

Juan has plenty of advice on how to proceed with my project, start-ing with a cautionary note about the terrain: "there's a few places up there where you can really get lost," he warns. Juan offers to take me up on the mountain tomorrow, after the Euro Cup match between Spain and Italy. I explain that I'm interested in analyzing the horse so-cial structure before and during the *rapa*. Juan has lots to say about the stallions around here, most of whom have names and reputations earned in previous years. He rattles off a list of them that I struggle to jot down—Castaño, Chulo, Ghano, Zepelin . . . Juan is less interested in the mares, but he understands what I'm after. He talks about the clashes in the *curro* and how the horses interact; less so about their relations up on the range. But he knows some locations that'll suit my interests, and I'm grateful to have him as an initial guide.

As the afternoon bleeds into twilight, Juan's talk about the *rapa* drifts into reflections on the hamlet's recent past and how the place has changed since he was little. "It's all so overgrown now," he laments, as we gaze across the road toward the thicket of greenery surging up from the banks of a little creek. "When I was a kid, the fields around here were full of cows and sheep," the land was worked thoroughly and doggedly. But starting in the early 1970s, young people left Quireza for the big cit-ies, as they did all across Spain. Today both Quireza and Sabucedo are emblems of *la España vacía* or "emptied-out Spain." As the countryside depopulated, agricultural lifeways declined. "We had a sawmill here. We had several restaurants and bars; those places were packed in the evening! Now everything has gone wild, it's all overgrown."

I notice that the terms he uses, *silvestre* and *salvaje,* are different from how the "wild" untamed horses are characterized, as *bestas* and *burras.* I ask Juan about this and he clarifies that the first set of terms are used only on nonhuman subjects. So, "like wildlife, in general, or an area can be a wild area, things in nature." In contrast, "We use *besta* for people, too, like when someone is acting crazy or out of control. We tell somebody, 'you're *muy besta* man.'" It's a subtle equivalence, but it helps me glimpse the various connotation of wildness in this region.

Also, as he's talking, I recognize gradually that I'm imbibing a different perspective on horses than I'd been acquiring with Laura and Victor. Juan draws from and conveys a nuanced form of knowledge linking horses and humans, in contrast to the population-level dynamics that interest Laura or the species-being view Victor has cultivated. In Juan's account, a key challenge facing organizers of the *rapa* is that the horses are too savvy. "They won't fall for the same trap twice," he insists. "When you go to trap 'em in the same way again, they know better, they avoid it." They catch fewer horses each year because the horses grow smarter about the human tricks. But this familiarity is a two-way street. "People know horses here," Juan stresses. Villagers grew up around horses and typically have a deft hand for controlling and directing their movement and behavior.

By way of illustration, he offers me advice on what to watch for in the movement of their ears, eyes, and angle of the neck, anticipating their actions or possible dangers. Unlike the guidance offered by Victor, who is concerned with unobtrusively observing them in the field, Juan's counsel is focused on how to drive horses from their redoubts and direct them into pens and catchment areas. But Juan also describes a very different *rapa* when he was young. "We didn't pen the horses back then. You were in the middle of them, all around you [before the shearing]. Six hundred to eight hundred horses, just grazing away." He painted a scene of families milling about the horses, picnicking on tables they set up in the meadow by the *curro.* "The horses were calm, they were used to it," he said of the process of the *rapa.*

Juan then expressed an additional dimension of this local knowledge that I'd not glimpsed in the field school. The *besteiros* know the lineage of the horses. In making claims to own a horse, they have to identify foals as the offspring of a particular mare. Beyond that, they frequently can trace parentage back through several generations of mares and often can identify her siblings going back many years. "They can look at a foal and tell what kind of future it might have." Is this an animal that might be sold as a riding horse someday, or is it only worth selling now, as meat? The *besteiros* that keep going manage to make a family tradition out of observing their horses. Several described to me taking their children up in the mountains a couple of times during the year to check on their animals. These *besteiros* know the horses' favored haunts and can usually locate them with ease. Juan's cousin does this regularly and is a good person to talk to about where the horses are right now. Observing them this way bears some similarity to the activities we pursued during the field school, but the focus is obviously different. Still, between Victor and Juan I recognized a shared pleasure in seeing untamed horses roaming unfettered in the high country.

The sky darkened from twilight to night, but as empty bottles of Estrella Galicia thickly populated the table tops, Juan had more to share. More advice on how to avoid dangerous situations with the horses, though he warned me far more about the threat posed by cows, especially those with young calves. He had much more to say—vent, really—about the envy and petty jealousy of locals vying to lay claim to the *rapa,* as well as what's wrong in how the ritual is conducted today. I listened to much of this as a well-worn lament about nostalgia-drenched "good old days" and the way things have gone down now.[1] Juan also laid into what he called the "church fairytale" about the origin of the *rapa.*

The legend goes that during a plague in the 1500s, when the village seemed at risk of being wiped out, two elderly sisters sought divine intervention. Taking refuge in a cabin not far from the hamlet, they made a vow to San Lorenzo, the town's patron saint, promising they would give their horses to his care if the hamlet was spared. When the plague subsided, they handed their mares over to the parish priest, fulfilling their promise. He decided the horses would be released up on the mountain after being marked as property of the saint by having their ears clipped. Each year thereafter the villagers would go up and bring the horses down to shave their manes and tails. For Juan, and many other people I spoke with, the tale is just an example of how the Catholic church lays claim to many ancient "pagan" traditions. He simply points to the petroglyphs just a few miles west of here, at Campo Lameiro, which show scenes of humans similarly trapping horses and driving them into an enclosure, to make it clear that this practice is likely thousands of years old.

Despite such awareness of the prehistorical roots of the *rapa,* the ritual is draped in spiritualist sensibilities, at least by way of the official depictions and narratives in promotional literature. The horses are construed as "spirits of the mountains" with which the humans are alternately communing or fighting. In this sense, "*besta*" transmogrifies from disparaged creature to mythically powerful entity, worthy of combat in the *curro.* Here instead of speaking of *besteiros,* owners of the beast, they identify as *aloitadores,* fighters, vying against the beast. They boast of fighting the horses by hand and mounting them bareback rather than using ropes and poles to control them, as in Serra da Groba. And most importantly, the ritual still commences with a mass in the village church, with the bells sounding at 6:30 a.m., echoed by loud fireworks. Following the mass, a procession of locals and tourists heads up the mountain to encounter the horses.

Through our time together, Juan could voice seemingly contradictory views. He lurched from opining that, "the horses are really wild now," to conceding that, "they're pretty much tamed now." I had to listen carefully for his shifting views and characterizations of an event he could see from competing perspectives, sometimes influenced by scenes from years ago and other times emphasizing how much things are changed today. He was a superb and generous guide for jumpstarting me on this stage of my project, especially because his experience with the *rapa* is so extensive. He talked late into the evening, a lot about stallions and how viciously they fight in the curro: "They try to bite each other's nuts off, man!" adding, "people don't realize, their most dangerous parts are their teeth." And about the mares on the mountain, how they build a defensive circle around foals when they're attacked by wolves, but how one will abandon her foal when they're being stalked by humans: "They don't care what's behind them, they just take off," leaving a foal behind, at times. But mostly about the intricacies of tracking and herding them on the mountain, especially when they disappear into thickets. "You can't see them at all—you have to be able to smell them." In the end he says, "You'll see for yourself up there," and we call it a night.

DAY 2

The next morning, anxious to get started, I head off on my own up the mountain rather than waiting for Juan. Before I left the Sheriff, he vaguely gestured toward a path at the west side of the hamlet that I could take. Starting from above the church in Quireza, I moved along an old farm lane up the slow rising slope. I soon could see what Juan meant about how overgrown the local fields had become. Not all of them, certainly, but I strolled by many that once held varieties of livestock and now were thick with ferns, brambles, and gorse. Gorse rules the hillside of the Galician ranges, typically decumbent and low spreading, but when it isn't burned back, the shrub can grow to seven feet in height. As the lane gave way to a trail and then to some vestige of a path, I found my way forward repeatedly blocked by thickets, some rising above my head, perforated by occasional dark passageways burrowed through by wildlife. My handy retractable walking stick worked well for whacking the chest-high ferns to shake loose any ticks; my keenest anxiety was over contracting a fatal tick-borne fever that had already struck a number of people that summer in western Spain. Facing the dim openings through the towering shrubs, I pictured ticks raining down on me from above and gave up trying to shimmy up the mountain by myself.

Fortunately, in the interim Juan realized the Spain–Italy match was slated for late afternoon instead of in the morning. So by the time I returned discouraged to the guesthouse, a message was waiting for me to meet him in front of the Sheriff and we would drive up together. Driving sounded convenient, but doing so in my dubiously insured rental car gave me the willies. But Juan wouldn't hear of walking, so we got into my red León Cupra and wound along the narrow eucalyptus-lined road to Sabucedo until we reached a dirt track to the west maintained by a lumbering operation. As I hesitated at the turnoff, Juan assured me, "It's like a highway up there." I was doubtful and anxious about damaging the rental car but figured if I kept it in a low gear we'd probably be alright.

At first, the track wasn't too rutted, though it was cratered with impressive puddles randomly distributed across the surface. Juan knows this way quite well, though he is without a car during his stays at his mother's house in Quireza. Driving up he counsels me on where the troubling holes are, since he'd recently driven up in a borrowed car that he claimed had lower clearance than the red León. My confidence grew as long as the grade didn't rise too quickly, but as the slope ahead angled up sharply and the side of the track dropped off more steeply to my left, my confidence diminished quite a bit. We halted for several minutes, waiting on a bulldozer/tractor to finish loading a logging truck parked on a narrow pullout. I'm silently grateful we didn't have to meet the loaded truck earlier in our ride, while Juan talks about the job he's getting ready to start in Berlin after the *rapa.* He assures me that just fifteen minutes along from here we can park the car and set out on foot.

Both the night before and as we drove along that morning, I conveyed to Juan my basic interests and plan. He understands the academic questions about the sociality of horses, and he certainly didn't dismiss the matter. But it was all oblique to his interests. Still, tagging along with me gave him a good excuse to do what he enjoys most: spending time on the range with the horses. Leaving aside the excitement of stalking, then corralling, and finally herding the *bestas* down to the village, Juan, like many of the *besteiros,* delights in watching and following them. He says his cousin told him some good spots for us to check out today.

Juan talks easily as we bump along, recalling how these slopes used to be dotted with oaks before industrial planting of the eucalyptus began. He only passingly curses the wide tires of the León because they're bad on sand. Juan says that a couple days ago he and a dozen other guys had driven roughly 120 horses from farther west on the range closer to Campo Lameiro. These are kept in a large fenced pasture and are getting "crazier" by the day from being penned. Again, he mentions the anxiety in Sabucedo over having enough horses for the tourist spectacle, but mostly he laments the "politics" this generates in the village. This talk gradually blurs for me, and as we rise higher I start scanning the ridgelines above, looking for horses. Before long I see the first silhouettes of raised heads gazing down toward the valley. We stop so I can begin my observational tasks.

My first efforts to observe this distant band are incredibly awkward.

Getting out of the car, I fumble with my binoculars and notepad, rehearsing my field school training. The horses are several hundred meters distant and mostly obscured by the ridgeline. Aside from two foals quite close to their mothers they're mostly spread out, taking in the rising warm breeze. Rehearsing the familiar pattern of surveying, I start trying to count them. But it feels clumsy in this situation, mostly because I'm not sure what I'm doing yet. Partly, too, it's standing there with Juan, who approaches horses rather differently, based on personal and local history. Catching a glimpse of a black stallion through my binoculars, he says, "That's Ghano," then adds, "he's not a top stallion." Juan explains that they name the stallions as they pass through the *rapa.* They are featured characters in the ritual, with distinct personalities, revealed as they battle each other. I ask if mares are named too and he says no, only the stallions.

Meanwhile, I'm frustrated by my uncertainty over how many horses there are and exactly where we are on the mountainside. Etched against the brilliantly blue horizon, floating above mats of lush green vegetation, these equine figures only slowly gel into numbers on my steno pad. I settle on an overall count of fifteen, but how many are yearlings is unclear. I'm sure of only one yearling; then three foals, seven bay mares and one black and one gray (the color of the other three is too hard to discern), plus the black stallion. Juan says he's young and has not made much of a showing in the *rapa* combats. He explains that you can spot the stallion even if their genitalia are obscured because they are typically larger boned and more muscled than the mares. This species dimorphism, he shows me, is most evident in the thick necks of the males. I decide, not wanting to leave the car on the narrow track nor wishing to scale the heights above us, to settle for my numbers and Juan's stallion identification, and we press on.

Two minutes farther along we turn off the track onto to a sandy path that makes me queasy about the vehicle's traction. Then we see a second band just ahead, in a shallow dell shaded by several short pines. There's room to pull off here, so happily it's time to leave the car behind and finally start walking; but that means I now have to grapple with my backpack and walking stick, as well as camera and binoculars. Juan strides unencumbered toward the horses packed close together less than fifty meters away, in contrast to the widely dispersed band we just saw. I guess that they are settling in and close to napping; several pairs are positioned face-to-tail, fending off the flies that settle more easily around their eyes and mouths in the tree-sheltered dell. None are grazing and their necks are mostly at rest. Because they're all very proximate—not a horse-length between any of them—it takes us several minutes to make out the stallion—a young bay, a bit on the small side, in the center of the cluster. Juan looks him over and regards him with disdain, muttering, "He's not very impressive." Juan then adds, "I don't even think he has a name," meaning he has likely only recently transitioned from a bachelor to a band stallion and has yet to prove his mettle in the *rapa.*

The stallion is rather obsessively grooming the neck of a black mare, in parallel but slightly behind her. Juan speculates she's in heat. But we've yet to close the distance between us and the band, so it's hard to be sure of much. As we slowly approach, Juan's assessment shifts; he guesses she may be the "lead mare," a phrase he seems to prefer over "dominant."[2] Juan elaborates as we slowly walk closer, "Often they're the ones in charge," deciding when and where to move, "and the stallion just follows." Such a situation shifts, he adds, if it comes to "a matter of brute force," as in breaking through the brush; then the stallion leads. As he's talking, I recall that earlier he interpreted band dynamics differently, emphasizing the leadership of the stallion. I wonder if his low estimation of this less than "impressive" male shifts how he considers the status of females within the band. Juan is quick to add that it's a matter of personality, too, with particular stallions or mares having quirky individual dispositions.

Regarding the mares, I do a quick count, which is challenging since they're clustered close together, each within about a nose-length of another horse. I count thirteen mares—dark browns, bays and blacks, one gray—then two yearlings and three foals, so nineteen horses in total. As I'm working on the count, trying to catch those obscured from view by intervening bodies, I notice the stallion is slowly shifting from east to west, leaving the black mare behind. After moving just a few meters, he's now nose-to-tail with a dark-brown mare with a distinctive brand: a circle transected by a vertical line that becomes a cross on top. It looks like a Christian inversion of the Venus symbol. Then another mare moves toward both of them; she has a rabicano tail, a color pattern streaked by light gray or an off-colored white. I ask Juan if she's one I noticed in the *rapa* last year—a very striking mare with shock of golden hair in the center of her black mane; her tail was similarly rabicano. "No," he says. "That was Sheila's horse," a woman in Sabucedo. He says they ended up having to move her away from the village to another part of the range because she was getting into the gardens in the village and developed a taste for kale. That leads to the problem they face with horses down on the highway. When I arrived yesterday, I saw half a dozen on the shoulder just outside of Sabucedo, plus the droppings of many more.

For a moment though, I'm lost in thought, remembering Sheila's horse from the *rapa*. She was part of the first group we caught last year. That mare fascinated me because, while the rest of the group occupied themselves with grazing in the chest-high ferns, she stood at the edge of the cordon around them and scanned the far hillsides. She, too, intermittently grazed, but kept returning to this stance. So she was at full alert before the next batch of horses came rumbling into view. The intriguing thing about her was how the arriving mares, yearlings, and foals responded to her positioning. Several strode right past her, casting deferential sidelong glances or greetings, but at least a dozen of the horses refused to slip by her, and avoided her stare by munching in the grass closer to the humans. This was my first clear glimpse of boundary work by horses. To be certain, I showed my video footage of the scene to my biological anthropology colleagues who study animal behavior, and they concurred; it was a clear instance of drawing a line between those she felt belonged—likely members of her band—and those who didn't. Probably the ones she welcomed had escaped the initial cordon and fallen in with this other band that had just been caught. I made plans to look for comparable forms of boundary work when the horses were herded this year.

Jarring loose from these reflections, I remember to start recording identifying features, and see no better way to start than with the mare with the rabicano tail, who I'll call Rabicana. She's about in the center of this cluster. Meanwhile, the young stallion moves on again; as he does, the dark-brown mare (with the circle/cross brand) starts circuiting the band in the opposite direction (west to east), shifting around and outside the other mares. Eventually, the stallion pulls alongside to the left of a brown mare on the edge of the cluster, and they start allogrooming. This lasts less than a minute because the first brown mare (who I'll call Circle/Cross, because of her brand) has worked her way around and assertively nudges her way in between these two. This is an act of intervention, when a horse disrupts a dyadic interaction to assert its social bond with a preferred partner.[3] I'm fascinated and my mind races through ways of characterizing prominence among mares—whether from her forceful displacement of the other mare or by claiming proximity to the stallion.

I suggest to Juan that she might be the "lead mare." He demurs and mutters something about "pushy mares" that "don't respect the stallion" and the trouble this causes. His interpretation of their respective roles and forms of status may be shifting again. While we mull all this, I'm jotting notes and noticing more as I scribble. For instance, there's a bay mare off to the left at a remove from the others, paired with her yearlings. But as I grow curious about her, there's more action back in the center. A male foal with a thin crescent-shaped star has inserted himself into the tight triangle formed with the stallion; forcing his way from in front of the two mares, then wrenching his body around until he's beside and against the face of Circle/Cross. They weren't together when we first came up, so I'm not certain she's his mother, especially since in a couple minutes he's on the move again. But before he goes the black mare and the one I call Rabicana both crowd in too, right behind the stallion. The black, the one the stallion was grooming when we arrived, has "half" a star, two lines at right angles, so I think of Twink for her name (half of "twinkle").

I'm wondering what these actions suggest about conventions of social distance and whether Juan would think the male foal is being "pushy" too. But I sense he's restless to spot other bands; a course of action that's for the best. So bundling up my notebooks under my arm, I suggest we move on.

As we walk, Juan wants me to get my bearings up on the range. So we head toward the basin where much of the action occurred at last year's *rapa*. One significant change is there's now a large fenced cattle enclosure that cuts rectangularly across one of the hilltops. We approach it from the southeast, angling north along its line, but we stop abruptly upon hearing a long, high-pitched whinny behind us to the east. Turning, we see on the opposite side of the band we just left a striking lone gray stallion on the south lip of the dell. "Who is this guy?" Juan exclaims, riveted by the stallion prancing and strutting back and forth along the high ground above the tightly packed band. "I've never seen

FIGURE 2.1. *Rabicana is on the right, facing away; the bay stallion is in the center (only his rear is in view). Circle/Cross's head is dead center, next to the foal, and Twink is in the back, facing the camera.*

him before." And then, after a minute of further consideration, Juan concludes, "He's not from around here." I ask how he knows and Juan replies, "I would know him by now," adding, "he's too stocky, too tall."

Juan is doubly perplexed because the bay band stallion is paying no mind to the gray. Indeed, he seems more interested in eating, grazing actively, studiously ignoring this other male. We can't tell from this distance whether the gray is a bachelor or perhaps has a band on the other side of the rise, out of view. But he's clearly pushing at boundaries that constitute the limit of the band, though the mares seem mostly to be ignoring him, too. Juan's bothered by the nonchalance of the young bay stallion. "Why would he let this other stallion get so close? It doesn't make sense." He is far less prone to champion nonconfrontational stallions than Victor is. Juan repeats his disparaging assessment of the bay:

"He's not very impressive." Leaving them to sort all this out, we resume walking north until we reach the far corner of the cattle enclosure. Now we can see out over a wide basin ringed by several low peaks. He points around, listing place names where I see only a swirl of vegetation and dips and rises in the undulating terrain edging toward the peak about a mile ahead of us.

Much of the *baixa* portion of the *rapa* unfolded here last year. Animals from several bands were herded together and pooled in the enclosure until we moved them to a catchment area where more were brought, before eventually all were driven down to the village. It's exciting to see the same terrain again, and as Juan retraces the action, pointing with his right hand to where each band was captured and brought in from the various hilltops around us, the drama all comes rushing back to me. After we recap the arguments and confusion from last year's efforts, Juan turns to a more pressing matter: making sure I can find my way around up here. Directly west of us, to our left, the highest point, formed by a long slowly sloping mantle, is known as O Peón. Its laterals are pockmarked with dells and small knolls, then scored by many firebreaks cut through the gorse. The cattle enclosure is known as A Chan do Peón (*chan* means ground or lower floor), for its proximity to this peak. To the east, the area is drained by a *barranca,* a shallow defile obscured by groves of eucalyptus which deepens as it runs down toward Sabucedo. There's another forest track that parallels the *barranca*; it's the one the villagers and tourists take up at the start of the *baixa,* and I make a mental note that I'd be better off coming up that way than the route Juan took us on this morning. Farther to the east, on the next range, there's a line of windmills—another park like in Serra do Cando. To the southeast, Juan points out Caseta de Corvo, a tiny old shepherd's shelter made from cinderblocks. We can see a small band there, though it's too distant to tell much about them. I count ten horses, with four foals.

Across the low ground before us to the north, about a kilometer away on a hilltop, we see a huge herd of horses flanked by cattle. "That's Chaparro," he tells me, "the old man up here." With my binoculars I try to make a rough count; it's hard because they're so far away but also because there are so many of them. After several recounts, I have to settle for "more than forty" as a rough estimate, and I'm amazed. Juan says such large herds used to be more common, when they were able to keep the number of stallions down to around four or five. He says there are eleven in this forty-five-square-kilometer range. "That's too many!" He diagnoses the problem as "not enough wolves." Laura would be amused and might well agree.

Juan suggests we check out Chaparro, so we trek down and across the basin. In about fifteen minutes we're at the lowest point and I can get another angle on a couple of hilltops along the flank of O Peón. I quickly spot yet another large band off to the west. That one has more than twenty horses and a black stallion, though we're too distant from them for Juan to identify him, even with my binoculars. He says there are two or three more bands in that direction and I start to despair over the size of the task before me—there are too many bands for me to do anything in-depth enough to characterize their social configurations in advance of the *rapa*. Looking off to the west, Juan talks again about how they drove more than a hundred in from out by Cadavo, and how they're already penned up below. But remembering Laura's suggestions to focus on just a couple bands, I take heart again.

As we edge closer, it's clear the mares in this big band on the hill ahead are watching us, perhaps because we quickened our pace after my effort to headcount the band, as we had yet a lot of ground to cover. Soon the mares, along with their foals and yearlings, begin churning about. I ask Juan what the strategy would be to go after Chaparro's band right now. "See how they're moving; that's where they'll try to escape. So you have to go around that side first." He and his companions read the landscape to find the routes the horses will likely take—then close some off and encourage the use of others. Through Juan's narrative about last year, I recognize those contours now, too; I can see where the action was and the logic of the catchment approach. It's then that I settle on my plan for observations. I'll focus most of my limited ethnographic attention on the bands most likely to be caught: these two, closest to where participants in the *rapa* arrive and to where we'll gather up the fragments of bands. I'll follow the logic of the terrain and the horses and the humans in their ancient drama. That will also give me a range of stallions to consider—from the young, "unimpressive" bay to the "old man," Chaparro.

Given how stirred up the mega band is up on the hill, we decide to head back rather than scatter them and set them further on edge before the *rapa*. Rising back up through the vale and passing through the rocky outcrop at the northeast corner of the cattle enclosure, we come upon an interesting sight. Two bands seem to be overlapping or in confusion—one with the young bay stallion we observed earlier and the other bunched near the gray stallion—roughly two dozen meters distant. So maybe he's not a bachelor after all; Juan wonders if "his" mares were just out of sight behind the rise. I work on recounting the bay stallion's band: thirteen mares, three foals, and two yearlings, so the same as earlier, but I ask Juan to check me on that count. He too comes up with nineteen total in this band. With the gray stallion are seven mares and two foals, though the way they're arranged makes it hard to count, and the gray keeps charging at the bay, rearing up or turning and kicking at him, then dashing away, stirring up all the mares, along with their foals and yearlings. Juan is bothered by this guy, who he now characterizes as a "city slicker." "He doesn't belong up here," he says, and adds, "he's acting crazy." Sure enough, as we look closer, sharing my binoculars, it's apparent he's wearing a halter, which must've broken off from its tether. He's also larger than the others, so a modern horse.

But his estimation of the young stallion, facing such an unusual threat, doesn't rise accordingly. Why doesn't the bay fight back? Generously, Juan suggests "He's afraid of that lunatic." Or, alternately, that "he can't get the smell" of the gray, perhaps because he's gelded. Without those olfactory triggers, the bay might not take him seriously. But Juan's assessment shifts eventually to, "he must just be submissive," or that it could be "the invisible fence of territory" around the gray's band that makes him afraid to return the attack. My concern with the "crazy" gray is that this interloper it going to disrupt any chance I have of making observations in a "natural" context. Off to the east we can see Sabucedo down below, and with the day diminishing and match time for the Euro Cup approaching, it's time to go.

We wind our way back down and head to the Sheriff. It's packed tonight because the match is on the big screen TV. As we settle in, tapas plates of chorizo or cheese and bread start stacking up, washed down by more Estrella Galicia. Intermittently, Juan asks around about the crazy gray, guessing that he has escaped from someone's pasture here below. But no one recognizes the horse from our description and no one has heard of one escaping. As Italy makes savage work of the Spanish team the crowd shades from disgust to resignation and finally into a boisterous "who cares" frivolity. Conversations swirled and were inviting, but

I couldn't stop thinking about the horses, wondering what they were doing, what was happening up there. So I said good night and went to type up my notes.

DAY 3

I rise early and am off up the mountain, anxious to observe the horses. The idea of doing so entirely alone animates me. I navigate the cumbersome car up the narrow track and find a wide enough spot in the woods where I can leave it for the day; then schlep my gear together and onto my back and start hiking. The air is chill and mist-drenched but brightening up ahead as the sun sharpens on the high terrain. Soon I'm sweating and heaving wind and cussing myself for not having rented a four-wheel drive vehicle that could carry me farther up the mountain. I fondly recall Laura's Terrano while pressing on. Passing through the stands of eucalyptus, though, my physical stress gradually is countered by the lushly tranquil setting. It's quiet and the air smells rich. I'm the only human around—an unusual situation for an ethnographer. But a surge of anxieties that rise as I climb is oddly reassuring. They're typical concerns of fieldwork: did I pick the right site, will I find interesting subjects, have I prepared for this fully, will something interesting happen?

Striding up a long grade and passing from the trees into a fairly flat opening, I stop to scan the landscape ahead, looking for horses. Sure enough, in the distance there are several on the knoll adjacent to the cattle pen, loosely spread across its apex. I'm relieved and start counting, but soon notice they aren't grazing or milling about. At least a half dozen of them have heads raised at attention, looking up and across to the north. They're watching some activity on the slope of land across the *barranca,* to the right of the track at least three hundred meters away, across broken ground. It's the crazy gray stallion churning about, trying to herd several mares with one foal. This is not a good development, I think, worrying that he's disrupting the established social structure. Then he stops abruptly. From this distance through my binoculars it's hard to see why. But the gray then flehmens, so it must've been mare droppings that caught his attention. Whatever scent he picks up leads him dashing thirty or forty meters to the east toward the knoll, the track, and the stream. While he's in motion the black mares he was driving slink off to the west toward a copse of trees. Crazy Gray (I decide to name him) gradually realizes this and charges after them; then they all drop from view down the backside of the slope. I need to find some higher ground to follow the action further.

A rock outcrop on the left side of the track seems promising, so I climb up to have a look around, shedding my pack and walking stick, taking only my binoculars draped around my neck. I'm absorbed with whatever is unfolding to the north with the gray stallion and mares, so I'm startled upon reaching the top of the boulders to notice there's a band right below me, hidden from the trail: ten adults, two foals. They appear equally surprised, since I was downwind and out of sight, quietly walking the track alone. The anxiety that consumed me at that moment was strange. Here I was, practically face-to-face with these animals—the goal I'd been striving for! But I didn't have my notebooks or camera to record the encounter. How would I make proper identifications without them!? This mattered intensely because they rapidly began moving to get away from me—not bolting in a gallop; more like a canter, eyeing me steadily as they shifted down toward the track I'd just left behind. My mind froze momentarily. If I moved at all toward my gear they would be gone even quicker. But I was desperate to record what I was seeing. In a frantic second, I realized I would have to form mental images of each one as they passed.

That might not seem like a challenge, or perhaps it shouldn't be. But it entails doing something I hadn't yet mastered: seeing a whole horse. Not just its age and gender, as with counting and tracking populations. But, in an instant, any of its distinguishing features—facially, on the legs, along the mane—and where the animal is positioned in relation to the others as they move. That is, a mental image of individual animals in motion, such that I could detail with certainty who, when, and with whom. And I would need this ability because of my aim of tracking horses in the *curro* during the *rapa*. The camera makes this kind of seeing easy—initially and after the fact—but had made me lazy about visualizing and memorizing what was before me. The lead mare doesn't seem to be similarly debilitated. She fixes her gaze on me as they circuit the rock outcrop and pass down to the trail. It is a strange sensation to be stared at this way. She may not have disliked me but she was leery, at the very least. My impression is that she's performing a stance for her bandmates to follow, though none do so as raptly or edgily as she does. As they pass, my mind is clicking "photos" and a distinctive kind of memory work has taken hold. Much as I first learned to memorize what people say when I was becoming an ethnographer, here, visually, my memory operates in a new way—selectively and somewhat assuredly seeing what I feared I might miss. Not perfectly nor expertly, but sufficiently, so that as they loped on by and trotted up the road out of sight, I didn't have to scramble frantically for my notebook. Their images lingered and stayed vivid.

The one in the front, as I replayed this in my mind, was a bay with a wide blaze that bends obliquely over the left side of her face, a large "bald" patch around her nostrils, and a right rear stocking. She was followed closely by a dappled gray who also has a large bald patch above her mouth, extending up and around her right nostril. The seven horses that followed—four mares, three foals—were a blur, though. What struck me sharply was that there was no stallion. Was this a mare band? I wanted to know more but decided to let them pass on by along the road; I would follow slowly, to not startle them, working patiently at getting close again while trying not to appear as though I was stalking them, with Victor's voice ringing in my head, "Don't disturb the horses!" As soon as the last of the column passes down onto the track and up around a bend ringed by tall pines, I slip quietly off the rocks, pick up my backpack—making sure to dig out my camera this time—and discreetly trail after them.

To my surprise and dismay, they are nowhere to be seen. Based on my limited experience with surveying the bands of Serra do Cando, they should have been right around the bend. The horses we tracked there moved slowly, casually grazing, drawn gradually toward ever more appealing grass. Perplexed, I couldn't understand why that wasn't the case here. I decided they must have left the track at a nearby spring just to the north, on the right side of the road. Picking up my pace, I made for this vale; yet they weren't there either. They had entirely vanished, likely into the thickets edging the *barranca* that descends from this spring down toward Sabucedo. The day had just started and I was already frustrated and concerned. But I decide to keeping heading up toward the band I spotted initially on the knoll.

Along the way I'm surprised once again by another cluster of horses—four black mares and one male foal, brown, off to my right on a rise above the track. They look like ones I had seen with the black stallion named Ghano in roughly this same area yesterday. But he's nowhere in sight and I'm hardly certain of this association. Strikingly, they're staring sharply at me. I don't look back; just cast my gaze back down from where I came and then up ahead again, eyeing them briefly in the process. It's the hardest I've ever been stared at and they seem quite on edge, heads at sharp alert. Not wanting to move and startle them, I slowly slough off my pack and start venturing more sustained glances at them. Eventually, I even risk a couple photos, since they're not moving. But this makes them more uneasy and they quickly coalesce defensively in a tight bunch around the foal. No sooner had they clustered this way, though, than one mare decides another is too close and aims a bite threat at her face, busting up the brief assemblage around the foal. Not wanting to cause further consternation, I resume my trek toward the knoll, leaving them behind.

Walking along, I wonder what I'm seeing. These two stallion-less groups seemed to contradict what I had learned so far and observed already in a quite limited manner in Serra do Cando. Mares on their own, in a group, don't surface in the literature. The defensive posture I just witnessed, too, seems counter to the assumption that they need stallions to protect them. For that matter, I started to think that Crazy Gray was responsible for the disquiet I had already observed. This thought

FIGURE 2.2. *Four black mares and foal.*

makes me depressed as Juan's remarks come back to me: "He doesn't belong up here." He's bigger, stockier, and seems a city slicker. As Laura pointed out, the "modern" breed horses are noticeably taller than these *garranos.* He clearly seems to be disrupting the conventions, acting in ways that strike both these horses and Juan as strange and warranting attention. This meant I would hardly get a natural view of horse sociality; I felt as though this project and my site were corrupted. After a moment of despair, anxiety, and confusion, an inkling slowly forms that perhaps this will be an opportunity to learn about local social conventions through their disruption instead of trying to formulate an ethologist's species-typical account of horses.

Meanwhile, I'm not the only one thinking about the gray stallion. The horses I spotted first are still up on the knoll and watching the direction I last saw him, at alert as they follow his movements. Not wanting to spook them, I follow the track as it loops around the base of the knoll; once I'm around it to the west I angle back and up, practicing the slow, halting zigzag gait I learned from Victor. This maneuver takes about ten minutes. But since they're focused on the stallion, the mares hardly notice as I sidle up the west slope and move up to the top, where the ground is cluttered with large stones laced with lichen peaking up through the short grass turf. The gorse that dominates the laterals of the hill has yet to encroach on its rounded zenith, probably kept in check by the active grazing of horses and cattle in this spot, favored for the hilltop breezes that help with the flies. Off to the southeast stands Caseta de Corvo, the old shepherd's hut; I'm close to where Juan and I left off yesterday—I just approached it from a different track.

As I'm taking all this in and starting my count, surprisingly, Crazy Gray joins us, back from his unsuccessful effort to herd those other mares. He pauses for a moment on the lip of the high point, gives me a glance, then enters into the loose ring of stones atop the knoll. Off to the north, where he just came from, there's a large cluster of horses, maybe twenty, about one hundred meters away along the east edge of the cattle enclosure. They're in view now because I'm on higher ground. But before I can give them any thought, I stop to watch what happens as he advances toward the mares.

The mares, in concert, abruptly turn away from him and move across to the southern slope. Crazy Gray continues encroaching until he comes face-to-face with a black mare with a small white star who

FIGURE 2.3. *Crazy Gray enters the knoll.*

has peeled off from the others as they keep moving. There's no exchange of niceties between them—they don't make contact with their noses, necks, or faces; it's really like a standoff. She's staring hard at him, ears alert and piqued forward—not lowered fearfully. They lock gazes and are frozen for about twenty seconds, then she whinnies and snorts, snapping her head up and down; he balks, his face veering away from her gaze, off to his right, and he takes up an animated interest in the ground, sniffing distractedly. She parallels his head movement, almost in a herding posture, until Crazy Gray bends around and away, back toward where he entered the knoll. So who are these mares without a stallion?

I count twelve horses, including two yearlings and one foal, but they've broken into two close clusters about twenty meters apart. As they separate, I'm startled to realize that one grouping is the four blacks and foal I observed ten minutes ago. They must've passed behind and around me, scaling the southeast flank of the knoll as I gingerly worked my way up from the north. Then who are these other mares and yearlings? Are they all bandmates or are these vestiges of two different bands? The second cluster of mares here—the ones I'd spotted initially as I was coming up the track—are a mix of dark browns and bays, one of whom has a large star that reminds me of the shape of Africa, with some discoloration around her mouth, a tall right rear sock, a left front cornet, and a rabicano tale. I realize she's Rabicana, from yesterday, and I recognize one of her bandmates, the dark-brown Circle/Cross, the one who intervened in the stallion's allogrooming of Twink. Another bay has a long scar on her right flank, which looks like the vestige of a wolf attack. Laura asked me to send her photos of any scars I see, so I snap several and decide to call her Scar. She's flanked by a two-year old, who sticks close to her side. Then there's a big bay with a star that ends in a long thin line, a narrow snip between her nostrils, only half a mane on her right, and a "JB" brand. The remaining mare is another dark brown with a similar circle/cross brand; I wonder if they're sisters. She has a male yearling sticking close to her. I'll have to check my photos from yesterday to be sure, but this seems like the core of the mares Juan and I observed with the young bay stallion a few dozen meters from this location.

The scene is quite tense. First, none of the mares are grazing, and the yearlings are sticking close to their mothers. Second, there's a great deal of movement in a fairly small space; the group around Rabicana is trekking but in a tight column and from one edge of the knoll to another. The group of black mares is pacing about, too, and keeping the foal surrounded. They configure themselves somewhat oddly at times, with several faces close together, heads erect, where before I've mostly seen horses pairing up. Crazy Gray now has his back to them, looking off to the north at the big bunch of horses he just left behind. Gradually, he seems to lose interest in these mares and finds a spot to take a long roll on his back. As he does, the black mares and their foal quickly start down to the south slope of the knoll. They haven't gone far in that direction when Crazy Gray notices and dashes over to head them off and back up the slope.

As they return, one of them slides over to the other bunch of mares, while her mates make a short loop and soon form two parallel clusters, all facing the same direction, vaguely looking off to the northwest. I check the time; all this took eight minutes. The black mares hold their position for a moment longer until Crazy Gray advances toward them; again, they turn in concert and pace away, now toward the east, refusing to look at him at all. Soon they slide in alongside Rabicana and the other mares, forming a dense cluster that keeps him out. I'm struggling here because the ethological units of analysis for social behavior don't seem relevant. Everything I've read about horse social structure defines it strictly in terms of "harem maintenance," "harem tending," or "harem formation strategies"—all focused on the role of the stallion in defining and maintaining the group's boundaries; mostly, it should be noted, against other stallions. The kind of cohesion here seems more of a resistance to or rejection of the stallion. Perhaps Crazy Gray has driven off the band stallion; but given the propensity for the group of blacks to leave, I'm not sure they were all one group prior to the gray's arrival.

The situation gets more complicated; after fourteen minutes I notice some movement way down below the angle of the mountain to the south. Several horses appear along a low outcrop of rocks: two mares, a brown and a bay, each with a foal. They're grazing steadily, which encompasses their movement. They seem only to have appeared in the course of following good grass. They're out of sight for most of the horses on the knoll, but surely scents announce their proximity. Now I'm really unsure what's going on. Who are these new horses below and are there more of them? Sure enough, over the next six minutes several more come into view—three more bays and a dappled gray with a foal. So there's nine horses below, moving up gradually. They loosely graze in pairs, no more than three horse-lengths separating each pair. That reminds me to check the spacing on the horses around me, which I've not done because there's been so much motion. Now that they've settled down a bit, they're still in one big cluster on the east side of the knoll—so maybe they're not vestiges of two separate bands, but I don't know why the group of blacks had left before (when I first encountered them) or why they seemed more keen to flee than the bunch around Rabicana. I'll need to work up more identifications and start tracking the social bonds evident between them all, which seems quite challenging.

Adding to my consternation, just then the cattle arrive. I had heard their clanking bells for some time and spotted them leisurely ambling down from the northwest corner of the fenced enclosure above. But I hadn't paid them any mind until the first wave lumbered up into view. They're showing up here for the same reason as the horses —this nice, breezy top is a coveted location for keeping the flies at bay. There are lots of calves among them, so I'm on alert and start thinking of moving on. Not only do I have to worry about the danger posed by edgy cows; once they settle in, they also obscure my view of identifying features on the horses. I wait, though, to see what the mares approaching from below will do. While I'm occupied, Scar's two-year old gets up close with the stallion as he's standing off alone. First, she nibbles a bit at the grass beside him; then nuzzles her head up under his neck. Soon their faces are side to side as they sniff and snort, but this contact is brief. Crazy Gray shifts again, keeping an eye on the perimeter of the gathered mares. I realize this two-year-old nibbling is the first I notice any of them eating, and it's been fifty minutes!

Gradually, the nine horses from below ascend, grazing the whole way. As they get closer, I recognize one of the bays—she has a "bent" or U-shaped blaze and large bald patch on her nose. Then I make out the patch of discoloration on the dappled gray with a foal. This is the batch of horses I surprised without my camera about an hour and a half ago! The gray is the first to enter the ring of the knoll and she makes her way over toward Rabicana, but stops short of entering the full cluster. Behind her, the other mares spread out along the south lip of the hilltop. I do a count, expecting to come up with twenty-one, with these nine adding to the original twelve. But I only see nineteen horses. A recount confirms that two are "missing" and likely escaped Crazy Gray's vigilance when these others arrived. I can't see Scar and her two-year-old, so I guess it was them.

The cattle settle in and many calves flop down to sleep, so the situation seems calmer. Indeed, soon the foals are crashing out hard on the ground, too. It's a drowsy moment in the warm sunlight and the breeze drops entirely. The stillness lasts close to ten minutes, then the bay with the bent blaze from below—I'll call her Bent—takes an interest in the stallion. It's conspicuous because to get to him she rouses two sleeping foals, who scramble to get out of her path. Another bay mare who came up with her also ends up shifting as Bent moves in alongside the stallion. It's only then that I notice he's not been sniffing their droppings, checking on who might be in heat as a band stallion would. There's great tumult as he mounts Bent and they engage in copulation for close to a minute. This eliminates one of Juan's speculations—that this male may have been a gelding. Once finished, Crazy Gray meanders around the knoll; Bent goes back to her sleeping foal and settles into a loose cluster with most of the other mares she arrived with. The ones who were already here are tightly bunched around Rabicana. In between is the gray and her foal who arrived with Bent but don't seem to fit into either grouping.

So far, none of what I've seen matches what I expected concerning horse sociality. Is the group of nine that arrived a stallion-less band? Given their edgy state earlier and their rapid effort to disappear, I guess they were perhaps part of a larger band that clove in two under Crazy Gray's attacks, like his assault yesterday on the young bay stallion. Speaking of which, is he not here with Rabicana and the others because Crazy Gray drove him off? If so, some mares must have fled with him, since even counting the four blacks this grouping would be seven fewer than the band I counted yesterday. I can make sense of what Crazy Gray is doing using ethology; he seems to be engaged in two typical "harem formation strategies": "raiding," or abducting mares from another band, and defeating another stallion in combat. Yet how the mares are responding to his efforts is more complicated. They're clearly socializing—I can see social bonds being performed and intimations of boundary work—but absent a "band structure." How would I determine the dominant or lead mare here? Is there more than one? JB seems bigger and so probably older than Rabicana, but Rabicana is more in the center of relations as that group resumes pacing the perimeter of the knoll. I see her using her muzzle to make contact with other mares in passing. And what of the bunch of horses down below and up by the cattle enclosure? Feeling overwhelmed, I gather up my pack and gear and trek down the knoll toward the cattle enclosure.

Within a few minutes I approach the next cluster of horses. They're bunched close together on shrunken, boggy ground, mostly snoozing; scattered around them is another congeries of cattle. I make my count—twenty total, with six foals and four yearlings. So there are over forty horses in this general area. It doesn't take me long to find the bay stallion from yesterday. He's on the south end of this bunch. I notice him because he's standing face-to-rear with a mare, allogrooming. He's working diligently at her backside, around the tail. It's Scar, with her two-year old on her opposite side. When the adults finish allogrooming their heads drop to a rest position, with only the tails swishing occasionally, driving off flies from each other's faces. Until he makes a languid gesture at a flehmen, then lowers his head again beside her.

So is this a band or a collection of mares, yearlings, and foals who were hived off of other bands? Since they're all quite still here, I draw up a position map. Starting from the right or southeast: a mare with a two-year-old right behind, both grazing; three body-lengths from them a pair of two-year-olds, side by side and face to rear; then the stallion and Scar and her two-year-old; behind them, within a body-length, is a bay mare (with a star) and her large foal, maybe a couple months old already; then two foals on their right, crashed out sleeping; adjacent to them are three dark-brown mares; two body-lengths distant from them, at the end of this line of horses to the northwest, are two dark-brown mares and a bay, all grazing, plus three foals, one of which is sleeping. Except for the three two-year-olds and the bay to the right, they're arrayed in three clusters. Then the foals stir and start nursing. Scar drifts left a few horse-lengths; the stallion follows but ends up on the opposite side of her two-year-old, whose rear backside he briefly grooms until her mother's head extends across her back, nuzzling the stallion's face, and he stops. They settle into this position without further grooming, while the snoozy portion of the band starts stirring.

Over the next forty minutes, as the foals finish nursing, the mares—in pairs or individually, with and without foals—fan out in a variety of directions, leisurely munching as they go. No motion seems to amount to a trek, just widely dispersed grazing. I decide this is a good time for me to eat my lunch of chorizo, cheese, and fresh bread. Perched on a boulder, I get everything out, greasing up my hands slicing the sausage. Then I start noticing little actions that warrant a photo—several of the proximate mares trade microaggressions as their heads get too close. But I also see a pair nuzzle each other, nose-to-nose, after a similar encounter. Then before too long—I've been sitting on the rock for twenty minutes—they're spread out far enough that I lose sight of the microinteractions, so I wipe off my fingers and generate another position map. I content myself with this task until I notice that three yearlings and the bay mare, who were off to the far right when I arrived, have moved north. The stallion is alone, rolling in the grass. When he finishes, he makes no effort at herding them back; rather, he moves in the opposite direction, toward the knoll. As he ambles slowly, grazing along the way, Scar, her two-year-old, and two other bay mares fall in along with him. They're at a distance from me so all I can make out of them are their brands, an AP and a PS. I decide I need a name for the stallion. As we're at the northeast corner of the cattle enclosure, lacking much imagination, I settle on Northeastern.

I've already spent an hour and a half with this group and am anxious to get to the band with Chaparro, off to the north. From the corner of the cattle enclosure, I can glimpse their contours. From what I can see with my binoculars, it's a huge group, over thirty horses by quick count—a mega band, which is what I settle on for its name. As I head out, I pass the yearlings, who nervously shift closer to the mare. The four of them bunch up for a brief moment. Two of the young animals nuzzle faces side by side; then they all start moving back toward the others, who now are widely dispersed across the small shallow basin. Behind me are three pairs of mares and their foals strung along a loose line, about a body-length from each other; about twenty meters from them is a pair of mares and their foals; the stallion and the other mares are almost out of view in a copse of pines.

The northeast corner rests atop a low knob. Facing north there's a taller hill about five hundred meters away, where the Mega band awaits. Between these two elevations is a wide, deep basin where most of these horses were initially held during last year's *rapa*. Off to the west, the cattle enclosure fence dips for fifty meters, then rises, working gradually up the side of the big peak, O Peón. Two hours from now, when I trek back from observing the large band, I will cross the basin in about seven minutes. But heading there now takes more than twenty-five minutes, stopping often, zigzagging regularly, so as not to make these horses nervous. The only trees in this basin are squat and bushy, bunched along a few springs in the low ground. The tall pines are behind me, within the enclosure; the hill ahead and the farther ones in the distance are arboreally bare, though matted thickly with gorse and ferns. I work my walking stick mostly to shake off possible ticks from the hip-high growth I'm trudging through.

The closer I get, the slower I move, until my pace morphs into motionless bursts of observation followed by a few steps of inching forward. Part of this maneuver, as Victor insisted, involves avoiding staring at the horses, which is a threatening gesture. So in addition to my zigzagging pace, I frequently look up, around, or down, so as not to look directly at the horses I'm approaching. This makes taking a count difficult until I settle into one spot. There's an array of mares ringing the lip of the high point, mostly on alert, heads raised watching me, ears propped forward, but turning away when I look back at them briefly. I practice this game of looking and not looking; the gaze pattern is quite predictable and conventional. As long as I abide by it by not staring, they play along, pointedly turning away when I look back so as not to be caught staring. This gesture is followed by a studied nonchalance, surely developed through a lifetime of social relations in which gazes must be cautiously moderated and monitored. This pattern is quite different from the cows pastured among them. They stare at me in long, unbroken stretches; glaring aggressively if their calf is nearby, or mutely curious in less edgy circumstances.

The counting task here is daunting. There are even more horses than I realized. My first count goes over forty, but I'm not certain whether I'm double-counting some or if I can even see them all, given their distribution over the low prominence of the hilltop. So I settle into taking pictures of the horses closest to me, holding off the count until I'm better positioned. Of the dozen or so mares I can see easily on this southeastern perimeter, I start with the most forward one—a flea-bitten gray with a bright enough coat to seem white, like her mane and tail. As an identifier, I note that her mane falls entirely on the right side, with a long forelock lying across her face. There are several mares and one foal near her. The flea-bitten gray mare whinnies and she's answered directly by a smaller voice—a foal I assume; hers I guess, though I can't see it.

One minute passes and the mare calls out another time, receiving the same response directly. As she returns to grazing, the other mares pass close alongside her, spreading out; none draw any threat gestures from her. After three more rounds of whinnying, the flea-bitten gray's foal appears and settles next to her, trying to nurse. But the mare moves along to catch up with the others, until they spool back into a close grazing cluster of five adults, two yearlings, and two foals. They graze almost nose-to-nose while the rest of the band is gradually dispersing. Eleven minutes have passed since I took my first photo of the flea-bitten gray mare.

Besides the quantity of horses, I'm intrigued by the soundscape here. They're so loud! Whinny after whinny lolls through the hot air, as mares call to foals or other mares. As one rings out and is answered, more follow. In contrast, the horses on the knoll were quite silent. I can't track how these neighs and whinnies link or pass between individuals, but I guess their frequency reflects the dispersed social expanse of so many animals in one place. I also notice multiple acts of allogrooming taking place intermittently across this huge band. Compared with what I've seen on this range so far, this is a very socially stable band.

Rather than head into the center of this group, I decide to circle its perimeter, identifying mares along the way. The idea of position mapping all of them seems untenable, at least initially. But I've already noticed that they seem to parse out into little clusters, like the one around the flea-bitten gray.

Walking less than twenty meters to the west, I get close to the next cluster, where three foals are sleeping on the ground and the mares are grazing. As I start mapping them, I realize that the stallion, Chaparro, is among them. He's larger and older than Northeastern or Crazy Gray, with a face so scarred it looks almost pockmarked. A dappled gray mare with a black mane and tail keeps close to his left side as he chomps through the gorse along the ring of the hilltop. There are thirteen adults here and one yearling. I decide that rather than mapping, I'll go straight to identifying mares. I'm starting here because I think the stallion gravitates toward the prominent mares.

Several catch my attention—a bay with a wide blaze and a "bald" face (entirely white discoloration); a dark brown with a full blaze that shades out or gets blurry around the edges; a bay with a large round star that seems to be shaded on her left side, almost as if it was a shadow; another bay with a star that looks like an open book propped up on a lectern, with two rear socks (Book strikes me as a good name for her); then a flaxen mare with a foal and another bay, this with a thin, almost whisper of a stripe, along with a male foal. These two—bay mother

FIGURE 2.4. *The cluster with the flea-bitten gray; facing south, the road marks the edge of the cattle enclosure, and O Peón rises on the far right.*

and foal, who has a blaze so wide it just about covers his forehead—start allogrooming. The foal follows the mare's lead, and I guess this is how the practice is socially learned. As the mother changes sides of the young one's neck, another foal approaches, and the first one greets it with a brief grooming of its forehead. Other nearby horses stand face-to-rear, taking advantage of each other's fly-chasing tails; two more pair up in allogrooming their respective shoulders and necks.

Working diligently, jotting notes on blazes, snips, and stripes, I also try to develop a general sense of how clusters seem to have broken out within the larger band. After starting the process of making identifications, I shift quickly to sketching the patterns by which social proximity is unfolding. In the fifteen minutes I've been here, Chaparro and bandmates seemed to pay little heed to me, so I feel comfortable circuiting the rest of the group. There's another big cluster at the rocky apex of the hill—nine mares, two foals, spread out in a long line covering roughly thirty-five meters, mostly all grazing (one pair is nose-to-rear). But they're all now moving and shifting a bit, starting into a fulsome graze, so the initial contours of their sleep clusters are dissipating.

When I get back close to Chaparro, I observe several developments. First, the dappled gray beside him has ambled up the hill alone. There's also a new configuration—the bald-face mare (I'll call her Baldface) has headed off and is being trailed at a respectful distance by several mares and a yearling as she drifts westward. I remember that identifying a mare involves more than jotting down her physical features; it also entails getting a sense of her social identity or position. If I had to guess right now, I'd tag her as the "lead" mare, given the deference others seem to show her.

The third development, an elaborate instance of herding, takes place quite slowly and helps me immensely in the difficult task of recognizing social position and the structure of sociality here. During the time I was mapping the cluster above—about eight minutes—six horses left the hill and now are down in the vale below: four mares, two with foals (one is the flaxen mare who was near Chaparro when I started). This presents an opportunity to think about **movement initiation**, a key unit of analysis in horse ethology and in studying herd species broadly. It's a means of gauging the social structure of a band by tracking how "decisions" are reached in a group in terms of how they synchronize their movements. The theoretical question turns on whether the movement of horses is "coordinated," as in swarming activity (e.g., insects, birds, fish, etc.), where a broad pattern emerges simply by individuals responding to the motion of directly adjacent conspecifics. Or is there a broader sense of social identity at work? Do horses perhaps have in mind a "global view" of the band as a social entity as they observe and respond to each other's actions?[4]

Konstanze Krueger developed a model for studying this by applying network analysis to systematic field observations of relationships among groups of feral horses near Frosinone, Italy.[5] She recorded data on affiliative interactions and paired this with information on agonistic encounters to develop an overarching sense of the connectedness of each group member. Krueger concluded that equids likely follow "a limited form of distributed leadership." Movement might be initiated by any individual—not just "high status" ones—but the higher status ones are followed most. Perhaps that accounts for the difference between the dappled gray, who no one followed, and Baldface. Marie Bourjade, working with Przewalski horses, further finds that "leadership" is not really a useful unit of analysis, since a "multiple step decision-making process" unfolds as mares display and interpret a variety of "pre-departure behaviors," such as shifting out to the periphery without foraging. Instead of a single horse performing leadership, Bourjade concludes "followers" enact a "partially-shared consensus" about their movements, as I was perhaps observing with the Capilla band on our last day in the Serra do Cando.[6] So though I don't know who initiated the movement that led down below, I can consider whether the followers are enacting a consensus on foraging so far away from the others.

While pondering all that, I keep at position mapping. There remains the first cluster around the flea-bitten gray, then a group up at the top, and the bunch following Baldface. But of the dozen or so mares loosely near Chaparro, several more have started threading down into the vale; meanwhile the six below have split in two: the flaxen mare (who I'll just start calling Flaxen), her foal, and two other mares are moving up the far southern slope of the vale in the direction of the cattle enclosure. The two they left behind—a mare and foal—are joined by another mare, and several more start shifting that way. Soon they roughly form a loose line strewn from the hilltop to the boggy low ground and up the far side. Over the next ten minutes more meander down, trailing the others and spreading out now over about one hundred and fifty meters. They've parsed out into separate clusters along two firebreaks below, where the grass is easier to access. I start wondering what the stallion thinks of this dispersal.

Apparently, he's unconcerned. I come across Chaparro again while retracing my path to check on the cluster around the flea-bitten gray mare (who I decide to call Fleabit for now). His head hovers close to the ground, munching away at little blades percolating up through the rocky surface. He shows no evident interest in much else, but I make note of his location and decide to check back with him soon. I'm anticipating at some point he'll engage in herding—the other significant form of movement initiation. Fleabit is now flanked by only two mares and a yearling; the foals are over playing among some large rocks, and two other adults are paired up nearby. One of the foals is using a boulder that tops out about head high to him as a local enhancement. Here, too, is another opportunity to think about sociality in terms of cognition more than structure.[7]

Ethologists debate whether horses are capable of social learning through observation of others, or are restricted to a more limited form

FIGURE 2.5. *Spreading out to graze. Flaxen is in the cluster on the far left, about one hundred and fifty meters away.*

of social transmission, **social facilitation**, when behavior like grazing is contagiously triggered by a similar behavior in others.[8] The former exhibits **cognitive complexity**, the latter simply reactive, instinctive impulses. Local enhancement tends to be construed as facilitation, in contrast to **imitation**, in which "the observer copies the motor patterns of the demonstrator," requiring "certain cognitive sophistication." In this view, as a behavior, local enhancement simply reveals a newly salient part of an environment, rather than calling attention to the action itself. But as Victor noted, a dimension often left out of such equations is that the social status of the initiator seems to matter a great deal—as with movement initiation, it matters who is doing it whether the behavior is learned and imitated or simply contagiously transmitted. The ethological terminology, I find, is burdened by a narrow focus on individuals, obscuring a wider frame of social relations and dynamics.

But what I notice now is that the second of the foals is imitating the first one's behavior on a different, similarly sized rock, suggesting it is imitating the actions of the first foal.[9] I make a note to keep focusing on this question of characterizing local enhancement.

Minutes later, Chaparro is still munching away as the portion of the band below grows larger and spreads further. There's movement being initiated all around. The widely dispersed cluster in the firebreak around Flaxen has grown to twelve; in the other firebreak they've formed up into a trek heading east: two mares, each trailed by a yearling and foal. Another four mares are turning away from them toward the west. While tracking all this, I take a few moments to watch the foals struggle at licking or nibbling at their own backsides, awkwardly twisting to reach difficult irritations. I think this challenge may be the origin of allogrooming, mirroring their own bodies on those of others.

Eventually, I notice the stallion positioning himself around fresh droppings from a nearby bay who is shadowed by her yearling. Chaparro investigates the pile attentively, then launches into a sustained flehmen. I'm close enough that I can feel the bellows of his lungs reverberate when he exhales. As this olfactory gesture waxes and wanes he seems unconvinced she's ready for sex. He settles for positioning himself above her droppings, letting forth a **marking** shower of urine, before turning around and ambling southward along the crest.

Chaparro's dispersed bandmates below finally catch his attention— it's been more than thirty minutes since I first noticed them heading south. Standing aligned with him, I count at least eighteen horses in his line of vision. He observes for over a minute. I watch him sizing up

FIGURE 2.6. *Chaparro takes notice.*

the situation—his head at alert, focusing directly on the mares spread out below, gauging their dispersion, with the scent of the mare most proximate to him still in his nostrils from the flehmen. He decides to start down the rocky incline.

Chaparro saunters unhurriedly toward them for about forty meters, then stops and again takes stock of their configuration. With a quick snort and roll of his head, he's back in motion again moving at a trot, with the pull of gravity on the descending slope showing jauntily in his churning shoulders. But only for another twenty meters, when his head dips down into the ferns and he takes up grazing. He's at this for almost a minute, giving me time to quickly sketch the band's dispersed positions. Chaparro resumes moving, turning sharply to his left initially, taking up a lateral line to the hilltop crest. His maneuver will take him out well ahead of the mares, about fifty meters farther to the east, the direction I came up from.

I can see Chaparro's backside sporadically as he surfs the deep thickets of fern that engulf him. He has covered at least one hundred and fifty meters heading east to get out on that distant side of the mares. Baldface too is in motion and the rest of the proximate horses—six adults, one yearling, and two foals—canter after her briskly down toward the basin. I see Fleabit by herself, off to the east, down from the hill and on the edge of the basin; she stops and watches as Chaparro cuts back west toward Flaxen and company. Through all this activity, the two groups below have not registered any notice of what Chaparro is doing. They leisurely attend to the grass before them as he's making his maneuver.

Only the lone mare farthest to the east recognizes his approach, spinning hastily off to her right, breaking into a brisk trot, heading back toward the more southerly grouping around Flaxen. Chaparro follows at a trot too, but only for a dozen seconds, then settles into a slow gait that parallels the mares still trekking east; he's out in front of them now from his lateral maneuver across the slope. In a matter of seconds he passes by them entirely just to the south, heading toward the cluster around Flaxen. Meanwhile the majority of the remaining horses on the hill cascade down, trotting toward what seems to be a rapidly coalescing center in the basin. About thirty horses are spread out below over at least a hundred meters from east to west, and maybe seventy meters from north to south.

As Chaparro emerges into the firebreak from the east, he first encounters Flaxen, who turns quickly with her foal and bolts back toward
the hill. But she's almost instantly at the end of a long line with the other
mares now in motion; the whole cluster files rapidly into a column moving at a quick trot eastward, Chaparro driving them briefly from the rear.
The others who just recently descend from the hill mirror this motion,
trotting east, where they pick up the small bunch that Chaparro had just
bypassed. Within seconds they form two lines jogging diagonally along
the floor of the basin. Their coordinated motion is mesmerizing. When
they begin to converge, out in front is Fleabit, who was waiting off to
the east near where Chaparro made his turn back west toward the two
clusters. She waits until they're close, then she turns toward the hill at
a trot, and they fall in behind her. Chaparro gallops to get ahead of this
flow; as he does, he rapidly heads off several mares who are not following Fleabit's lead. They dash to comply and then they all stream west in
a long fast column with Fleabit out in front. They dig into the slope at
an angle, climbing on a line that comes out well west of me on the high
ground. But there are stragglers.

From the smaller trekking group, one mare with a foal and yearling
are barely moving. Chaparro heads back to coax them along as the band
flows up out of the vale. Fleabit's bunch leads this motion; they open

FIGURE 2.7. *Baldface on the left; Flaxen is on the far right.*

up a gap as they advance and a couple dozen horses slow to a gentle gait. One mare is cutting a less westerly line, more directly for the top. I hear a foal crying out above me; her mother is heading straight toward me, stopping just ten meters away, hesitating, as the foal dashes around me and toward her. When they're reunited, the foal nurses briefly, but then they too head back up the slope. I turn to see Baldface again; she's now taking up the rear of the group, having stopped to watch until the stragglers followed the rest up the slope off to my right.

Once Chaparro returns to the crest, the band is again in the basic position I found them in when I arrived one hour and fifteen minutes earlier. His herding maneuver took approximately ten minutes. But clearly it was not his alone; in this instance of herding, two mares played a crucial role, both of whom stood out when I first arrived. Considered in terms of "movement initiation" their role would be negligible—they didn't instigate the motion. But they displayed a canny capacity to position themselves so that this unwieldy mass of horses would end up back where they "belonged." Perhaps this was an enactment of what Bourjade characterizes as "partially-shared consensus." In this sense, herding is not just a matter of demonstrating the stallion's dominance: it's an instance of boundary maintenance to which the group responds. A social dynamic is on display here involving several horses who similarly

grasp the boundary being enacted and participate in its performance. They bind the group into a coherent collective. If so, then they perhaps share an idea of how the group should be configured and anticipate the stallion's actions and intent.

I want to stay and map the new configuration that unfolds, curious about the roles of Baldface and Fleabit. But it's getting late and I'm also hoping yet to check on the horses back at the knoll to the south. So after a quick position map, I'm off and down, reversing the course this band just traced.

Crossing the low ground easily in the afternoon, soon I come across the large cluster of horses near the northeast corner of the cattle enclosure, snoozing, interspersed with cows. Since they're static, it's easy to make a head count—seventeen adults, seven foals (half are lying on the ground), and four yearlings: twenty-eight in total. Checking my notes, I realize that some have been added since I last passed through. With only a couple of identifications in hand, there's little basis for me to tell who is here now that wasn't earlier. But the bigger question is where these additional six mares and two foals came from. My guess is that they had been corralled by Crazy Gray on the knoll; I can see most of its contours from here, just to the south, and it's empty now. It's easy to spot Northeastern; he's by Scar, who is standing over her sleeping two-year-old lying on the ground. Mostly cattle are around them, but two mares are standing over their crashed out foals a few horse-lengths away.

As they start to wake and the foals find their mothers, I cautiously loop around the east side of the assembled horses and cattle—a trajectory of sixty curving meters. There are enough calves here that I'm uneasy about getting closer. I take just under thirty minutes to circuit around to the south side, back toward the knoll near Caseta de Corvo, south of the enclosure. Stopping along the way to make a couple of identifications, I track social bonds as they branch out in pairs, triads, or clusters. Here, too, the females gradually spread out from their contracted sleeping configuration. One mare heads south, followed by her foal and yearling and another mare, also with a foal. The pair of yearlings I saw venturing northward earlier are now trekking south too, followed by two older mares. When Northeastern stirs, he pays little attention to any of this movement. Eventually he meanders closer to the fence where several mares and foals are clustered. After sniffing and urine-marking two of their dung piles, he makes a herding gesture toward the mares, trying to move them. But it's a far more modest effort than Chaparro's. Rather than being driven by this young stallion, these mares let him go past and only briefly trail behind him for a few meters before stopping. Northeastern then ambles on alone.

I'm jotting all this down when I hear movement behind me—the sound of large bodies crashing up from the *barranca* that drains down toward Sabucedo. In a moment, several mares emerge from the thicket of pine. It's Rabicana in the lead, followed by the dappled gray who was in between the clusters of mares when I left the knoll. Her foal is following. Looking at the large pinkish blotch covering most of the gray's nose, I think of Mancha ("stain") as a name for her. Coming up behind is Circle/Cross, the dark bay, and another bay, JB, bringing up the rear. Behind them and then soon alongside them is Crazy Gray. I wonder what happened to the rest of the mares that were on the knoll with these three earlier. Perhaps they all scattered at once and Crazy Gray just chose to follow these three. Perhaps he's fixated on or drawn to the dominant mare. Crazy Gray pauses for a moment on the open ground, looking me over; right then Rabicana dashes to the left at a hard gallop, accompanied by Mancha. Crazy Gray charges too and heads them both off before they cover forty meters. A standoff follows: the mares start chewing at the grass and he stands in front of them, looking back over his shoulder toward the knoll.

Then Crazy Gray, seemingly losing interest in Rabicana, dashes and drives at the outlying mares in the large group near the enclosure. With one hammering lunge he scatters most of them but pries loose two mares, a foal, and a yearling. They sprint along the fencing until they reach a thicket of trees and stop, with Crazy Gray right behind them. From among the others, I see Scar and her two-year-old peel off from the rest and reunite with Rabicana. After a few moments Northeastern charges into the thicket, and the two mares, yearling, and foal turn and race back with him a few meters along the fence. But Crazy Gray closes in rapidly, charging at Northeastern, who turns sharply and gallops away. Crazy Gray gives chase, closing fast; as he prepares to bite, Northeastern rears both hind legs and kicks while still running. Crazy Gray avoids this blow and delivers fierce bites to Northeastern's rump and flank. Northeastern turns, rears, and bites Crazy Gray's face; then directs another blow at his throat. They crash into several of the mares— one bolts but another stands her ground, front feet assertively splayed.

The stallions contort in a neck wrestle, both shrieking and twisting. Then Northeastern gallops to the south, fleeing his attacker. Crazy Gray pursues until he reaches the mares he'd just left, while Northeastern vanishes from view.

Amid this tumult, Rabicana and her mates slink back toward the *barranca*. But in less than a minute, Crazy Gray leaves off chasing Northeastern and seeks them out again. He follows their trail for about twenty meters, but turns back instead to make another go at Northeastern. The mares have disappeared to the east as the two stallions clash again, but this time Crazy Gray breaks off the combat and heads down for the *barranca* once more. I assume their conflict is over and start packing up, when Crazy Gray comes charging back up one more time and again drives Northeastern off, away from this big cluster of mares, before resuming his search for Rabicana and her mates.

Seeing this frenzied series of attacks, I guess at what happened earlier to create the confusing scene on the knoll. It seems likely that Crazy Gray similarly drove off Northeastern; perhaps most of the mares scattered too, such as the group of four blacks. Rabicana, Circle/Cross, JB, and others stayed behind. As for Bent, who copulated with Crazy Gray on the knoll, and the other later-arriving mares, perhaps they were a fragment from another band whose stallion was also driven off by Crazy Gray.

There's so much disruption here I despair of ever sorting out a clear band structure that I can observe prior to the *rapa*. But what I have observed so far is fascinating: both stallions are failing at the most basic forms of reproducing horse social structure. Crazy Gray's efforts at these two harem formation strategies are not working, because he's unable to keep or contain the mares he's pursuing or hiving off. The mares decidedly resist. And Northeastern's efforts at maintaining "female defense polygyny" are meager at best; the brief gesture he just made at herding some of these mares was ineffectual.

I speculate that there are two aspects to their challenges. The first has to do with socialization: Crazy Gray, as a city slicker, hasn't been socialized into the ritual conventions around managing relations within and between bands; Northeastern, as a young stallion, likely is not experienced enough at performing this role, either. Then there are the mares: their rebuffing or resisting these stallions' efforts suggests that their interest or willingness to participate in social organization matters. They may refuse to do so based on dislike (in the case of Crazy

Gray) or disinclination (with Northeastern). In neither case are they simply instinctually responding to the stallions' efforts, and they're certainly able to keep together despite the absence of "their" band stallion.

It's been nine hours since I spotted the first group on the knoll and I realize, despite all the excitement, that I'm tired and should be heading back. Trudging toward the track and glad to be out of the tangled underbrush, I think I'm done for the day. But I've not gone more than three hundred meters down toward the village when I come upon the four black mares and their foal, trekking east of the knoll. Another hundred meters on, I see Bent and her bunch off to the north side of the track, down in a dense thicket around a spring. It's fascinating, like running the day in reverse, or repeating the highlights, by passing back through the terrain I previously covered. Stallion-less by accident or intention, these two groups of mares leave me further intrigued about the social order that exists up here.

That evening I review my notes and photos, initially discouraged by how uncertain and shifting the situation is because of Crazy Gray. But it's also a familiar confusion to me, as an ethnographer, especially at the onset. I'm cheered, too, because despite the chaos, my use of ethological techniques generated plenty of data for me to pour over now. I begin by looking over photos from yesterday. Around the stallion Northeastern I make out Rabicana, Scar, Circle/Cross, JB, and even Mancha. There's also Twink, who I don't think I saw today. This was prior to the onslaught from Crazy Gray, so I think this will give me a baseline for their band structure; I'll have to see if this is borne out tomorrow. Combining these with the mares I identified in the Mega band—Baldface, Fleabit, Book, and Flaxen—I have thirteen identifications (ten mares, three stallions). Tomorrow will still be challenging, but I feel better about it by the time I close up my photos and notebooks. Before I go to bed, I call Juan to check if he's been able to identify Crazy Gray's owner; but he's not found out yet.

DAY 4

As I head up the next day, the high terrain is eerily empty. I don't see any horses as I slog my way toward O Peón, the high peak. This is unnerving, but I don't panic. I speculate that there might be several bands circulating on the lower slopes, passing below on the flank of the mountain, not yet having risen up to the peaks to avoid the flies. But rather than scout them out I decide to go directly to the Mega band and settle into observations. The knoll is entirely empty, as is Caseta de Corvo and even the spring by the road. No cattle in sight either.

Before long I spot Crazy Gray, far up the road beyond the southeast end of the cattle enclosure, with three mares and a foal. Well off from them there's a small cluster: four bay mares and two foals. They're waiting, it seems—certainly not driving to go elsewhere. Then I hear the frantic calling of a horse off to my left. Following the sounds, I'm surprised to find three mares are inside the cattle enclosure. I can't imagine how they got stuck in there—no human would've driven them in and the pen's design impedes entering as well as exiting: a "cattle guard" of horizontal pipes is embedded in the road, spaced apart to unnerve four-footed animals and with the unsettling capacity to roll under their hooves. One of the prisoners is Twink, who was being groomed by Northeastern on my first day up here. I recognize another mare from yesterday on the knoll among the four blacks; she has a distinctive star-shaped brand. So perhaps Twink was there yesterday too and I just couldn't see her oddly shaped half-star under her long thick forelock. The fact they're in the enclosure now and quite frantic to get out suggests they must've been spooked and fleeing and somehow leaped the fence yesterday, probably to escape Crazy Gray.

I don't dwell long on their predicament, resuming my trek up the range toward the Mega band. After crossing through the basin to the north I'm most of the way there when the herd of cattle appear too, coming up from off to the east, similarly heading for the big hilltop. I take this in stride, hoping they pass through quickly. But they're in no hurry. While I wait, I scan the nearby peak and, sure enough, spot a band off to the west. A gray mare, long mane on left, w/ foal; five adults (two black, one bay, one brown), and three foals total. From this distance—maybe a kilometer away—I can't make any identifications, but I wonder if they're a refugee group from another band, perhaps driven apart by Crazy Gray.

The cows just stop, so there's no other option for me than to work my way around them. Initially this doesn't seem challenging, but I'm quickly in a bind. A cow realizes her calf is missing. She stands facing off in the direction I'm circuiting and calls for it, over and over; very gradually, she moves a few steps toward where I'm heading. But while

I'm waiting for her to pass by me, I hear a foal calling from off to my left, from somewhere lower on the slope, hidden in the gorse. In quick response, the mother trots toward the cry, crossing roughly sixty meters hurriedly from deep among the band, accompanied by her yearling, also moving briskly. I hadn't noticed the foal as I was in motion, but I see it plainly now—it's very young, just a few days old. A large swath of its hide is missing on the right flank. Its face, too is ripped. The foal must've been attacked by wolves in the night. The mother nuzzles its forehead and takes up a position alongside it, skirted by her yearling.

As I wait for the worried cow to separate from the group enough that I can cross behind her, I ponder the species differences in mothers and the spacing and care of offspring. I'm curious why the cow doesn't head down at a clip to find her calf, like this mare has done. At that moment, I see a cow repeatedly chastising a calf for getting in the way of the bull trying to mount her. By contrast, horse foals and yearlings can stay quite close during copulation, as long as they snap deferentially around the stallion. What surprises me most, though, is watching cows mount each other. I find out later that the females are similarly excited by the pheromone that attracts the bull. I'd love to study their sociality, too. But that's a different project.[10]

Finally settled in among the cows and horses, I take stock of what I'm seeing. Once again the size of the Mega band and their dispersal over uneven ground amid dozens of cows makes this a challenge. The outliers are the clearest ones initially. Fleabit is clustered out on the edge just like yesterday, with four adults, two foals (one is hers), and two yearlings. I again spot a somewhat distant pair on the outmost eastern point. I used them yesterday as a base point for my position mappings. Today I notice that one of them is taller than the other— perhaps a modern horse—and her ears are clipped. Maybe she went through the *rapa* when they were still clipping ears. Everything else about the band seems muddled, though, in contrast to the clarity of social structure that unfolded with yesterday's grand herding maneuver. I look for Baldface and spot her but can't make out anything distinctive about her positioning vis-à-vis her bandmates. I notice Book, too, but she hardly stands out either.

If their positioning is scarcely revealing, an interesting behavior quickly catches and absorbs by attention. Twenty meters away, two mares are allogrooming. One is the dappled gray that I thought was an outlier yesterday, when no one followed her movement. The other is a large bay with a sun-bleached mane that almost seems flaxen, but I can't get a good enough look at her identifying features. I decide to shift around to get a better view, which takes more than five minutes. Before I start, Chaparro approaches from the dappled gray's other side. He has just left the side of a mare with a long blaze shaped like a large golf tee, but haloed by a lighter shading. Later I decide to designate her Haloed Tee. When Chaparro arrives at the dappled horse's rear, they form a triad. I'll call the middle horse Dapple. While cautiously circuiting cows and horses, I think about what I'm seeing and the differences between how I'm approaching these observations and how an ethologist might proceed, starting with the status of allogrooming as an interactional data point and a fixed action pattern or innate behavior.

Fixed action patterns are important to ethological observation; instinctive, species-typical behaviors facilitate observational precision and reliability. These patterns are envisioned to be "hard wired" (produced by an innate releasing mechanism) and discretely objective: a characteristic action construed as unique and clearly bounded from all other behaviors so that its observation can be readily confirmed by anyone, since there is no subjective dimension. At the edges of a fixed action pattern, behaviors shade off into arbitrary, peculiar, or random manifestations—the various things an animal might do that are not fully representative of characteristic actions of its species. Against such vagaries, this unit of analysis allows ethologists to shift perspectives across an observational repertoire: scanning, sampling, or focused modes of attention that generate different records of behavioral activity.

Amid the more than forty horses around me, behavioral units of analysis are a means by which I can see patterns and features of sociality. They range across a behavioral continuum from *events*—short duration, gauged by their frequency, to *states*—prolonged activities, measured by their duration, as I shift and develop my observations of this band. Against the vast backdrop of a state like "grazing," an event like allogrooming stands out as interactional and distinctively social. So the frequency of this behavior offers a means to assess the social cohesiveness of this band. More diffuse is the set of relationships that allogrooming performs or reproduces: the series of social effects that reverberate from this one data point.

Yet sociality does not easily conform to this observational convention. Perhaps the most fundamental aspect of sociality, from an ethno-graphic perspective, is that it involves a continuous flow. Interactions and relationships certainly begin and end, but those transitional mo-ments are often tinged with ambiguity. That's why many social species have ritualized forms to clarify these liminal inevitabilities: greetings and farewells.[11] By contrast, in order to achieve clarity and objectivity, behavioral units of analysis follow a binary logic. Acts are distinguished between aggressive and affiliative, threatening and submissive, vigilant or self-directed (absorbed in self-grooming, for instance). Compiled and calculated, such observations lead to depictions of individual animals as dominant or subordinate, assertive or submissive.[12] Such characteri-zations are typically assessed as fixed identities (status) even though so-cial positions of dominance and subordination are constantly shifting; or they're construed as "personality" traits, again potentially missing much of the flow of sociality. Among horses—a species characterized by fission-fusion dynamics at the band level—such positionality seems far more fluid and less fixed. Not surprisingly, their interactional behaviors feature plenty of opportunity for ambiguity and interpretive efforts.

In the seven minutes it takes me to move closer to the triad of Dap-ple, the bay mare, and Chaparro, they've intensified their interaction. But what is it exactly? Technically, it's no longer allogrooming: though the bay and gray mares are still facing each other with necks roughly overlapping, only the bay is doing the work with her teeth of digging through Dapple's mane. Though not for long. Soon she too stops grooming; now she's stroking her left nostril up and down Dapple's neck energetically. At one point, Dapple passes her head under the bay's, briefly presenting her right side to the plunging and rising nose. But this positioning is awkward for both, underscoring how cumbersome faces can be in close contact; and since neither shifts their feet, Dapple's head passes back again to its original position.

The bay resumes her attentions, then steps a few feet forward, still alongside Dapple. This movement ends with the bay pressing her face against Dapple's flank, burying her nose in the fold where hip and torso meet. Meanwhile Chaparro has yet to move at all; his face is still close to Dapple's opposite rear flank. Two foals off to his right, press near his face; perhaps one belongs to Dapple. Chaparro takes no notice, nor does the bay, who is inhaling deeply from Dapple. After just over a min-ute, Chaparro shifts his face to Dapple's left side, coming nose-to-nose with the bay. Both sniff each other, though without making contact. Then he turns back again and the trio settle into a static state of rest.

What am I seeing here? Something more excessive and peculiar than a fixed action pattern. That reification of behavior demands consistency and clarity; this interaction is anything but. Of course, such excessive activities are manifold among animals, so they are bracketed off, falling outside the domain of observable, recordable events or states. As an ethnographer, I am drawn exactly to such elusive, ephemeral moments; their accretion in relation to a place—both reflecting and constituting a locality—are the staple of ethnographic accounts. Also, it's axiomatic in my field that reifying a thing or behavior obscures the tangle of relationships that constitute sociality. That's why I dwell on this interaction, which is interesting in part because it's emblematic of how much of sociality escapes or eludes ethological quantification or objectification.[13]

But how can I characterize what's occurring here? Around me are many instances of such intimacies among mares, though none as intense in terms of duration and focus. And beyond these momentary couplings I see outlier mares singly scattering around the loose edges of the band. Perhaps they've been pushed out through agonistic be-

FIGURE 2.8. *A trio in a fixed action pattern. Chaparro is on the right and Dapple is in the middle.*

haviors, the principal means by which dominance is analytically established for ethologists. But what of the other, more numerous social bonds expressed through these intimacies? As an ethnographer, I can sketch outlines of the social texture; I can attend to the wide range of relationships among mares, those that fall from view in observations oriented around the stallion when using him as the principal identifier of a band—even though his tenure is typically short-lived—while the mares endure, daily sorting out their affections and dislikes.

At the same time, still speaking as an ethnographer, I'm feeling uncomfortably bound to traditions of "thick description" as articulated by Clifford Geertz. For this to be ethnography in that mode, I would need to be able to access the subjective states of these horses through elaborate hermeneutical procedures that rely upon the intersubjectivity of languages as encapsulated in interpretable "texts." Instead, I am drawn to what I can take from ethology: an attention not to inner thoughts and experiences but to the observable range of interactions that generate sociality through bonds and boundaries, affiliations and agonistic gestures that amount to a continuous performance of group identity through socially situated selves, signaling and responding to the signals of others. This is close to the idea of "thin description," as described by John L. Jackson or a "flattening" of the ethnographic subject by way of resisting what Bruno Latour characterizes as too-quick jumps to abstract "society."[14]

Jarring loose from these reflections, I decide to shift my location, moving a few meters north and centering myself more within the band, perching on a boulder that gets me up a bit higher. It's then I notice how much the horses have been compacting as a group, gradually moving closer together. By the time I look back at the two mares, the bay has turned around so that her head now snuggles deeply against the neck of the gray, both slipping into a snoozy posture. Sleep seems to be a contagious behavior, because soon they're all drowsing, heads at rest, eyes shuttering, faces pressed close to rears to take advantage of fly-swatting tails. Those moving in close to another reach out and make contact with a smell gesture or a light lift and extension of the face; none of these are rejected with a threat of a bite or even a warning forward pitch of the ears. It's 11:45 a.m. and the band slips into stillness.

Thanks to the days spent in the mountains, I recognize this as an advantageous moment. Not in itself—there's very little to observe when they're all napping, though it is a great opportunity for a head count and to map positioning. I do use it to detect potential relationships (the clipped ear mare has nestled in between a bay with only a trace of a star and a dark brown with an "S" brand; near her is a mare/yearling pair, both with "PO" brands). Rather, it's most revealing and fascinating for what follows next, when they wake. Proximity within these bands contracts as they move toward sleep and expands as they wake and graze. Each repetition of this periodicity offers a panoply of opportunities to assert social distance or to close that elusive boundary.

After twenty minutes, their bodies begin to shift slightly and heads start to rise. When they do, the ones around me make a quick transition to alert; they seem startled to see me still there, as if they forgot about me as they drifted off. But only a couple direct long stares my way, including Clipped Ears. Most faces drop back to inattention, except for Book, the bay with a large star like the pages of an open book who caught my attention yesterday. Book keeps her eyes on me for more than fifteen seconds before eventually turning away. The duration gives me a sense that she's performing "attention" here, not just for my benefit but for her bandmates as well, who can see someone is being vigilant and so they can concentrate on grazing.

Chaparro does much the same as he too wakes. But his focus on me doesn't last as long; he soon engages a four-foot-high stone as a local enhancement to rub the left side of his face. He's flanked by a male foal, whose mother—a black with a distinctive face who I also noticed yesterday—is some ten meters away, keeping close to Book. She has a large star that morphs into a full, bending, hazily shaded stripe. It looks something like a palm tree, so I'll call her Palm. I remember that yesterday she was also close to Book, so I wonder about their relationship.

Collectively, what unfolds now is a series of small shifts and slight jostlings; at their sharpest, these would be recordable as aggressions or threat gestures, and they're manifold. Horses who sought or tolerated closeness in the snooze now signal that proximity is annoying. Mares snort or flick their heads and others back off or slide away, movements that impact neighbors, especially foals and yearlings. The social life of bands is an endless series of these gestures, and affiliative ones as well, asserting and collapsing social distance and projected boundaries. Cumulatively, some of these may amount to "movement initiation," but they are really more about asserting *distance*. And while I'm trying to

assess "status" among horses, they're doing the same through this panoply of microaggressions and affiliations, the fodder for establishing
social position. Is there a dominant mare; does she mirror the male
or is she subordinate to him; which mares follow others? Perhaps the
mares and I share these questions and interests, which are intriguing
because they're so difficult to determine; beginnings and endings, as
causal connections, can be ambiguous and often vague.

Over the next hour, a series of treks unfurl. They're each distinct,
suggesting the individuality of the animals involved, but they also repli-
cate a common pattern or dynamic. In the midst of all this, the stallion
is largely unmoving. As he works a tall stone as a local enhancement,
he's shadowed by Palm's male foal, who mimics his actions. About three
horse-lengths in front of him stands Baldface; the two mark the puta-
tive loose center of this band. Neither are grazing, though all around
mouths are nosing the ground, filling with greens ripped brusquely
from their roots.

The stasis first breaks when Book shifts from the far left of Chaparro
and ambles forward and past him. Instantaneously, at least half a dozen
horses are in motion—I can't make them all out—following in her wake.
Book angles to her left, around Flaxen and her foal, who've been on the
perimeter the whole time I've been here. But one of the following mares
directs an open-mouth bite threat at Flaxen's rear, sending her lurching
forward. Yesterday, when Flaxen was in the advance party down in the
basin, I thought she might have played a role in leading; now I think
maybe it's more like she was pushed away and along through gestures
like this; or even that she might be thinking about finding another
band. After about twenty seconds, Book stops in a dense wedge of gorse
and defecates. The other mares stop and clutter up behind her. Clipped
Ears presses forward and smells her dropping; then she generates a rear
kick-threat that sends the mare closest to her—she has just a wisp of a
crescent star, so Wisp—jumping high and away. Meanwhile, Palm and
her foal reverse course and step back the way they came. While Book
stays still, Clipped Ears too turns back and soon overtakes Palm, nudging her out of the way at first, but then seeming to drive the pair from
behind, keeping them at least a dozen meters ahead.

Nothing decisive or profoundly insightful here; it's one of numerous such movements that comprise a band's day. The next one is instigated by Fleabit—the gray who seems to center her own cluster. She

juts forward, dislodging several bays in front of her, who fall into a loose trek that curves around and ends up behind Fleabit. She then strides forward and the bays follow, but have to move around Chaparro, who's still in the same position, though now he's joined by a bay who seems interested in sex. As those two stand paired, Fleabit and three mares, one yearling, and two foals head out and away from the rest of the band. Another trek involves Dapple, who once again is the recipient of keen attention from the same bay who allogroomed with her earlier. This mare's star narrows into a thin blade, so I'll call her Stiletto. This development is complicated. As Dapple starts moving, Stiletto and two two-year-olds start following, but she stops and looks me over—though I've not changed positions for more than an hour and a half. We're now about ten meters apart. Stiletto tries to get around the two-year-old on Dapple's left side; the young horse surges ahead to get out of the way, instead; this startles both the other two-year-old and Dapple, and all four of them spring forward. This sets off an ancillary movement as several rattled mares and foals ahead of them fall into a linear motion. Stiletto comes up behind them, driving them farther, while Flaxen and her foal drop in hopefully, too. Dapple adopts this direction too, but at a remove, so they walk in parallel for about ten seconds; then Stiletto breaks from her column and turns toward Dapple, who stops and they pair up again.

The backdrop of all this is a diffuse collection of foals and yearlings, all working out where they belong and how they fit in; jostling to be closer to mother, responding to the distancing gestures made at them by other adults. A young horse moves to avoid a menacing older one and that sets another mare pair or trio in motion; a mother looks for sweeter forage and her movement attracts the interest of another mare with yearling and foal in tow. The trek has coherence as a fixed action pattern; "movement initiation" has the potential to reveal status, but these are moments of legibility in a dense mass of socializing. I take note of how these treks fracture as individuals perhaps respond to the gravitational force of others' social orbits. The movements generally don't "go anywhere" because the band all remain powerfully oriented toward each other, observing constantly what anyone else nearby is doing. The movement of a trek, then, isn't directional, rather it's relational; they're not heading toward goals, they're responding to what others are doing and who's up ahead or off to the side before they settle in to graze. That is, they're "reading the social" while reproducing it, responding as other horses engage in movement that entails performing proximity and distance: distance not as ground covered, but social distance that opens and closes around each horse, adult or youth.

The last trek I record involves Baldface. I'd forgotten about her entirely, but as space gradually clears out in the center through all this movement, there she stands—about twenty meters from Chaparro, so she has not been caught up in any of this kinesis. Chaparro, it seems, has noticed her too. He jaunts up and sniffs carefully at her face, getting a partial erection. But she rears her head and shakes him off. He persists in sniffing her rear, which she turns and positions to deliver a kick, so he slides away. Seconds later she turns and moves off at a slow gait; directly, another mare and two yearlings fall into line behind her, and Chaparro falls in too, taking up the rear. He follows until he comes across a fresh dung pile, which absorbs his attention as Baldface moves on. It's the only time I've seen him participate in any of this directed motion, so I take this as another indicator of her prominence within this band.

I've been here for just under two and a half hours, so it's time to go check on Northeastern and the mares I saw yesterday. I do one more quick sketch of their positions. Dapple now is draped by several different band mates. If I had only observed her today, I would have a completely different sense of her position in the group than I did when she trekked alone yesterday. I also note that Flaxen is peripheral again to the group. So too is the third gray here, another flea-bitten one with a "CF" brand. CF seems to be gravitating toward Flaxen, though in a sort of parallel-exclusion stance. As I make my way down off the hill, I come across the wounded foal again, not far from where she was when I arrived this morning. She's trying hard to stay close to her mother, who wants to get back to the rest of the band. A cloud of flies halos her bleeding hip and raw facial wound. That's the last time I see her.

Passing back across the basin heading south, I arrive at the northeast corner of the cattle enclosure, but there are no horses where they had congregated yesterday. I see a band up on the knoll so I make my way there. Without much effort but in slow, zigzag fashion, it takes me about thirty minutes to edge up the lip of the north side of the knoll without stirring any of the animals. I count twenty-seven horses, with eight foals and three yearlings. Northeastern is easy to spot, standing about in the center, flanked by Rabicana and Circle/Cross; a few feet away is Mancha, the dappled gray, with a foal sleeping at her feet. So is JB, and Scar is here too, with her yearling, as are the mares branded AP and PS that I saw with Northeastern down below yesterday. With the exception of Twink, stuck in the enclosure with two other mares, this configuration closely matches what I observed with Juan when I started up here. But I counted nineteen horses then, with three foals. If this is the reconstitution of that band, there are several more mares and foals now. I decide to call it the Knoll band since this is where I've most frequently encountered these mares and this stallion.

Where all was churn and motion in the Mega band, this configuration seems surprisingly staid and solid. Maybe they're all exhausted from yesterday's run-ins with Crazy Gray. Circle/Cross's face is buried in Northeastern's left flank, but she moves her nose up and down against it, like Stiletto did on Dapple. I work out a few more identifications, but the air is drowsy here and I've had quite enough of standing in one place after my long stint with the Mega band. The flies are quite active, surging and feeding on the moisture around the animals' mouths and eyes. They also animatedly attend to the copious manure piles. I realize a good initial indicator of how fresh a dropping might be is the volume of flies swirling around it—the most recent ones are swathed with a buzzing that reminds me somewhat of a rattlesnake's warning. The fact that this occupies my thoughts conveys the serenity of naptime. The three foals here are all sprawled across the ground, utterly crashed out; a mare, too, is asleep on the ground. Since little is moving, I decide to look for some of the other mares from yesterday; pressing on, I work my way up the logging road farther than I've gone before, rising up along the south side of the cattle enclosure. Though I've opted out of more surveying, I figure it would be good to spot a few more horses that might be caught up in the *rapa* in two days.

The climb is hot work and I doubt my decision several times, especially as I stop to catch my breath and scan for horses, seeing none. I'm standing under the last pine on this stretch, hugging its shade, steadying myself for the climb ahead, when I see Crazy Gray barreling down the track; behind him are three black mares and a foal, who look like the ones I saw him with up here yesterday at the start of the day. They're following, I note, not being herded. I'm actually startled at how fast the distance between us closes; they're coming down at a hard trot and he's heading straight for me. Somehow, instinctively, I turn and look askance, nonchalantly diverting my gaze off to the north. Crazy Gray slows and then stops maybe twenty meters from me and just stares. I realize this diversion of the gaze mimics something I've seen some of the mares do when ostensibly challenged. They look away and it somehow blunts the confrontation, draining it of momentum. Sure enough, he turns from his standstill and trots over to get a better view of the lower flanks of the slope, ignoring me for the time being.

As he loses interest in me, the blacks behind him fan out and graze in a southerly direction. They've been grazing quietly for four minutes when another batch of horses trots down along the track: a brown mare and foal, a bay with a foal, then two more bays. They pull up about thirty meters from Crazy Gray, who's midway between them and the black mares. Both groups turn casually to grazing. This second bunch wants to get to the spring just behind me, so after four minutes they move in concert, around the stallion and down to the water gurgling up through a thin stand of young pines. He follows them slowly. As he does so, the blacks seize an opportunity to escape and in a flash are down the plunging slope. He doesn't seem to notice as he tags along with the bays into the lush shade of the trees. But they don't want to be with him and surprisingly leave almost as quickly as they arrived, without even drinking. That's when he notices the black mares are gone. Crazy Gray picks up their trail directly and dives down the slope after them, but is not well received when he gets there. I watch them for a bit until he takes off back up the mountain, passes me again, and heads toward the cattle enclosure, where the mares I saw trapped earlier have reappeared. Crazy Gray trots up and down the fence line, whinnying vociferously, but to no avail.

He may not be tired, but I am and decide to call it a day. Looking back down the track to the east, the knoll is in view, and since there's now some movement there, I figure to stop and check on the Knoll band on my way down. Impressively, Crazy Gray gets there first. After trotting back and forth with the mares in the enclosure for a bit he stops and looks at the band up on the knoll. I watch him watching them; then he decides something. He changes course and charges down through the funnel of pines toward the knoll. I go by the road and reach an opening in time to see him take the hill and clash with Northeastern, rearing and biting, driving him off. He caps this off with a vigorous flehmen directed toward Northeastern's retreating form. He has won **King of the Hill**—a game or ritual by which one drives the other from a hilltop. Just as impressive, though, is how the mares, yearlings, and foals fan out away from him, leaving a wide empty arc. The cattle have cleared out too, which is favorable for me. The nearest horses to Crazy Gray are Rabicana and Mancha. He starts to approach Rabicana but turns away as she glares at him in a defiant stance; he opts instead to inspect the lower reaches of the knoll, around which Northeastern is now frantically circuiting.

Paralleling Northeastern's movements below brings Crazy Gray up against a bevy of horses on the east lip—five mares, four foals, and a yearling. In a moment they turn in concert from a static, clumped formation to a hurried shift away from him. This is different than the treks I observed this morning; it lasts longer and is more cohesive. As they move, I can see that the bunch around Rabicana, seventeen in total, are not moving. The group in motion stops when Crazy Gray gets out in front of them; then they reverse course. When they finally come to rest, they do so at a remove of several horse-lengths from the others. Northeastern shrieks from below and feints at rising up the south side, but Crazy Gray is there to meet him and he recedes again. I see him below, deep in the brush, scanning the ring from which he's been expelled. Above him, Crazy Gray stares imperiously down at his predicament. Perhaps curiously, I only see one mare do so as well, but only for a few seconds. Sometimes, when Northeastern's cries waft up on the stiffening wind, mare heads will pop up and register his location. But mostly they focus on what's happening up top and moving away whenever Crazy Gray approaches.

At the core of the seventeen horses are Rabicana, Mancha, Circle/Cross, and JB. After being fairly sedentary for the first twenty minutes of this ordeal, an interesting motion develops. The mares start moving, slowly circulating, also very different from the trekking earlier. They form a series of loops, circling around and around, basically pacing. What's notable too is that they're passing close to each other, close enough to reach out a nose and sniff or make physical contact. They do so with their eyes as well, glancing at each other as they shuttle past, not stopping or staring but looking from one to another, pacing and pacing. This restless energy is turned inward, not probing for a break to escape the high ring of rock and grass. Three times when Northeastern tries for the high ground, Crazy Gray plunges down to meet him. The mares, though, keep up their circling, not looking to exploit his inattention and escape. They're walking and watching and waiting, thinking, I suppose, about what to do next. This is an intensely heightened mode of sociality.

Below, the bays who had escaped from Crazy Gray earlier come into view, passing along the base of the knoll. Northeastern makes one more effort at the top, but the big modern stallion easily drives him back. Northeastern then turns and joins up with these mares, their two foals, and a yearling. He sniffs at dung in the road but finds nothing notable. As they move off to the north, he falls in alongside them, not looking back again that I can see. Meanwhile, the mares above are still moving, slipping between and across each other. This is striking because none of these close passes is accompanied by a threat gesture of any kind—no feigned bites, head thrusts, or kicks. It takes a great deal of concentration, I imagine, to condense so, in such a tense setting—everyone is on edge; no one is grazing—and to sustain this exchange of glances and gazes, circling, looping, avoiding Crazy Gray and turning time and again toward each other. Any of them could easily bolt, like the two batches of mares I've just seen, the blacks and the bays. But these mares primarily seem focused on staying together and staying put on this spot.

I'm not sure what I'm seeing but I'm fairly certain they will keep this up for as long as Crazy Gray is pacing the perimeter. After an hour on the knoll, and a total of nine hours up on the range, I decide I'm tired and that I'll just have to find out what happens in the morning.

DAY 5

Again the slopes are quiet and desolate as I hike up and in. The knoll is empty and I encounter no horses along the track. I walk out to the flanks of the mountain and scan the lower reaches but see nothing there either. Finally I spot Crazy Gray, higher up than I've seen him before but not far beyond where I encountered him on the track late yesterday. He's driving six mares and three foals. They could be the remnants of the Knoll band, maybe fled in the night. Taking him as my mark, I start the steep climb wondering, if that's the case, where all the other mares are. They're so distant when I first spot them that I can't make out any identifying features, even with my binoculars. So I resign myself to a long hike before I can begin observations. I climb up past the trackside spring and grove, past the now-empty knoll and the vacant northeast corner of the enclosure, huffing along the track until it reaches the logging road that Juan and I drove on in my rental car on the first day.

I catch my breath at the higher spring just off the road south of the enclosure, where Crazy Gray came running toward me yesterday. He's up ahead still, maybe three hundred meters, when I notice two mares and two foals in the thicket of pines around the water source. They're skittish and bolt as I get closer. I wonder what band they belong to, and I'm curious why Crazy Gray doesn't seem interested in them, though they're fairly close by. Having caught my breath and taking my bearings on where he's positioned, I strike up a steady stride again. I cover only fifty meters when off to my left, beside a larger boulder about eight feet high, I see three horses wedged close against it as if **sheltering** against bad weather, though the day is clear and bright. They seem to be sleeping—heads at rest, unmoving.

They're so close together I can't identify them. I worry they'll be skittish too and hard to approach. Then I notice yet more horses here, down in a relatively flat depression flanking the road, a low spot previously obscured from view. I can only just make out their upper bodies: more than half a dozen are bunched together, with roughly four horse-lengths between the trio by the rock and the closest bay in the bigger cluster. In the distance, on a crest to the west, I see two dark-brown mare pairs, each with foals.

To get a better look, I leave the road—which at this point enters the cattle enclosure through an open gate barred only by a cattle guard—and head across the stony terrain around the backside of the boulder, aiming for a taller outcrop of broken granite just south of these animals. Moving obliquely, it takes several minutes to edge around the first boulder, very slowly, so as not to seem threatening. Reaching the outcrop, I set down my pack and walking stick, then pull myself up the lichen-draped crag. From my new perch I'm surprised to see more than ten horses in loose array on the west side of the rock outcrop. Then I spot Crazy Gray closing in, maybe sixty meters away; he moved down while I was hiking up. He's struggling to coax the two dark-brown mares back up the slope, sauntering between the pair, but having no luck in catching their interest or getting them to move. The six mares I saw him with previously remain grazing farther up, on the high promontory jutting from where the ground rises more steeply, approaching the peak.

In the sharp morning light, lushly glistening greens of gorse and ferns cast the animals in bright relief. Against the backdrop of Crazy Gray's movements, the three horses wedged up against the boulder seem like they've assumed a defensive position, with one side entirely shielded; the fence of the cattle enclosure roughly seals off another possible direction of attack by Crazy Gray. From my high perch, I survey the setting. Ringing the outcrop is a broad stretch of stubbly grass and stones bounded by an encroaching expanse of ferns. Farther west are three ridges cluttered with a dense brush of small trees and undergrowth. Turning east, I'm able to focus easily on the trio, less than twenty meters from me. It's Rabicana, right next to Northeastern, who's close against the boulder; perpendicular to them is JB, about a body-length away. How did they end up here overnight?

Pondering that, I start to identify the others here and to map this wide configuration of horses. They're mostly sleeping or drowsing, so this shouldn't be hard. The cluster about fifteen meters west of Northeastern has four mares, two yearlings, and a foal; one of them is Scar, with her yearling and I also recognize AP with her foal, so seven total. Oblique to them is a dappled gray, off at a remove, with a sleeping foal—it's Mancha. Twenty meters past her is a trio of mother, yearling, and foal, closets to the cattle enclosure fence. I don't recognize them.

FIGURE 2.9. *Northeastern (facing away), Rabicana (facing forward), and JB.*

Then at least thirty meters farther west and a bit to the south is another bunch of eleven, with five foals. They're spread out in a rough line, grazing in a southerly direction, moving behind me if I face the triad by the boulder, and so out of sight of Northeastern. This formation garners my attention because it's the biggest cluster at the moment but there's no stallion directly associated with it. As far as the distant dark-brown mare pair on the adjacent ridge, before I can identify them Crazy Gray gets forceful and drives both up and over the ridge to the west.

All told, there are twenty-six animals here, so this is likely all of the Knoll band plus a few extras. My original count for them, on the first day, was nineteen. That leaves seven more horses than I'd expect for this band, so I decide to attend closely to forms of boundary work that might be revealed in how they've clustered or positioned themselves.

First, I take note of what's not happening. Despite Crazy Gray's menacing proximity, Northeastern is doing nothing to check his actions. Nor does he seem concerned that so many mares have drifted out of sight, moving closer to Crazy Gray. Northeastern is not exhibiting "normal" stallion behavior, such as herding or "harem maintenance."

FIGURE 2.10. *The line of grazers facing south; Circle/Cross is on the far left.*

Rather, he's motionless in a defensive position against the boulder sheltering, his face pressed low against Rabicana's right flank. Over the next hour and forty-five minutes I spend observing this scene he moves no more than four or five body-lengths from the rock's shadow, returning to its shelter quickly. I wonder what all this might reveal about this band's structure, particularly the mares. Given how this band, or at least its stallion, has been repeatedly assailed by Crazy Gray, I've had difficulty mapping its social structure.

Mentally rummaging through the ethological toolkit I picked up in Serra do Cando, I opt for focal-animal sampling: recording a particular horse's behavior. But since time is short—the *rapa* commences tomorrow—I'll have to maximize my efforts and focus on more than one. Who should I choose? Seeing Rabicana in the position she's taken up, practically shielding the stallion, I start with her, especially given her prominence in all the observations I've made. JB is next to her and I wonder again at their relationship, but I want to spread my view more widely. I've been most curious about Circle/Cross, so I scan for her now. She's easy to spot amid the grazing horses; she's the farthest advanced

along their loose, southerly line. So I'll keep a close eye on her too. For an opposite sense from these two prominent mares, who might be the most peripheral? Based on their current configuration and what I've seen previously, I decide to go with Mancha, who's alone with her foal on the "edge" of this assemblage. I'll follow her, too. The rest should hopefully sort out in between, giving me an overarching sense of their band structure.

I settle in to observe the interactions and relationships this morning by keeping an eye on these three mares. Since Northeastern isn't doing any boundary work, I assume the mares will be instead. Even though Crazy Gray has been hugely disruptive, his antics have fortuitously presented an excellent opportunity to think band social structure, certainly, but also sociality more generally and how boundaries manifest and are negotiated.

Ten minutes from when I first spotted them, I see some movement. AP rouses from the bunch of seven and steps sluggishly toward the trio by the boulder, her male foal tagging along. She stops more than a body-length from JB, though her foal advances, filling up the intervening space. JB does not noticeably gesture to acknowledge her approach. Meanwhile, Mancha's foal awakens and starts grazing in the direction of the trio, too. Mancha grudgingly follows, but AP, now in between her and the trio, stares hard at her. Mancha reverses course but also steers clear of the cluster of bays, grazing by herself over toward the fence, facing away. I wonder how she fits in. She was with the Knoll group when I first observed them, but she was with Bent on the second day early in the morning; then when that group climbed up the knoll Mancha was the only one to join the cluster around Rabicana—the others kept apart. And later that afternoon she was traveling with Rabicana, not with Bent's group. But she doesn't seem to fit easily in the band. I think about the contrast to the situation, say, with Monk and the Capilla band in Serra do Cando: instead of the stallion trying to include her, perhaps Mancha has some kind of tie with Rabicana.

Then I notice motion from above. The two dark-brown mares and their foals are barreling back over and down the slope from the west. They've escaped from Crazy Gray, who is not bothering to give chase. Within a minute both pairs have fully descended, but one stops with her foal at the edge of the grassy flat where the rest of the horses are strewn. The other mare approaches the cluster of bays that AP just left. Several whinnies of greeting ring out and she replies similarly, trotting directly to the middle bunch, taking up a position alongside one of the bays and snatching at the grass animatedly. The whinnies are how this boundary is acknowledged and negotiated. Those I just heard are greeting rituals, quite common among horses. They remind me of how Goffman characterized such rituals in humans: "Our relationship is the same as it was." The other dark-brown mare, though, remains on the fringe. This is striking because, isolated, she remains at risk from Crazy Gray, but she makes no effort to join the others, and they show no interest in her fate. She's not one I've seen in this group, so I get a clearer sense of the boundedness of these mares. The lack of welcome for the outlier dark brown underscores that sociality is predicated on the extension or withholding of recognition, which allows or prevents an animal from taking its place in the social setting among the group. This dimension of boundary work is highlighted by the disruptions caused by Crazy Gray.

The dark-brown mare, along with the lone bay with a yearling and foal grazing by the fence, appear to be fragments of other bands. Given that Crazy Gray has been peeling mares away for several days now, it's likely that he's assembled a loose collection of females rather than taking over a band as he did with the Knoll group yesterday afternoon. Given the hesitancy of the other returnee to get closer to this concentration of mares, and the continued peripheral positioning of the lone mare with her yearling and foal, I can see that the boundary around a band isn't just asserted by the stallion in herding; it's recognized by adults from other bands, who, even in this risky situation, are loath to cross it.

Slowly another source of motion is developing, perhaps offering more clarity on the social contours here. After the dark-brown mares escape, the line of eleven grazers gradually reverses course. To observe them I have to turn around on the granite outcrop to face southwest; in this position, my back is to Rabicana and company. Circle/Cross, the farthest away (about seventy meters from the stallion), was nosing south, but now turns north; as she passes, the others fall in to this flow, loosely trailing her. I wonder if they've been waiting on this last horse to rejoin them. Giving that some credence, the middle cluster where the dark-brown returnee settled in, just a few meters below me, is starting to dissolve. First, the bay branded "PS" peels off with her dark yearling and walks toward the bunch by the boulder—Northeastern, Rabicana, JB, and the bay AP with her foal.

As she approaches, Northeastern shows some interest and advances a few meters to meet her, while Rabicana peels off, faces the boulder and glides the right side of her neck up and down against its coarse surface, repeatedly; then she scratches the crown of her forehead along the lower portions of the boulder. PS and Northeastern make facial contact but the yearling's face is also there—she deferentially snaps to the stallion as he moves to smell PS's rear end. The yearling tries shifting out of the way entirely by sliding around to her mother's opposite side. But this brings her quite close to Rabicana, who, at the moment, is still avidly using the boulder. Once that activity ends, Rabicana turns toward the others; the anxious yearling, now in her path, briskly avoids her by cutting across between Northeastern and her mother, who then also finds herself facing Rabicana. PS makes a similarly deferential movement, turning to her right rather than face Rabicana directly, who now has interjected herself alongside Northeastern's right flank until they stand rear-to-face. JB also settles back in by Northeastern, sniffing his face. Notably, in the background, AP has followed Rabicana's example and is engaging in local enhancement with the boulder's rough sides. There's a lot of rocky surface area, but AP chooses the exact spot Rabicana had been using. I suspect her scent lingers there.

Three minutes later, Scar and her yearling also move toward the growing cluster, but they loop out in a longer pattern that takes them by Mancha and her foal, though steering clear of the lone bay close by. The remainder of the middle bunch—a bay mare, the dark-brown returnee, and her foal—follow this circuit, gradually grazing over by Mancha and her foal, who parallel the unidentified lone bay, yearling, and foal trio, about six meters distant. As that lone mare grazes, a bubble of space radiates around her—in contrast to the deferential space afforded prominent mares, this is a product of the other mares doing boundary work against her, distancing by the group.

The cluster around the stallion has both grown and concentrated, now with eight horses near him: Rabicana and JB, who were recently joined by AP with a foal, and Scar and PS, both with yearlings. They're each close enough to make physical contact by extending their noses; none are grazing, but they're all standing in a relaxed posture.

FIGURE 2.11. *Northeastern is in the center, flanked in front by PS (on the right) and Scar (her two-year-old is behind her, to the left); JB and PS's yearlings are behind him; Rabicana (with blaze) is by the boulders; behind her is AP and her foal; cattle enclosure in the background.*

Meanwhile, the movement of the distant grazers behind me has elaborated. As Circle/Cross treks closer to the bunch by the boulder, about half of the horses with her hive off: a pair of bays, each with a foal, and a bay with a yearling. These six meander over by the lone bay, yearling, and foal trio, while Circle/Cross heads on, trailed by two dark-brown mares and two foals. They join up with Mancha via a casual graze; it's been five minutes since Circle/Cross reversed course. This seems like an inclusive gesture, since Circle/Cross is the second mare to swing by her on the way to the bunch around Northeastern. But there might be particular mares who don't like her and drive her off. I focus on this as Mancha now falls in, too, behind Circle/Cross, who has shifted direction and now is trekking toward the group by the boulder.

This motion is unified for a few moments and then it splinters into two trajectories, one following Circle/Cross and the other involving Mancha and her foal. Circle/Cross is trailed by a dark-brown mare who looks so similar I thought they were sisters; she bears the same brand, too. These two, both with foals, amble around the periphery of the group, sidling between JB and PS, who are about four body-lengths apart. Circle/Cross heads for the eastern or far side of the boulder; there she turns and comes up alongside AP. Both of their foals engage in sniffing each other's faces. They're standing less than two horse-lengths from Rabicana and Northeastern, the core of this cluster; to his right is Scar and her yearling. Now as Mancha tries to edge inward, she is rebuffed by a hard stare from Scar and so stops right at the edge of the cluster, still only a horse-length distant from Scar.

Now this group has fifteen horses, and Rabicana is at the center. From being spread out, they've slowly contracted and moved closer together. The resulting configuration is similar to the result that's achieved by herding but, notably, the stallion is not effecting this. He has made no gesture at "harem maintenance" and certainly none at "protecting" the mares. When Circle/Cross arrives finally at the group near the boulder, she doesn't make contact with him at all. The mares have assembled themselves, perhaps using the stallion as the focal point for their mutual attraction and interest in being close together. But they're doing so without being herded.

As they contract, it's clear who is left out. The horses that didn't take part in this contraction configure in two groups: one with five (with two foals) about twenty meters to the west; the other with eight (two foals) maybe forty meters farther west. Orbiting the most distant group (the eight) is the returnee who hesitated on the edge of the grazing area, with her foal. As she gets closer, grazing slowly, she gradually turns south, heading around the rock outcrop, basically reversing the course taken by Circle/Cross earlier. Four horses follow her—the two bays with foals—but they only go a few dozen meters before they peel off and stop. The one in front turns abruptly and directs a bite threat at her partner behind, who backs off quickly but stays close. Those two bays end up in parallel, more than a body-length apart, standing still while their foals both nurse. But the lone mare continues on her way unhurriedly. Meanwhile the group of five has grazed closer to the big bunch around Northeastern, but cautiously so, hewing very close to the fence of the enclosure, advancing no nearer than a dozen meters behind Mancha's rear. Notably, as the big grouping around Rabicana and the stallion contracted, Manchaca drifted farther away. Now there's a tight core with Circle/Cross and her partner, Rabicana, and AP, all within inches of each other; PS and JB are proximate too.

Then, just as it contracted, the group begins to expand again. Circle/Cross is back on the move after several minutes hanging out by Rabicana, who goes back to her local enhancement with the boulder. In this new trek, Circle/Cross is followed again by the nearly identical dark-brown mare with a foal. As they move back in the direction they came from, several of the outlying five horses either move in behind them or edge closer to the dissipating cluster. Northeastern demonstrates an interest in one of the mares who's drawn to the trek. But he only advances far enough to sniff a pile of fresh droppings, and he doesn't flehmen. This is the farthest he's been from the boulder since I arrived, and quite promptly Rabicana joins him. As she moves the other mares fan out in front, giving her room. One of them is displaced by Scar and her yearling, who move in the direction of Circle/Cross's trek. As she goes, Mancha slides quickly into the opening cleared by Rabicana and the others.

This movement is brief, though. In less than a minute Circle/Cross abruptly veers to her left and looks around the back side of the boulder, ending up about where she was before, and takes up the local enhance-ment Rabicana has vacated, rubbing the left side of her face and neck up and down the rock face. The horses behind her stop to graze on the far side of the boulder. As they're all spread out now, Mancha and her foal make a move. Over the course of forty seconds, Mancha slides into a space opened as AP shifted away, arriving at the boulder right in front of Circle/Cross, who is still at the spot Rabicana was using ear-lier. Mancha's foal tries to join Circle/Cross in the local enhancement but she drives it away. Meanwhile Rabicana moves toward Northeast-ern, opening up a great deal of space, but also jostling other mares as she moves. In her wake, I no longer see distinct gaps between clusters of horses. Northeastern responds, meeting her advance, until they're again rear-to-face, while the other horses start spreading out a little farther as they continue to graze.

The five horses along the fence steadily encroach through this breach, moving toward what remains of the center, now occupied only by JB, who was there with Rabicana when I arrived. As these mares edge inward, Rabicana takes note and asserts herself by striding back from the stallion's side toward the boulder with her ears menacingly low-ered. When she does, these encroachers scramble to make way, displac-ing horses in front of them, including JB, who lurches out of the path of one of them. The only one who doesn't move, surprisingly, is Mancha, who seemed so peripheral before. She's grazing facing into the boul-der, and is not startled or reactive as Rabicana comes up from behind.

The two are standing comfortably when Northeastern decides to follow Rabicana, seemingly uneasy about standing alone and exposed. He stops just behind Mancha, who takes little notice of him, even when she reaches around to bite at a bug on her right flank, facing him briefly. Eventually Mancha carries her grazing forward a few feet; as she does, Rabicana turns around in that vacated space and slides along Northeastern's right flank, as if she was just waiting on Mancha to move.

Over the next five minutes, the horses roughly maintain this position, with either Northeastern or Rabicana shifting and the others adjusting accordingly. Their responsive awareness of her, as well as Rabicana's assertions of position, strongly indicate her prominence. How does she stand relative to Circle/Cross, who has drawn so many followers? When Circle/Cross leaves off rubbing on the rock and starts another trek, she has to squeeze past Northeastern; scooting around him brings her right into the rear of Mancha, who is unruffled and unmoving. Circle/Cross casts her gaze over at Rabicana, who is nibbling at her own left flank. When her head comes back around, Circle/Cross deferentially shifts her face away and with half-lowered ears walks out away from the boulder. But Rabicana's ears are pitched forward, not threatening. Circle/Cross is followed by several other mares until the only ones on the west side of the boulder are Northeastern, Rabicana, and AP with her foal.

Over the next ten minutes I watch them expand and contract like this, milling and shifting about. AP's male foal, who seems weeks older than the others, flehmens and then urine-marks a pile of mare droppings, but this draws no rebuke or even notice from Northeastern. Circle/Cross is restless and stays in regular motion, rarely grazing. Her next circular treks expands farther and more mares follow. Mancha and her foal join this latest round, though at distance, at least for thirty meters, then she pulls off and grazes while the others move on. In the distance the lone mare trio is drifting off to the east. In mid trek, two of the mares with foals stop and look in her direction, while Circle/Cross and her partner and foals travel on, back toward the boulder.

Just then, two horses appear in the cattle enclosure. I hear them before I see them. Northeastern does too, and he trots to the fence. It's two of the dark-brown mares I saw earlier, and the one in the lead is Twink. Northeastern is finally animated and trots over to the fence. Twink and the stallion try to make contact through the wire, sniffing nose-to-nose.

Northeastern stamps and shakes his head in frustration; Twink sounds stressed and desperate to rejoin the group. But there's nothing to be done, and Northeastern returns to Rabicana's side against the boulder.

In this series of contractions and expansions, what's legible is what I've known all along but only gradually learned to see among horses: social space is generated through a series of mutually informing relationships that are performed as much as assumed. The horses' movement involves and manifests interpretive sensibilities about proximity and distance conveyed and read through glances and gestures, as with humans. The density of these interactions may be somewhat more legible now because their subtlety has largely dissolved; the taken-for-granted forms of dailiness in a band are all churned up.

If I am seeing this band reconstitute, the social work is all being done by the mares. This certainly is far from a "natural" ethological setting, but it's absolutely revealing of a dimension of their capacity to socialize that might not be legible in "normal" circumstances. Importantly, too, this mare-driven sociality is why they are all gathered here. Crazy Gray could drive off Northeastern by winning at King of the Hill, but he had no social skills with which to keep the mares together, and the threat of violence was not enough to make them cohere socially. And they clearly were not afraid of his potential for violence, in that they all ran off.

Also interesting here: they're doing the work of boundary maintenance by refusing to extend greetings. This is very active work, while the stallion is passive. Ethologists tend to believe that the stallion keeps the band together, but there's clearly more to it. I think of what might be missed about horse sociality through the process of quantifying instances of fixed action patterns or behavioral mapping focused on stallion behavior and the misnomer "harem." Ethologists might dismiss attention to the mares as just another layer of dominance, this one emanating out from the oldest mare. Or they might assume all we would gain from this view is a "soap opera" of infighting and jostling.[15] That's a particularly gendered characterization, one that maps with the disturbing depiction of mares as forming a "harem." And it's dismissive of the idea that paying attention to an intense cluster of volatile, changing relationships can reveal something significant about sociality. That conceit (and its gendered assumptions) stems from an emphasis on "social structure" as an edifice that funnels through countless individual lives. But for all its durability and coherence, sociality still needs to be performed and reproduced through everyday "dramas."

For that matter, they aren't just "bickering"; there are copious forms of affiliation as well, perhaps even "alliances," though that concept might be too abstract and make this all seem political more than social—resources aren't at stake, just belonging. The stallion may work to "capture" mares and keep them together but it's the mares who police who stays or not, as I observed with the Capilla band. Mares monitor and maintain the boundary of belonging, both at its fringe or edges and interactionally, face-to-face. What I've observed this morning came from focusing on several mares. I would've missed these dynamics if I was following the stallion or dismissive of the "soap opera" of their everyday interactions.

The ethnographic or cultural question turns on whether these social relations vary enough by place or time to warrant more analytical attention, instead of falling under the "species-being" descriptive regime. Or perhaps it's not a matter of time/space distinctiveness as much as what these disruptions reveal of the plasticity of horse sociality, which would otherwise be obscured. The capacity to see this mode of sociality as performative—relations asserted, accepted, or rejected—requires interpretive work on the part of such subjects, not just instinctive reactions. I see these mares not as bound to a stock set of instinctual "moves" or gestures, but as interpretive subjects, reading and responding to the actions around them.

In the big picture, I'm trying to understand the local forms of sociality in order to analyze how they are impacted by the pending *rapa*, which will churn everything up drastically tomorrow. But Crazy Gray has already accomplished much the same thing. For that, I'm both deeply bothered and grudgingly appreciative. The sociality of the mares arguably is more durable and significant than the behaviors the stallion impacts or centers. The mares know each other longer, as stallions come and go; they sort out who to follow and play out a continuous string of interactions conveying alternately affiliation and aggression. That's what's most evident now, I realize. As Northeastern is immobilized and Crazy Gray is largely being ignored, this large number of mares is moving about, orienting to each other as they reverse the group's contraction toward sleep by expanding out now to graze in the clear, warming light on this rocky slope. Several are choosing to cluster near the stallion, while others are fending for themselves, moving away.

I am noticing a periodicity to their sociality that's not easily captured by tabulating and quantifying fixed action patterns. They get closer when they sleep, collapsing social distance, only to reassert it again when they wake and spread out. Some move toward something (grazing) or perhaps just asserting distance, "leadership," or independence, while others are moved—pushed away or following in a trek. So "initiation of social distance" kind of works, as in trekking or clearing out space. Conversely, when the band contracts the issue is who the dominant mares will accept close by. It's not an absolute; the horses perform tolerance, just as they do aggression or affiliation. And likely these affects change over the course of the day, month, season, and lifetime.

As it becomes apparent that these horses are remaining stationary, I decide it's time to check on the Mega band. I hike back around the eastern side of the cattle enclosure, then turn north. I'm ready to move briskly, but as I round the northeast corner to drop down into the dell, I'm startled to see a bevy of horses. They're grazing languidly, so I stop to figure out who they are. I can see two mares and three yearlings and guess they were peeled off from their band by Crazy Gray, but if that's the case they don't seem anxious to rejoin their group. I note the absence of a foal here and wonder how that factors in. I spend fifteen minutes working out identifications and then head off to the Mega band. But I only go about forty meters before I come across the carcass of a freshly killed foal. It doesn't have the wounds of the one I saw yesterday. Its stomach is ripped open and its entrails are strewn about. This must've been a wolf attack, but I don't know why they didn't finish eating the foal; its insides are cavernous and the muscle around the ribs is a dull red. Perhaps the other horses drove the wolves away after the kill. Unable to know for sure, I continue my trek.

In contrast to the churn among the Northeastern's Knoll band, everything is drowsy among the Megas. They're slumbering as I approach. Cows are mixed in as usual, so I move extra cautiously to get into position, aiming for the western slope of the hill, where most of the forty or so horses are clustered. They're on a little pointed clearing that rises to disrupt the descent of this west flank. By the time I find a boulder to perch on, it's been forty-five minutes since I left the other band. I take my bearings by working through my identifications. The first ones I recognize are Dapple and her friend Stiletto, again braced close together, head-to-tail. Chaparro is facing Dapple but from three body-lengths away. He's nestled alongside a mare I can't initially identify from behind. They're all wedged so closely together, with heads at rest, pressed against adjacent rears, that I can't yet make out many more. There are nineteen horses within ten meters of Chaparro, each just about touching another. Off to the east, about forty meters from him, there's a second cluster around Fleabit, who I identified first two days ago and who rolled out ahead of Chaparro in his long herding effort. There are six adults, including her, one yearling, and two foals. The rest of the horses are more dispersed, in trios or pairs with other mares, accompanied by their younger charges. The only others who stand out are literally standing on the edge of the band—Flaxen and her foal on one side, to the south, and the other flea-bitten gray I identified previously as CF.

My timing is good; less than five minutes later they're stirring awake. I draw little attention as they readjust spatially; the compressed constellation unwinding as they take tentative steps forward or backward or away. Now I can see Book in the crowd, right next to Clipped Ears; her head bobs up, again eyeing me assertively. She is on the opposite side of the mare standing beside Chaparro. Later, as they fan out, I recognize her as Palm. Her foal is crashed on the ground a few feet away. And I see Baldface. She was obscured by cows, but once she stirs and starts backing up aggressively the cows scatter, leaving her a wide berth. Then she moves forward, head bobbing energetically, and mares clear out too.

She's standing alone in a circle at least ten meters in circumference. It's a distinctive social space—in contrast to the bubble around the lone mare trio on the fringe of the Northeastern band, Baldface is ringed by her bandmates who are quick to move out of her way if she gestures in their direction. So she most certainly is the lead or dominant mare. How do the others stand relative to her?

The most proximate to her is Haloed Tee and her yearling; I noticed her yesterday, when Chaparro moved toward Dapple and Clipped Ears as they allogroomed. They're both snoozing, about two body-lengths away. Then there are the mares near Chaparro, starting with Book, Palm, and Clipped Ears. Since I've consistently noticed these females, which is why I have identifications for them, I'm guessing they're all fairly central to this band. Literally—over the two and a-half hours I'm in this position they never veer from this central spot near Baldface. Then who are all the others? I take time to develop more identifications. There's a bay mare with a foal near Dapple; no distinguishing marks other than tufts of sun-bleached hair on the top of her tail and the back of her mane, so Tufts. Another one, a dark brown beside Book and Clipped Ears, has just a thin wisp of a stripe on her forehead, so Wisp. More striking by far is a black who is roaning out, with a distinctive star/stripe combination. The color of her coat, flecked with roan, reminds me of a calico cat so, Calico. She has a foal. Then there's a bay with a star that curves at the end, sort of like a scimitar, so Scimitar. She has a yearling and a foal. The yearlings interspersed here are more of a challenge, mostly because their heads are down, sleeping.

To be more certain about these mares, I need to see some interactions. And before long, an interesting series of movements develops. It begins with the group around Fleabit. In concert, they advance a couple dozen steps forward from east to west, where I'm perched on a boulder. I'm curious because they start with a jump but stop almost as sharply, as if they're facing a wall I can't see. Tufts—no more than five meters in front of me but at least forty meters from this bunch—moves in their direction within ten seconds. As she does, Dapple, Stiletto, and Calico fall in behind her sprightly. Tufts pauses for a moment until they form a loose line, then she strides toward the encroaching bunch, stopping just a few feet away. Her move is paralleled by Baldface on the opposite side of the line from me, her head outstretched menacingly. In response, Fleabit and company turn quickly back, two bays clashing as their heads and necks nearly collide in reversing course. As they do, Tufts and her mates return close to where they started from; in doing so, Calico carefully steers wide of Baldface. Meanwhile I see Haloed Tee, relatively close to Baldface's space, back up and deliver a low kick at the closest cow, sending her skittering forward.

Soon they're all roughly back where they were when I arrived but now I can see clearly a boundary that wasn't evident before. Also, I'm forced to rethink my assumptions around centrality and periphery in relation to mare identity and status. Tufts struck me at first as peripheral, because spatially she was. But her trek to enforce the boundary was followed by others and it made Fleabit's bunch recede. So clearly

she can lead. That said, the spatial dimension of being peripheral remains telling of who belongs. I conclude this not only from seeing it
policed, but from the way Flaxen keeps getting rebuffed whenever she
tries to draw closer. At one point she nears Stiletto and Calico, who
look her off, and she veers away. So spatial positioning signifies and is
legible, but only in relation to seeing how the horses respond in concert
in reaction to the movements of others.

Through this brief churning, I'm able to make a couple of other observations. Dapple's left front leg is injured; she's avoiding putting any
weight on it. As she steps painfully back from the confrontation, Stiletto settles beside her again and they are alone in space, until a two-
year-old comes along Dapple's opposite side. Stiletto won't have it and
drives her off; but when Calico comes alongside, occupying the same
spot, Stiletto doesn't stir in response. As the horses rouse from their
slumber, I make out another mare I hadn't identified earlier—a two-
year-old bay with an odd star that juts obliquely to the left, so Juts. I also
note that CF is moving in synch with a black mare with a bloated star.

The next movement comes as Palm shears off from Chaparro and
steps among her bandmates moving easterly; Book, who's been close
by the whole time, follows her directly. Their movement is blocked by
a mass of cows, so Palm swerves, bringing her close to Baldface, who
stares at her, unmoving. This is enough to stop Palm entirely. After a
few seconds, though, she resumes her motion, but by circuiting the
bubble projected by Baldface, who lurches forward, paralleling her
every step around it. After a dozen meters like this, Baldface cuts toward Palm directly, who veers off; this trajectory brings her up against
Flaxen, who scrambles to get away quickly. Palm stops, with Book right
behind her, once Baldface bends back to her spot. But Flaxen and her
foal keep moving, displaced once again.

And so the afternoon goes. I watch a series of such moments and
displacements—one or more mares rebuffing another, asserting space
and distance. Or, one draws close to another: they touch noses, sniffing, or glide against an open flank, touching that way. Such affiliative gestures are far more numerous, but I often miss them because
they're not as flashy, more subtle. Through it all—two hours plus—
Chaparro barely moves. Amid all this boundary work, he's drowsily
static. Nor have I moved, since I've not had to; all the motion circulated

around the slightly elevated ground where Baldface stands. As I think about heading out, I notice some rustling down by a spring about seventy meters away below this west flank of the hill. It's a family of javalinas: two adults and six pups. They emerge from the brush and make for the spring. They splash about for almost ten minutes before disappearing again. Since they don't notice me at all, I think for a moment that I've achieved the state Victor exalted—becoming a piece of gorse. But I realize that's too narrow an understanding of this situation; the horses know I'm here; it's not like I've just blended into the flora. Rather, they've become *habituated* to my presence, at least for this moment.[16]

Reflecting on the scene in front of me, I'm of two minds. One part of me fixates on what I don't yet know about this band—all the nuances of interhorse relations. It would take me weeks to develop detailed sketches on each of these mares, ranking them relative to each other, as they do themselves. My second state is more tranquil. I have in hand a substantial set of identifications and a general understanding of this band's structure, how the mares sort out and position themselves, and their yearlings and foals along with them. Thinking of the task ahead— tracking the impacts of the *rapa* on the structure of their sociality—I have a sufficient basis for proceeding. I feel I'm ready for tomorrow.

FIGURE 2.12. *Baldface is center right; Haloed Tee is to her left with her yearling, facing away; then Wisp, Book, and Palm, with her male foal; Chaparro is behind them, alongside Clipped Ears.*

— 3 —

Ritual Shearing

DISSOLUTION AND CHAOS

DAY I

The *rapa das bestas* in Sabucedo commences every year with the *misa da alborada* (dawn mass) at the Church of San Lorenzo, a Romanesque building on the south side of the village. They used to stage the *rapa* in a stone-walled *curro* right beside the church, but in 1997 they built the current arena, which holds upwards of four thousand people. I can faintly hear the report of large bottle rockets firing off to celebrate the mass and the day. I'm perched on a nub of high ground across from the northeast corner of the cattle enclosure, about thirty meters from where the track from the village crosses the lip of the basin between the enclosure and the tall hill where the Mega band mostly resides.

I'm up here, foregoing the ceremony below, in order to get a base-line for the horses' behavior before the ritual commences; but also to observe what happens as the humans arrive on the range. It's a quiet, chill morning, with clouds draping ridgelines and saturating shallow vales. About a dozen horses are gathered down in the basin around the spring, but they're mostly obscured by a dense thicket of small trees and tall bushes. At a distance of two hundred meters it's hard to make out identifying features, but I see Dapple and Stiletto from the Mega band, off by themselves a bit; then I spot Flaxen trailing a crowd of bays I can't yet distinguish, positioned on the periphery, much like she was on the jaunt that prompted Chaparro's great herding exercise. They don't seem to notice the faint rolling booms from outside the church down below, foreshadowing my conspecifics' pending arrival.

The humans will proceed in a long procession, winding up the mountain through the woods, arriving at this point beside the cattle enclosure

and basin where I'm waiting. The previous year when I joined in forming
the human cordon that surrounds the horses before driving them to
holding areas, the first stop was here on the south slope of the basin.
This year, guessing they'll again be driven here and held temporarily, I
want to track what happens as fragments of different bands arrive.

Over the next hour, the mares from the Mega band graze in stillness
broken only by scattered strands of fleeting bird song. The depth of
the damp quiet is most apparent to me just as it's broken by the arrival
of the people up from Sabucedo. This is an interesting bunch. At the
head is Ghelo, an emblematic *besteiro,* with a shaved head and a bent
right arm that doesn't swing well; a vestige, I assume, of a poorly healed
break. He's barely breathing hard, though the crowd behind is mostly
heaving from their exertions. Ghelo, perpetually garbed in a dark tank
top, hardly seems to notice the nippy air. Many of those following in
his wake take this pause as an opportunity to put on light jackets or add
an extra layer. About fifty people are with him: a mix of locals—lightly
clad—and tourists in various shades of sportswear, dangling cameras,
canteens, and backpacks. Juan, when he arrives with his friend Jose and
Jose's father, sports only a small plastic water bottle in the back pocket
of his jeans. He's wearing a T-shirt and seems unbothered by the dank
mist drenching the ridge.

The horses below, of course, have noticed us. They take off up a
firebreak that slices across the gorse, and in less than a minute they've
ascended the height of the north hilltop. Three mares linger above,
looking back at the array unfolding around me. Then they too slip from
sight over the curve of the hill. Meanwhile, the human side of all this
is getting complicated as a horse-riding club arrives, in matching light-
blue jerseys. A few other single riders who were camping down below
show up as well.

The hallmark of this stage of the *rapa* in Sabucedo, as I've realized
after attending several others in the south and the north of Galicia, is
a lack of coordination. This ritual was designated a Fiesta of International Tourist Interest by the Spanish government in 2007, so it draws
lots of visitors, who are curious but completely unfamiliar with this
terrain. But the biggest problem is diverging opinions among the locals.
The *aloitadores*—Sabucedo's more ample version of *besteiros*; people
who "fight" and/or drive the horses—differ on where and how to start
and how best to proceed. There are sharply different views over which

bands to target and where to hold them until the collection can be shifted to a temporary corral on the west side of the cattle enclosure, at the foot of O Peón along the logging road. Juan and Ghelo confer with several others on encircling the Mega band; meanwhile word circulates among the assembled crowd to start spreading out in a line, the cordon.

This is the basic technique and the simplest part. When I came to Sabucedo the year before, I couldn't imagine how the herding worked—how could humans on foot catch a horse? As Juan explained it to me then, as I found my place among the tourists who turned out that day to run the horses down the mountain, the cordon works on two principles: the horses' fear and their desire to stick together. Horses are easily frightened by humans and they react by running away as a group. The trick is to direct that motion toward an enclosed location, using the horses' sociality against them. Humans' lack of size and speed is compensated for with long sticks that extend our profile and fearfulness. This dissuades the animals from aggressively driving at the people, and it guides them in a direction of the humans' choosing. This requires humans moving in synch, in a practice that dates back millennia.

Watching the cordon develop now, I think back to the wolf trap we visited with Laura Lagos, about sixty kilometers to the southwest of here. I cast my mind back centuries, to when humans waving burning torches or shaking various noisemakers moved in long lines across the mountain slopes, driving the wolves before them into the funnel of the ravine, where the speed of their escape hurtled them into the tower's opening. After they tumbled down onto each other, they were beaten to death. Horses trapped in a similar topography faced a different fate—domestication.

Along the mountain above Sabucedo, a cordon once again takes shape this foggy morning, as the humans unspool in a line running north to south. All I can see of the Mega band now is six distant heads (mostly bays) closely watching us, their bodies obscured by the rough edge of the crest. I wonder what they're seeing as they watch us—a form or a pattern taking shape? Are they remembering this time and this movement from past years? Locals say yes, at least to the latter question. But all this makes me newly attentive to the social space among humans, as I watch them try to spread out along the rolling terrain, trying to become a form, the cordon.

Most of them have never done anything like this; they're tourists, here to participate in the spectacle. It's intriguing to watch the micro-interactions by which they are establishing and testing who knows what's going on. Who's asserting knowledge, barking directions about placement and spacing and direction? How far apart is a big uncertainty: they're wondering about spacing and how to establish it. At this moment, I get why Goffman thought of applying ethology to people.[1] He would also be quick to recognize the dual way spacing matters, for horses and humans, reprising an ancient ritual of companion species interactions. Horses will break through a gap between humans if they're bold or desperate. But how large an opening does that require? The people who are here for the first time have no idea, and they also are not privy to the various tactical discussions among the *aloitadores*. So they're left to their own devices for sorting out how close or distant to be from the next person. But they also have to decide who's authoritative and whose directions to follow, since the *aloitadores* are heatedly voicing contrasting opinions.

I can't dwell on this too long. The expanding line has spooked some of the horses on the hill. Juan is certain they know what's happening—many of the mares have been through previous *rapas,* and a few are savvy about avoiding such traps. As the cordon advances, one bunch tears down the slope toward the thickets in the lowest portion of the basin. In the lead is Fleabit; trailing her are the bays and dark-brown mares that congregated around her and her one foal. Running parallel to the cordon, they don't try to slip through it; rather, they crash into the dense thicket around the swampy ground by the springs below and disappear. Ghelo looks for help to roust them out, so I volunteer, along with two other guys, one wearing shorts. He's soon unhappy with that choice as the gorse slices his bare legs. I'm not particularly happy either as we crash through chest high ferns; nor is it an enticing option to follow the horses into a thicket so dense we can't see them at all nor detect traces of their movement.

We follow Ghelo's lead, trying to roust the hidden animals, until he's distracted by the second wave of horses coming down from the hilltop. They're responding to the encroaching cordon that snaked around the north side and rose in a line, driving them down toward the humans strung along the firebreak to the east that intersects the path to the village. Chaparro is in this bunch of more than a dozen. He was the *aloitadores*' principal target, since they want lots of stallions in the *curro* to fight each other dramatically. He and the mares surge down and then veer as they approach the cordon across the east lip of the basin. Their momentum carries them up to the enclosure fencing, where they turn west along the firebreak lining the fence and then are brought to a halt in front of the humans lined up across that trajectory. Ghelo is livid over this development; he argued for pooling them down in the vale, where we contained them initially last year. He tears off to intervene, leaving the three of us wondering what to do about Fleabit and her companions. After a few minutes, it's clear Ghelo has lost the argument, so I head to the impromptu catchment zone, formed in a dip along the north side of the cattle enclosure.

The climb from the spring takes six minutes of slow walking up the steep incline, but once there I take a place in the thin cordon around the "*bestas*"—about twenty of us are enough to seal them off against the cattle fence along a wide spot in the firebreak. I have to step in since many of my conspecifics are drawn more to the chase and start drifting off, looking to join the pursuit of horses still on the range. Meanwhile, people are taking photos and slide in and out of the cordon, making it rather flimsy. Several men with expensive cameras on tripods muscle in for close-ups and then head off in search of more photogenic shots than these captive horses. But the arrested animals make little effort to escape; only occasionally over the next thirty minutes does a mare or two advance toward a gap in the line—one that is easily sealed off with raised arms and a few shouts. Mostly they settle in to reestablishing a social structure in an odd and anxious setting.

A quick count gives me sixteen adults, four yearlings, and three foals. But a modest high point, where the firebreak and enclosure rise up the next ridgeline, intermittently obscures my view, depending on how I'm able to move about. So who's here? Some mares are easy to spot, both because I'm familiar with them and because of how they're behaving. The first one I recognize is Baldface, who positions herself in front of a lone scraggly pine tree that screens her off from the press of bandmates. She then paces around the perimeter and looks at me several times, while the others eat. No one gets close to her. Then I spot Book along with Palm and her foal. It strikes me suddenly that she'll surely lose him when they cull the males. A few meters off from them is Tuft, who led the trek that turned back the encroachment by Fleabit's cluster yesterday. In fact, in a few minutes I recognize most of yesterday afternoon's configuration around Baldface. Clipped Ears is in there too, close to Chaparro. I notice Haloed Tee when she and her yearling make a move down the short grade, again paralleled by Baldface, just like yesterday.

There are a couple of mares I need to consult my notes on to be sure, like Wisp and Jut, who I only identified the day before. Wisp again seems drawn to Book. But what's striking, as this social core coalesces, is the periphery it reproduces. Flaxen skirts it and receives a bite threat from Clipped Ears when she edges too close. Surprisingly, she has two foals now—her own and another who must've followed her. Juan had told me that when the cordon approaches, mares will bolt, leaving foals behind. I wonder which mare it was; this gets me thinking about who's not here. Besides Fleabit, in the thicket below—and no one is interested in the challenge of rousting her out—Dapple, Stiletto, and Calico also eluded the entrapment. At least eighteen horses escaped—so not a very efficient system. But finishing up with my scan of the nascent periphery shaping up here, I also notice the other flea-bitten mare, CF, who I only identified yesterday; she's again intermittently alongside that black mare with the bloated star, who I'll quickly settle for designating as Bloat.

After eighteen minutes, the first instance of allogrooming occurs—a mare I don't recognize and her foal. Soon Baldface and a yearling I've not noticed before also commence allogrooming. This is the first horse

FIGURE 3.1. *Baldface in foreground; Flaxen in center rear.*

I've seen her engage with affiliatively. They get quite deep into it, for more than two minutes; after they both work each other's forefront Baldface starts in on the yearling's shoulder blades, affectionately and vigorously nibbling at that most hard-to-reach spot. In quick succession, two more instances occur: another mare and foal, then two mares begin allogrooming. This flourish is capped by Chaparro grooming the shoulders of Palm's male foal, who learns quickly to respond in kind, though he only reaches Chaparro's flank. This is the most concentrated allogrooming I've yet seen, so it must be a social response to a stressful situation. Allogrooming tends to be an isolated dynamic between a pair. But here its prevalence seems restorative of a calm social collective at a disturbing moment. This is most notable with Baldface, who has been loath to let other horses too near her.

But this intensive surge of affiliative gestures also underscores the boundedness of the social core. When CF approaches the others, they signal threateningly with lowered ears or move away. I watch her try to nose in beside a mare and her yearling; after first ignoring her, both walk away instead. Flaxen is not finding any friendliness either. A moment later, I see her have to raise her head to avoid being brusquely shoved by a passing bay.

This spate of allogrooming might have blossomed further, but soon their attention, and the humans', is riveted off on the horizon, where sounds are emanating from another band being pursued and trapped. The noise is distant and shifting, hard to read through the mist that still covers the ridgelines ringing the basin. My hearing is not as good as the horses' but I can detect faint shouts and commotion. As the sounds ebb and surge, most of the animals here go back to grazing. But a knot has formed at the highest point, right behind the small pine, where Chaparro, Book, and Palm stand scanning the horizon and intermittently making contact by sniffing each other. Eventually Baldface joins them to get a better of view of where the other horses are. These could be the rest of the Mega band or another that's been trapped and is now being herded toward us.

Five minutes pass before the situation becomes clear. Another bunch is being driven hard from the east, galloping along the firebreak. As they pass the northeast corner of the enclosure about a hundred meters from us, our cordon pushes back against the curious animals before us, compressing them into a tight concentration nearer the fence. Then the people on the east side peal back, making room for the new arrivals to pass through. "*Rapido, rapido,*" several of the old men shout, and "*cuidado, cuidado!*" encouraging the young tourists to clear the way quickly. The incoming batch picks up speed as they approach, partly from momentum but also from the extra effort to gain this higher ground. I make out Rabicana and Mancha among the mares in front, so it's the Knoll band. They're hurtling forward impressively; then, in a moment, there's a mashup of large bodies as the two bands converge.

Rabicana and company stream along the fence but have nowhere further to go. The mass of the Mega band gives way—Tufts heads out for the space opened by the new arrivals; she's trailed by CF and Bloat; Baldface leads most of the other mares along a parallel reverse trek, but then drops off the firebreak and stops. I only realize how quiet the horses have been when there's a startling shriek. It's from Northeastern, trying to clear space amid the crunch of bodies. He fails and instead lumbers down the grade, only to confront, in turn, Tufts, who's aiming a rear kick at JB from the Knoll band, and Baldface. He turns away from both, lurching back up into the mass, though most mares get out of his way. JB, also turning away, encounters Chaparro and so turns yet again. There's jostling all around as the two groups mix; a swirl of threat gestures ensue, but also a few extended faces and curious sniffing of rumps.

The stallions are quite ill at ease. Chaparro maneuvers to have a better view of Northeastern, who's shrieking again, driving off several more mares. When they're only a few meters apart Chaparro too screams but also rears. They both veer away and mares shear off from their trajectories. I recognize two immediately—Circle/Cross and her sister (I'm guessing), and Twink, who I last saw trapped in the cattle enclosure; she must've been freed during the roundup. Northeastern circles down by them, then heads back toward the high ground, with both of them now trailing him. Meanwhile, Baldface is standing her ground a few feet away, and Book, Palm, Haloed Tee, and Tufts are joining her. Chaparro is just above, several meters distant. Northeastern is restless and passes very close to Chaparro, from behind, about three horse-lengths removed; Chaparro turns his head to watch where he's going, then turns his whole body. He ends up nose-to-nose with a mare from the Knoll band, who cautiously extends her nose toward his, which is reciprocated with ears pitched forward, curiously or welcomingly. Then they fall still, and movement becomes minimal for a moment.

Ghelo leads the group that brought in the Knoll band, and now he's debating with others whether to move the whole bunch now or wait for more to come in. But I follow little of this discussion as I'm concentrating on the horses. Northeastern paces about nervously; he approaches Baldface, who drives him off curtly. Redirecting his motion, he unexpectedly comes across Chaparro, who was hidden from view by several mares. Chaparro shrieks and Northeastern reverses course. They're both moving now, stirring up mares as they shift away from each other. Interestingly, they each clear away mares from the other band, with glares or sometimes bite-gestures. The writing on stallions stresses their need to collect mares in "harems," but here I only see the boundary work of males driving off females from another social group. That basic dynamic soon develops into a striking spatial arrangement.

I'm standing just below the firebreak, close to the back side or north end of the cordon around the horses, so they're mostly either slightly elevated on the road or right in front of my face. I notice JB, with Circle/Cross right behind her. As she moves, JB directs a bite threat at a mare from the Mega band, who skitters out of range, setting a yearling and foal in motion, moving away. Northeastern slides in alongside JB and Circle/Cross briefly; they make facial contact, then he turns back, climbing up the road, where I can just make out Chaparro's head, keeping a close eye on him with his ears pinned low. There are about six mares and foals in between them, and in Northeastern's flustered state he doesn't recognize he's heading right for Chaparro, who rears fiercely but doesn't strike. Northeastern, startled, reverses course, disrupting JB and Circle/Cross, stopping right in front of me. The two stallions eye each other from a distance of about ten meters, then Chaparro turns into the wedge of mares. He screams once and kicks, clearing out space as Northeastern moves in an opposite direction.

What unfolds next is startling in its clarity but subtle in its development, even though I'm alert for interband boundary work. Without any direct effort from the stallions—as in herding—mares from the two bands gravitate away from each other. Several moments are decisive. Initially, Book, Palm and her foal, and Clipped Ears shift in concert, moving downhill, developing a trek that forcefully displaces mares from the Knoll band, who dash upwards to where their mates are standing fixedly. They're starting to coalesce around Rabicana, who I've not seen much of because she was obscured on the other side of the pine. But as some separation emerges, I glimpse her again. I shift to see her better and focus on what seems to be evolving. Meanwhile, Baldface starts moving; when Chaparro notices, he falls in behind her. Baldface steps along until she reaches the firebreak and stops maybe fifteen meters from Rabicana, with half a dozen mares loosely arrayed in between. Baldface quickly draws the attention of her bandmates, who, keeping a close eye on what she's doing, shift their bodies away from the Knoll group mares above.

Northeastern is far removed from all this; he has found a spot behind most of the mares at the west end. In between, the mares around Baldface have turned so their backsides are toward the mares around Rabicana; Mancha is right beside her, with her foal. The emergent "line" between the two groups is made emphatic as Flaxen, still trailing two foals, bumps along it, not garnering acknowledgment from the Mega mares and then sharply receiving a bite threat from Rabicana, who reaches past Mancha to strike.

Flaxen turns immediately, wedging herself between her reluctant bandmates; Rabicana and Mancha rotate too, and melt in among their bandmates. And just like that, a gap about five meters wide has clearly emerged, delineating the two groups.

FIGURE 3.2. *Rabicana and Mancha, center, in the firebreak; Flaxen is avoiding Rabicana's threat.*

FIGURE 3.3. *A boundary emerges.*

What punctuated it? In addition to Rabicana's threat, Baldface's gaze is doing a lot of work—driving back mares from the other band; locking in the attention of her bandmates. This buffer held for eight minutes. Then a bay mare I don't recognize makes eye contact with Clipped Ears across the line. She sniffs and the two edge over the buffer toward the Mega band side of the firebreak opposite the fence. As they pass, Clipped Ears moves in parallel but nudging through her proximate bandmates. This course brings her face-to-face with Chaparro, who shrieks and rears mildly. But she doesn't give ground as the stallion flashes his face close to hers, and her ears never lower. Chaparro turns and drifts away from the mare. As others move out of his way, the boundary space dissolves, and curious mares from each side inch forward. Rabicana and Mancha move away, in the process opening up more social spaces. Little fraternizing unfolds; it's only that the space has lost the polarizing charge that kept them physically apart and distinct as groups.

Over the next ten minutes the horses relax considerably, and those along the dissolved boundary intermingle with curious sniffs and forward-directed ears. Gradually, the boundary becomes indistinct as the horses spread out on the lower ground in the direction from which they entered. Mancha moves loosely and freely through the others. Rabicana follows her and, in turn, Northeastern follows Rabicana. Soon he's less than twenty meters from Chaparro, who looks over at him. Northeastern seems startled when he catches sight of the other stallion. He averts his gaze, but then sneaks a peak back at Chaparro, whose neck drops at rest with his nose nestled into Clipped Ears's flank. More mares are intermingling. I see AP and Circle/Cross both within a few feet of Chaparro. Most of these interactions are obscured by the mass of horses. Over the next eight minutes, Northeastern slowly turns toward the uphill slope, and Rabicana realigns with him, face-to-rear. Chaparro's attention is devoted to Clipped Ears through all of this collective motion, but something jars him, and we're all startled when he suddenly screams and rears.

Turning around toward Northeastern, Chaparro knifes his way through the mingled horses, ears pinned back and head hostilely low; he swiftly cuts across the firebreak to the fence and then back again, parting the mares and their yearlings in an aggressive herding gesture. He stops, glaring at them; then turns toward Northeastern, but drops his head and feigns nibbling at sparse strands of grass rather than making a direct confrontation. Northeastern turns away too but tries to go around the backside of Chaparro, who then charges him swiftly. Both stallions rear and kick wildly in the air; descending, they each turn toward their respective bands. Northeastern mimics Chaparro's herding by directing head threats toward the vulnerable legs of the mares above him, driving them rapidly back.

Chaparro's movements are more measured but just as effective. Working methodically over a few dozen seconds, the stallions have inscribed an absolute divide between the two bands; horses in both direct their gazes away from the others. In less than a minute, the boundary

FIGURE 3.4. *Chaparro, center, draws a line.*

FIGURE 3.5. *Northeastern herding.*

is reasserted, but this time with its sharpness heightened by the actions of the two males.

This is an impressive instance of boundary work, for two reasons. First, it drives the horses closer to us humans, from whom they've been trying to maintain a distance. But even more so because it is not articulated in defense of a resource. This is not one band asserting or defending control of a position on the range. This is an effort to re-establish social cohesion and differentiation. The boundary extends to forty meters by the time the males stop herding back and forth. The open expanse in a confined area illustrates the symbolic importance of differentiating these two now-captive bands.[2]

The stallions maintain this boundary for at least ten minutes. At one point, a pair of female yearlings try to cross over from the uphill side. Northeastern initially drives them back against the fence of the enclo-sure, but when he's distracted at the opposite side of the line they scurry past. I'm surprised to see, though, that Chaparro won't let them slide over to his group. The ethological literature is clear that "species-typical" behavior for stallions is to collect mares, especially young ones like these. But Chaparro exhibits far more interest in maintaining the social bound-ary of his band. The two yearlings are stuck in the liminal zone between the groups until Ghelo and the others decide it's time to move this batch

FIGURE 3.6. *Chaparro, on left, back turned to Northeastern, in front on the right.*

of animals up higher along the road, to the main catchment site where horses from farther west on the range are being brought.

I mull what I've witnessed as our mass of horses and humans stir up dust in a slow march to the catchment area at the foot of O Peón. The sharp social articulation dissolves as soon as we begin moving—horses surge forward to avoid the shouting, stick waving humans ringing them; foals and yearlings struggle to stay close to mothers and familiars. Progress is slow as we stop every few minutes to stall the momentum of the horses, which could easily overwhelm our efforts to contain them. After twenty minutes, turning the corner at the far west side of the cattle containment area we arrive at the collection zone, where a large kitchen has also been set up for the humans.

This site is prepared for the horses with a wall of fencing made from green tarps, creating a half circle against which dozens of horses are already loosely confined. With whoops and hollers we drive ours toward them and they merge in a swirl, circling around and around, trying to avoid each other and unable to escape—or unwilling. Again, any one determined horse could overpower a human or find an opening in the cordon, or probably even leap this five-foot fencing. Fear is a constraining factor, but likely even more powerful is the social sensibility of sticking together. This thought tempers my initial impression that the social configuration I had observed simply collapsed when the band structure boundary dissolved and these animals were forced back together. Rather, sociality at a broader species level asserts itself, and

despite the ripples of aggression that crackle through this herd, they prefer the company of others over chancing a solitary escape.

Following their movements, though, proves challenging. There are so many humans here. Most have driven up the logging road, and the big kitchen with a grill is set up with a dozen people making *bocadillos.* Young men on motorcycles zip by, driving back and forth to check on the progress of other groups still out gathering horses. Several riding clubs are assembled here, dismounting to eat lunch and let their horses graze. Before too long I hear excited shouts as another batch of animals approaches; Juan is leading this group. After they are added to the swarm, I catch up with him to hear of his travails tracking and herding horses in from the western side of this range.

Alongside all this activity, the *besteiros*—those who claim ownership of particular mares—are studying the horses. These are men in their sixties and seventies, bent and creaking, but limber enough to navigate the rocky, uneven ground. They're here to see their horses and especially to ascertain if any of them have birthed foals this season. If so, they can claim that offspring. They do so through a long process of observation, which involves getting these beasts to move out of the way so they can properly appraise mother-foal connections. They move methodically through the mass of horses, whacking at rumps to clear a path. These elderly men are also watching and listening to each other, summoning up and confirming their respective genealogical knowledge of the horses and adjudicating claims informally through studied consultation. When a foal is claimed, they summon eager grandsons or more experienced middle-aged sons to corner the creature and pin it to the ground so it can be marked with spray paint. Later, during the *rapa,* they will receive the owner's brand and either be released again for another year if female, or sold for meat if male.

After lunch and the final arrivals, the horses number 157, a very small haul overall. In the early 2000s they were bringing in 600 horses each year. But it's time now for the *baixa,* or "lowering" the horse from the mountain. This operation has all the chaotic elements of the earlier efforts at forming cordons on the slope. More people are involved now, since many more were able to make it up the logging road in someone's truck. The scene is boisterous, with young kids jostling to make up the line of humans that will funnel the equines along the narrow track and down to the village. This jaunt, too, features frequent stops to keep the horses from moving too fast and garnering their natural advantage of speed and mass.

What's different now is that the horses are quite loud. Earlier there were few scattered whinnies, but most of the creatures could stay in visual or olfactory contact with the ones they cared about, even if they were temporarily pushed apart. In a far larger mass and strung out along a more protracted line, the air reverberates with neighs and whinnies and cries. The descent is unsettling enough, but not being able to find each other in the crowd prompts many of the horses to sound out, calling for others or announcing their location or presence. Their voicings elongate and extend with greater duration than previously, above on the range. When we pause in the dense eucalyptus grove about halfway down, the aural commotion is churning and pressing.

As we walk, I see that Crazy Gray has been captured. A young man has him tethered to a lead off the road. His owner has been identified and is coming to claim him. Juan tells me he escaped from Fondos, the village south of Quireza, where he killed an older stallion in a shared pen, likely breaking the fencing in the fight. His adventure in the mountains over, Crazy Gray agitatedly twists on the side of the road as the herd lumbers past. Intermittently as we slope downward a pair of stallions rear and clash, but most of that kind of conflict is squelched by the tumult of the descending mass of animals. Within forty minutes we reach Peche do Castelo, a large pasture where the horses will spend the night. They're joining others who were driven in by Juan and his companions earlier in the week, worried that they wouldn't have enough horses to fill the *curro*. I think about staying to watch what happens, but the pasture is huge and tree-choked; so I decide I'm better off waiting to observe them after they've settled down and slept.

DAY 2

Early the next morning I approach Peche do Castelo to observe the horses. Fog hovers in the hollows and laces through scattered stands of eucalyptus. From the gate, they can't be seen; there are too many trees and the terrain is corduroyed with low ridgelines. I also suspect they're as far away from the gate as possible, to keep their distance from the humans. I'm enthused to get started observing them but the task is daunting. Broadly, my goal is to analyze how their modes of sociality are impacted over the course of the *rapa*. For a baseline I have two sets of band identifications, my mapping of their structures, my observations in the field, and what I've learned of horse ethology. But the scale here is drastically different, since there are about three hundred horses penned in this pasture—this is a huge herd now.

I'm not sure how best to proceed or whether the observational techniques I've adopted will be useful in this context. I settle on trying to find members of the Mega or Knoll bands, while also sketching aspects of how the horses configure themselves and how they socialize. First, though, I walk the four hundred meter lane along the west side of the enclosure so I can enter from the high point at the far north end. Soon I'm drenched from dew-soaked ferns draping the narrow path. The topography here is a jumble of shallow ravines where many horses are hidden from view.

The top of the pasture, though, is an open-faced slope, and here I count more than seventy animals at rest—a dozen of these are foals. I work at a distance with my field glasses so as not to set off a startled flight before I can map their configurations. My effort is limited by sightlines and because there are so many animals I've not seen before. They are loosely clustered together in a large mass, making identifications challenging. Eventually, I climb through the fence and enter the huge enclosure quietly; then proceed as I would up on the mountain: advancing a few steps; stopping, looking around, not taking direct aim at any one target; counting and jotting notes, then moving again.

Before long I recognize Rabicana by her distinctive tail. Sure enough, to her right is Northeastern and also Twink, but I'm not sure of the other proximate mares. To Rabicana's left is Mancha and her foal but at a remove of several horse-lengths, as I saw her initially yesterday, in the configuration by the big boulder. But there are dozens of horses between me and them and I can't get closer without startling them, so I shift my course upward again, angling for a view from on high to try to spot Chaparro. Unfortunately, other humans begin arriving as I do so. Their voices carry but they're not yet in view; several families are working their way up from the gate, coming out to see the horses. I make quick work of spotting and mapping, hoping the horses don't rouse. No such luck. My approach has already caused sleepy heads to rise, alert. Once the other humans close in, the trigger is tripped and in a sudden swell all the animals before me cascade forward, plunging down and toward the distant gate.

My disappointment is tempered by the sight of them streaming away at a canter, then driving down through the tree-choked ravine. For over a minute they pour past, and before long I'm watching them rise up on its far side in long lacing lines slicing through trees and glades, and then out of sight again. The delicate configuration of proximate bands and stragglers flushes past in a rush, energetic in the front but slower at the rear, where a few horses step along unhurriedly. There are more than I thought. They keep coming, spilling past. Pausing the demanding work of mapping and counting frees me up to admire how they move in unison.

After the last horses trail by, I head toward the gate as well. Along the way small knots of horses, hidden in the trees, jostle loose and follow in the herd's wake, until the middle stretches of the pasture are entirely drained. I'm not completely surprised by the scene awaiting at the bottom, though it takes me awhile to register: a mass of horses is standing stock still in a giant wedge formation in front of the gate. It's stunning to see them go from dispersed to compressed so quickly. The play of social distance and proximity I glimpsed briefly and all the movement just moments ago has been replaced with another configuration—compact and static. It's striking how they manage this, since, as yesterday's boundary work between the Mega and Knoll bands made clear, their penchant is for maintaining band structures through boundary work. Whatever their group differences or efforts to hew closely to friends or kin, now their overriding focus is a shared one of getting out of their confinement.

But they have a long time yet to wait. About an hour and a half passes before the gate is opened. In the meantime, they stand there expectantly, concentrating their attention on escaping this confinement. In doing so, they have the challenge of managing their physical compression, which largely means avoid staring at others even though most of their bodies are touching. Some of this is handled by aligning proximate heads in opposite directions. Several times, I can trace a rough line of ears inversely posed—pointed to my left or right—running across more than a dozen heads, each staring forward or looking down. Toward the rear, foals start crashing out on the ground and there's some light socializing in the rear—extended noses, smelling. But it's mostly still and quiet, with no calls or whinnies.

On the opposite side of the gate, humans are strung out along the fence, several people deep, looking at the horses and also waiting for their release. These people have turned out for the spectacle. Eventually, Ghelo and his compadres, Ruben, Ramon, and Diego, whom I met at the dinner with Victor in Sabucedo, arrive to begin moving the horses down through the village and up to another large pasture, Peche do Cataroi, where the horses will wait before being brought into the *curro* to start the *rapa*. As they mass up outside this enclosure, I leave to find a position along the descent to the village to take some photos.

I'm not the only one. Photographers drape the edges of the dusty track that trickles down to the paved country lane below that leads into Sabucedo. More are arriving, anxiously vying to get a vibrant image of horses in motion. Before the mass gets moving, Ghelo and two dozen others (including several women) with long walking sticks that have a bulbous knob on the top form a line to keep the horses from moving too quickly. They pause twenty meters before me, tightening up their contour, then advance about forty meters down slope. The horses cautiously descend, pushed forward by another cordon in their rear. A few try to twist back uphill and others try shifting sideways, but there are humans strung all along the descent, so their advance is inexorable. It takes them two-and-a-half minutes to lurch past, in staggered fashion; people stream by too, trying to capture the procession on cell phones.

At least fifty people stride down past the animals churning down the hill. Once they're gone, I decide it's best to move much farther ahead, to where they'll all end up.

The route from here through Sabucedo and up to the next pasture covers two kilometers, and it's lined most of the way with humans waiting to see the *bestas.* Descending through the first stretch, I start passing the thousands camped in the woods for the weekend; some have brought horses of their own, who are tethered to trees beside tents set against old stone walls or beside the narrow creek. Along the paved lane a thin line of people wait, many with children, anticipating the animals' arrival. At the bottom, where the two-lane highway cuts through between the mountain and Sabucedo, the fields are densely packed with parked cars and campers. Crossing over and into the village, a huge crowd is assembled. They take up cramped positions along the lane, some atop the stone wall outside the social club and many more above the rocky cutaway where the road turns left through the north edge of the village and toward the *curro.* The day is already hot and I feel for the parents trying to keep their children amused. The few houses along here are adorned with massive black-and-white photos of fierce combat between stallions in previous *rapas.* This route is clearly curated to cultivate an image of the village as equated with the *rapa.*

Eventually I reach the turnoff, a rutted track leading up to Peche do Cataroi, an enclosure ringing a steep hill where the horses will be kept before and after the daily shearing. The track is lined with fields where yet more people are camping on either side. They crowd against a tall wood-rail fence that keeps them off the steep, stony route to the *peche*; behind them are many more tents, these side by side, and some beneath blue tarps. After huffing a bit, I reach the open gate and enter the large, sloping pasture. I take up a position beside a narrow stand of eucalyptus to observe what happens as the animals arrive. I'm curious about how they will socialize. Will the band structure reemerge, much the way I saw it in the first catchment area? How will these horses negotiate social interactions with so many unfamiliar conspecifics penned together? What will the mares do? How will the stallions react to each other and to the mares they know best?

I trace the yet-unseen procession mostly through the shouts of the humans: "*vamos,* let's go, ho, ho!" The meadow is tranquil before they arrive. The first horses through the gate are tentative, stopping from a hot trot, sizing up the space before them. From the rear they're pushed forward as the humans drive the column up and in. A few start to gulp at grass; they've been moving for about an hour now on asphalt lanes, and there was little eating while they waited to get out at the gate in the first pasture. Their hunger is high, but the press of motion behind sweeps them along. Now the air reverberates with intense whinnies, tinny and shallow from the foals, long and deep from the adults. Many of the yearlings and foals try circling back, looking for mothers, but the onward rush is too strong to negotiate. They fall back in with the surge that leads onward. Crisp peals of eucalyptus bark and branches on the ground crackle underfoot as they stomp ahead; the air is drenched with the tang of its oily aroma, drifting dust, and horse sweat.

After five minutes, the last of roughly three hundred horses (I count 312) are through and the gates are closed and chained. But it's easy for humans to access the *peche* through a narrow passage on the side, and many are making the trek to see the horses up close. The first wave is the photographers, fanning out for shots; then a couple dozen spectators arrive to get a look. After them, the *besteiros* will show up to pursue their age-old task of identifying mares and their foals.

Based on my experiences in the *peche* from the year before, I know the best place for observation is on a wide hummock just above the two long concrete watering troughs. The horses will slowly spread out and some will move to the top, but most initially congregate on the fairly flat glade in front of the water troughs. Here the grass is best; the slope above is mostly a mat of ferns until you get to the top, where it thins into patchy, pebbly soils. So I start my mapping, looking for clusters to form.

For a long time, though, most of the movement is mares trying to find foals. They reunite fairly quickly. After ten minutes I only see one unattached foal, though judging from the whinnies circulating above and through the herd, at least a couple others are looking for their mothers. Gradually the intensity of the whinnying wanes, with fewer of the short sharp bursts from the foals; now it's mostly calls between adults: preferred partners, siblings, or familiar bandmates. Their vocal tones are less stressed and more reassuring. Even these whinnies diminish as they mostly turn to eating.

From my perch, I'm watching for several things: animals I recognize, treks or directed movements, and the formation of clusters. But it's hard to make out much over the first fifteen minutes as the horses

FIGURE 3.7. *Peche do Cataroi; the troughs, in the center, are mostly obscured by the horses.*

settle in. One group of easily forty or more starts drifting up a low gully off to my left, oblique to the gate; above me on the hill, a strand of about two dozen stretches up, mostly singly or in pairs; but the largest mass sprawls out before the troughs. I focus on the biggest grouping, trying to gauge for two dynamics. First, proximity: how long do the horses stay closely packed together; and as they dissipate, do they do so singly, in pairs, or in clusters of several horses? Second, I watch for affiliative gestures and microaggressions, the staples of life in a band, as they sort out closeness and distance through bodily positioning, looks, and gestures. Both sets of observations are challenging—a rough count gives me just over two hundred horses directly in front of me; if I turn around and look up the hill I count another twenty-five. So there's little hope of focusing closely on subtle individual interactions. At the same time, because they form such a thick cluster it's easier to see the abrupt ruptures of a threat gesture and the subsequent reaction. I observe only one, at twenty minutes in, between two mares. Notably, the horses—after the stressful trek through the village, and though there is no evidence of the social structure of bands remerging—are socializing with ease. To remain this proximate, they have to be socializing.

They mostly stay within a body-length of each other. Gaps open and close as grazers shift, but there's a continuity to this large mass, such that there are only a few outliers—several mares with their foals and one black stallion, who I notice after five minutes. He's the only horse looking around; he's relatively small and looks young. Four minutes later, as a few more gaps open, I notice another stallion, a bay, also alone, with head elevated, also looking around. It dawns on me that after almost ten minutes I've yet to see any herding action on the part of the males. Since I'm waiting to see if bands will reconstitute, I anticipate that soon, especially after seeing it play out so sharply yesterday with Chaparro and Northeastern. But perhaps the sociality of the herd is such that it overrides their instinct to hive off mares. Still, these two stallions are noticeable (there are ten total in the herd) because they are the only ones looking around for bandmates.

Meanwhile, some mares are starting to angle off on their own in pairs or trios, trekking toward removed spots within the *peche,* trailed by their foals and yearlings. They're not heading purposefully in a certain direction; they don't look up or around, as in scanning for a stallion or identifying threats. They're following tasty bits of grass. I count more than a dozen of these sets before I lose track. Foals try to nurse, limiting their movements, but they hardly appear hurried anyway. But I notice as these clusters take shape that they move away from the herd, largely heading to higher ground or more distant spaces, like a band might move; and I wonder what is shifting socially in such movements.

After twenty-two minutes in the *peche,* a third stallion emerges. He is a bay; distinctive because his is the only raised head, straining to look toward the west edge of the grounds where some horses are taking up shady spots under the trees along the fence line. A minute later the young black stallion hurries up from my immediate right and rushes toward a bay mare behind and above me on the slope. He sniffs deeply along her flank but yanks back his head, bellowing briefly, then dashes over to a cluster of mares. They move quickly away as he approaches, and he seems consternated over not locating mares he knows. I decide to keep tabs on his efforts at finding bandmates and settle on calling him Young Black. Over the next hour he passes in and out of view, searching unsuccessfully.

Two minutes later I finally spot Chaparro down in the big gathering of horses; he stands out mostly because five photographers are moving through, and the horses part as they approach. It's interesting that the easily two dozen people drifting among the horses now cause little consternation. The horses hardly seem anxious or antsy. After locating Chaparro I spot a second black stallion grazing solitarily along the slope above me. His big round star is a bit off center, and he has a pink snip on his nose. I'll identify him as Star Black. He makes the fifth stallion I've spotted in this *peche*.

Down below, Young Black approaches yet another clump of mares, who also move briskly away as he nears. Meanwhile Chaparro is on the move. He's found the flea-bitten mare, CF, who I had pegged as somewhat peripheral when I mapped the Mega band two days ago. She's the only mare I've recognized from that group so far. The only other mare I spot with certainty is Rabicana, because her tail is so distinctive; I see her along the trees edging the west side of the pasture, but she's alone. Chaparro is following CF as she moves across the glade; then he actively begins herding her. The behavior is unmistakable and accentuated because she's somewhat reluctant. As she angles away from the mass, he follows; when she tries to cut back into the herd he lowers his ears, menacingly pinning them back, paralleling her step-for-step until she reverses course. This motion plays out until he has her isolated in a large opening.

Scanning the herd again, I make out two more bay stallions. That makes seven out of the ten in this herd, so I'm feeling well positioned in the *peche*. I notice one because a mare is sniffing his genitals; he rears back initially, but then turns toward her. They pose for a moment in the mating ritual maneuver with deep olfactory investigations, but abruptly part ways. When they do, I see the other stallion less than six body-lengths away from him. He too is approached by a mare. They meet nose-to-nose to make familiar contact; then he matches her slow turn, coming alongside her left flank. Overall, I'm surprised by two things: that these stallions are so singular in their focus on a particular mare (rather than herding to reconstitute the band structure), and that they are not challenging each other, even though they're so proximate.

My attention shifts to the mares as smaller clusters start taking shape. One has formed up to my left: seven adults, two yearlings, and two foals. They're not moving, just eating, but their heads are quite close together: with so much available space, this indicates affinity. This proximity is evident in more than a dozen mare pairs—affiliative, but also showing an absence of aggression and threats. The way these clusters are taking shape, without a stallion involved, suggests mare sociality is foundational to the social dynamics that characterize the larger config-uration of the band. Eventually, a trek of sorts unfolds; a gray flanked by six other mares approaches the water trough determinedly. But they halt when the horses in front of them don't give way. Each of them hives off and probes for openings to reach the water individually. The only other distinctive movement is from CF. She slipped away from Chaparro at some point (I didn't see), but now she emerges from the tree line flanked by her buddy Bloat, who tagged close to her when I first observed them. They march across the glade and find their way to Chaparro, who's grazing near some mares I don't recognize.

It's been an hour and twenty minutes since the horses entered the *peche.* Tuning back to the stallions, I notice Young Black is still keenly looking around. His traipsing brings him close to Chaparro, who sees Young Black and makes an aggressive approach. Both stallions lower their heads and stamp the turf with their right legs. From about a body-length apart, the black makes a strike threat with his front right hoof; Chaparro shrieks and dashes off. Though he's larger and looks more powerful, he seems more concerned with CF, the flea-bitten mare, who's a few a meters away and on the move again. In his wake, Young Black stands alone in a large bubble of space cleared as other horses moved away. The brevity and singularity of this exchange highlights how little interest the stallions have shown in challenging each other. It was an abrupt encounter and broken off before the ritual conflict interaction could develop.

The aftermath of this brief dustup is telling, too. When a dark-brown mare with a long stripe moves across the cleared space, followed by her yearling and another mare, Young Black makes a herding gesture to-ward her. He sustains it for only a few seconds as she accelerates on her way, ignoring him. As they break off contact he notices a large cluster of mares (ten adults, two foals) alongside the watering trough. He ad-vances, and one black on his side of the cluster raises her head at alert. When he gets close and tries to sniff her, she aims her left front hoof at his face. He gives a head toss, then tries her right side, pulling his face in close as she whips hers around to confront him again. They lock in this position for a moment, but whatever he's trying to communicate is not accepted. When she turns her entire body into a rear kick-threat posi-tion he reluctantly leaves, heading up the hill to continue his search.

After an hour and a half, the only sounds from the horses are their massive jaws grinding grass into pulp; foals are crashed out on the ground and adults start dozing. The black stallion's struggle to identify his bandmates makes me think trying to find Northeastern would be futile and exhausting, wasting the limited time I have before the *rapa.* He's not by Rabicana. Since the action here is slowing down, I decide to head over to the *curro* to prepare for the evening event.

An hour or so later I'm settled in with my fellow humans in the *curro,* packed in tightly on concrete benches that rise in rows around the sandy arena, which is shaped like a rectangle crowned in a crescent. It's made of low stone walls about five feet high. Across the straight edge, on the west side of the *curro,* the walls are much higher and topped with two viewing platforms: one for the media and the other for the announcer, locals, and the day's musical performers. Between the two platforms a double-door wooden gate is open, awaiting the arrival of the horses. But first the folkloric group Tequexeteldere plays. The performance includes about a dozen dancers and a chorus of women singers; the music comes from a pair of pipes and an accordion, clarinet, and drum; all of them are dressed in traditional garb. The dancers glide back and forth across the sand through several numbers, to appreciative applause.

After the folk band finishes and leaves the arena, the announcer tells us to observe silence as the horses arrive. The crowd indeed stills, to the point that I can faintly hear recorded music playing over at the carnival games. Ghelo, in a white tank top and army fatigue pants, and another *aloitadore* are by the large gates to drive the horses all the way in, keeping them from slipping back out. Their task is not challenging. The horses enter one bunch at a time, so they have a few moments to adjust to the too-tight confines of the *curro.* The announcer quietly intones, "These are beautiful animals, the savages (*salvajes*) of the mountain." The first wave has roughly fifty horses; the lead ones enter at a quick trot, well spaced out from each other, not making contact. But that social distance is unsustainable as the rest of this batch pours in behind. Those in the lead confront the walls at the curved end of the *curro* (where I'm sitting, to the east) that confine their movement. They turn northward along the arc of the wall, only to collide with others who are now streaming through the gate.

It's a tense moment because the horses are forced to be face-to-face

FIGURE 3.8. *Tequexeteldere, a Galician folkloric group.*

with others while being roughly pressed to keep moving toward them. But both streams meld and turn southward. The herd ends up confronting that wall, to my left. Remarkably, with only a few exceptions they manage to face the same direction, demonstrating the "elevator effect" (see figure 3.21) as observed in primates.[3] Those that can't physically avert their gaze crane their necks obliquely and probably uncomfortably; keeping their torsos and feet static so they don't push up against another conspecific. These avoidance techniques mirror what Erving Goffman characterized as civil inattention. Just as people will avert their gaze from awkward matters in order to avoid conflicts or challenges, these horses are doing so too. Briefly and impressively, they do manage to turn and reorient so they're almost all roughly facing in the same direction, which alleviates the potential for unintended threats. The stallion Star Black takes up a position in the center and starts clearing space with threat gestures, pressuring the mares forward—an example of dominance being performed by asserting social distance.

The second incoming surge brings more horses awkwardly face-to-face with others, further disrupting the delicate social balancing act they've maintained over the last several minutes. The new arrivals bend hard to their left to avoid those standing in the center, hewing tightly against the high west wall. This effort abruptly brings them to the northwest corner in just a few meters. So they turn right, overwhelming

FIGURE 3.9. *Star Black clears space.*

the bubble that Star Black has asserted. As more animals enter they become increasingly unsure of where to look and how to stand in order
to maintain social distance between themselves. Most ears are pitching forward in an inquisitive, responsive stance. But others are pitched
back aggressively. This is most evident closest to Star Black, as if his
aggression has become contagious. Complicating all this are the foals,
who are clumping up underfoot, trying to stay close to their mothers
but plainly anxious and flitting about to avoid being crunched. By the
time the last of the second group is in, maintaining social distance is
impossible; they're all unavoidably in physical contact now.

The stallions detest this most, or at least are the most aggressive in
reasserting a buffer space around themselves. Chaparro conveniently
pops up right in front of me and immediately begins casting threat
gestures around. Facing north, he glares at a mare ahead of him, who
backs up as best she can, while others to his left and right also give way.
Quickly a small spatial pocket forms around him. It doesn't last long.
The mares are now pushed toward him from competing directions;
unable to keep clear, Chaparro rolls to his left, heading back toward

the gate, where he's wedged into the mass again. Meanwhile, Star Black is stamping about, clearing space around him. The gate stays open as Ghelo and the other *aloitadores* wave their arms and push the horses away, making room for the next batch.

Now the ring is packed with more than a hundred horses, heads snapping back and forth to avoid facial confrontations. Already there are some awkward situations with faces wedged cheek to cheek, or heads perched uneasily above the back of another horse positioned at a right angle. Here the "problem of face," as described by Goffman, is quite legible—the horses increasingly can't put their face anywhere without rupturing the projected personal space around others' faces. For the moment, though, these discourtesies are tolerated and for the most part civil inattention prevails. Some of the foals lift their faces, seeking reassurance from a yearling or a mare. Otherwise, they all avoid socializing through nose-to-nose contact or other forms of olfactory investigation.

Compression starts to dominate the herd; that's the principal of the *rapa*—to deny the horses the capacity to maneuver. But the lack of space to retreat deprives them of a foundational avoidance technique. They cannot back away because they have nowhere to go. Instead they twist in a steady churn, as yet another batch is driven into the *curro*. Chaparro is back in front of me again, hedged in by a foal and yearling, who he does not threaten. In front and to his left, Star Black is asserting space with rear kick gestures. The stallions' pockets of space overlap and they're in parallel, about a horse-length apart; their ears pressed low, aggressively glaring at each other. In response to Star Black's kicks, an adjacent mare directs a bite threat at another mare's face, against whom she's been pressed. This is the first I notice of mares engaging in blatant aggressive gestures, which will soon spin into open violence. On the range and in their bands, mares assert space or achieve proximity with fairly subtle signals, relying on the strength of signaling and behavioral conventions to convey their intention or will. In the *curro*, as the possibility for maintaining social distance disintegrates, gestures are no longer sufficient, and threats become actual bites.

More bites follow quickly as this third batch pours in. Star Black directs a bite threat at a mare in front of him. As her head snaps to the left it collides with that of another mare, who was turning to avoid hitting the mare to her left. The spaces around Star Black and Chaparro, who's parallel but facing the opposite direction, overlap and open up briefly. As Star Black turns toward him, Chaparro twists rapidly and sends a rear right kick at his face. Star Black twists away, biting at two bay mares to clear an exit path. Along the edge of the briefly opened bubble mares grimace, faces arched high to avoid another kick or antagonizing Chaparro further. He lurches forward, crashing into the mass to his left, and his wake is swiftly filled by mares, yearlings, and foals.

On the south side, to the right of the big gates, a mare viciously bites the mouth of another, whose face was crunched against hers, both facing the same way. The capacity for civil inattention is dissolving. Heads are snapping back and high to my left and right as more horses pour in, crashing against those closest to the gates. Star Black appears in front of

FIGURE 3.10. *Chaparro in the foreground, kicking at Star Black in the center.*

me and delivers a double barreled rear kick at an encroaching mare, who has nowhere else to turn. The sclera or white of her eye flashes; her terror amplified as another mare's face approaches, just glancing off to her right side where it comes to rest. But all is not yet chaos. I notice a mare in Star Black's path who doesn't retreat. They stand face-to-face for a long moment, both extending their noses, making contact, ears erect and attentive, where his have mostly been lowered threateningly. Two foals and a yearling appear in the space around Star Black, while he and the mare turn and look in tandem toward the south side of the *curro*.

The horses closest to the gate and in the center are jostling as the ones along the walls have largely adjusted to being compacted. They are managing to stand stock still in this miserable crowding. I see one affiliative gesture, strained and overstated: two mares reach their faces toward each other, nostrils dilated widely, across two intervening bodies; but it's too hard to sustain. I glimpse other such gestures, with noses working tactilely as means of contact or offering reassurance. The gestures are all greatly exaggerated compared to how these interactions manifest in everyday life.[4] Meanwhile Chaparro has grown more tolerant, once he manages to wedge his rear against the north wall. Though they're unable to avoid face-to-face confusions along that wall, those horses stabilize their positions and manage to stand still. Chaparro briefly rests his head on a mare's back, also an affiliative gesture. Then the fourth batch is driven in and the gates close. It's been five minutes since the first batch entered.

This last group fills the *curro* entirely with about three hundred animals, allowing no social distance, and the roiling horses become frenzied. Increasingly desperate to avoid facial contact and confrontation, horses are rearing all around the arena; the plane of backsides irrupts jerkily with efforts at avoidance; torsos inevitably coming down atop or alongside another horse, who either cringes or lashes out with bites—kicking is now quite difficult. Then the distress bleeds into panic as the humans begin to extract the foals. The idea is to keep them from being injured in the melee to follow. They'll be sequestered in a stable underneath the announcer's platform beside the gate. The room has vent openings above the stone wall for air, but it will also transmit their frantic cries.

The humans work in father-son teams, with an occasional daughter or two participating. Three to four kids work in the *curro* at a time, each aiming to capture and remove a foal. The fathers help them maneuver, casually smacking the rears of horses in their way as they push through the mass toward a foal. The children grab it by the ears, or sometimes around its neck, and with father's help, yank it along until they clear the arena. As each father–child pair moves through, the foals cry out and the mares futilely try to keep close to them. The humans brusquely part the horses as they move, jolting them forward inexorably into another horse.

The *curro* is now a frenetic cacophony. The desperate bleating of foals echoes; mares whinny, stressed and anxious; stallions shriek threats as they are pushed too close to each other. Two near the center clash, with one rearing and delivering a double kick, and the crowd roars; this is what they most want to see. A mare bites another's face repeatedly, only to be bitten in turn by a different mare who was roused by the victim's efforts to escape the first one's blows. Soon I'm no longer able to track this in detail—it's too rapid and frequent. Aggression and violence are breaking out all over. The speed and force of the bites is stunning—mouths flashing forward faster than a punch, drawing back just as quickly. I remember Juan's remark: "people don't realize, their most dangerous parts are their teeth." There are moments when the thrashing subsides; but then another pair of humans move across and a current of aggression crackles through the beasts. I'm riveted as I watch Chaparro again pass nearly under my feet along the wall. He's biting savagely at the backsides and buttocks in front of him—I count six in rapid succession. One mare bites back at his face then peels off away; another kicks him, but he continues biting across her withers.

Even though I observed this event last year, I'm astounded by the ferocity and viciousness on the blows. On the range, I didn't once see sclera flashing from a frightened horse, nor did I see nostrils flare so widely nor observe actual bites other than when Crazy Gray was clashing with Northeastern. The texture of everyday social life is full of microaggressions. But they're almost entirely gestural—a feigned bite or kick, but often a glare is sufficient to carve out social distance. Aggression is mediated and managed through dynamics such as the social gaze or forms of civil inattention, compounded by assertions of, challenges to, and acknowledgments of status and position. In social species, primal forces can be expressed and responded to via conventional expressions that alleviate the explosion of physically unbound force. Among the horses in the *curro,* as conventions around social space collapse, violence surges. Here I see teeth glinting in the late afternoon sun streaming through rising columns of dust; I see them landing with shocking directness on sensitive faces. It makes me think that these animals' capacity for sociality has collapsed entirely.

Perhaps this violence would not irrupt if the horses were able to stabilize themselves. Even when physically compressed, some of them demonstrate remarkable restraint in not aggressively responding to forms of contact that would be threatening out on the range. But after all the foals are cleared and the shearing begins, the panic among the horses becomes acute. The *aloitadores* work in teams: one jumps on the horse from behind while another grabs its tail and one tries to get alongside it, grabbing at its head and obscuring its vision. It looks artless and clumsy at times, but there is a technique at work.

There are many variations of this basic technique, all sharing the same principle. The rider aims to disorient the horse so it can't resist;

FIGURE 3.11. Aloitadores *grappling with a mare.*

he may also do this by smacking the animal's head while driving it into the mass of its conspecifics. Once a smaller horse tires from this ordeal, they can tackle it to the ground and commence shearing it, using large, bulky metal clippers. But on the big beasts like the stallions, the men may settle for immobilizing it in a standing position. This is what happens with Chaparro.

He is the first one to be sheared. They target him because he's large and powerful; a struggle with him casts the *aloitadores* in a bold light. Six of them approach him where he's clogged up on the north side. Whether because he has been through this ritual before or because their intentions are obvious, Chaparro tries to flee. He rears up to drive the animals from in front, only to land clumsily on a mare's back. The men advance inexorably, one mounting him deftly while the others close in, trying to grab for tail, mane, and face. The rider, wearing a white bandana and T-shirt, grabs his mane as Chaparro surges again and again until the mass no longer gives way. Also fighting through the throng are the trailing crew members. When one finally secures Chaparro's tail the rider dismounts and pins the stallion's head to his chest. They lock

FIGURE 3.12. *Chaparro being sheared.*

him in this position until the others arrive. One takes the shears to his mane and another does the same with his tail. In about four minutes, he's sheared and released.

This process continues for an hour and a half. It is hardly efficient; only a few dozen are sheared in this period. But it is dramatic, as the riders make increasingly bold efforts at mounting and the horses grow more terror-stricken. People cheer as the announcer calls out the names of the riders, all local men. There are moments when one section of the animals manage almost entirely to face the same direction. This is what they struggle for as each one shifts to avoid confrontation. But its duration is terribly brief, as another rider leaps onto the back of another scared horse, driving into the others. As Star Black is being sheared, I start noticing faces buried under the shoulders and flanks of others, wedged down where the air must be stifling but free from confrontation. Finally it's time to release them back to the Peche do Cataroi for the evening. The stable door is opened; disoriented foals flow out; the tall gates swing wide and the horse careen from the *curro,* through the lane ringed by kitchens and carnival games, back to the hilltop pasture.

They return to the *peche* shattered. The air shivers with desperate cries from lost foals and foal-less mares. Again they eat ravenously, but now they maintain a heightened sense of distance. A few mares graze close to each other, but there is very little clustering, if only because most of the mares are running around. In stark contrast with their earlier behavior, many now elevate their heads, looking for foals or yearlings. The whinnies are copious and distressed; the air rattles with them. I see pairs of foals—in one case, one foal has followed another, but not to its own mother. It seeks to nurse but is refused; still it lingers, confused.

Most distressing are lone foals following mares who do not recognize them and walk away; or mares sniffing at foals who are not able to identify them as their mother. The problem is scent and its confusions. Most of these offspring are only days old. The mothers largely identify them by smell. But in the stable for so long, their aromas become thoroughly muddled and masked. They smell like a combination of all the other foals. The mares' aromas, too, are melded with those of other adults. So their searches go on and on. Amid this desperation, I see plenty of threat gestures now, in contrast to early in the afternoon, when they were practically absent. I track the frenzy for an hour. But as twilight deepens, I leave and let them rest.

DAY 3

Most of the horses are sleeping when I arrive at the *peche* the next morning. It's a strange scene—the sharp, crisp light silhouettes dozens of mares across the hillside above the trough. First I notice the ones standing singly beside a sleeping foal. Across the slope and the flat ground, the young ones lie completely sprawled out, unconscious. Most have their mother standing guard nearby, but I notice that several are alone; they were not reunited overnight. What surprises me more is to see quite a few adults also sleeping on the ground—a sign of sheer exhaustion after yesterday's ordeal. Most are sternal recumbent, with their head raised above folded forelegs, tucked against their torsos, but a few are lying on their sides, laterally recumbent.

Absent any evidence of social structure, the horses initially appear mostly isolated and adrift. I don't see much evidence of huddling as they slept. But as I start mapping their positions and moving around, I see sociality manifesting in various ways. In contrast to those on the hillside, there's a large cluster below the trough and more horses bunched up nearer to the trees that hedge the stone-wall fence. Among

FIGURE 3.13. *The morning of day three, looking up the hilltop in the* peche.

them adults are slumbering standing close together. Though I move slowly and infrequently, my approach jars some awake. I worry about this and stop moving but most are already stirring; and I realize this is a moment like one of the most generative on the range: after naptime. On the mountain, watching them wake reveals displays and performances of social identity and status; stirring, each animals' movement begins asserting or responding to gestures insisting on distance, or continuing proximity.

There's little of that now, since the band structures are dissolved and many adults are standing only with a single foal or yearling. Gesturing toward others is infrequent; rather, a slow checking on the young ones and then a desultory turn to grazing. In several instances, though, it seems mares that were sleeping close together ended up that way haphazardly in the night. These proximate horses wake with something of a start, perhaps surprised to be so close to an unfamiliar animal. Instead of gesturing toward each other, one or both quickly walk away; not grazing immediately, only moving in an opposite direction, perhaps to locate a missing foal, a preferred partner, or to gain distance. I suppose that sleep found them near each other in the dark, a proximity that felt different in the morning.

A rough count comes out at 130 or more in my direct line of sight. There are more in the trees that I can't see, and others are obscured because they're standing in a cluster—side by side or face-to-rear. So more than a third of the animals are in this large bunch. I can see several stallions as well, distinguishable quickly because they are isolated, not close to any of the mares. One is a bay, shorn; about ten meters away is Star Black, alone. This is the area where most of the horses congregated the day before; their concentration today is not as dense, and they seem to scrunch up closer to the shelter of the trees along the fence line. So I head in there to continue my task of identifying and mapping.

Under the oaks are several adjacent clusters of mares, but none I recognize. I find Chaparro by himself, backed up against the stone wall, gazing out stolidly, not moving—just static. There's another bay stallion about five meters away; they're actually facing toward each other. The bay is close to a flaxen mare with a foal and they appear quite familiar. It seems odd that these two males would have slept near each other without fighting. But they certainly don't seem on guard this morning, and I don't see any threat gestures. All through this tree line the horses are quite close together, so that it's difficult for me to maneuver without disrupting anyone. So I turn back toward the troughs and the slope.

That's when I see the first act of allogrooming I've observed since these animals came down from the mountain. It's two mares; I guess a mother and her two-year-old, though I can't be sure. The interaction is sustained and energetic. Seeing allogrooming only now is a good indicator of how collapsed sociality became, or at least the band structure—especially seen in contrast with its prevalence among members of the Mega band after they were first captured on the roundup day. Nine minutes later, another pair of mares also engages in allogrooming nearby; and five minutes on, two others commence this reciprocal behavior. I also see a dark-brown mare with her head across the shoulders of a bay. So if sociality did collapse in the *curro,* it is slowly percolating back up through such affiliative gestures and the spatial proximity of many of the mares. Or maybe what happened in the *curro,* more precisely, is that space as a socially signifying medium dissolved; and now it's being reasserted and expressed through reciprocal acts of allogrooming.

But not only through such vigorous activities; sociality is also evident in the way mares are forming pairs or trios, with or without foals, across the hillside. Meanwhile, with the rising sun there's more motion down below, especially around the trough. As horses converge, I see gestures of recognition—extended snouts, sniffing and touching. Following affiliative acts, they fall in closer, side by side, eating or drinking in unison. These acts of relating look much like what I observed on the range: the mares perform a great deal of sociality apart from what the stallions do. What makes this more pronounced here is that the males are either maintaining social distance from others or not latching onto any of the groupings of mares.

While watching the allogrooming pair, I notice a dark-brown stallion slowly emerging from the cover of the trees. That brings my count to six, so I've spotted just over half of them. Only one was close to a mare; the others I saw, like this one, are isolated. He's dangling a half erection but making no moves toward particular mares. These stallions are not making any effort at herding or even looking about for mares they know. I also realize I've yet to see any fecal marking displays. On the range band stallions do this with frequency; it's also part of how they claim possession of mares in relation to other stallions. They actively examine mares' dung in a ritual sequence—sniffing, performing a flehmen, perhaps pawing the pile, stepping over or pivoting around it to defecate on top of it, stepping back to smell it again, and then possibly repeating all or just parts of this series. It dawns on me how profoundly absent this behavior is, providing another indicator of the thorough collapse of the social structure. Again I think it odd that these males are so close to each other without provoking conflict. I don't observe any of them engaging in boundary work.

As I mull all this, a collective movement is developing. Up across the slope, mares have been grazing—a few singly, but mostly in pairs or trios. As they slowly synchronize their socially facilitated eating motion, a fairly close formation takes shape as they parallel each other, grazing in the same direction. There's a cluster of eight mares and five foals, while fanning out in front are another eight, with three foals; there's no stallion present. This makes me think about the important concepts of "basic social unit" or "core unit," which are the building blocks of multilevel societies like horse herds. The idea is that fundamental groups are formed from subunits. With horses, there's a long-standing belief that the basic social unit is the **family group** (or "harem bands") consisting of one stallion and one or more mares.[5] But I'll venture here that a more accurate formulation is that the core unit is made up of mare pairs or trios, whether matricentric (comprising a mare and one or more subadults), siblings, or based on friendship. These long-term relationships seem to constitute the basis for the social organization of bands, given that stallions come and go with some frequency. Yet there are still several mares missing foals; with morning their search resumes in earnest. Whinnies start sounding out across the *peche* achingly. In front of me, a mare's calls are answered by an unattached foal. But she doesn't recognize it, so she turns away; the stumbling foal follows, unconsoled.

As the day warms, more humans arrive to view the herd. As they do the horses grow skittish and start moving farther up. Soon the largest cluster, located in the most accessible part of the *peche,* dissolves and the animals move into the trees or high across the slope. In their shifting movements, a few more gestures of recognition and **parallel prancing** emerge. What I don't see over the course of an hour and a half are any acts of aggression. As the close formation in the lower *peche*

FIGURE 3.14. *Grazers in motion, exhibiting socially facilitated behavior.*

unwinds and as other mares begin grazing closer together, there's no eruption of the hostile interactions that were prevalent in the *curro* and on display in the *peche* as evening fell the day before, or even that might be observed in a band over the course of a morning. I wonder at how that intensity of antagonism from yesterday has managed to dissipate. But before much else is able to unfold, the village men arrive to begin driving the horses down below.

Another musical act opens the festivities, but this is a small affair—two men, one with a harp, the other with a tambourine, both singing. Once they're done and their equipment is cleared away, it's time for the horses to return. Again, a batch of about fifty horses enter initially. They circle the *curro* and spread out, renewing their effort to create spatial buffers between them. As the dust settles, the second batch enters. In the shifting and turning of animals accommodating each other, two stallions end up in front of where I'm positioned, on the north wall today. I recognize Northeastern, and he's yet to be shorn; the other is a dark brown, also unshorn, with two long scars on each side of his rear haunches. They'll both be targets today. Right now they are targeting each other. Northeastern launches his rear legs in a kick at the dark-brown stallion, which clears ground as mares, yearlings, and foals compress at the edge of his radius. Northeastern then presses into the crowd, but as more horses enter he's pushed back toward the other stallion—I'll call him Dark Brown—who returns the rear kick, opening a semicircle around him. This projection of social distance compacts the mares, while Northeastern stands unmoved, facing him. Now the third batch pours in

and that space dissolves. Northeastern again turns southward and I lose sight of him; Dark Brown is able to stand roughly on the same spot, using glares to keep other horses from approaching his face.

Amid the swirling that ensues, my attention is drawn to a bay mare I saw with her foal in the *peche* that morning. Her face is oddly colored, like the lower half has been powdered white—so, Powderface. She's noticeable now because she's worked to stay with her foal, which she has managed to pin protectively under her chin and against her chest. Her effort comes undone before long, but she's able to push against the other animals to keep it in view . . . as it is slowly pushed toward Dark Brown. He's fiercely clearing space again, biting another bay's buttocks

FIGURE 3.15. *Dark Brown creating social distance.*

until she springs away, leaving a gap soon filled by a flaxen mare who is
being pushed from behind. The foal slips into this space, too. Behind it,
Powderface is energetically pushing forward, until she has the stallion
in her sights.

I'm riveted as the foal pops up right before the stallion's angry vis-
age; Powderface is right there, too—ears pinned, glowering at him. She
lunges a bite threat at his face. Dark Brown does not retaliate; he just
lowers his head and bestows on the foal a reassuring snort between its
shoulder blades, then turns to his right as a crush of beasts surge into
his left flank. Powderface pushes forward enough to make face-to-face
contact with her foal before they both are separated by the surge. I see
her strike at the right cheek of a flaxen mare prior to being driven back
by the other horses. The human children start taking the foals, so the
pace of motion is ratcheting up again. During this anxious moment,
the foal sidles up to the dark-brown stallion and attaches to his side;
soon he is taken away with the others.

Now bites are flying and heads are snapping back. Powderface is
pushed farther and farther away, toward the gate. I don't see her again
that afternoon. Interestingly, amid the fury, three other foals are soon
bunched on Dark Brown's right flank. They shelter there for a matter of
moments, drawing the attention of the father–child extraction teams.
One is taken quickly while the others churn back in the maelstrom. The
humans work methodically over the next fifteen minutes as whinnies
of fear and desperation ratchet up.

While the foals are being extracted, I gradually begin attending to
the announcer. Each day in the *curro* he maintains a steady banter
with the audience and a running commentary on the action with the
horses—much like at an American rodeo. I had mostly tuned him out
because I was focusing on the horses. Since he speaks in Castrapo—
mostly Castilian but with Galician vocabulary and syntax—that wasn't
hard to do. But as he talks about the generational transition occurring
with the children, I could no longer resist tuning into his discourse.

> Look at these brave young boys and girls. Give them an
> applause! They are taking up the family tradition. Look
> at them wrestle with these foals. Soon they will be strong
> *aloitadores.* Give it up Sabucedo! Let's do the wave, starting
> from this side.

FIGURE 3.16. *Removing a foal.*

The crowd boisterously rises and falls around the concrete bleachers of the stone arena and then sits back down. As he calls out names of kids, who range from eight to twelve years old (though one father has a one-year-old in arms to grab at a foal's ears and then sit on its back) people shout out encouragement and praise. The parallelism between

the youths, human and horse, underscores the extent to which we are
companion species gathered here, reproducing a ritual practice that
dates back several thousand years. Yet it's the horses who are the center
of attention:

> There are only a few foals left already. As soon as all of the
> foals leave, the *rapa* will start, they will start fighting the
> horses. There they are, there they are already! . . . Look at
> those stallions, what beasts!

As he calls attention to the stallions, he lists famous horses from past
rapas, who have become *bestas míticas,* or mythical beasts.

> Look to see if Makelele is there . . . the stallion of the
> monte Cabado, from my point of view the most beautiful
> woodlands of Sabucedo . . . the tallest woodlands from
> where you can see the *rias. . . .*

Makelele is famous locally for his fighting prowess; I had seen him in
last year's *rapa.* He was named for a Claude Makélélé, a French soccer
player renowned for sexual exploits—or so I was told—who played for
Real Madrid. But he was not caught this year, so the announcer asks the
crowd, "What other famous stallions are there? The people of Sabucedo
are telling me something here. . . ."

Names ring out around me—El Chulo, El Solitario, El Zapatero—but
he can hardly hear them and so turns to a more general point, "The stallions are the bosses of each band, very territorial. All of the stallions belong to the saint, they have their ears cut, you can search and see them."

Then he speaks of the horses more generally.

> For the *aloitadores* of Sabucedo, the horses are not, are
> not horses, are not beasts, they are not livestock. For these
> people, the horses are free spirits that live in the wood-
> lands. Three days every year, they have the privilege of
> sharing in this village of Sabucedo with us, and sharing
> with you, all this marvelous party. They are . . . the horses,
> the beasts . . . they are noble and powerful beings, and that

is why the fight must be fair and with dignity, body to body, with respect.

This characterization is a lot to take in: the *bestas* are not beasts but "free spirits," simultaneously degraded and ennobled; they are sharing the village and "this marvelous party"; they are being "fought" fairly and with dignity. This is the core of what makes the *rapa* in Sabucedo distinctive: in contrast to the workmanlike practices in the south and north of Galicia, here the horses are on display as full of symbolism, not just of the mountains but of our species' encounters with wild beings of the mountain. The notion of "nobility" is also invoked in some of the promotional literature, where the horses are referred to as "kings" (*reyes*) of the mountain. And the *aloitadores* are construed as those who manage and channel this potent mixing of "powerful beings" with humans in the village. The *aloitadores* are congregating now, about three dozen young men and a couple of women, waiting in front of the gate as the more practiced *aloitadores* like Ghelo start setting the stage.

As the last of the foals are cleared from the *curro,* the announcer calls out, "Come on, as they remove, as they remove the last foals already, as the fighters get ready to start this beautiful dance, we are going to ask you again to make another wave. . . . Come on Sabucedo! Come on the wave! And let's make it return, let's make it return, let's make it return! There we are, that wave of the *curro* of Sabucedo. There they are, there we have the *aloitadores,* Ghelo, Diego, Fernando, there they are, come on Sabuceeeeedo!"

He calls out Diego, in particular.

> Diego, who was not going to fight today because his girlfriend is pregnant, and said: "No, I am going to take care of myself." And eventually he is already here, because this is a poison, and this is something that we carry in our blood. . . . Sabucedo people, boys, girls, all together, fighting, here, one more year, in the best party of the world, Sabucedo!

The *aloitadores* work as a team to coordinate their attacks on the horses. Fernando is the first to choose one and then leap onto its back.

The announcer narrates the action as Fernando tries to hold tightly to the mane.

> There is Fernando. There you have him. Come on, you got
> it, come on, you got it, grasp it, grasp it well, very well. . . .
> The affection they feel for them is not only because they
> shave them, but also because they rid them of parasites.

As the stallion Fernando has selected is tackled, the announcer turns to themes of camaraderie.

> What is true, what is true, there's always . . . a big applause,
> of course, a big applause for Fernando (*boisterous applause*).
> Since the first horse, since the first beast, you see how all
> of the fight-mates are ready to help out a colleague who is
> struggling with a *besta*.

Camaraderie weaves together, then, with technique and antiquity.

> Force is not enough for, for being able to shave these an-
> imals; the technique is essential. . . . The technique, team
> work, everything is necessary. Also necessary is the deter-
> mination of the jump [onto the horse's back], the pressure,
> the direction, changes in steering opportunities. . . . You
> already saw how she tossed a fighter up and down. It is
> also very important to know when to mount and dismount
> the horse, one must avoid kicks, and above all, above all,
> protect oneself from the wall and from the other, the other
> animals that are in the *curro*.

As a series of rides and subsequent shearings unfold, the announcer calls attention to Ghelo.

> If you pay attention, the fighters, most of them pull the
> tail up, and for Ghelo, in this case, it is easier for him to
> throw the beast off balance by pulling it down. Each fighter
> has his own technique. There we are, watch out, the wall!
> Watch out, the wall. . . . And there you see the fighters.

Camaraderie among fighters is essential. All of them know how powerless one feels when it is not possible to fight due to injury. . . .

As Ghelo moves onto the next target, the announcer continues.

In this *corte de* Sabucedo, in this dance, in this fight of man and beast, the most important, apart from technique, is above all collegiality; the team that the fighters form, how they and the beasts understand each other when it comes to the fight.

He then explains how the cordon, which is formed on the mountains to corral the *bestas,* is also employed in the *curro,* as a few *aloitadores* will hold hands to protect their mates engaged with one horse from being trampled by others. But mostly the announcer wants to dispel the notion that the actions in the arena are perhaps haphazard and clumsy. He explains the effort to control the horse's head and obscure its vision.

There we go, there we go, let's go, Sabucedo! They are covering the beast's eyes. . . . Got it. A big applause! Look how they pull its tail, bringing the beast up so that it does not kick, throw it off balance. We will see how they get the beast and calmly shave the mane, because whenever beasts are shaved as they are standing up, the beasts get more nervous.

It is also important to choose the beast. There they are, all of them, taking a look. If you notice, they do not fight with two beasts at the same time, for respect and to avoid problems, they fight them one by one.

Then he adds, "The stallions mark their territory both in the wood-lands and here, in the *curro.*" This is inaccurate, I think, or certainly a distortion, as was his earlier suggestion that they are "territorial." Stal-lions police the boundaries of a band but they do not claim and defend distinct locations. But his commentary highlights something notable here: the stallions in the *curro* are not deploying their principal mark-ing technique of fecal displays. I've yet to see any of these horses empty their bowls in these tightly packed quarters. But I'm hooked on the patterns of his speech and imagery, so I just keep listening, especially when he draws the following parallel:

"We are all more packed than the beasts. . . ." It's an astute observation. We spectators are wedged uncomfortably close together, with shoulders, hips, and knees involuntarily touching. We certainly couldn't stay this way for long if not for the spectacle of the horses below. Before I can ponder this parallel further, the announcer calls out, "There it is the line of safety [cordon] that I mentioned before, while three shave the beast, the other fellow fighters protect them. A big applause, another beast shaved! There we go, there we go, riding that beast, let's go! They grip the tail while they shave it." Then he calls on the band to strike up a tune: "How about Retrouso playing another song? Come on Retrouso!"

He bellows, "There we go! There!" as another *aloitadore* lines up a horse for a jump. "He was aiming for one and eventually ended up with a different one. . . . Yes sir, an applause! It usually happens, it usually happens. . . . And there it is, there it is, how they pull the beast, how they hug it. There it goes. . . . Tumbling head to the ground, and there they lay hugging the beast because what these men feel for these animals is mostly affection."

Photographers rush from along the wall to snap close-ups of the downed assemblage of humans and horse. The next ride seems to go wrong from the start, partly because the humans are becoming a bit disorganized with the photographers dashing about. After the rider leaps on, Ghelo grabs the mare's tail with both hands, but one slips loose when he is tossed sideways into another horse, who gets between him and the mare he's holding. Ghelo regains his grip but the rider flies forward over the mare's head and disappears between the animals ahead. Two men charge out to clear the horses away from the prone rider, while Ghelo remarkably tackles the mare from behind. But she rises and surges, leaving him dangling, grasping her tail but dragged across the sand as the mass closes over him. Several other men from the wall leap forward to move the horses away; in tandem they have to pry Ghelo from his grip. As he stands blood gushes from his forehead. His comrades start ushering him out of the arena, but he has to be tugged along, resisting all the way. "Applause, applause for Ghelo," the announcer's voice rings out and the crowd responds appreciatively.

As the *aloitadores* resume their work, the announcer returns to another theme I've heard him invoke multiple times:

> Very close to here, in Campo Lameiro, you will see petroglyphs showing humans riding horses, just as you see here, bareback. Have you seen them? Have you seen the figures? Riding the horses just like the *aloitadores* are doing today. You must go see the petroglyphs.

I had indeed gone to see them, as had others around me in the stands. What's more, just a couple of weeks prior I had seen a recently uncovered collection of petroglyphs, thanks to Laura Lagos, who took us to visit a site being developed by archaeologist colleagues, Xosé Lois Vilar Pedreira and Xilberte Manso de la Torre. On a tree-dense hillside overlooking the river Minho, we crowded around a granite rock face to view a scene chiseled some three thousand years ago, of several horses being driven toward a circular enclosure, one that resembled the structure in which I now sat with several thousand conspecifics.[6] The historical trajectory between then and now is certainly dense, but what occupies my thoughts is how this particular cultural form and the rituals around it, of human and horse locked in a "dance," endures so animatedly.

Finally, after this dose of discourse and symbolism, I turn my attention back to the horses, for whom none of what the announcer has been saying matters at all. The violence today is just as intense, with rapid strike bites crackling around the *curro*. As with yesterday, their efforts to get facing the same way and to avoid facial contact are undermined each time a rider drives one of the herd crashing backward. Or as two stallions clash—rearing, shrieking, kicking, biting, crashing back to the ground. Or as another animal is driven to the ground to be sheared, and the humans clear space with a small cordon so the shearers won't get stomped. They are pushed repeatedly into the faces, backsides, and flanks of others. Still, even in the chaos I'm fleetingly able to make out individual horses.

Northeastern turns up for a minute or so almost under my feet as he's making for the north wall. I notice him first with his head resting on the back of a flea-bitten mare; rather than biting her, he seems the least aggressive of the stallions. Perhaps he recognizes her, though I don't. The throng shifts and now they're side by side; then it shifts again and she's perpendicular to him, initially twisting her head awkwardly out of his facial space. But as he doesn't bite, she relaxes and lowers her head beneath his nostrils. Suddenly Baldface pops up between them, also too close, but without any bites or bite threats from him; I assume because they recognize each other. But she's gone again in an instant and disappears from view. Northeastern too is shoved forward and I lose sight of him for a moment, until I see him off to my left, rearing up in a brief clash with Dark Brown.

Northeastern's **head-rest gesture** struck me, and I start looking for this affiliative signal around the *curro.* There's a mare resting her head on the back of a yearling not far to my right, and across the expanse of the herd I start recognizing it sporadically, mostly between mares. I also notice more widely dilated nostrils, reaching out, signaling inquisitiveness or interest, rather the opposite of aggression. Ears around the arena are pitching forward or angling to the side, conveying attentiveness, in contrast to the pressed low ears that indicate pending aggression. Snouts are extended not just as threats but to make contact across another horse's withers or buttocks. The difference is the mouth stays closed, the ears unpinned, and the nostrils open wide. I glimpse this briefly as a dark brown and a bay reach out to each other in a momentary lull from the churning. Then I see it again a couple minutes later; one mare's right nostril strokes the left side of another's face, who is pinned close by. I can't tell if it's a gesture of recognition or of comfort, but it is manifestly affiliative and not an act of aggression.

The nostrils seem to act much like the social gaze, taking in information while projecting interest; the nose, too, is an active social organ. As I grow more attentive to the expressive aspects of their nostrils, I realize how much sniffing is going on. They extend their heads not just to bite but to smell each other—to recognize a familiar scent, to check in with them: that's you; I'm here. What prompts and aids me in focusing on smell is the pressing scent of this hot, surging mass of horses and swirls of sand and fear and reassurance. Hours later, in the night, it's still seared into my nose, layered in with the aroma of eucalyptus. Sitting above them, I see the effort they expend sniffing and sensing. Notably with the stallions, too, who I now notice sniffing at the mares, refraining from biting some though they're crowding. The mares are doing this, too. I suspect at such moments familiarity mitigates aggressive acts or gestures.

I realize that, in tracking the violence, I am missing the face-work—the tactile and visual signaling seeking to sound out or reestablish social connections. That's partly because I initially thought of face in terms of abstractions of self, as a mental, internal image, from and against which a "line" is projected and gauged. But taken in concert, the active, expressive movement of ears and nostrils, along with the restraint of mouths and hooves, matches what Goffman referred to as face-work. It was hard for me to notice when I focused on aggressions, but I also hewed too closely to Goffman's formulation of the concept in relation to the assertion of status among humans.

"Face" involves the tenuous social self in coordination with other selves, supporting or challenging its "line." In humans, it operates in relation to representations we project of ourselves and perceive in others, and is subject to copious potential mistakes or failings. In horses, this social activity is likely less representational and more sensorial. Spatial dynamics underlie face-work for both species, but in the *curro,* I can see between these animals a range of expressive gestures that exactly support a performance of self and sociality. "Face" requires affiliative gestures to be sustained, and it is imperiled by aggressive challenges or responses. In this sense, these horses are both asserting and maintaining face through their sensitive social organs—eyes, nostrils, and ears—which comprise a larger signaling repertoire than humans possess. This is also evident in how exaggerated the facial expressions are in the *curro,* in contrast to daily life on the range. Where sociality is assured and stable, slight signals are sufficient; here it needs to be expressed in an exaggerated manner, lest any ambiguity be misconstrued as aggression.

Still, violence remains rampant as bites surge left and right. The stallions draw the most attention—Northeastern and Dark Brown rise again in a furious collision—but the mares bite those in their way with great gusto. They bite back against each other, responding to violent acts, but also against stallions. Yesterday I saw Chaparro receive several retaliatory bites to his face; today it's Dark Brown who gets crossways with a bay mare off to my left. Like yesterday, once the riders begin driving their charges into the mass, the ability to stabilize any social space around each other collapses. There was one exception that seemed to prove this rule: The flea-bitten mare whose head was up against Chaparro's seems to have a sister in the herd. I noticed them reaching out and touching nostrils as they pass close to each other. Roughly five minutes later, as this section of the mass stops churning for a moment, the two of them, from a distance of thirty meters apart, move toward each other. They manage to embrace, in a sense; their necks cross and heads rest on the other's backside. They stay entwined for almost thirty seconds, until a big bay stallion crashes in between them. I don't see them manage to get close again, but this instance of directed action is notable—though perhaps only to underscore how difficult such gestures are.

Now Northeastern is targeted by an *aloitadore*. Soon he's caught and secured, though they can't tackle him to the ground. After he's shaved and released I follow his trajectory, curious to see if the shearing changes his disposition and makes him more aggressive. He passes

FIGURE 3.17. *Two flea-bitten mares reach out across the malestrom.*

FIGURE 3.18. *Northeastern about to be sheared.*

off to my right, close to the high west wall underneath the media platform. His face gets wedged in between several mares, but he doesn't
bite them or kick at those behind him. His ears are angled a bit lower,
but not wedged down menacingly.

Even when he comes up against Dark Brown again, Northeastern
doesn't appear noticeably more belligerent. Mares clear the way as the
two draw close, faces just a few feet apart. For a moment they settle into
a parallel stance with a spatial buffer between them. As mares eventually crowd in, they still resist clashing. Dark Brown bites heartily at
those who press too close. But then they're at it—Northeastern rises
and kicks; Dark Brown rears too. Northeastern falls back and turns
away; Dark Brown bites his buttocks viciously. As mares press in again,
Dark Brown turns his full attention to biting at their encroaching faces.
Over the next ten minutes he repeatedly and animatedly keeps biting,
menacing, and kicking until a large bubble opens and endures around
him. By then the *aloitadores* are done.

The last ride and shearing completed, it's time to turn the horses back to the *peche,* after an hour and a half in the *curro.* A half-dozen men, including Ghelo, who returned bandaged, hold hands and form a cordon, steering the animals toward the just-opened gate. In a couple of minutes they're gone. The announcer explains to the crowd, "There are again all of the beasts mixed together, freed and going back to the *peche.* Once they get out of here the beasts go to the *peche,* on Cataroi, where they can drink and rest; it is the *peche* that you have up there, on the uphill road that turns left after passing by the *pulpeiros.*"

Despite his encouragement, only a handful of humans make the trek with me. The scene in the *peche* is familiar—the whinnies of foals and mares ring out as they repeat their desperate efforts to reunite. The elevated, searching heads belong to mares, not stallions. This time, though, I see more aggression, at least initially; more bite threats or kick gestures, especially as faces draw close around the trough at the foot of the hill. This time, I quickly spot Chaparro. He's hard to miss, both because he's big and because now he has a full erection. He's facing a mare's rear; it's Baldface! I'm glad to see her again, so from a distance of fifteen meters or so I settle in to see what unfolds. Over the next minute and a half, Chaparro loses his erection. I don't see proximate threats to him that might be a distraction. Baldface finally turns to her left, looks askance at him, then turns to her right, meandering past and up behind him. When she's back there, Chaparro makes a kick threat, but Baldface is unperturbed. Instead, she's stock still as he gradually turns around and comes up on her right side. They stand stationary like that for minutes, so I start up the hill to see what else is going on.

A quick scan of the slope suggests the horses are more dispersed than this morning. The vast majority are several body-lengths from each other, excepting yearlings and foals with their mothers. I quickly spot Star Black, following a flaxen mare whose foal is trying to nurse as she keeps shifting upward. He follows her for several minutes before peeling off to the far right side of the *peche.* I start mapping the configuration on the lower part of the *peche* when I hear a stallion shriek.

Star Black has settled in next to a white mare, bookended by her yearling and foal. But Dark Brown is charging up toward him from down nearer the gate, maintaining his violent disposition from the *curro.* But what unfolds is unlike the formless combat there; his approach is greeted with an arched neck threat from Star Black. The stallions lock into the ritual agonistic sequence—the first I've seen in the *peche,* amid all these stallions—bending around each other, sniffing intensely at the genitals, then neck wrestling briefly. Star Black positions for and then delivers a double rear kick; Dark Brown steps back but then thrusts alongside his rival before churning back down the hill as the mares scatter from the pair of clashing males.

With this unfolding of a conventional interaction, I wonder if perhaps the social structure is reemerging. Eventually Star Black moves out across the *peche.* I spot another stallion, alone, down in the flat of the meadow; then another one, also alone, above me low on the hill. They're both just grazing. Then below I see Baldface, also alone, moving toward the trough. I wonder that Chaparro hasn't followed her. Then I also spot Circle/Cross and her sister, heading toward the tree-line boundary on the west side of the *peche.*

Gradually I'm drawn upward, following the diffuse drift of the animals away from the lower *peche.* I pick a spot halfway up the slope and map the movement that unfolds over the next thirty minutes. To the west of me are four grays, three bays, and a dark-brown mare, focused on munching grass. One gray directs a bite threat at a bay, but she doesn't flash her teeth or make a grimace with her mouth, though her ears are pressed. It's an instance of a return to the symbolic assertion of social distance, and it's effective in moving the bay away. The heads of all these horses are askew to each other. Within two minutes, though, two of the bays and the dark brown have aligned their grazing efforts, facing in the same direction. To the left and right of this loose cluster are more than a dozen mares, each well spaced from the other. To the east are about twenty lone mares, all grazing. When I turn back from taking this count, the grays and bays, the dark brown, and the other horses off to the side are all grazing in the same direction, heads in parallel, slowly eating their way toward me. They're arrayed as pairs and a couple of trios. Over the next few minutes the space between them narrows gradually, until they cohere as a large cluster, moving in parallel.

I look around for the stallions. Below, I see Star Black has again found the flaxen mare and her foal. He contentedly grazes behind her as she rises up the hill. Above me on the slope, a flaxen mare has pulled alongside the lone stallion there; though the bay stallion down on the flat is still solitary. Of the six males I've spotted, two are following mares—both dangling half erections—and the others show little interest in anything like herding or even doing fecal displays. That they are content to follow mares underscores how little a social role they are playing at this moment.[7] The socializing that is occurring mostly involves mares positioning themselves in relation to each other.

It's time to leave them to rest and head back to review my photos and notes. Before I go, though, I do one last mapping from the entrance, looking out and across the *peche.* There are over one hundred and twenty horses in view. More than a dozen are in a loose grazing line in the center—the cluster of bays and grays. Behind them six more, moving in the same direction. Across the crest, horses are strung along but starting to bunch up a bit near the apex. Below, there are at least four clusters of six or more adults. Aside from these, the rest are mostly in pairs or trios. All of the foals seem to be accounted for now and trailing attentively behind mares, though there are fewer than at the beginning, since some have been culled for sale. I can't know if any of these clusters are reformulated bands, but in the two hours I'm in the *peche* it's clear that they've shifted from highly dispersed to more bunched together. So, absent a reemergence of their social structure, the capacity for sociality persists and is being enacted.

As evening descends, I start down the hill toward the village. After only a few steps I notice a tick on my right knee, then another just below it. Stopping to brush them off and check myself for more, I have a moment of rumination on the concept of *umwelt.* This idea was developed by ethologist Jakob Johann von Uexküll (1864–1944); using the tick as a model, he theorized that species uniquely perceive and experience "their" world in such a thoroughgoing manner that we can hardly speak of an objectively shared world. Though this is a subject of intense speculation for philosophical ethologists, I recognize now why it has so little bearing on my analysis. First, as Vinciane Despret notes, "the theory of the Umwelt is mostly fruitful for relatively simple animals."[8] It's deployed to identify perceptual cues that trigger certain behaviors in relation to environmental stimuli—such as the odor of butyric acid that prompted these ticks to leap on my leg as I brushed past them in the tall ferns.

For horses—as a highly social species—social context and structure matters as much as, or in a different register than, the environment. And this is the key reason why I don't rely on umwelt: because I'm analyzing these horses as social subjects. I don't need to access their subjective, perceptual experience of the world; I only need to observe their social interactions and reactions. Their sociality—as a subset of equids broadly—is one rendition of many versions of sociality across a range of species. Homologous with the social lives of zebras and donkeys, analogous with aspects of primate social dynamics, the sociality they manifest is an evolved capacity to maintain cohesive groups through affiliative bonds while also mediating forms of competition.[9] These parallels interest me more than using umwelt, as Despret proposes, "to divest the objective world of its familiarity and to make ourselves feel less at home in it." Rather than trying to comprehend or enter into the "strange" world of another species, the social subject inhabits a readily familiar one.

DAY 4

I reenter the *peche.* The stillness is deeper than the other mornings. Repeated rounds in the *curro* must be taking their toll. I move gingerly, not to rouse any sleepers. More horses are concentrated near the gate than before, so I start my mapping right away. At least forty horses are snoozing here in several clusters amid the fallen fronds and shed bark of the towering eucalyptus trees scattered around the low portion of the field. I've been jotting notes for only a few minutes when I spot Baldface. It looks like she's alone, but she's not; maneuvering around to get a better view I see Chaparro backed up against the fence just about where I saw him last, and he's ringed by about half a dozen mares. Who are they? In a minute of craning, I start making them out. There's Scimitar and Book; then I see Haloed Tee and her yearling flanking him closely on his right; Tufts is doing the same on his left, shadowed by her foal. Two yearlings I can't make out are standing beside Scimitar, and I think that's it. But it's not. About fifteen meters to the right are CF and Bloat and another dark-brown mare I've seen in the Mega band. After the extent of dissolution of social structure over the past couple days, I didn't expect to see a band reformed. Yet here they are.

Taking this in, I think about what I'm seeing. Yesterday Chaparro, like most of the stallions here, was isolated and defensive; today he's at the core of a partially reconstituted band. Remarkably, too, they've approximated the spatial formation I last recorded for them on the range (see Figure 2.12), as Baldface casts a distancing screen through

FIGURE 3.19. *Baldface on the left; Chaparro third from right; flanking him on his right are Scimitar, Book, and Haloed Tee and her yearling (both facing away); Tufts and her foal on his left.*

her relative proximity, and CF and Bloat, who were peripheral before, are so again. The band structure that had been shattered has coalesced once more. But how? Since I've not seen any herding by a stallion after Chaparro's initial effort two days ago with CF, I have to think the mares accomplished this. Perhaps Baldface played a key role after she found Chaparro at the conclusion of yesterday's *rapa*. Mulling all this, I start thinking about who's not here. Checking my notebook, reviewing my identifications, one missing mare that surprises me is Palm. She's nowhere around. Then I remember her male foal, who would've been culled already. Perhaps like the mares Laura talked about who leave a band when they lose a foal, she chose not to be here.

Now I decide to find Northeastern. The last place I spotted him was in a similar defensive position, backed against the fence but on the west side of the *peche*, so I head there next. Along the way, I see that band formations are still the exception—the hillside is strewn with lone mares, some with their foals. I pass one huddle of four mares and a foal; then I spot one of the dark-brown stallions in another cluster, standing close to and facing the rear of a bay mare. I notice he has one right rear cornet, so on the fly I name him Corny. Thinking I've found another band, I stop and take some pictures. But as I do, the mares get leery and start moving away—leaving behind the stallion and the bay he's right behind. So it wasn't a band after all. I pass one more stallion, a big bay, but he too is standing by only one mare. The males seem only interested in being companionate, not reconstituting bands.

As soon as I get close enough to start making out horses along the west fence, which here follows the remains of an old stone wall, I immediately spot Rabicana—her tail is so distinctive. And sure enough, there's Northeastern, hugging her left flank. But not just him; Circle/ Cross is there, too, a body-length behind Rabicana. Then I recognize Twink, on the other side of Northeastern, standing face-to-tail. Off to Rabicana's left, AP is standing also, at a respectful remove with her foal. And Mancha is nearby too, also with her foal, farther along the fence, but at a similar distance as when I came upon the Knoll band the last day on the mountain. Seeing Northeastern in this location along the fence reminds me of how he sheltered against the boulder that morning, with Rabicana and JB shielding him from Crazy Gray. I wonder where JB is, and in a moment I spot her too, standing a few feet from Circle/Cross, well behind Northeastern.

A lot of mares are missing from the ones caught up in the cordon three days ago. But the mares surrounding Northeastern are those I had noted as prominent in that band. Similarly with Chaparro, the mares around him were also prominent in the Mega band; and those that

FIGURE 3.20. *Circle/Cross far left (head only); then Twink and Rabicana, flanking Northeastern (compare to Figure 2.1 of Knoll band, with Twink facing camera); Mancha and foal, far right. AP and her foal are in the foreground.*

weren't, like CF and Bloat, were close but kept a distance. These are the mares who demonstrated the most agency in policing group boundaries or asserting social distance within these bands. So I have to assume that they are the ones who are reassembling the social structure here, given that I've seen them do that with consistency, and absent evidence of stallions herding. Indeed, in just a couple of minutes and with hardly moving a step, I observe other largely inactive stallions.

Corny has ambled over this way, alone; and he did so without riling that bay stallion I passed on the way over here, who's about thirty meters from me, still standing with that one mare. He's approaching the length of fence that laces north to the hilltop slope, where there are two small knots of horses. The closest is five mares (no foals) clumped almost touching under a tall broad pine. Over several minutes he noses closer, grazing as he goes, but they offer him no opening or contact. Gently glancing off this cluster, he eases toward the next bunch, twenty meters farther along the fence; low beams of the rising sun slicing through the oaks here are sharp in my eyes, so I have to shift a bit to watch what happens next. He pulls up alongside a dappled gray, who doesn't show much interest; but he stops and waits for a bit. As he does, three of the mares from under the pine move over to check him out.

As the mare in the lead approaches, they seem familiar. Their extended noses greet and he begins lightly grooming her neck. The dappled gray moves away, though, and to his surprise and mine, there's Star Black, lurking in her wake. That stallion lunges sharply at Corny, who scampers off about ten meters back toward me. Star Black gives a half-hearted chase and then turns back, but he's gone long enough that I can see in that small cluster another stallion; he's on the other side of two mares—one dark brown and the other gray. He may be familiar with them, but it's not obvious. Then, as Star Back strides back to the wall he comes in close with one of the mares who came over from the pine. When she doesn't move away, he drives a vicious bite to her right rear flank, and that does the trick. He next turns menacingly back toward the two mares along the wall who haven't moved. They shift away and that sets the bay stallion in motion, out toward the meadow. Only the gray mare follows him, though.

Besides Northeastern, who is ensconced between Rabicana and Twink and bracketed by Circle/Cross and JB, there are four other stallions right here. Two show interest in only one proximate mare. Corny may have found his band—the mares under the pine. The one bit by Star Black goes up to sniff at Corny afterward, but she's the only one; the others are proximate but don't pay him much attention. If this is a cluster of his band, then he found it already assembled. I consider for a moment if that might've been the case with the core remnants of Mega and Knoll, but I realize those situations are different. I'd consistently seen those two stallions hunkered down in those spots; it makes more sense that the mares sought them out and, finding them, slowly coalesced again. Or maybe the mares from the Mega band found Baldface yesterday as she moved across the *peche* after returning from the *rapa*. In any case, what struck me as a state of complete social dissolution yesterday has been significantly reversed in these two cases. Given that I'm sure about the prior prominence of these mares, again I have to assume they are the ones reconfiguring the social order.

Unfortunately, I don't have time to ponder this further. Several men have already arrived to start driving the horses down from the high pasture. I hadn't paid them much notice as they strode in, but soon I hear their whoops and hollers from above and I watch as the animals gush down from the hilltop. I hadn't realized so many were up there, and once again I'm mesmerized watching them flow past toward the gate. They dash past in several twisting strands, a couple hundred horses in motion, in loose unison over the ragged ground. They're all beyond me before I see even one of the men coming down from the top. The horses move together and stay well clear of these two-footed threats. It's time for the last round of the shearing, so I head to the *curro,* arriving just ahead of the herd.

The crowd has substantially thinned; less than a third of the seating is occupied. It's Monday and the celebration is winding down. I find a seat easily on the south side of the *curro* and enjoy a group of pipers through several tunes until they stop to let the horses enter. The first batch spreads out, but the two stallions, Star Black and Dark Brown, find each other quickly. They slide into the ritual of sniffing, with their necks locking together briefly, both snorting at the end before turning away. It's the first instance of conventional conflict I've seen in the *curro.* Star Black moves back toward the gate, while Dark Brown approaches the south wall; mares hurry away from him. One seems oblivious, though, until he glares at her; then she sidesteps to her left to clear out of his view. With the large amount of space they have at the moment, they're able to return to more conventional forms of signaling. Only about fifty horses are in the *curro* right now. But another batch enters before I can give this more thought.

More than a hundred arrive in the next wave, a very large batch. They try spreading out but space collapses rapidly. One entering mare gingerly extends her nose to a bay who was already in the *curro,* standing stock still. It's an interesting gesture—she reaches out with her nostril, touching briefly the other's left ribs, leaving plenty of space between them, then moves on. The bay stays still as the arrivals flood past her. She only moves when the swell of horses that reached the back of the *curro* have turned around, coming back toward her. Impressively, within seconds they are all facing the same direction; the only exceptions are in the bunch in the southwest corner near me, where faces are still being adjusted as they turn from their entering orientation. They are very quiet today, so far.

Then something surprising occurs. Dark Brown, who's maybe ten meters from me, defecates. It's the first I've seen that in the *curro,* and he does it deliberatively, first clearing space and then circling around the droppings afterwards. This is a fundamental gesture of boundary work for a stallion, and I've not seen it over the last few days. Within seconds, another stallion—a large bay—approaches assertively. He too circles the dung, sniffs it, then unleashes his own contribution, adjacent to Dark Brown's pile. Dark Brown aggressively jabs his nose toward the

FIGURE 3.21. *The "elevator effect" in the* curro.

other's genitals until a swift kick threat separates them both into parallel stances. The mares around them recede and then close back in. The bay angles off to the east, where he confronts another dark-brown stallion; Dark Brown circulates more toward the center, where he crosses paths with Star Black again. They both are rotating, trying to keep space cleared around them, but their efforts falter within moments. For all their edgy forcefulness, though, they've yet to explode in a clash. They seem to have settled into more ritual forms of contending with each other. Indeed, this seems a clear indication that conventions of sociality are reemerging within the *curro.*

The next batch entering has little room to do so; they have to push into the mass across the entrance. As they do, I notice a considerable difference from the first day of shearing. As the *curro* filled for the first time, bites accelerated quickly; their recipients reacted frantically, reeling backward or offering up an exaggerated head toss. Now there's little of all that. The collisions that occur near the gate are being absorbed fairly calmly. There are fewer bites in this choke point than previously. One entering mare ends up with her neck crossing that of another's; shifting her head to avoid that position brings her face alongside that of a bay mare turning to escape a bite threat from Star Black. In an instant the two are shoulder to shoulder though their torsos are oblique to each other's. Their faces are too close, side by side, but they both push forward away from the various threats without turning and biting each other's face. It's a moment of heightened civil inattention, underscoring the reemergence of conventional sociality in this fraught setting.

As Chaparro enters in this last wave, I take stock of the subtle differences I'm noticing today. He can't or is unwilling to push forward, though a trickle of mares angles past just to his left. They stall until another push from behind sends the whole mass of animals forward. A bay mare is distributing bite threats to everyone around; these are closed-mouth jabs, not bites, yet. After about a minute, Chaparro bites the buttocks of a mare and that section of the mass gives way, with a few intrepid horses finding a little room against the wall to my right, but soon they too are crunched shoulder to shoulder. What's different today is that the horses are better at holding their ground, using a combination of more muted responses to threats and bites and an apparently greater ability to hold steady in the face of constant competing pressures. In other words, they're finding and maintaining their footing.

This realization puts me in mind of Goffman's concept of footing, which he characterized as the "bodily orientation" of speakers and hearers, which alters frequently as speech flows through a series of code-shifts. "A change of footing," he writes, "is another way of talking about a change in our frame for events."[10] As a speaker shifts through a series of distinct speech types (direct or reported speech, interjections, separation of topic and subject, and so on), both speaker and hearer register these through alterations of bodily posture. Footing involves a participant's "alignment" or "stance" regarding a "strip of behavior," one that exceeds or falls just below the coherence of a single sentence; it operates along a continuum "from gross changes in stance to the most subtle shifts in tone," and "brackets" a "phase or episode of interaction." These brackets play "a liminal role, serving as a buffer between two more substantially sustained episodes."

Footing works remarkably well as a frame for thinking through how the horses are contending with and responding to this maelstrom where social distance is again dissolving. Goffman developed the concept of footing as he critiqued the "two-person arrangement" for modeling speech acts, in favor of acknowledging "that much of talk takes place in the visual and aural range of persons who are not ratified participants," that is, bystanders, people on the periphery, perhaps only in passing, as we speak to one another.[11] "Their presence should be considered the rule, not the exception." Goffman's invocation of a "physical arena" to model this larger, englobing "social situation" resonates well with the *curro* and helps me think about its challenging confusions: a mare might react to a bite from another mare only to crash into a third, who in turn either strikes or reels backward, setting off a cascade of unintended consequences. On this third day of shearing, what I notice most is that the horses seem far more cognizant of bites striking or directed at *adjacent bodies.* As the frenzy induced by extracting the foals commences, repeatedly I see roughly synchronized head snaps, as a horse three bodies over reacts to a bite hitting a neighbor. In Goffman's sense, they are "overhearing" or "eavesdropping" on violent acts and responding accordingly. The relevance of footing is heightened by his insistence that "in managing the accessibility of an encounter both its participants and its bystanders will rely heavily on sight, not sound" (132).

Like participants in social situations of speech, these horses are "constantly changing their footing" (128); they do so without relying on social space as a signaling medium. What they have instead are exaggerated gestures and a heightened responsiveness to the encounters of others around them. This brings a second dimension to thinking about footing here. Goffman found that the "management" of code-shifts between modes of speech and turn-taking operate "in the assessment of reception through visual back-channel cues, in the paralinguistic function of gesticulation, in the synchrony of gaze shift, in the provision of evidence of attention (as in the middle-distance look), in the assessment of engrossment through evidence of side-involvements and facial expressions—in all of these ways it is apparent that sight is crucial" (130).

With footing in mind, I focus on the knots and corners of stabilization, which are more plentiful than the zones where horses are physically clashing. One just to my left contains five faces in a rough line, inches from each other. To their right, a bay with a round star is biting the rump in front of her, pushing that horse forward while the dark-brown mare next to her responds by kicking at the face of the round-star bay, who, in turn, bites her backside. The dark brown lurches ahead to escape that bite—she can't advance, but her motion further compresses the five faces. At their center is a bay with a long star that almost connects to her longer stripe; let's call her Starstripe. I focus on her against a backdrop of constant jostling behind her. Directly in front of her is a two-year-old, wedged between a flea-bitten gray and a bay. To Starstripe's left is a big bay mare; to her right are two dark browns, one with a wide blaze and the other with a big stripe and a mustache. After these horses expand back in the wake of the first dark brown's incursion, Starstripe focuses on the two-year-old. She delivers two short, light nudges with her left nostril to the right back side of the younger horse's neck. The effect is direct: the two-year-old dutifully pushes forward, leaving slightly more space around Starstripe's face while forcing her own more uncomfortably into the flanks of the two horses in front of her. It's the subtlest gesture I've seen in the *curro,* and it's effective.

Meanwhile, the dark brown to Starstripe's right extends her neck over that of the dark brown with the mustache. She's moving her head, it seems, to get out of Starstripe's way but also to offer an affiliative gesture to Mustache, who is now being bit by the aggressive dark brown behind them. I notice too that the large bay on Starstripe's left is nuzzling her backside affiliatively with her right nostril, as is another mare behind both of them. Then in the gap opened by the raised neck of the dark brown, another head surfaces, also escaping from the round-star bay's continuing attacks. Starstripe briefly extends her nose affectionately to this mare's face, then turns back as the head of the wide-blaze dark brown comes down, not threateningly but abruptly. As the pushing behind all of them intensifies, they manage to hold their footing. The large bay extends her face to nuzzle the pinned two-year-old, then she rests her head on the rump of the flea-bitten mare just ahead. This requires twisting her neck to the right, so it's an intentional gesture, not simply a reflex. As this occurs, the horse that pushed in alongside Starstripe has pulled parallel with the horses to the right side of the two-year-old; this horse reaches her neck over the intervening backside to deliver a jab at the younger horse's face. Then she uses her right nostril to make an affiliative gesture to the rear end just ahead.

All this takes less than a minute. There's too much happening to account for it all at once, but I see here a Goffmanian "frame," one that emerges from their stabilized footing. These horses receive and extend a range of gestures, aggressive or affiliative, in a manner that starts resembling a highly compressed, concentrated version of how such signaling takes place in the generally languid settings of everyday life in a band. The presence of a clearly subordinate younger horse here probably helps ratify a sense of structure, which the older horses can assert, but this is also buttressed by the large bay mare's affiliative contact with several of these animals, including the two-year-old. Within a moment this frame shatters, as the pressure behind them swells with the first rider crashing up from that direction. The configuration is lost and the individuals are impossible to follow. But the footing of these horses briefly allowed them to stabilize something like a social order, and it revealed their dexterity in responding to countervailing threats and pressures.

As I'm thinking about how sociality is playing out here, I have a sudden "channeling the ancestor" moment. Maybe it's an effect of the heat of the day and the writhing horses, but I imagine Clifford Geertz sitting down next to me. I sit up straighter as he intones, "This isn't ethnography that you're doing, you know." Surely I've conjured him here through the resemblances to the Balinese cockfight, which are very much on my mind since animals are at the center of that ritual, too. As in Bali, the humans are ringed around the arena watching the horses intently, waiting for the outbreaks of violence that crackle through the herd. The "themes" of animality and fury are present here, too. Like the cocks, the stallions also clash in what Geertz described as an "explosion of animal fury so pure, so absolute, and in its own way so beautiful, as to be almost abstract, a Platonic concept of hate."[12] And there is no doubt the violence of these animals is seen as dramatizing many themes of cultural life for those who have traveled here to watch the horses' ferocity rise and fall. But that's not how the horses see it.

"This *is* ethnography," I retort. I'm observing and analyzing social subjects as they contend with a rapidly changing setting, one where their reliable social frames have largely been shattered. It's easy to channel Geertz's voice in response; I can draw, chapter and verse, from his classic work, *The Interpretation of Cultures.* "The proper focus of ethnography," I imagine him rejoining, involves emphasizing that this ritual, like the cockfight, "provides a metasocial commentary upon the whole matter of assorting human beings into fixed hierarchical ranks and then organizing the major part of collective existence around that assortment."[13] But horses too engage in this sorting process almost constantly, though ethologists vary in how "fixed" such hierarchies prove to be. Horses' lives, too, are lived "in a haze of etiquette," learned through lessons following directly from their birth into a social order that, like ours, precedes them. What's fascinating here, and fully worth ethnographic attention, is what happens to that social order in the thoroughly "unnatural" cultural setting of the *curro* and the *rapa.*

But Geertz is insistent that the proper focus of ethnography be on representations. The cockfight, he reminds me, is "an image, fiction, a model, a metaphor"; "the fight is a means of expression; its function is neither to assuage social passions nor to heighten them . . . , but, in a medium of feathers, blood, crowds and money, *to display them.*" As the announcer chimes in once more about how the *bestas* are also spirits of the mountain, I recognize how I could easily offer up that rendition of ethnography. But should ethnography be reserved for analyzing such displays? I think not. Ethnographic method has allowed me to avoid reproducing yet another account of representation and instead learn something about the social lives of these horses. And it's these social lives that are on display as much as the status concerns of men.

Geertz confidently concluded in his essay: "It is only apparently cocks that are fighting there. Actually, it is men." The cocks were relegated to symbolic status as representations: "cocks are viewed as detachable, self-operating penises, ambulant genitals with a life all their own"; and "the fact that they are masculine symbols par excellence is about as indubitable . . . as the fact that water runs downhill."[14] Horses here certainly perform similar representational roles, as the announcer reminds me, but think of what we miss in fixating only on that. Instead of regarding them as "symbols," I see their efforts at restraint and composure in this crushing mass of horse flesh, muscle, and sweat; efforts that parallel if not resemble the form of restraint Geertz highlighted among the Balinese.[15] Indeed, the horses' performance of restraint is emblematic of how ethologist Frans De Waal describes emotional self-composure in animals.[16]

Around me the crowd cheers as two stallions rear and clash—it's Chaparro and one of the bays. At my feet, on the rim of the rock wall of the *curro,* several mares contort and twist to get away. Geertz had to avert his attention from such distractions to arrive at the "sociological" truth of the cockfight, but that choice is no longer mandatory for ethnographers. He delineated his analytical object by asserting that the "crosswise doubleness of an event which, taken as a fact of nature, is rage untrammeled and, taken as a fact of culture, is form perfected, defines the cockfight as a sociological entity."[17] But in cultural anthropology, the confident opposition of "nature" and "culture" has collapsed; and for ethologists, the idea of "animal cultures" is taking hold. And the sociality of these horses opens an attention to what Geertz rather dismissively characterized as the "really real."

"The cockfight is 'really real' only to the cocks—it does not kill anyone, castrate anyone, reduce anyone to animal status." Rather, "it catches up these themes . . . ordering them into an encompassing structure . . . [and] puts a construction on them, makes them, to those historically positioned to appreciate the construction, meaningful— visible, tangible, graspable—'real,' in an ideational sense."[18] This representational sheen has been cultural anthropologists' analytical focus. But what of the "really real"? Why shouldn't that interest ethnographers, as well; why shouldn't that be part of what we analyze? We've formed our creed solely around representation and its construction for too long. Here, the "really real" of the horses is both legible and fascinating. Here, in the "small, cleared off space"[19] of the *curro,* they display their capacity for sociality in a wholly unnatural situation—confined and compressed, absent the signifying mediums of spatiality, which has collapsed in the brute fact of constant churning proximity and contact. Such **behavioral plasticity** generally falls outside the purview of ethology, which fixates on the opposite end of the spectrum Geertz lays out—"nature" rather than "culture."

I am not promoting a full-scale repudiation of Geertz's articulation of ethnographic "thick description" and how it has honed "the precision with which we vex each other" over decades. Certainly, we can continue "plaguing subtle people with obtuse questions, which is what being an ethnographer is like."[20] But what more can we learn about the world and others' social lives? The answer lies in detaching ethnography from the theoretical apparatus that informed Geertz's articulation: a text-based model focused on discourse analysis. As in, "The culture of a people is an ensemble of texts, themselves ensembles, which the anthropologist strains to read over the shoulders of those to whom they properly belong."[21] Or his assertion that ethnographic description involves interpreting "the flow of social discourse" and trying "to rescue the 'said' of such discourse from its perishing occasions and fix it in perusable terms."[22]

I won't rehearse here in full the turn away from this model, which has been underway for some time. John L. Jackson writes about it at length, championing "thin description" as a model to replace the "thick description" Geertz derived from Gilbert Ryle. What I will underscore is that Geertz's version of ethnography as an interpretive science (or perhaps art) was developed in response to the "observation-heavy" social science that dominated up through the 1970s and certainly remains prominent yet today.[23] For Geertz, "deep" and "thick" opened up subjectivities that were exquisitely aligned to place and fluent in subtle forms of signaling and response, engaging via perplexing and fascinating "texts." The nuance of such subjects is captured in the "wink," which Geertz also adapted from Ryle. When I first presented this project to my departmental colleagues, one asked me, also channeling Geertz, if horses wink. I don't know if they do but physically they can—they have three eyelids which they can variously contract. But this question turns more on why winking mattered for Geertz: he made the case for interpretive analysis by contrasting the wink with the twitch, which "carries no message." Geertz asserted that the target is the representational meaning of such messages. But horses use their eyes to signal and assess social relationships continuously, reproducing or preempting them with a glance, whether or not they wink. And such social signaling is both legible (it's intended for an audience) and worth studying in nonhuman subjects. This is why horses can be ethnographic subjects.

In turning from "thick description" I'm turning back, in a sense, to a more observational model of ethnography that Geertz was rejecting as "a matter of mere recording."[24] "Thin" is a reminder of how much we can actually observe of sociality, its boundedness, plasticity, and reproducibility; the legibility of horses as social subjects because the effects of their "looks" and presentation of "face" are quite observable. All via Goffman, who analyzed social dynamics by focusing on the observable "strips" of behaviors (gesture, spacing, timing, eye contact, and posture) without opening up the "deep" domains of an interpreting subject. In this regard, it bears noting that Geertz, too, drew upon Goffman in analyzing the Balinese cockfight, in characterizing it as a "focused gathering," easily mapping "a set of persons engrossed in a common flow of activity" for the formation Geertz struggled to identify: "searching for a name for something not vertebrate enough to be called a group and not structureless enough to be called a crowd."[25] But Geertz would surely understand this, for he warned in the closing passage of his essay "Thick Description" of "the danger that cultural analysis, in search of all-too-deep-lying turtles will lose touch with the hard surfaces of life . . . and with the biological and physical necessities on which those surfaces rest."[26]

This "dialogue" with Geertz absorbs my thoughts as the last round of shearing for the year wraps up. Today's conclusion is different. The *aloitadores* leave and the horses remain. Instead of letting them run up to Peche do Cataroi they'll be moved in a procession back to Peche do Castelo, across the highway, and to the base of the trail that leads back up to the range. I wait with the horses as the humans make their arrangements.

The wait stretches on past thirty minutes. The horses stay focused on the gate the entire time. Left on their own, they mostly all get facing the same direction. The rate of aggression drops drastically. The only bite threats and kick gestures I see are from the horses closest to the gate as the animals behind them push incrementally forward. The stillness of the *curro* now, still filled with horses, is striking.

Finally the gates open and the horses are led again through the village, out across the highway, and to the larger *peche*. From there, after a few hours rest, it's time to return them to the range. The *aloitadores* work them back up the track we all descended three days ago. They lumber up the steepening grade with quickening steps. Once they reach the lip of the basin where I waited for the humans on Friday, the horses fan out, with twilight falling, and the *rapa das bestas* is over for another year.

FIGURE 3.22. *Civil inattention reemerges, as horses manage a dearth of social space while waiting to be released back to the mountains.*

Conclusion

SPECIES-LOCAL ANALYSIS

This book is the result of fusing ethology and ethnography to study the social lives of wild horses in Galicia, Spain. This fusion was largely accomplished through melding their respective methodologies. A greater challenge arises in addressing the contrasting theoretical frameworks informing these fieldwork techniques and methods—evolutionary and social theory. By way of concluding, I will briefly sketch the contours of that challenge, but only after summarizing how I see this study contributing to rethinking ethological and ethnographic subjects. First, ethology.

When ethologists observe animals, they think and write in terms of "species-typical behaviors." This framework highlights the uniform characteristics of a species—observable and verifiable in any setting where its members may be encountered. These characteristics result from evolutionary processes and a species' interactions with particular environments, and they are largely construed as fixed behavioral dynamics. But if recent theorizing on animal cultures is to advance, it will need to attend to the more variable, diverse, and contingent aspects of social behavior: exactly what is meant by "cultural."[1] I characterize my approach here as a "species-local" account of horse sociality, formulated through an ethnographic attention to how horses responded to disruptive and unsettling situations.[2]

The value of a species-local account is that it can call attention to an elasticity, variability, and dynamism in social behavior that would not be evident in naturalistic settings, or that might be overlooked because of prevailing assumptions about behavior. For example, my observations on the importance of mare sociality were possible largely because of the unusual circumstance before and during the *rapa das bestas* in Sabucedo. But mare sociality also seems obscured by an overemphasis on stallions and the suspicion that dominance in mares may not confer

253

an evolutionary advantage.[3] Through a species-local framework, it was possible to see the active roles mares play in establishing and maintaining band social structure. My point is not to suggest that this is characteristic of all horses; rather this finding offers up a speculative means to reexamine horse sociality in other contexts.

The species-local account emerges from an ethnographic orientation toward the field. Some ethologists—ethnoprimatologists in particular—have been trying out various ways of adopting ethnographic techniques or theories in their field observations.[4] Broadly, this involves a more expansive sense of data and observation, a relational understanding of behavior, and a reflexive stance toward units of analysis and theoretical assumptions.[5] These efforts are particularly generative for thinking about forms of habituation between animal subjects and their human observers.[6] Here I will add that ethnography is more than a set of techniques or methods; it's an orientation toward sociality, seeing it as both emerging from and informing performances of relationships by interpretive subjects.

Context is foundational for these performative, interpretive interactions, as subjects are continually reconstituted through place-based interactions. Context is social, in contrast to the environment or genetics, the dominant explanatory frameworks for ethologists; as well, it is fundamentally subjective, which poses a great challenge for the objectivist methods and orientation of ethology. What I hope to have demonstrated in this book, though, is that these subjective dimensions are legible and observable, to the extent that they are expressed interactionally and are oriented toward or informed by a larger sense of group identity through dynamics of boundary work related to belonging within the group.

The other contribution I hope this book makes pertains to multispecies ethnography. Over the last decade, an attention to multispecies dynamics and relations has led ethnographers to see anew the nonhumans that reside within human worlds, opening up novel sites and lines of inquiry. This development is leading to a gradual opening up of the ethnographic subject. Initially in multispecies work, humans remained the centerpiece. Ogden, Hall, and Tanita observed in their 2013 review of these projects that, "rather than a topical redirection to the study of animals, plants, and other beings, or specific methodological innovations, multispecies ethnographers are making theoretical contributions by reconceptualizing what it means to be human."[7] Much of this reconceptualization turned on the ability to see and construe animals as "ethical subjects," analogous to humans. This marks a shift from initial "ethical concerns over the consequences of human exceptionalism" to seeing nonhumans as posing and possessing equivalent rights and forms of being. My concern is that the relatively easy transposition of an ethical framework from humans to nonhumans is foreclosing a greater engagement with ethological methods and knowledge, as I have pursued here. Without such an engagement, I worry that the insights and relevance of multispecies ethnography will be limited.

Radhika Govindrajan's *Animal Intimacies: Interspecies Relatedness in India's Central Himalayas* illustrates this transposition of the ethical subject to nonhumans. Setting out "to understand the complicated entanglements of people and animals in Kumaon," in the eastern portion of Uttarakhand, Govindrajan focused on how villagers engaged "with the difficult question of how to live an ethical life in relation to animals."[8] She found that villagers drew "inspiration for ethical conduct in the everyday knots of relatedness that drew them into a web of mutuality with animals," which served as a resource "to shake off the yoke of a (post)colonial imaginary that located backwardness and savagery in their very nature." But pursuing a broad concern with how relatedness is constituted across species lines required developing an ethnographic attention to the animals as well as humans. Govindrajan describes immersing herself "in the lives of animals much as I immersed myself in the lives of people: by spending long periods of time with them; by closely observing their preferences and habits; and by learning how to 'talk' to them through 'messages exchanged in gestures,'" referencing Donna Haraway. Govindrajan "came to really appreciate how paying attention—that is, sustained and careful attention—to what individual animals do over the course of their daily lives could yield valuable insight into their lives as empathetic, intentional, interpretive, and intelligent beings." Yet for all this inclusiveness of "animal subjects," orientation to the human remains foundational and irrepressible in this ethnography; this is an "ethnographic exploration of how relatedness is extended by humans to other-than-humans in Kumaon." In the end, her account is about "what it means to live an ethical life in relation to animals."

Animals, in this approach, are knowable to the extent they enter into constitutive relations with humans; in contrast, for ethologists, knowledge about animals is predicated on regarding them apart from human-dominated settings. Govindrajan examines "how reflexive exchanges between particular humans and animals, facilitated through an embodied, touchy-feely, language of mutual recognition and response, were crucial to their co-constitution as subjects." Including animals as ethnographic subjects also entails, for Govindrajan, rendering them as familiar ethnographic subjects, with a capacity for reflexivity "that is simultaneously intrinsic and relationally produced" and with an aptitude for narrative, "as crafters of stories about the world they inhabit."[9] Up to a point, though, a point that is also foundational to the ethnographic project generally: the "recognition of difference." Within relatedness, "difference had to be constantly and imperfectly negotiated"; and as "deep" subjects, their "inner lives and affective states" remain elusive and ever-receding, as Clifford Geertz would recognize. Govindrajan stresses, too, that these forms of relatedness do not "overcome or erase the ontological differences between human and nonhuman animals."

Confronting the perils entailed by the "translation of difference," Govindrajan invokes the partialness of ethnographic accounts, a point that I wish similarly to underscore with my own account of these horses in Galicia. But I also want to highlight what I gained by opting for epistemological concerns over ontological ones, by adopting and relying upon ethological method and analytics. For ethologists, animals are knowable as social subjects more than "deep," affective ones. However entangled the *garranos* are with humans, their sociality is an evolved capacity, one that is homologous with other equids and analogous to a range of other species, including humanity. Ethologists rely upon an evolutionary perspective, one that is also fundamentally about "relatedness," but across vast time scales. "Our biological kinship" with horses stems from our divergences from a common ancestor maybe 56 million years ago, but also crucially reflects our species' similar respective adaptations to savannahs.[10] The innovations in sociality this more "recent" development required, differentiated aspects of our sociality from our arboreal primate "cousins" and eventually brought us closer to horses.

This opens onto a broader concern than ethnographers typically address: what is sociality and how does it shape individual lives, whatever the species? Attention to humans alone cannot pose—let alone answer—these questions; our principal resource, "social theory," has for too long been construed solely in relation to our species. In theorizing sociality, social scientists have insisted upon the uniqueness of its manifestation in humans. But research on animal cultures, radiating out through our fellow primates to the cetaceans and even the birds, suggests the plasticity of "traditions" in other species is quite similar to that which characterizes our own version of culture. Humans have culture as a conserved feature of our primate lineage, but it is analogously paralleled in a range of other taxa. Cultural anthropologists' long-running fraught concern with defining culture is becoming yet more complicated, and multispecies ethnographers can open an intriguing new chapter in this discussion, if we are able to step out of our disciplinary comfort zone and attempt a far more radical interdisciplinary engagement with ethology.

The host of theoretical issues at stake in such an engagement are too elaborate and intricate to address here, but they are the subject of my forthcoming book *Social Theory for Nonhumans*—a companion book to this one and the capstone for a multispecies trilogy I began with *Care of the Species*.[11] What I will succinctly address here is a key methodological issue facing ethnographers pursuing multispecies subjects of how or whether to tap scientific expertise in developing our accounts and analyses of animals. As Govindrajan's work shows, this is not requisite; nonhumans can be made to fit the frame of a humanist subject. For that matter, cultural anthropologists are generally loath to draw upon or deploy scientific frameworks. In terms of multispecies ethnography, this is well illustrated in Juno Salazar Parreñas's ethnography of orangutan rehabilitation centers in Borneo. *Decolonizing Extinction* examines the relationships that develop between orangutans and the people who care for them.

Across richly detailed encounters, Parreñas narrates and thinks through how the question of the orangutans' point of view is a matter of uncertainty. Parreñas suggests, "We could turn to different kinds of experts to help us piece together what orangutan perspectives might be," but in purveying these, she cautions that "privileging a primatologist's perspective over all others limits our imagination to those with technoscientific expertise."[12] This is not just about ceding authority to science. Ethnographers are not disposed to make authoritative knowledge claims, preferring instead to offer up detailed accounts of the situatedness of relational lives in everyday life. Parreñas contrasts her account to ethnographies that "incorporate the vantage point of scientists or conservations," which end up reproducing the privilege of "environmental cosmopolitanism." Instead, she lays "emphasis on geographic specificity and what that entails by way of history, culture, sociality, and ecology, even when that specificity might lead to an emphasis of one species over others." I hope to have shown, through my ethological ethnography, that such specificity is not antithetical to scientific accounts of species; indeed, this characterization is emblematic of what I mean by a species-local account.

My first effort at formulating such an account is detailed in the last chapter of *Care of the Species*, "How to Interview a Plant." In the Jardí Botànic de Valéncia, I strove to render up several plants as ethnographic subjects. I did so by drawing on a range of techniques for observing plants, some from philosophers but also from botanists. To an extent my efforts were stymied; what interests me most—their sociality—remained largely inaccessible, circulating in their rhizospheres underground and slipping past me aromatically on the breeze. But I succeeded on two fronts. One was in formulating an account of species formation in a dense urban setting, in a register that diverged from how botanists would describe and characterize species. The second was in making a case for using ethnography to theorize species. Part of the resistance to tapping scientific forms of expertise, I think, lies in not recognizing exactly this potential and capacity to formulate theoretical accounts of nonhumans beyond the penumbra of human social relations.

In this book I attempt both to model how ethnographers might take up and deploy other forms of expertise—ethology especially—and to show what might be gained from doing so. But I have also transposed concepts from social analysis on humans—such as face, civil inattention, and footing—to highlight the conventional aspects of horse sociality. When the social structure dissolved in the *peche* and when social space as a signifying medium collapsed in the *curro,* sociality became unmoored and undermined. This situation was reversed as mares reassembled the social structure and as stallions returned to more ritual forms of combat, and conventional modes of signaling distance and proximity both reemerged and were sufficient for reasserting and navigating relationships. Using Goffman's concepts, as horses regained their footing, they were able to practice civil inattention more widely, and the dynamics of projecting and maintaining face reemerged. I stress "conventional" here because, in contrast to acts of open violence, these behaviors and gestures are principally symbolic or signifying: they engender responses that reproduce or contest the social organization but do not undermine it. The role of conventionality is both a reflection of and response to the plasticity and multiperspectival aspects of social dynamics, where social subjects are co-constituted and incessantly engaged with interpreting others' actions and positioning.

In this regard, I hope to have modeled how ethnography may be both useful to and adoptable by ethologists. The basic contribution that ethnographic approaches can make is providing a nonmechanistic perspective on social dynamics across a range of taxa. This would enhance current stimulating discussions of animal social behavior. Ashley Ward and Mike Webster frame this epistemological moment in *Sociality: The Behaviour of Group Living Animals*: "Despite the fact that we are able to identify social attraction as the fundamental unifying mechanism underlying social groups, there is an apparently bewildering diversity in the expression of sociality both within and between animal species."[13] Species largely vary across an axes of two continuums: the tendency to associate with conspecifics (from weak to strong, or facultatively to obligatorily) and difference in the structure and organization of social groups (more or less restrictive membership). Each of these continuums offer potential entry points for ethnographic approaches. With the first, Ward and Webster highlight how "individual members of a social species can vary in their overall sociality"; here, ethnographers could be attentive to how this varies not just by "animal personality," but as an outcome of relational dynamics within or between groups. Certainly, "individuals may adopt sociality to a greater or lesser extent according to their immediate environment and in particular the level of threat"; but they may also do so in response to boundary work and dynamics around social space playing out between coalescing or dissipating clusters of individuals.

The second continuum, concerning social organization, is more pertinent to the subject of this book, particularly in relation to the fission-fusion dynamics of equids. As Ward and Webster note, fission-fusion has been studied across the vertebrates, from ungulates to cetaceans, bats to elephants, and of course primates. That's because "fission and fusion provide a highly responsive means for social animals to adapt to changes in proximate social and environmental conditions."[14] Though they champion a progression from initial qualitative formulations to more quantified ones, I hope to have made the case here that an ethnographic perspective can still be part of this analytical discussion, if only because ethnographers are astute about all that might fall from view in the process of quantification. Efforts to delimit observable behavior and objective conditions potentially obscure relational dynamics that are fundamental to sociality. Consider the central challenge of understanding fission-fusion, as posed by Ward and Webster: "Determining the relative roles played by environmental factors, such as resource distribution, and *socially mediated decisions of individuals* to remain with or to leave a group is a current challenge in social behavior research." These "relative roles" are not discrete; they are enmeshed in what social actors understand to be *context*: this can be formulated abstractly, in advance, but it should also be approached as something interpretively perceived and constituted by social actors sorting out their relationships to each other and to conspecifics in other groups. This requires an openness to such interpretive processes that are at the core of ethnography.

Working out the dynamics of attraction, repulsion, and alignment in social group formation is perhaps most interesting when we broach questions of self-organization and emergence. These "rules of interaction" or "social forces" are where we can add a third continuum to the above axes—degrees of conventionality or "culture." As Ward and Webster relate, self-organization involves the emergence of group-level patterns through multiple local interactions: "Patterns manifested by groups cannot be predicted on the basis of a full knowledge of the local interactions between individuals"; "the outcome of a process is not directly proportional to its cause," which may be amplified or dampened as a reaction "spreads between individuals within the group."[15] This version of emergence, they add, is predicated on "the important caveat that each individual animal acts in response to local information and without reference to the global pattern." But if "animal culture" is to have any real bearing as a concept guiding observations of animal behavior it must be in positing or at least considering the opposite proposition—that individuals have imbibed and are well aware of the "global pattern," that is, their culture. Collective dynamics and forms of identity need to be seen as emergent in a social sense; not simply as "interacting individuals [who] cause patterns to emerge at the group level" but as a set of forces conditioning those very interactions.[16] That is, the "rules of interaction" not in terms of the "biological realism" that Ward and Webster emphasize, but in terms of the forms of habituation that precondition the constitution of biological individuals in any group context or social milieu. This is something ethnographers are keenly trained to observe and analyze.

I will close by noting that the version of ethnography I have infused with ethological techniques in my study of *garranos* above the village of Sabucedo is rather narrowly focused on interactions. I have used this version purposefully, because it provides the most affordances for transposing concepts like face across social species. But as Parreñas makes clear, ethnography is more commonly associated with a specific attention to the historical, political, and economic forces shaping localities and infusing particular social contexts. Wherever animals reside, however their social groups are constituted, they are in some manner—great or small—already impacted by humans. These impacts can be both tallied and factored into accounts of how animals behave in the wild.

Acknowledgments

This book was instigated by Jaime Mata-Míguez, to whom I am forever grateful. Jaime was a graduate student in our biological anthropology program when I was developing a rather pedestrian next-project on efforts to rewild horses in Extremadura and Cantabria, Spain. Jaime encouraged me to check out the *rapa das bestas* in his native Galicia, and he helped me make initial arrangements to visit the one in Sabucedo. Without his prompting and encouragement, this book would not have come about. But I would not have had the wherewithal to undertake and complete this work without the expert guidance of horse ethologists Laura Lago and Victor Ros. For my time in Sabucedo and Quireza, I am indebted to Juan Carlos Bouzas for introducing me to the horses on the Montes de Montouto range, and to Jen Kemp and Tracy Mulligan for their hospitality and good cheer. ¡Abrazos a todos!

I also received encouragement and inspiration from a host of horsey colleagues in the United States. Erica Tom, Sarah Elizabeth Platt, Karen Dalke, Lee Deigaard, Claire Brown, and especially Jeannette M. Vaught all played roles in helping me formulate what this project would eventually be about.

For the real grinding-it-out work of making sense of what I observed and rigorously analyzing these dynamics, I am indebted to a number of wonderful colleagues. The quality of all I do continually stems from and reflects the expertise of the members of my department of anthropology at the University of Texas. Conversations and debates with Rebecca Lewis, Chris Kirk, Tony DiFiore, and Aaron Sandler (on the biological side), Jason Cons, Courtney Handman, James Slotta, Craig Campbell, and Kelsie Gillig (on the cultural side) pushed me to think more clearly about what it was these horses were doing in Galicia. Ranging a bit more widely at UT, and particularly the American studies department, I drew inspiration, as usual, from Janet Davis, Randy Lewis, and Steve Hoelscher. Without all of their prompting and prodding, this would have been a lesser book. Finally, a word of thanks to Jean Langford, who was an excellent reviewer of the final manuscript, and to Mary H. Russell, who did a superb job of copyediting.

As always, my love and gratitude to Rebecca Lyle for putting up with me through all these intellectual forays.

Notes

1. See Vilar Pedreira (2014) and Xilberte Manso de la Torre (2016); both of these archeologists allowed me in 2016 to view additional recently uncovered petroglyph scenes.

2. For more on the distinctive features of these horses, see Iglesia Hernandez (1973) and Bárcena (2012).

3. On the history of breeding horses in Spain, see Alves (2011), and more generally, Derry (2003).

4. Zoologist Felipe Bárcena (2012) speculates that these horses, which he terms *garranos,* are a subspecies of wild horse, *Equus ferus atlanticus,* since they are morphologically distinct from European domesticated horses: smaller in stature, yet stockier. Also see Manso (2016).

5. According to European Union regulations, they are "Equidae living under wild or semi-wild conditions," thus exempt from receiving mandated Universal Equine Life Numbers, but the Galician government has not applied for this exemption and regulates them as feral livestock. More broadly, on redefining "wild" in the Anthropocene, see Lorimer (2015).

6. See Laura Lagos Abarzuza, Picos, and Valero (2012).

7. For a contemporary account, see Laura Lagos Abarzuza (2013 and 2014), as well as Nuñez (2016). Historically, see Iglesia (1973). These techniques are indicative of interspecies dynamics, as described by Coulter (2016) and Orr (2016); on dynamics of herding more broadly, see Fijn (2011) and Ingold (2009).

8. On domestication dynamics in northwest Iberia and especially nearby Campo Lameiro, see González-Ruibal (2005) and Estévez and Veiga (2018).

9. The *rapa* in Sabucedo sporadically generates media protests by animal rights groups, but none (to my knowledge) have demonstrated in person.

10. These men are construed as wrestling with the "mountain spirits" embodied in the horses and illustrate the heavy symbolic emphasis placed on the horses, a discursive form of mythmaking surrounding this particular event—quite in contrast to other *rapas* in Galicia, which are regarded principally as labor.

11. On the distinctive history of the *rapa* in Sabucedo, see Manuel Cabada Castro (1992).

12. Many attendees are also sons and daughters, along with grandchildren, of villagers, returning for family vacations.

13. For other ethnographic approaches to animals under stressful circumstances, see Langford (2017), Parreñas (2018), and Blanchette (2020).

14. On the uses of horse hair, see Iglesia (1973).

15. Drawing on foundational work by Robert Hinde (1979) and Hal Whitehead (2008), Prox and Farine define social structure as "the emerging property of the ways of interaction between individuals" (2020, 792). They discern three levels to this structure, beginning with the "surface structure," which is "the social structure as perceived by the observer. The two layers leading to this are interactions and the relationships that arise out of such successive interactions. Social structure emerges from relationships of individuals and determines them at the same time." Here I emphasize the latter point, that individuals both generate and are shaped by this emergent form.

16. Multispecies ethnography is a rapidly developing area of inquiry. For overviews see Kirksey and Helmreich (2010), Ogden, Hall, and Tanita (2013), Wilkie (2013), Smart (2014), and Watson (2016). In addition to individual ethnographies referenced below and discussed in the conclusion, see Moore and Kosut (2013), Jerolmack (2013), Van Dooren (2014), Baynes-Rock and Thomas (2015), Locke (2017), and Moore (2018).

17. This development is strongest in primatology. See Malone et al. (2014), Jost Robinson and Remis (2018), and Riley (2018).

18. See Lestel (2006), Lestel, Brunois, and Gaunet (2006), Lestel (2014), Van Dooren (2014), and Chrulew, Bussolini, and Buchanan (2017).

19. Ritual analysis offers two prominent openings for multispecies ethnography. First, since many rituals feature animals, they are choice domains for incorporating nonhumans in a social analysis, revising or expanding upon their delimited roles as either food or food for thought; see Remme (2014), Peterson, Riley and Oka (2015), and Govindrajan (2018). Second, since all vertebrates have rituals—conventionalized behaviors that are more communicative than functional—they are a leveling analytic that applies across species. For biologists, ritual references "behavioral patterns and accompanying physical features which do not serve any immediate purpose but exist for communication." The ethological theory of ritualization examines "development of signals and symbolic actions" in nonhumans; "the biological term may denote the stylization of any perceptible element of animal shape or behavior under the selection pressure of communication" (Baudy 2006, 347, 349). For an intellectual history of the ethological attention to ritual, see Burkhardt (2005).

20. Though it remains prominent, Geertz's account has been the subject of two broad criticisms—one in the 1980s, by way of articulating key positions in the emergent self-reflexive turn (see Roseberry, 1982; Crapanzano, 1986, 68–76; and Clifford 1988, 38–41), and another addressing problems or

limits to his rendition of ritual analysis (Bloch, 1986; Bell, 1992; Turner, 2006; and Baudy, 2006).

21. This and the following quotes from Geertz (1973a) are on pages 417, 437, 443, 420, 424, 444, 447, and 448.

22. On how cultural anthropologists have rethought the opposition of "culture" to "nature," see Strathern (1992), Descola (2013), and De la Cadena (2015). In *Aesop's Anthropology* (2014), I articulate my own effort at a "post-dualist" definition of culture.

23. On broad formulations of animal culture, see Laland and Janick (2006), Laland and Galef (2009), Snowdon (2017), Schuppli and van Schaik (2019), and Brakes et al. (2019).

24. On culture among cetaceans, see Whitehead and Rendell (2015); among birds, see Aplin (2019).

25. This stance is more fully articulated in Geertz (1973b), "Thick Description: Toward an Interpretive Theory of Culture," but it is abundantly evident in the Balinese cockfight essay, as well.

26. By Geertz's own account, this is a distorting exaggeration; the Balinese men are "cock-crazy": they "spend an enormous amount of time with their favorites, grooming them, feeding them, discussing them . . . or just gazing at them with a mixture of rapt admiration and dreamy self-absorption" (418–19) and could as easily be read as models for thinking through multispecies relating. Further, see Hugh Raffles' account of the "deep ontological connection between people and crickets" that informs cricket-fighting rituals in China (2010, 74–115).

27. Horse ethology is quite developed and amply cited below, but initially, for overviews, see Berger (1986), Godwin (1999), McDonnell (2003), Waring (2007), and Krueger (2008).

28. Fission-fusion refers to the plasticity or dynamism of social systems where spatial cohesion and individual belonging to a group shifts over time, "vary[ing] from highly cohesive with stable group membership to highly fluid with either relatively stable or flexible subgroup membership" (Aureli et al. 2008, 628). Konstanze Krueger writes, "The social lives of equid herds can be compared to the fission-fusion model of other social mammals. Like groups of apes, elephants, and dolphins, they frequently split and reunite again. The social groups of most equids are much more stable, even though stallions may change their reproductive strategy and therefore their social affiliation several times throughout their lives" (2008, 196). Mares, she notes, will change groups too, depending on predation pressure and resource availability, even later in life.

29. Social distance is an old concept in sociology, originating with Georg Simmel (best expressed in his essay, "The Stranger") but elaborated and applied by Robert Park (1924) and Emory Bogardus (1925). Park and Bogardus developed this unit of analysis to examine white Americans' fierce

anti-immigrant sentiments in the late 1910s and early 1920s. White "race consciousness," they found, was expressed through both a geometric and metaphorical sense of "social space," such that, for whites, people of color are projected to be more distant—physically and symbolically—from the unmarked "in group." Erving Goffman (1959) used the concept to characterize efforts to draw physically closer to those we perceive to be similar in status, while insisting on a greater remove from those deemed lower. I use social distance here to convey the interpretive and performative work of social subjects to position themselves relationally within the band social structure. I find that prominent mares both assert and are recognized to have a status constituted through a malleable distance from others. On the combined geometric and metaphorical dimensions of this concept, see Ethington (1997), and Wark and Galliher (2007).

30. Efforts to find a modern identifier for this potentially quite ancient population are inflected by varied interests in developing breed horses from this stock. That aside, the field research on these horses is developing quickly. See Morais et al. (2005), Ringhofer et al. (2017), Matsuzawa (2017), and Inoue et al. (2019).

31. See Lagos (2013).

32. On face see Goffman (1955); on civil inattention see Goffman (1972); and on footing, see Goffman (1981).

33. Chriss (1993, 476–77).

34. Goffman (1989, 125).

35. Krueger finds that eavesdropping—when uninvolved bystanders "listen in" on dyadic encounters between other group members, which is evident among birds, fish, and bats—is widespread among horses: "horses appear to similarly observe their social environment and utilize information they draw from monitoring interactions among others" (2008, 202). I also use Krueger and Heinze's discussion of social cognition. They find that horses, like other animals that live in stable social groups, "need to gather information on their own relative position in the group's social hierarchy, by either directly threatening or by challenging others, or indirectly and in a less perilous manner, by observing interactions among others" (2008, 431). They note, too, that such indirect inferences of dominance relationships have previously been reported from primates, rats, birds, and fish.

36. Wathan et al. find that, in the complex anatomy of horse facial muscles, "there are a surprising number of similarities with humans and other primates" (2015, 16).

37. On horse visual acuity, see Timney and Keil (1992), Murphy, Hall, and Arkins (2009), and Tomonaga et al. (2015).

38. On analyzing modalities of horse attention, see Wathan and McComb (2014), and Waring (2007).

39. On the social gaze in humans see De C Hamilton (2016), Shepherd (2010), George and Conty (2008).

40. On the social gaze in nonhumans, see Schilbach (2015); Shepherd and Platt (2012, 537–539); and Emery (2000).

41. This point is summarized succinctly by Fureix et al., "Horses have a repertoire of graded visual signals that enable other animals to assess the intentions of the emitter" (2012, 219).

42. These quotes from De Wall (2016) are on pages 71, 73, 75, 148, 200, 176, 221, and 222.

43. My use of sociality is informed by Sally Anderson's discussion of this concept (2015). Her definition builds off of a formulation by Tim Ingold (2000, 196), which construes it as "the resonance of movement and feeling, stemming from people's perceptual monitoring and mutually attentive engagement in shared contexts of practical activity." She adds that it manifests "in observable patterns of relationality," such that "we ought to think of sociality as the constitutive potential of always emerging relational fields" (2015, 100), though she cautions it works best "as a heuristic device . . . rather than becoming an analytical category" (101). I add to this formulation the recognition that sociality is evident in social species broadly, not just humans. For ethologists, sociality is framed in mechanistic terms and equated with "rules or interaction" or "social force" covering attraction, repulsion, and alignment (see Ward and Webster 2016, 33–34). In "animal studies," the concept draws more upon "psychological studies of emotion and affect" and is formulated as "affective attunement" (Willett and Suchak 2018, 371). But this rendition is part of a larger framework that can overlap with an ethological perspective; as in "Animals synchronize through multiple sensory modalities to forge social fields where cooperation, competition, and predation are at stake" (380).

44. Social space is a concept with many facets and a long history in social theory; it refers to localized interactions through which group identity is produced and reproduced. I use it here to analyze perceptions and positioning related to distance and proximity by which social identities are established or contested, and boundaries of group belonging and exclusion are navigated. This entails ongoing interpretive and performative work by social subjects. For an overview of this important concept, see Reed-Danahay (2015), and for ethnographically informed analysis of social space, see Reed-Danahay (2019).

45. Quoted from De Waal, *Mama's Last Hug* (2019, 230).

46. I draw my use of this concept from Michèle Lamont (1992), who defines it as a dynamic, ongoing process of demarcating group belonging in variously exclusive or inclusive manners. Boundaries are negotiated and performed by differently situated social actors, who are continuously assessing relative differences between themselves and others. On boundary work over "biological" and "social" explanations in evolutionary and social theories, see Meloni (2016).

47. For horses, spatial proximity and distance comprise a signifying medium by which they interpret and express relationships through conventional signaling gestures and acts. Wolter, Stefanski, and Krueger write: "Spacing behavior demonstrates social bonding, as horses that stay close to each other are more likely to prefer each other"; they also exchange information about other "bonded and potentially bonded group members" through affiliative approaches, as well as mutual grooming (2018), 8.

48. Waring (2007, 61–62).

49. This assertion is also made by Govindrajan (2018); Birke and Thompson (2017) and Coulter (2018), do so too, particularly with horses in mind. For other recent ethnographic work involving horses, see Vaught (2018), and McKee (2014).

50. With animal signals, "conventional" identifies behaviors that evolved to be communicative rather than functional (as in sustaining an organism). John Maynard Smith developed this perspective by focusing on conventional aspects of mating rituals, which allow animals to avoid the violence of engaging in "total war" without restraint during a competition (Smith and Price, 1973; Smith 2003). Bradbury and Vehrencamp, in *Principles of Animal Communication*, offer this definition: "Conventional signals are those in which the coding scheme's assignment of alternative signals to alternative conditions is *completely arbitrary*. . . . The assignment of these signals is a coding convention that is shared by senders and receivers" (2011, 296). This formulation of arbitrary signs, while close to a linguistic definition of convention, covers a far wider gamut of visual features and nonverbal behaviors.

51. In framing violence ethnographically, my sources range from Bloch (1986) and Daniel (1996) to Parreñas (2019).

52. On politeness in other species, see Haraway (2007) and Kirksey (2015), along with my use of the concept with plants in Hartigan (2017).

53. Dominance, as will be discussed on these pages, is an enormously complex concept, especially with horses. I began with a mistaken assumption that ethologists construe it in reductively biological terms; instead, they regard it as "an attribute of the pattern of repeated, agonistic interactions between two individuals, characterized by a consistent outcome in favour of the same dyad member and a default yielding response of its opponent rather than escalation"—even stressing that "dominance is a relative measure and not an absolute property of individuals" (Drews 1993, 283). Yet the objectivist tendencies of ethologists—observationally and analytically—often reduce its nuance and contingency. The in-text quote is from Feh (2005).

54. For an initial critique of this use of "harem," see Linklater (2000). For more nuanced accounts of how various factors (e.g. personality and affinities) play a role in horse social structure, see Briard et al. (2015), Krueger et al. (2014), Heitor and Vicente (2009), Heitor et al. (2006b).

55. This finding is not entirely novel. As Konstanze Krueger comments,

"Whether mares form alliances against other mares or with stallions has as yet not been demonstrated, though mares play a much larger part in the social lives of horse herds than stallions do" (2008, 202). But this basic fact often is overlooked, ignored, or obscured by research fixated on stallions, or the degree to which "harem maintenance" remains the staple of observation and analysis. The original aspect of my finding is that I reach it through observing the collapse of horse social structure during the *rapa das bestas* ritual; this allowed me to recognize mares' roles in reconstituting the social organization of bands, absent efforts at "harem maintenance" by the stallions. Hence, I argue that the maintenance and reproduction of social cohesion should not be equated with what stallions do.

56. The contrast between behavioral models in the natural sciences (inherited and innate) and those in the social sciences emphasizing the performance of mutable social roles and identities is clear but should not be overdrawn. Ethologist Dorothea Baudy writes, "performativity is at least an implicit feature of ritual behavior that has been seen since [Sir Julian] Huxley's earliest research." Among animals, she finds that, "insofar as ritual is usually interactive, ritual communication has nearly always a performative sense" (2006, 356). In particular, she aligns this with anthropologist Victor Turner's notion of "social dramas."

1. INTO THE FIELD

1. My ethnographic approach to such populations draws from Lorimer (2015), Kirksey (2015), and Tsing (2017).

2. "Dam" is typically used to identify a foal's female parent, but neither Laura or Victor used the term as we worked.

3. Terms for behaviors and behavioral patterns characteristic of the horse ethogram, as well as those that are ethological units of analysis, will be in boldface on first use.

4. For examples, see Stewart (2007) and Berlant and Stewart (2019).

5. The term "subadult" covers yearlings and two-year-olds; we used it when this age difference was difficult to discern, generally at a distance.

6. Sally Anderson distinguishes these two definitions. One, "focusing on evolutionary and ontogenetic developments of cooperative behavior, treats sociability as universally recognizable and measurable behavior generic to animals and humans." The other, "referencing modern concerns with social cohesion and concord, treats sociability in the plural as a wide range of organizational forms, joint activities, venues, hierarchies and norms of social behavior among particular categories of people living in different places and eras" (2015, 99). However, my biological anthropologist colleague Rebecca J. Lewis is convinced every aspect of the second definition pertains to primates broadly, not just to humans.

7. Briefer et al. (2015).

8. On the prevalence of friendship in nonhumans and its substantial health benefits see Brent (2015) and Brent et al. (2014).

9. On the philosophical dimensions of such naming practices, see Hearne (2016); on the history of ethologists developing the capacity to identify individual animals in field studies, see De Waal (2016).

10. As described by George Waring, "Interactions between stallions commonly involve ritualized displays, unlike other forms of agonistic behavior in horses. . . . Ritualization has provided a means for horses to interact and to demonstrate dominance without resorting to violence" (2007, 262).

11. Berger reported that "dominance appeared inconsequential in Granite [Range] females," dismissing its relevance to mares, since "dominance seems to be of little biological importance and had no effect on female reproductive success" (1986, 158–59). He suggested this "probably stemmed from the fluctuating ranks held by females at different periods of the year," further noting that "dominance relationships changed regularly and most often over periods that spanned a few days to several weeks" (158).

12. Lorenz characterizes three basic functions for aggression: "balanced distribution of animals of the same species over the available environment, selection of the strongest by rival fights, and defense of the young." Lorenz found it "hard to say whether it is a paradox or a commonplace that, in the most intimate bonds between living creatures, there is a certain measure of aggression." In the social structure "of society among highly developed animals," he emphasized the role of "ranking order" in limiting open fighting among conspecifics (1963, 43–44).

13. Waring notes, "Foreplay and time for full arousal are necessary for successful horse breeding" (2007, 165).

14. Waring: "Expressions of forward attention are characterized by anteriorly directed orientation for reception of visual, auditory, olfactory, and sometimes tactile cues. The ears are up and rotated forward. The eyes are directed forward and appear to emphasize the binocular visual field. The neck and head angle adjusts to facilitate use of the sensory receptors. An elevated neck with head flexion is used for distant visual inspections" (2007, 274).

15. On staring by stallions, see Waring (2007, 262–63).

16. Waring notes, "Most aggressive interactions between stallions are the result of bands passing too close together or because of disputes over male status and conflicts over mares" (2007, 264).

17. The components of this "ritualized interactive sequence" between males are characterized by McDonnell as: 1) stand and stare (alert); 2) posturing (arched neck threat); 3) olfactory investigation; 4) strike threats, pushing, squealing, and snorting; 5) fecal pile displays; 6) repetition of previous elements, often with increasing intensity (2003, 166).

18. Fecal pile display is a behavioral sequence in which two or more stal-

lions approach a mare's dung pile, paw and sniff it, then flehmen, stepping forward over the pile and defecating on top of it. The whole sequence or just parts of it may be repeated. See McDonnell (2003, 158–65).

19. Also detailed in McDonnell (2003).

20. On mare dominance and alliances see Hartmann el al. (2017).

21. Berger (1986) noted a similar disinterest among mares for the outcome of stallion contests. Ethology is changing considerably through deployments of social network analysis, particularly in herd species. But with horses, the attention to social dynamics beyond a limited concern with establishing dominance hierarchies is becoming well established. Part of this shift involves greater attention to mares and their investments in building and maintaining social bonds. Behaviors like "dominance" or "leadership," which were staples of early field observations, either don't work well or look quite different in relation to mares rather than stallions. Subsequent work by ethologists Konstanze Krueger, Marie Bourjade, and Machteld Van Dierendonck focuses more on the maintenance of social bonds, alliances, and distributed leadership.

2. BANDS

1. See Stewart (1996, 48–53).

2. "Lead" is also used some in the literature, instead of dominant. See Feist and McCullough (1976) and Krueger et al. (2014).

3. As Machteld van Dierendonck et al. find, "The active protection of preferred affiliative relationships, by means of interventions, shows the high motivation of the horses to safeguard their social network" (2009, 73).

4. Studies of collective behavior in social species tend to assume that large-scale movements or formations result from "local information" generated through "nearest-neighbor" interactions. In contrast, the concept of "animal culture" should suggest that individuals are capable of adopting a "global view" of group boundaries and recognizing a "global pattern" in their interactions. I address this question more fully in the conclusion.

5. Krueger et al. (2014, 91).

6. "We conclude that the decision-making process was shared by several group members a group movement (i.e., partially shared consensus) and that the leadership concept did not help to depict individual departure and leading behaviour across movements in both study groups. Rather, the different proxies of leadership produced conflicting information about individual contributions to group coordination. This study discusses the implications of these findings for the field of co-ordination and decision-making research." From Marie Bourjade et al. (2015).

7. "Social structure" focuses on how relationships are established and maintained, while "social cognition" opens onto the broader question of

thought processes within a group. Social cognition is assumed in humans, but its contours and dynamics in other species are still being tentatively explored. See Krawczyk (2018, 289–94); De Waal (2016, 156).

8. See Krueger and Heinze (2008) and Røvang et al. (2018).

9. Brubaker and Udell (2016) argue that "inconsistent evidence of social learning in horses to date may have more to do with study design, coupled with a shortage of research on this question, rather than the absence of observational learning skills on the part of the horse."

10. For the contours of a such a project, see Petitt (2013); Petitt and Eriksson (2019).

11. On horse greeting and departure rituals, see Briefer et al. (2015), Yeon (2012), Waring (2007), and Kiley (1972). On "greeting ceremonies" and "departure rituals" in mammals generally, see Bradbury and Vehrencamp (2011, 551–53).

12. In her essay "H for Hierarchies," Vinciane Despret critiques how ethologists have formulated the concept of dominance (2016, 57). She allows that, in a naturalist perspective, "hierarchy makes for a good object. It confirms the existence of species-specific invariants; it assures the possibility of predictions that are reliable and may be subject to correlations and statistics." Yet she notes, "the conception of a society arranged according to the principle of dominance is also taken from a social conception that primatologists borrowed from sociology, according to which society preexists the work of actors." Invoking the work of Bruno Latour, she highlights "the incessant work of stabilization that is necessary in the act of making a society"—in contrast to a "frozen image" of dominance. She then asks, "Does a hierarchy that fluctuates every three days still merit the name of hierarchy?" This is an open question on the pages ahead, and especially in chapter 3.

13. Matei Candea addresses this issue in his discussion of how behavior is differently constituted as an epistemological subject. He writes of behavior that "the concept's power, but also its elusiveness, lies in its ability to tack back and forth between two visions: on the one hand behaviour as materialized, objectified action, regular, repetitive and rule-bound, and on the other behaviour as a placeholder, a word to index something we do not yet know or understand. Those are two ways of being a 'thing'" (2019, 1).

14. On "thin description" see Jackson (2013), and on "flat ontology," see Latour (2007).

15. For instance, Wendy Williams, in *The Horse,* writes, "Like humans, horses in a band are notorious squabblers. . . . When you watch wild horses, it's like following soap opera" (2015, 20).

16. Habituation—a key and complicated concept and concern for ethologists—refers to the process by which wild animals gradually accept human observers as a neutral element in their environment. Primatologists Katherine T. Hanson and Erin P. Riley have redefined habituation "as

a mutually modifying process that occurs between human observers and their primate study subjects." Their approach combines ethnography with ethology, allowing them to see habituation "as a bidirectional, intersubjective experience, and come to understand habituation as a dynamic spectrum of tolerance rather than a state to be 'achieved'" (2018, 852). Donna Haraway also refashions this key concept in a commentary on primatologist Barbara Smuts's foundational fieldwork on baboons. Smuts characterized her effort to blend in to the background as trying "to be like a rock," but Haraway sees this as ignoring important social cues from the baboons. "I imagine the baboons as seeing somebody off-category, not something, and asking if that being were or were not educable to the standard of a polite guest. The monkeys, in short, inquired if the woman was as good a social subject as an ordinary baboon, with whom one could figure out how to carry on relationships, whether hostile, neutral, or friendly. The question was not, Are the baboons social subjects? but, Is the human being? Not, Do the baboons have 'face'? but, Do people?" (2007, 24). Also see Candea (2013a and 2013b).

3. RITUAL SHEARING

1. James Chriss points out that Goffman developed key aspects of his conceptual approach from ethology. Chriss writes, "Three of Goffman's most important concepts—presentation, claims, and ritual—can be considered appropriations from the corresponding ethological concepts of display, territory, and to a lesser extent, ritualization." But further, Goffman worked his mode of analysis as a parallel to ethology: "Just as ethologists have observed a range of 'territorial claims' among animals, so too Goffman observed a range of 'territorial claims; among humans." Chriss also notes that, for all his attention to speaking, "Goffman preferred to observe how people behaved rather than listening to the talk about how they behaved" (1993, 476–77).

2. My use of "symbolic" here draws from the ethological uses of the concept, as in the biological "development of signals and symbolic action" (Baudy 2006, 347). As used with "ritualization," "the biological term may denote the stylization of any perceptible element of animal shape and behavior under the selection pressure of communication." Such 'signs' are "visible, audible, or in any other way perceptible," evident in a single movement or gesture or as "a series of such elements" (349).

3. De Waal, Aureli, and Judge report on results from a variety of experiments to gauge the impact artificial crowding has on several primate species. They refer to the "elevator effect" as a means of diffusing social tension in tight spaces: "During brief periods of crowding, people often limit social interactions—a way of avoiding any conflict" (2000, 81), for example facing forward and not making eye contact or talking in an elevator. If the crowding situation is of brief duration, they find "threats" are more prevalent than open

violence. "Threats serve to keep others at bay, forestalling unwanted contact. The monkeys also avoid one another and limit active social engagement, as if they are trying to stay out of trouble by lying low" (81). With Rhesus monkeys, crowding induces conflict between matrilines: "Normally, friendly contact between matrilines is rare and antagonism common. But reduced escape opportunity makes the risk of escalated conflict greater in a confined space." A similar reduction in escape opportunities, and the collapse of avoidance techniques through social distancing, is evident and consequential among these horses.

4. On dynamics of exaggeration in animal signaling and ritual inter-actions, see Baudy: "To make sure that the signal arrives at its destination, it is stylized in a more impressive manner than the expression of an emotion itself would normally require" (2006, 350).

5. See Klingel, 1982.

6. Their findings were published the following year. See Manso de la Torre et al., 2017.

7. Analysis of social organization in mammals differentiates three aspects of social systems: social structure, mating system, and care system. In this case, I'm contrasting mating activity with efforts to reconstitute a band social structure. See Prox and Farine (2020).

8. Despret (2016, 162). Though she expresses disappointment in the con-cept, Despret offers the following as a potentially useful formulation of its effect on thinking.

9. In terms of homology, King et al. observe that "equids have developed an array of multifaceted social behaviors that have both similarities and dif-ferences across species" but that foundationally all turn on the capacity for individual recognition; as in, "individuals navigate a complex social land-scape among familiar and unknown individuals and groups" (2016, 23). On parallels between primate and horse social systems, see Ringhofer et al. (2017) and Matsuzawa (2017).

10. Goffman (1981, 128, 132, and 130).

11. On eavesdropping in horses and the social knowledge generated through such activities, see Krueger (2008).

12. Geertz (1973a, 422).

13. Geertz (1973a, 448, 444, 417–18, 424, and 443).

14. Geertz (1973a, 417–18).

15. Geertz characterized the Balinese as "controlled masters of indirec-tion and dissimulation." He continues, "Enveloped elsewhere in a haze of etiquette, a thick cloud of euphemism and ceremony, gesture and allusion, they are here expressed in only the thinnest disguise of an animal mask, a mask which in fact demonstrates them far more effectively than it conceals them" (1973a, 446–47).

16. On animal self-control, see De Waal (2016, 226–29). Also pertinent

here, De Waal, Aureli, and Judge find that chimpanzees demonstrate a great deal of emotional control in artificial crowding situations: "If crowding did induce social tensions, our chimpanzees seemed to control them directly" (2000, 80). Also, even when crowding intensified, "aggression increased only slightly. In fact, the effect of crowding was not entirely negative: friendly grooming and greetings, such as kisses and submissive bowing, increased as well." They suggest that a kind of "coping culture" arises in such circumstances, which I believe is evident here as horses find their footing and reassert conventional social signaling even in tight quarters.

17. Geertz (1973a, 424).

18. Geertz (1973a, 443).

19. Geertz (1973a, 420).

20. Geertz (1973b, 29).

21. Geertz (1973a, 452).

22. Geertz (1973b, 27).

23. As Heather Love observes, "Geertz's insistence on interpretation against observation in "Thick Description" should be understood as a polemic against prevailing norms in the social sciences" (2013, 409). Love's detailed analysis of how Geertz drew from Gilbert Ryle (for whom "an account of a wink . . . is incomplete without an account of the layers of meaning that separate it from a twitch") and how this stands in contrast to Goffman's approach to microanalysis informs my analysis in this section. I particularly want to underscore her finding, "that the dismissal of empiricism has blocked humanities scholars from using a range of potentially useful tools: morphology, ecology, observation, natural history and description" (419). To this list, I have in this book added ethology.

24. Love (2013, 408).

25. Geertz (1973a, 424). This quote continues, "what Erving Goffman has called a 'focused gathering'—a set of persons engrossed in a common flow of activity and relating to one another in terms of that flow."

26. Geertz (1973b, 30).

CONCLUSION

1. In addition to earlier references, see Carl Safina's recent book *Becoming Wild: How Animal Cultures Raise Families, Create Beauty, and Achieve Peace.* He offers the following characterization of culture in animals: "Cultural learning spreads skills (such as what is food and how to get it), creates identity and a sense of belonging within a group (as distinct from other groups), and carries on traditions that are defining aspects of existence (such as what works as effective courtship in a particular region)" (2020, xii).

2. Multispecies ethnographers offer excellent guides to such settings. See Kirksey (2015) and Tsing (2017).

3. The larger issue with understanding sex and dominance lies in problems with conceptualizing female power across species. As Rebecca J. Lewis observes, "The phenomenon known as female dominance encompasses multiple types of female-biased power. Research on all types of power will continue to be problematic until the underlying sources of variation in social relationships are analyzed independently rather than as a unitary phenomenon. This shift will require greater specificity in the analysis and reporting of power characteristics, dynamics, and structures" (2018, 546).

4. See Riley (2006); Fuentes (2010); Malone et al. (2014); Peterson, Riley, and Oka (2015); Parathian et al. (2018); Dore et al. (2018); Jost Robinson and Remis (2018); and Riley (2018).

5. Jost Robinson and Remis find that multispecies ethnography "allows ethnoprimatologists to simultaneously situate our work within multiple ecological, social, anthropological, and philosophical frameworks. Shifting our perceptions of an interface as merely a point of physical contact allows researchers to begin to reassess the notion of subjectivity and agency in primate studies. This approach acknowledges issues of subject representation while simultaneously tending to the process of knowledge production where human and nonhuman subject meet" (2018, 789–90).

6. See Hanson and Riley (2018); Riley (2018).

7. Ogden et al. (2013, 7).

8. Govindrajan (2018, 5, 16); subsequent quotes are from pages 17, 21–22, 177, 20, and 25.

9. Conforming to the traditional ethnographic subject via attending to "individual animals," Govindrajan (2018, 25, 177).

10. Wendy Williams recounts this evolutionary heritage (2015, 48–72, 193–217).

11. *Social Theory for Nonhumans* is being produced as an open-access book; early iterations of it are available now at https://manifold.umn.edu/projects/social-theory-for-nonhumans.

12. Parreñas (2018, 14–16).

13. Ward and Webster (2016, 2, 4).

14. Ward and Webster (2016, 5).

15. Ward and Webster (2016, 6).

16. Ward and Webster (2016, 40).

Bibliography

Alves, Abel. 2011. *The Animals of Spain: An Introduction to Imperial Perceptions and Human Interaction with Other Animals, 1492–1826.* Leiden: Brill.

Anderson, Sally. 2015. "Sociability: The Art of Form." In *Thinking through Sociality: An Anthropological Interrogation of Key Concepts,* edited by Vered Amit, 97–127. New York: Berghahn.

Aplin, Lucy M. 2019. "Culture and Cultural Evolution in Birds: A Review of the Evidence." Animal Behaviour 147 (January): 179–87.

Aureli, Filippo, Colleen M. Schaffner, Christophe Boesch, Simon K. Bearder, Josep Call, Colin A. Chapman, Richard Connor, et al. 2008. "Fission-Fusion Dynamics: New Research Frameworks." *Current Anthropology* 49, no. 4: 627–54.

Bárcena, Felipe. 2012. "Garranos: Os Póneis Selvagens (*Equus ferus* sp.) Do Norte Da Península Ibérica." In *Libro de Actas Del I Congresso Internacional Do Garrano,* edited by N. Vieira de Brito y G. Candeiras, 75–96. Portugal: Arcos de Valdevez.

Baudy, Dorothea. 2006. "Ethology." In *Theorizing Rituals, Volume 1: Issues, Topics, Approaches, Concepts,* edited by Jens Kreinath et al., 345–59.

Baynes-Rock, Marcus, and Elizabeth Marshall Thomas. 2015. *Among the Bone Eaters: Encounters with Hyenas in Harar.* University Park, Pa.: Penn State University Press.

Bell, Catherine M. 1992. *Ritual Theory, Ritual Practice.* New York: Oxford University Press.

Berger, Joel. 1986. *Wild Horses of the Great Basin: Social Competition and Population Size.* Chicago: University of Chicago Press.

Berlant, Lauren, and Kathleen Stewart. 2019. *The Hundreds.* Durham, N.C.: Duke University Press Books.

Birke, Lynda, and Kirrilly Thompson. 2017. *(Un)Stable Relations: Horses, Humans and Social Agency.* New York: Routledge.

Blanchette, Alex. 2020. *Porkopolis: American Animality, Standardized Life, and the Factory Farm.* Durham, N.C.: Duke University Press Books.

Bloch, Maurice. 1986. *From Blessing to Violence: History and Ideology in the Circumcision Ritual of the Merina of Madagascar.* Cambridge: Cambridge University Press.

Bogardus, Emory S. 1925. "Social Distance and Its Origins." *Journal of Applied Sociology* 9: 216–26.

Bourjade, Marie, Bernard Thierry, Martine Hausberger, and Odile Petit. 2015. "Is *Leadership* a Reliable Concept in Animals? An Empirical Study in the Horse." *PLOS ONE* 10, no. 5: e0126344, https://doi.org/10.1371/journal.pone.0126344.

Bradbury, J. W., and Sandra Lee Vehrencamp. 2011. *Principles of Animal Communication.* 2nd ed. Sunderland, Mass: Sinauer Associates.

Brakes, Philippa, Sasha R. X. Dall, Lucy M. Aplin, Stuart Bearhop, Emma L. Carroll, Paolo Ciucci, Vicki Fishlock, et al. 2019. "Animal Cultures Matter for Conservation." *Science* 363, no. 6431: 1032–34.

Brent, Lauren J. N. 2015. "Friends of Friends: Are Indirect Connections in Social Networks Important to Animal Behaviour?" *Animal Behaviour* 103 (May): 211–22.

Brent, Lauren J. N., Steve W. C. Chang, Jean-François Gariépy, and Michael L. Platt. 2014. "The Neuroethology of Friendship." *Annals of the New York Academy of Sciences* 1316, no. 1: 1–17.

Briard, Léa, Camille Dorn, and Odile Petit. 2015. "Personality and Affinities Play a Key Role in the Organisation of Collective Movements in a Group of Domestic Horses." *Ethology* 121, no. 9: 888–902.

Briefer, Elodie F., Anne-Laure Maigrot, Roi Mandel, Sabrina Briefer Freymond, Iris Bachmann, and Edna Hillmann. 2015. "Segregation of Information about Emotional Arousal and Valence in Horse Whinnies." *Scientific Reports* 5 (April).

Brubaker, Lauren, and Monique A. R. Udell. 2016. "Cognition and Learning in Horses (*Equus caballus*): What We Know and Why We Should Ask More." *Behavioral Processes* 126 (May): 121–31.

Burkhardt, Richard W. 2005. *Patterns of Behavior: Konrad Lorenz, Niko Tinbergen, and the Founding of Ethology.* Chicago: University of Chicago Press.

Burns, Tom. 2002. *Erving Goffman.* London: Routledge.

Byrne, Richard W., Philip J. Barnard, Iain Davidson, Vincent M. Janik, William C. McGrew, Ádám Miklósi, and Polly Wiessner. 2004. "Understanding Culture across Species." *Trends in Cognitive Sciences* 8, no. 8: 341–46.

Cabada Castro, Manuel. 1992. *"A rapa das bestas" de Sabucedo: história e antropoloxía dunha tradición.* Vigo: IR Indo.

Candea, Matei. 2013a. "Suspending Belief: Epoche in Animal Behavior Science." *American Anthropologist* 115, no. 3: 423–36.

Candea, Matei. 2013b. "Habituating Meerkats and Redescribing Animal Behaviour Science." *Theory Culture & Society* 30, no. 7–8: 105–28.

Candea, Matei. 2019. "Behaviour as a Thing." *Interdisciplinary Science Reviews* 44, no. 1: 1–11.

Carrithers, Michael, Louise Bracken, and Steven Emery. 2011. "Can a Species Be a Person? A Trope and Its Entanglements in the Anthropocene Era." *Current Anthropology* 52, no. 5: 661–85.

Chriss, James. 1993. "Looking Back on Goffman: The Excavation Continues." *Human Studies,* January, 469–83.

Chrulew, Matthew, Jeffrey Bussolini, and Brett Buchanan, eds. 2017. *The Philosophical Ethology of Dominique Lestel.* London: Routledge.

Clifford, James. 1988. *The Predicament of Culture: Twentieth-Century Ethnography, Literature, and Art.* Cambridge, Mass: Harvard University Press.

Coulter, Kendra. 2016. *Animals, Work, and the Promise of Interspecies Solidarity.* New York: Springer.

Coulter, Kendra. 2018. "Challenging Subjects: Towards Ethnographic Analyses of Animals." *Journal for the Anthropology of North America* 21, no. 2: 58–71.

Crapanzano, Vincent. 1986. "Hermes' Dilemma: The Masking of Subversion in Ethnographic Description." In James Clifford and George Marcus, eds., *Writing Culture,* 51–76. Berkeley: University of California Press.

Daniel, E. Valentine. 1996. *Charred Lullabies.* Princeton, N.J.: Princeton University Press.

Davis, Dona, and Anita Maurstad. 2016. *The Meaning of Horses: Biosocial Encounters.* London: Routledge.

De C Hamilton, Antonia F. 2016. "Gazing at Me: The Importance of Social Meaning in Understanding Direct-Gaze Cues." *Philosophical Transactions of the Royal Society of London. Series B, Biological Sciences* 371, no. 1686: 20150080.

De la Cadena, Marisol. 2015. *Earth Beings: Ecologies of Practice across Andean Worlds.* Durham, N.C.: Duke University Press.

Derry, Margaret Elsinor. 2003. *Bred for Perfection: Shorthorn Cattle, Collies, and Arabian Horses since 1800.* Baltimore: Johns Hopkins University Press.

Descola, Philippe. 2013. *Beyond Nature and Culture.* Chicago: University of Chicago Press.

Despret, Vinciane. 2016. *What Would Animals Say if We Asked the Right Questions?* Minneapolis: University of Minnesota Press.

De Waal, Frans. 2016. *Are We Smart Enough to Know How Smart Animals Are?* New York: Norton.

De Waal, Frans. 2019. *Mama's Last Hug: Animal Emotions and What They Tell Us about Ourselves.* New York: W. W. Norton.

De Waal, Frans, Filippo Aureli, and Peter Judge. 2000. "Coping with Crowding." *Scientific American* 282: 76–81.

Dore, Kerry M., Lucy Radford, Sherrie Alexander, and Siân Waters. 2018. "Ethnographic Approaches in Primatology." *Folia Primatologica* 89, no. 1: 5–12.

Drews, Carlos. 1993. "The Concept and Definition of Dominance in Animal Behaviour." *Behaviour* 125, no. 3–4: 283–313.

Emery, N. J. 2000. "The Eyes Have It: The Neuroethology, Function and

Evolution of Social Gaze." *Neuroscience and Biobehavioral Reviews* 24, no. 6: 581–604.

Estévez, Manuel Santos, and Yolanda Seoane Veiga. 2018. "Rock Art and Archaeological Excavation in Campo Lameiro, Galicia: A New Chronological Proposal for the Atlantic Rock Art," in *Narratives and Journeys in Rock Art: A Reader,* edited by George Nash and Aron Mazel. Oxford: Archaeopress Publishing.

Ethington, Philip J. 1997. "The Intellectual Construction of 'Social Distance': Toward a Recovery of Georg Simmel's Social Geometry." *Cybergeo: European Journal of Geography* 30, https://doi.org/10.4000/cybergeo.227.

Feh, Claudia. 2005. "Relationships and Communication in Socially Natural Horse Herds." In *The Domestic Horse: The Origins, Development and Management of Its Behaviour,* edited by D. S. Mills and Sue McDonnell, 83–93. New York: Cambridge University Press.

Feist, J. D., and D. R. McCullough. 1976. "Behavior Patterns and Communication in Feral Horses." *Z Tierpsychol* 41, no. 4: 337–71.

Fijn, Natasha. 2011. *Living with Herds: Human-Animal Coexistence in Mongolia.* Cambridge: Cambridge University Press.

Fuentes, Agustín. 2010. "Naturalcultural Encounters in Bali: Monkeys, Temples, Tourists, and Ethnoprimatology." *Cultural Anthropology* 25, no. 4: 600–624.

Fureix , C., M. Bourjade, S. Henry, C. Sankey, and M. Hausberger. 2012. "Exploring Aggression Regulation in Managed Groups of Horses (*Equus caballus*)." *Applied Animal Behaviour Science* 138, no. 3–4: 216–28.

Geertz, Clifford. 1973a. "Deep Play: Notes on the Balinese Cockfight." In *The Interpretation of Cultures,* 412–53. New York: Basic Books.

Geertz, Clifford. 1973b. "Thick Description: Toward an Interpretive Theory of Culture." In *The Interpretation of Cultures,* 3–30. New York: Basic Books.

George, N., and L. Conty. 2008. "Facing the Gaze of Others." *Neurophysiologie Clinique / Clinical Neurophysiology* 38, no. 3: 197–207.

Gobel, Matthias S., Heejung S. Kim, and Daniel C. Richardson. 2015. "The Dual Function of Social Gaze." *Cognition* 136, Supplement C: 359–64.

Godwin, Deborah. 1999. "The Importance of Ethology in Understanding the Behaviour of the Horse." *Equine Veterinary Journal* 31, no. 28 (May): 15–19.

Goffman, Erving. 1955. "On Face-Work." *Psychiatry* 18, no. 3: 213–31.

Goffman, Erving. 1959. *The Presentation of Self in Everyday Life.* New York: Anchor.

Goffman, Erving. 1972. *Relations in Public: Microstudies of the Public Order.* New York: Harper & Row.

Goffman, Erving. 1981. *Forms of Talk.* Philadelphia: University of Pennsylvania Press.

Goffman, Erving. 1982. *Interaction Ritual: Essays on Face-to-Face Behavior.* New York: Pantheon.

Goffman, Erving. 1989. "On Fieldwork." *Journal of Contemporary Ethnography* 18, no. 2: 123–32.

González-Ruibal, Alfredo. 2005. "The Need for a Decaying Past: An Archaeology of Oblivion in Contemporary Galicia (NW Spain)." *Home Cultures* 2, no. 2: 129–52.

Govindrajan, Radhika. 2018. *Animal Intimacies: Interspecies Relatedness in India's Central Himalayas.* Chicago: University of Chicago Press.

Hanson, Katherine T., and Erin P. Riley. 2018. "Beyond Neutrality: The Human–Primate Interface during the Habituation Process." *International Journal of Primatology* 39, no. 6 (December): 852–77.

Haraway, Donna J. 2007. *When Species Meet.* Minneapolis: University of Minnesota Press.

Hartigan Jr., John. 2014. *Aesop's Anthropology: A Multispecies Approach.* Minneapolis: University of Minnesota Press.

Hartigan Jr., John. 2017. *Care of the Species: Races of Corn and the Science of Plant Biodiversity.* Minneapolis: University of Minnesota Press.

Hartmann, Elke, Janne W. Christensen, and Paul D. McGreevy. 2017. "Dominance and Leadership: Useful Concepts in Human–Horse Interactions?" Proceedings of the 2017 Equine Science Symposium. *Journal of Equine Veterinary Science* 52 (May): 1–9.

Hearne, Vicki. 2016. *Adam's Task: Calling Animals by Name.* New York: Skyhorse Publishing.

Heitor, Filipa, and Luís Vicente. 2009. "Affiliative Relationships among Sorraia Mares: Influence of Age, Dominance, Kinship and Reproductive State." *Journal of Ethology* 28 (January): 133–40.

Heitor, Filipa, Maria do Mar Oom, and Luís Vicente. 2006a. "Social Relationships in a Herd of Sorraia Horses, Part I: Correlates of Social Dominance and Contexts of Aggression." *Behavioural Processes* 73, no. 2: 170–77.

Heitor, Filipa, Maria do Mar Oom, and Luís Vicente. 2006b. "Social Relationships in a Herd of Sorraia Horses, Part II: Factors Affecting Affiliative Relationships and Sexual Behaviours." *Behavioral Processes* 73, no. 3: 231–39.

Hinde, Robert A. 1979. "The Nature of Social Structure." In *The Great Apes,* edited by David A. Hamburg and Elizabeth R. McCown, 295–315. Menlo Park, Calif.: Benjamin/Cummings.

Iglesia Hernández, Pedro Jesús. 1973. "Los caballos gallegos explotados en régimen de libertad o caballos salvajes en Galicia." Dissertation: Facultad de Veterinaria, Universidad Compulense de Madrid.

Ingold, Tim. 2000. *The Perception of the Environment: Essays on Livelihood, Dwelling and Skill.* London: Routledge.

Ingold, Tim. 2009. *Hunters, Pastoralists and Ranchers: Reindeer Economies and Their Transformations.* Cambridge: Cambridge University Press.

Inoue, Sota, Shinya Yamamoto, Monamie Ringhofer, Renata S. Mendonça, Carlos Pereira, and Satoshi Hirata. 2019. "Spatial Positioning of Individuals in a Group of Feral Horses: A Case Study Using Drone Technology." *Mammal Research* 64, no. 2: 249–59.

Jackson, John L. 2013. *Thin Description: Ethnography and the African Hebrew Israelites of Jerusalem.* Cambridge, Mass.: Harvard University Press.

Jacobsen, Michael Hviid, and Soren Kristiansen. 2014. *The Social Thought of Erving Goffman.* Thousand Oaks, Calif.: Sage Publications.

Jerolmack, Colin. 2013. *The Global Pigeon.* Chicago: University of Chicago Press.

Jost Robinson, Carolyn A., and Melissa J. Remis. 2018. "Engaging Holism: Exploring Multispecies Approaches in Ethnoprimatology." *International Journal of Primatology* 39, no. 5: 776–96.

Kiley, M. 1972. "The Vocalizations of Ungulates, Their Causation and Function." *Zeitschrift für Tierpsychologie* 31, 171–222.

King, Sarah, Cheryl Asa, Jan Pluháček, Katherine Houpt, and Jason Ransom. 2016. "Behavior of Horses, Zebras, and Asses." In *Wild Equids: Ecology, Management, and Conservation,* edited by Jason I. Ransom and Petra Kaczensky. Baltimore, Md: John Hopkins University Press.

Kirksey, Eben. 2015. *Emergent Ecologies.* Durham, N.C.: Duke University Press.

Kirksey, S. Eben, and Stefan Helmreich. 2010. "The Emergence of Multispecies Ethnography." *Cultural Anthropology* 25, no. 4: 545–76.

Klingel, H. 1982. "Social Organization of Feral Horses." *Journal of Reproduction and Fertility,* Supplement 32: 89–95.

Kockelman, Paul. 2016. *The Chicken and the Quetzal: Incommensurate Ontologies and Portable Values in Guatemala's Cloud Forest.* Durham, N.C.: Duke University Press Books.

Kockelman, Paul. 2017. "Semiotic Agency." In *Distributed Agency,* edited by N. J. Enfield and Paul Kockelman, 25–40. Oxford: Oxford University Press.

Krawczyk, Daniel C. 2018. "Social Cognition: *Reasoning with Others." In Reasoning: The Neuroscience of How We Think,* edited by Daniel C. Krawczyk, 283–311. Cambridge, Mass.: Academic Press.

Kreinath, Jens. 2006. "Semiotics." In *Theorizing Rituals, Volume 1: Issues, Topics, Approaches, Concepts,* edited by Jens Kreinath et al., 429–70.

Kreinath, Jens, J. A. M. Snoek, and Michael Stausberg, eds. 2006. *Theorizing Rituals, Volume 1: Issues, Topics, Approaches, Concepts.* Leiden, Netherlands: Brill.

Kreinath, Jens, Jan Snoek, and Michael Stausberg, eds. 2007. *Theorizing Rituals, Volume 2: Annotated Bibliography of Ritual Theory, 1966–2005.* Leiden, Netherlands: Brill.

Krueger, Konstanze. 2008. "Social Ecology of Horses." In *Ecology of Social Evolution,* edited by Judith Korb and Juergen Heinze, 195–206. Berlin: Springer Science & Business Media.

Krueger, Konstanze, and Jürgen Heinze. 2008. "Horse Sense: Social Status of

Horses (*Equus caballus*) Affects Their Likelihood of Copying Other Horses' Behavior." *Animal Cognition* 11, no. 3: 431–39.

Krueger, Konstanze, Birgit Flauger, Kate Farmer, and Charlotte Hemelrijk. 2014. "Movement Initiation in Groups of Feral Horses." *Behavioural Processes* 103 (March): 91–101.

Lagos Abarzuza, Laura, Juan Picos, and Enrique Valero. 2012. "Temporal Pattern of Wild Ungulate-Related Traffic Accidents in Northwest Spain." *European Journal of Wildlife Research* 58, no. 4: 661–68.

Lagos Abarzuza, Laura. 2013. "Ecología del lobo (*Canis lupus*), del poni salvaje (*Equus ferus atlanticus*) Y delganado vacuno aemiextensivo (*Bos taurus*) en Galicia." Interacciones Depredador-Presa: tesis doctoral: memoria presentada para optar al Grado de Doctor, Universidad de Santiago de Compostela.

Lagos Abarzuza, Laura. 2014. "O sistema tradicional de aproveitamento dos ponis atlánticos aalvaxes nos montes da Groba, Morgadáns e Galiñeiro. Retos No Século XXI." *Revista de Estudos Miñoranos* 12: 13.

Laland, Kevin N., and Bennett G. Galef. 2009. *The Question of Animal Culture.* Cambridge, Mass: Harvard University Press.

Laland, Kevin N., and Vincent M. Janik. 2006. "The Animal Cultures Debate." *Trends in Ecology & Evolution* 21, no. 10, 542–47.

Lamont, Michèle. 1992. *Money, Morals, and Manners: The Culture of the French and American Upper-Middle Class.* Chicago: University of Chicago Press.

Langford, Jean. 2017. "Avian Bedlam: Toward a Biosemiosis of Troubled Parrots," *Environmental Humanities,* 9, no. 1, 84–107.

Latour, Bruno. 2007. *Reassembling the Social: An Introduction to Actor-Network-Theory.* Oxford: Oxford University Press.

Lestel, Dominique. 2006. "Ethology and Ethnology: The Coming Synthesis, a General Introduction." *Social Science Information* 45, no. 2, 147–53.

Lestel, Dominique. 2014. "Toward an Ethnography of Animal Worlds." *Angelaki* 19, no. 3, 75–89.

Lestel, Dominique, Florence Brunois, and Florence Gaunet. 2006. "Etho-Ethnology and Ethno-Ethology." *Social Science Information* 45, no. 2: 155–77.

Lewis, Rebecca J. 2018. "Female Power in Primates and the Phenomenon of Female Dominance." *Annual Review of Anthropology* 47, no. 1: 533–51.

Linklater, W. L. 2000. "Adaptive Explanation in Socio-Ecology: Lessons from the Equidae." *Biological Reviews* 75, no. 1, 1–20.

Linnell, John, Petra Kaczensky, and Nicola Lescureus. 2016. "Human Dimensions of Wild Equid Management: Exploring the Meanings of 'Wild.'" In *Wild Equids: Ecology, Management, and Conservation,* edited by Jason Ransom and Petra Kaczensky, 121–32. Baltimore: Johns Hopkins University Press.

Locke, Piers. 2017. "Elephants as Persons, Affective Apprenticeship, and

Fieldwork with Nonhuman Informants in Nepal." *HAU: Journal of Ethnographic Theory* 7, no. 1, 353–76.

Lorenz, Konrad. 1963. *On Aggression,* New York: MJF Books.

Lorimer, Jamie. 2015. *Wildlife in the Anthropocene: Conservation after Nature.* Minneapolis: University of Minnesota Press.

Love, Heather. 2013. "Close Reading and Thin Description." *Public Culture* 25, no. 3, 401–34.

Malone, Nicholas, Alison H. Wade, Agustín Fuentes, Erin P. Riley, Melissa Remis, and Carolyn Jost Robinson. 2014. "Ethnoprimatology: Critical Interdisciplinary and Multispecies Approaches in Anthropology." *Critique of Anthropology* 34, no. 1, 8–29.

Manso de la Torre, Xilberte. 2016. "*Equus ferus atlanticus*: As burras do monte da Serra da Groba." *Revista Del Instituto de Estudios Miñoranos* 14–15: 107–36.

Manso de la Torre, Xilberte, Eloy Soto, Cándido Verde Andrés, and Xosé Lois Vilar Pedreira. 2017. "O Proxecto Equus: un novo paradigma nas escenas de caza da arte rupestre Galega e do norte de Portugal." *Revista de Estudios Miñoráns (REM)* 16–17: 23–75.

Martínez-Cortizas, A., M. Costa-Casais, and J. A. López-Sáez. 2009. "Environmental Change in NW Iberia between 7000 and 500 BC." *Quaternary International* 200, no. 1: 77–89.

Matsuzawa, Tetsuro. 2017. "Horse Cognition and Behavior from the Perspective of Primatology." *Primates* 58, no. 4: 473–77.

McDonnell, Sue. 2003. *The Equid Ethogram: A Practical Field Guide to Horse Behavior.* Lexington, Ky.: Eclipse Press.

McKee, Tamar V. S. 2014. "Ghost Herds: Rescuing Horses and Horse People in Bluegrass Kentucky." PhD diss., University of British Columbia.

Meloni, Maurizio. 2016. "From Boundary-Work to Boundary Object: How Biology Left and Re-Entered the Social Sciences." *Sociological Review Monographs* 64, no. 1: 61–78.

Moore, Lisa Jean. 2018. *Catch and Release: The Enduring Yet Vulnerable Horseshoe Crab.* New York: NYU Press.

Moore, Lisa Jean, and Mary Kosut. 2013. *Buzz: Urban Beekeeping and the Power of the Bee.* New York: NYU Press.

Morais, Joana, Maria Oom, Joana Malta-Vacas, and Cristina Luís. 2005. "Genetic Structure of an Endangered Portuguese Semiferal Pony Breed, the Garrano." *Biochemical Genetics* 43 (August): 347–64.

Murphy, Jack, Carol Hall, and Sean Arkins. 2009. "What Horses and Humans See: A Comparative Review." *International Journal of Zoology.* https://doi.org/10.1155/2009/721798.

Noske, Barbara. 1993. "The Animal Question in Anthropology: A Commentary." *Society and Animals* 1, no. 2, 185–90.

Noske, Barbara. 1997. *Beyond Boundaries: Humans and Animals.* Buffalo, N.Y.: Black Rose Books.

Nuñez, Cassandra MV, Alberto Scorolli, Laura Lagos, David Berman, and Albert J. Kane. 2016. "Management of Free-Roaming Horses." *Wild Equids: Ecology, Management, and Conservation.* Baltimore: Johns Hopkins University Press, 133–48.

Ogden, Laura A., Billy Hall, and Kimiko Tanita. 2013. "Animals, Plants, People, and Things: A Review of Multispecies Ethnography." *Environment and Society: Advances in Research* 4, no. 1, 5–24.

Orr, Yancey. 2015. "Animal Magnetism: Perceiving Environmental Objects as Social Subjects among Balinese Looking at Roosters." *Visual Anthropology* 28, no. 2, 127–36.

Orr, Yancey. 2016. "Interspecies Semiotics and the Specter of Taboo: The Perception and Interpretation of Dogs and Rabies in Bali, Indonesia." *American Anthropologist* 118, no. 1, 67–77.

Parathian, Hannah E., Matthew R. McLennan, Catherine M. Hill, Amélia Frazão-Moreira, and Kimberley J. Hockings. 2018. "Breaking Through Disciplinary Barriers: Human–Wildlife Interactions and Multispecies Ethnography." *International Journal of Primatology* 39, no. 5: 749–75.

Park, Robert Ezra. 1924. "The Concept of Social Distance as Applied to the Study of Racial Attitudes and Racial Relations." *Journal of Applied Sociology* 8: 339–44.

Parreñas, Juno Salazar. 2018. *Decolonizing Extinction: The Work of Care in Orangutan Rehabilitation.* Durham, N.C.: Duke University Press Books.

Peterson, Jeffrey V., Erin P. Riley, and Ngakan Putu Oka. 2015. "Macaques and the Ritual Production of Sacredness among Balinese Transmigrants in South Sulawesi, Indonesia." *American Anthropologist* 117, no. 1: 71–85.

Petitt, Andrea. 2013. "Cowboy Masculinities in Human-Animal Relations on a Cattle Ranch." *ELORE* 20, no. 1: 67–80.

Petitt, Andrea, and Camilla Eriksson. 2019. "Breeding Beyond Bodies: Making and 'Doing' Cattle." *Society & Animals,* 1–19.

Platt, Michael L., and Asif A. Ghazanfar. 2012. *Primate Neuroethology.* Oxford: Oxford University Press.

Prox, Lea, and Damien Farine. 2020. "A Framework for Conceptualizing Dimensions of Social Organization in Mammals," *Ecology and Evolution* 10, 791–807.

Raffles, Hugh. 2010. *Insectopedia.* New York: Pantheon Books.

Ransom, Jason, and Petra Kaczensky, eds. 2016. *Wild Equids: Ecology, Management, and Conservation.* Baltimore: Johns Hopkins University Press.

Rappaport, Roy A. 2000. *Pigs for the Ancestors: Ritual in the Ecology of a New Guinea People.* Grove, Ill.: Waveland Press.

Reed-Danahay, Deborah. 2015. "Social Space: Distance, Proximity, and

Thresholds of Affinity." In *Thinking through Sociality: An Anthropological Interrogation of Key Concepts,* edited by Vered Amit, 69–96. New York: Berghahn.

Reed-Danahay, Deborah. 2019. *Bourdieu and Social Space: Mobilities, Trajectories, Emplacements.* New York: Berghahn Books.

Rees, Lucy. 1985. *The Horse's Mind.* New York: Arco Pub.

Remme, Jon Henrik Ziegler. 2014. *Pigs and Persons in the Philippines: Human-Animal Entanglements in Ifugao Rituals.* Lanham, Md.: Lexington Books.

Riles, Annelise. 2001. *The Network Inside Out.* Ann Arbor: University of Michigan Press.

Riley, Erin P. 2006. "Ethnoprimatology: Toward Reconciliation of Biological and Cultural Anthropology." *Ecological and Environmental Anthropology* 2, no. 2: 75–86.

Riley, Erin P. 2018. "The Maturation of Ethnoprimatology: Theoretical and Methodological Pluralism." *International Journal of Primatology* 39, no. 5: 705–29.

Ringhofer, Monamie, Sota Inoue, Renata S. Mendonça, Carlos Pereira, Tetsuro Matsuzawa, Satoshi Hirata, and Shinya Yamamoto. 2017. "Comparison of the Social Systems of Primates and Feral Horses: Data from a Newly Established Horse Research Site on Serra D'Arga, Northern Portugal." *Primates* 58, no. 4: 479–84.

Rørvang, Maria V., Janne W. Christensen, Jan Ladewig, and Andrew McLean. 2018. "Social Learning in Horses—Fact or Fiction?" *Frontiers in Veterinary Science* 5. https://doi.org/10.3389/fvets.2018.00212.

Roseberry, William. 1982. "Balinese Cockfights and the Seduction of Anthropology." *Social Research* 49, no. 4: 1013–28.

Rubenstein, Dustin R. 2012. "Sexual and Social Competition: Broadening Perspectives by Defining Female Roles." *Philosophical Transactions of the Royal Society of London B: Biological Sciences* 367, no. 1600: 2248–52.

Safina, Carl. 2020. *Becoming Wild: How Animal Cultures Raise Families, Create Beauty, and Achieve Peace.* New York: Henry Holt.

Schilbach, Leonhard. 2015. "Eye to Eye, Face to Face and Brain to Brain: Novel Approaches to Study the Behavioral Dynamics and Neural Mechanisms of Social Interactions." *Current Opinion in Behavioral Sciences* 3 (June): 130–35.

Schuppli, Caroline, and Carel P. van Schaik. 2019. "Animal Cultures: How We've Only Seen the Tip of the Iceberg." *Evolutionary Human Sciences* 1. https://doi.org/10.1017/ehs.2019.1.

Shepherd, Stephen V. 2010. "Following Gaze: Gaze-Following Behavior as a Window into Social Cognition." *Frontiers in Integrative Neuroscience* 4, no. 5 (March).

Shepherd, Stephen V., and Michael L. Platt. 2012. "Neuroethology of Attention in Primates." In *Primate Neuroethology,* edited by Asif A. Ghazanfar and Michael L. Platt, 525–50. New York: Oxford University Press.

Simmel, Georg. 1977. "The Stranger." In *Georg Simmel: On Individuality and Social Forms,* edited by Donald Levine. Chicago: University of Chicago Press, 143–50.

Smart, Alan. 2014. "Critical Perspectives on Multispecies Ethnography." *Critique of Anthropology* 34, no. 1: 3–7.

Smith, John Maynard. 2003. *Animal Signals.* Oxford Series in Ecology and Evolution. New York: Oxford University Press.

Smith, John Maynard, and G. R. Price. 1973. "The Logic of Animal Conflict." *Nature* 246, no. 5427: 15–18.

Snowdon, Charles T. 2017. "Introduction to Animal Culture: Is Culture Uniquely Human?" In *The Handbook of Culture and Biology,* 2–104. John Wiley & Sons.

Stewart, Kathleen. 1996. *A Space on the Side of the Road: Cultural Poetics in an "Other" America.* Princeton, N.J.: Princeton University Press.

Stewart, Kathleen. 2007. *Ordinary Affects.* Durham, N.C.: Duke University Press Books.

Strathern, Marilyn. 1992. *After Nature: English Kinship in the Late Twentieth Century.* New York: Cambridge University Press.

Timney, Brian, and Kathy Keil. 1992. "Visual Acuity in the Horse." *Vision Research* 32, no. 12: 2289–93.

Tomonaga, Masaki, Kiyonori Kumazaki, Florine Camus, Sophie Nicod, Carlos Pereira, and Tetsuro Matsuzawa. 2015. "A Horse's Eye View: Size and Shape Discrimination Compared with Other Mammals." *Biology Letters* 11, no. 11: 1–4.

Tsing, Anna Lowenhaupt. 2017. *The Mushroom at the End of the World: On the Possibility of Life in Capitalist Ruins.* Princeton, N.J.: Princeton University Press.

Turner, Terence. 2006. "Structure, Process, Form," in *Theorizing Rituals, Volume 1: Issues, Topics, Approaches, Concepts,* edited by Jens Kreinath et al., 207–46.

Turner, Victor. 1969. *The Ritual Process.* New York: Penguin Books.

Van Dooren, Thom. 2014. *Flight Ways: Life and Loss at the Edge of Extinction. Critical Perspectives on Animals.* New York: Columbia University Press.

Van Dierendonck, Machteld C., Han de Vries, Matthijs B. H. Schilder, Ben Colenbrander, Anna Guðrun Þorhallsdóttir, and Hrefna Sigurjónsdóttir. 2009. "Interventions in Social Behaviour in a Herd of Mares and Geldings." *Applied Animal Behaviour Science* 116, no. 1: 67–73.

Vaught, Jeannette. 2018. "How to Make a Horse Have an Orgasm." In *Living with Animals: Bonds across Species,* edited by Natalie Porter and Ilana Gershon, 157–67. Ithaca, N.Y.: Cornell University Press.

Vilar Pedreira, Xosé Lois. 2014. "Escenas de Caza Nos Petroglifos Galegos E Portugeueses." *Revista Del Instituto de Estudios Miñoranos* 12–13: 119–34.

Ward, Ashley, and Mike Webster. 2016. *Sociality: The Behaviour of Group-Living Animals.* 2016. Cham, Switzerland: Springer International Publishing.

Waring, George. 2007. *Horse Behavior,* 2nd ed. Norwich, N.Y: William Andrew.

Wark, Colin, and John F. Galliher. 2007. "Emory Bogardus and the Origins of the Social Distance Scale." *American Sociologist* 38, no. 4: 383–95.

Wathan, Jen, Anne M. Burrows, Bridget M. Waller, and Karen McComb. 2015. "EquiFACS: The Equine Facial Action Coding System." *PLoS ONE* 10, no. 8: e0131738.

Wathan, Jennifer, and Karen McComb. 2014. "The Eyes and Ears Are Visual Indicators of Attention in Domestic Horses." *Current Biology* 24, no. 15: R677–79.

Watson, Matthew C. 2016. "On Multispecies Mythology: A Critique of Animal Anthropology." *Theory, Culture & Society* 33, no. 5: 159–72.

Whitehead, Hal. 2008. *Analyzing Animal Societies: Quantitative Methods for Vertebrate Social Analysis.* Chicago: University of Chicago Press.

Whitehead, Hal, and Luke Rendell, 2015. *The Cultural Lives of Whales and Dolphins.* Chicago: University of Chicago Press.

Wilkie, Rhoda. 2013. "Multispecies Scholarship and Encounters: Changing Assumptions at the Human-Animal Nexus." *Sociology* 49, no. 2: 323–35.

Willett, Cynthia, and Malini Suchak. 2018. "Sociality." In *Critical Terms for Animal Studies,* edited by Lori Gruen, 370–82. Chicago: University of Chicago Press.

Williams, Wendy. 2015. *The Horse: The Epic History of Our Noble Companion.* New York: Scientific American / Farrar, Straus and Giroux.

Wolter, Riccarda, Volker Stefanski, and Konstanze Krueger. 2018. "Parameters for the Analysis of Social Bonds in Horses." *Animals* 8, no. 191: 1–11.

Yeon, S. C. 2012. "Acoustic Communication in the Domestic Horse (*Equus caballus*)." *Journal of Veterinary Behavior* 7, no. 3: 179–85.

Index

John Hartigan Jr. is professor of anthropology and director of the Américo Paredes Center for Cultural Studies at the University of Texas, Austin. He is author of *Aesop's Anthropology: A Multispecies Approach* (Minnesota, 2015) and *Care of the Species* (Minnesota, 2017).

driver. She'd be a mosquito feast before that happened.

"This is all *your* fault, you know." She jabbed a finger in the moose's direction with enough emphasis to rock her body forward.

The bull's ears dropped as its hooves shuffled against the road. More than a decade had gone by since Tessa last encountered a moose, but she remembered what those signs meant. Her heart thundered in her chest. Escape was impossible. The road sat several feet below the ground level of the forest surrounding the path. Her city shoes would never help her scramble up the dirt wall in time.

"Always thought it would be a bear," she muttered, easing toward the car door. The moose could ram the Mustang, and might. But shelter in the cramped backseat floor was better than standing out in the open as his target.

The moose's shoulders squared in her direction as his steps grew more deliberate. Time gone, Tessa dove in through the open driver's window. She scrambled for the back seat, but the strap of her ankle boot caught outside the window. "Crap!" She hugged the bucket seat on the passenger side, bracing herself for the impact.

Which didn't come.

The roar of a diesel engine gave her both relief and panic. She hoped the driver would have more warning than she did. A dog let out a few sharp barks. Tessa tried to twist herself around to see what was

3

happening, but she was too tangled up. Outside of the leather seat and convertible topper she'd smartly left up, she could only view a sliver of light out the window.

Heavy footsteps crunched against the gravel. "You all right there, miss?"

Tessa's heart lodged in her throat. More than a decade had passed since the summer that changed the course of her life, but she would never forget that voice. "I'm fine," she called, desperate to hide her face. "Just fine."

"You know, usually people drive with their feet *inside* the car."

"Go away. I've got it all under control."

The easy, amused laugh that had haunted her dreams for years echoed through the window. "Tell that to your radiator."

"Triple A's on the way."

"No, they're not."

Tessa let out a frustrated groan. Liam Davies was always good at calling her bluff. "I don't need your help." But the sad truth was that she did. If she turned him away, it might be hours—even tomorrow —before someone else came by to save her. She could probably wriggle her ankle free of its trap. But her feet would be blistered and maybe even a little bloody if she attempted the trek into town with her current footwear.

"Your foot's caught, miss."

Tessa breathed a tiny sigh of relief. Liam didn't recognize her. "I hadn't noticed."

If she could just get him to leave without seeing her face, he might never know she came back to Sunset Ridge. Last she knew, he was traveling the world in the Army. She didn't plan on staying long. Only enough to figure out how to prove her innocence and return to Vegas to win the competition. But she would have words with her sisters for their failure to mention Liam had moved back to town.

"I'm just going to loosen this strap," he said. "I promise I won't try anything funny."

"Right."

"What's that?"

"Nothing." The graze of his fingers left a heat trail on her ankle as he undid the offending strap. It wasn't fair that after all this time a simple touch had an instant effect on her. The second her foot was free, Tessa yanked it into the car and crawled into the far bucket seat. "Thanks, got it from here."

Hope that she might keep her return a secret dimmed as Liam lowered himself to peer in through the window. Time had only done favors to the man. More than stubble dusted his tanned chin, but the beard only made him more attractive than she remembered. "You're still just as stubborn as I remember."

Tessa let out a sigh. "What are you doing out here anyway?" Last she knew, this was a private road. Trespassers weren't exactly welcomed. She forced herself to look away from those mesmerizing green eyes. They'd been her greatest weakness that summer. Her gaze fell to his thick forearms resting on the car door. *Big mistake.*

"Nice seeing you, too." His eyes traveled up and down her body, quickly the first time. Leisurely the second. "Not hurt, are you?"

"No." *Just my stupid pride.*

"You sure?"

"I was outside the car—standing—before that creature tried to charge me." Tessa unbuckled the other ankle boot. She'd be better off barefoot even if Liam wasn't holding the opposite one hostage.

"Ed."

"Excuse me?"

"That was Ed."

"Am I supposed to think it's cute that you named a moose?" Annoyed that Liam still hung in the open window dangling her shoe, Tessa attempted to exit the passenger door. But it only opened a couple of inches before it caught the embankment.

"I didn't name him. Ed's our moose."

"This feels like I'm in the Twilight Zone," she mumbled.

Liam opened the driver's side door and stepped back. "Need a ride into town?"

If there had been any other exit option—even climbing through a sunroof the convertible didn't offer—Tessa would've leapt at it. Instead, she was forced to shimmy on her rear toward Liam. "What about the car?" She cringed, hating to think how much this would cost. She'd been the brilliant one to waive the special coverage when she rented the car. And because she'd lived in New York City for the past five years and didn't own a vehicle, she didn't have insurance of her own.

"I can come back. Tow it to my shop."

"Your shop." He used to talk about someday taking over his grandpa's auto body shop. Maybe he'd done it. Tessa had no idea how long he'd been out of the military, or what he had managed to accomplish in the years that passed.

"Yeah, I can get the truck out here later."

She almost asked him *why* he would, but she knew. Liam would never turn away someone in need. It was one of the things she had loved the most about him. "I can have someone else do it. I don't want to be a bother."

"It's no problem." He held out her shoe. "As it turns out, I have extra time on my hands today."

She started to tell him no again, but a dog barked from his truck. A mostly black husky with flares of white and gray poked its head out the window, the tallest ears she'd ever seen pointed toward the sky.

"Why don't you go wait in the truck? Raven won't bite. She's harmless."

"I need to get my stuff." She'd only been allowed to bring two suitcases to the reality show—two that had been thoroughly checked upon arrival. The memory of the staff riffling through all of their luggage flashed through her mind. For the hundredth time, Tessa wondered how her ex had managed to sneak that recipe in; the same one that got her booted for cheating. The suitcases sat in the trunk now; one of them held her knives. No way she was leaving those behind.

"I'll grab them," Liam said after Tessa's attempts to pop the trunk with the door lever failed.

"I didn't hit the trunk." She pulled on the lever some more, as if repeated attempts might change the result. "It should open."

"You're lucky you didn't deploy the airbag. Tessa, let me."

Tessa wanted to argue, out of *principle*, and almost launched into a small tirade. But she was exhausted. The sooner her suitcases were loaded, the sooner she could find refuge at the lodge.

Raven let out another bark, her long furry tail in full motion. She looked like the perfect snuggle-monster—much more appealing than an argument right now. Tessa wondered whether Liam would notice if she borrowed his dog for a few days. "Thanks."

Refusing to look over her shoulder at the man with too many sculpted muscles, Tessa focused on the happy dog hanging halfway out of the massive truck's window. If Tessa lived to be a hundred, she would never understand why some men had to have trucks taller than skyscrapers. The floor of the cab went clear up to her hips.

As Liam worked at the trunk of her car, she catapulted herself inside the cab.

"Hi, Raven." The cheerful dog stood on the
center console in greeting, licking Tessa on the cheek
once she was settled in her seat. She took a cautious
step onto Tessa's thigh. "C'mon, girl. Lap dogs are my
favorite."

Living in New York and working demanding
hours for four- and five-star restaurants didn't leave
time for pets. But Tessa'd wished for a dog she could
snuggle more times than she could count. It was the
only wrinkle in living out her dream life. Well, it *had*
been the only wrinkle. "Raven, I should've known
better than to trust that rat."

The dog gave a gentle whine, then snuggled
deeper in her lap, smoothing Tessa's worries and
fitting rather well for a larger dog. Raven was smaller
than any husky she'd seen before, but still large
enough to consume Tessa's entire lap and then some.
"Want to stay with me, girl?" She hugged the dog,
feelings she'd suppressed from the last forty-eight
hours rushing back. One minute she was scrubbing
countertops, planning her menu for the next challenge. Next, she was being escorted from the
premises.

Once in the truck, Liam mentioned, "You two are
sure cozy." He'd loaded both suitcases in the bed,
making Tessa a little crazy. The bags themselves,
though quality, weren't her concern. It was the
contents. "Don't go stealing my dog, now."

"It's crossed my mind."

They shared a light, easy smile, and for a solitary moment, it felt like only yesterday that they'd been young and carefree together. Then Liam hit a bump in the road and the moment shattered.

"My knives are back there. Be careful."

"Sweetheart, I promise the airlines were rougher with your bags than this road could be."

Tessa fixed a glare on Liam, but the man didn't have the decency to look over at her to witness it. The way that nickname carried from his lips in that irritatingly sexy voice sent shivers throughout her body. She fought it with every fiber she could. "Don't call me sweetheart."

He flashed her a mischievous smile. "No promises."

Moments like this were quicksand she had to avoid at all costs. No matter how short a stay she expected to have, Tessa had to guard her heart. Because Liam Davies had always been her biggest weakness.

CHAPTER TWO

Liam

After a winding mile of silence down a road neither of them should have been on, Liam asked, "How long you in town for?" He acted calm and indifferent with his hand relaxed on the steering wheel, but inside he was wound up tighter than a line with a hundred-pound halibut on the other end. He thought he had until Christmas before he'd see Tessa again.

"Just a couple of days."

Liam wanted to ask about the show. It obviously had something to do with the reason she was here. But asking would expose the fact he'd been watching *Order Up: Las Vegas*. It was much too risky to let her know how much leverage she had over his heart.

"Did I miss a birthday?" He didn't. Liam remembered odd things, one of which was that the Whitmore sisters all had birthdays in March.

"No."

Raven remained curled in her lap, content to nap rather than look out the window. Though Tessa's words had a bite to them, her eyes fell gently upon the dog. Liam accepted that she wasn't going to admit a thing right now, so he changed tactics. "Raven's a retired sled dog," he told Tessa. "Ten years old."

"She's a sweetie."

"You can't kidnap her, Tess."

For a single beat, the heavy tension in the cab of the truck dissipated. Liam felt transported back in time, to the summer when Tessa riding shotgun in his truck was commonplace.

"Don't worry. I can't smuggle her back to Vegas."

Though tempted, he didn't take the bait. It would drive her far crazier for him not to ask than it would Liam not to know. Eventually, Tessa would burst all about the reality show. He just had to wait it out.

Instead, he said, "I won't charge you for the tow."

"Uh . . . thanks."

"But for me not to rat you out to Old Man Franks for trespassing, it'll cost you lunch."

Tessa huffed out a laugh. "Always a *but* with you, isn't there?"

Raven's ears perked as the truck slowed at a stop sign on the edge of town. If he turned right, Liam could have Tessa to the lodge in less than three minutes. He made the trip in under ninety seconds back when curfew was a concern. But he wasn't ready to let her go. Not yet.

"You're going the wrong way."

"I'll take you to the lodge after we eat."

Eyes front, still he saw her head turn toward the door handle. But the lounging dog in her lap kept Tessa from fleeing. That, and Liam possessing her luggage in the truck bed; including her almighty chef's knives. She was smarter than to let him hold those hostage. "I didn't agree to that."

He wasn't ready to let her out of his sight. Tessa was good at hiding when she didn't want to be found. "I can send you the tow bill instead." Liam's heart pounded in his chest, waiting to see whether she'd call his bluff. If it wasn't for Ed, the sly devil, he might never have been alerted she was in Sunset Ridge.

"How much?"

"Two-fifty." He took a chance and continued toward Warren's Sea Shack. There was a to-go order waiting for him. It was more than enough to share, food he'd planned to last him two meals, maybe three. Liam expected to work through dinner on a boat motor and had planned ahead.

"Two *hundred* and fifty?"

"I'm sure your insurance will cover it."

Tessa got awfully quiet after that, and Liam didn't have to guess. "Didn't take out insurance on that rental, did you?"

"Didn't think I'd need it."

The chips were stacking in Liam's favor the longer this conversation went on. If Tessa didn't have insurance, she'd have to cover repairs out-of-pocket or the rental company would send her a major bill.

"Why were you on that road anyway?" he asked, though he wasn't any more willing to answer the same question more than she likely was. The dirt road, hardly wide enough for two vehicles to squeeze past one another, was private. Though it did lead into town, not many people risked upsetting Old Man Franks by traveling down it. Certainly no one in a Mustang.

"I was trying to slip into town. Quietly."

Liam let out a hearty laugh. "You thought you would sneak into Sunset Ridge driving a cherry-red GTO Mustang convertible?"

"I wasn't trying to *sneak*," she retorted. "I just don't want the media to find me."

More dangled bait. *Media?* Though harder to resist this time around, Liam fought his urge to ask what that could possibly mean. To the best of his knowledge, the show hadn't finished airing. Not according to the timeline Sophie mentioned to him. Yet he couldn't bring himself to believe it was popular enough—especially in this remote Alaskan town—for anyone to recognize her, let alone have paparazzi follow. "So, you thought a red convertible would be just the ticket."

"I had the top up."

"Could've driven a tank for as discreet as that car is." He'd missed their bantering, maybe more than he missed anything else. They pushed each other's buttons, and nothing excited him more. The way they riled themselves up made for the best kisses. As consequence to his thought, his gaze dropped to her lips.

"Okay, so maybe it wasn't the *best* choice," Tessa admitted.

He almost made a comment about the flashy car being a consolation prize from *Order Up*, but Liam didn't want her to know he knew anything about it. Certainly not that he'd watched every episode so far. "What's with the secrecy anyway?"

"I'm surprising my sisters."

Liam didn't buy that answer—not a chance that was all there was to it. He did believe Cadence and Sophie had no idea their oldest sister was in Alaska, but he wouldn't press. Liam shifted his hand on the wheel. "I'll get the truth out of you sooner or later."

Tessa didn't have anything to say to that, for once, and instead let her head to fall against the window. He gave her the rest of the drive through town to take in everything—all that had changed, and all that had stayed the same.

Liam pulled into a spot outside Warren's Sea Shack. Nodding to the snoozing dog in her lap, he asked, "Watch Raven?"

Confusion lingered in those crystal-blue eyes.

Eyes that had haunted his dreams for more years than he could count. "I thought—"

He gave her a wink before he shut the door, saying through the open window, "We're not eating here."

Liam's feet couldn't carry himself inside fast enough. A cool blast of air conditioning hit him, making him realize his shirt had started to stick to his skin. Tessa always made him a little nervous. More so now that she was all grown up, and a very attractive woman. More attractive even, he suspected, if she got rid of that face full of makeup.

"Warm day out there," Jett, Warren's main host, said about the air conditioning running. It was an usually warm day for Sunset Ridge. Mostly A/C was in the bank and Freeman's Grocery. Most homes didn't have it, and few businesses did either. Liam felt relieved to be in one of the rare restaurant establishments that did.

"Supposed to be warmer tomorrow, I heard," said Liam.

Jett nodded. "Think your tacos are just about ready. Let me grab 'em."

"Thanks." Liam ducked off to the side to avoid anyone he might know. Usually he was a social creature, happy to chat with anyone. *Not today*. He studied the announcements pinned to the bulletin board in hopes of slowing his thundering heart. Some were old, like the flyer for the Alaskan Woodsman competition that he and his buddy Ford won last month. It was the reason Liam now owned a Super Cub.

He saw another flyer for the upcoming Blueberry Festival. *Sunset Ridge sure does like their summer festivals,* he mused. "Clam chowder contest. That's new," he mumbled under his breath.

"Here you go." Jett handed him a brown sack, weighted down with ten of Warren's finest halibut tacos and all the fixings. Liam paid and headed back to the truck.

A small sense of relief came over him when he saw Tessa still in the passenger seat. It wouldn't be unlike her to grab her suitcases and flee. But he'd lifted those bags of hers, and wondered if she'd stashed a couple of dead bodies in one of them. Doubtful she'd want to lug those all the way across town and up that last steep hill in her impractical shoes.

"How did you know I would be eating *with* you?" Tessa asked, eyeing the oversized bag when he climbed into the truck.

"I didn't."

She dipped her head to peer inside as Raven stirred from her slumber, nose lifted into the air before her eyes peeked open one at a time. Her ears perked and her nose wiggled a little, but she wasn't one to beg for table food. "There has to be enough in here to feed a family of four."

"You're lucky I'm sharing. You know Warren's halibut tacos are like currency around here."

"As if I could forget." A ghost of a smile crossed

Tessa's lips. Enough to make him hope the rift between them could be repaired. He had so many things he wanted to show her. "I don't suppose he's gone public with that sauce recipe?"

Liam laughed. "Yeah, right."

"Why aren't we eating here?"

"Because Raven and I have a better lunch spot." He wasn't sure how long Tessa would really stay this time, but he'd been waiting years for her return. Liam wasn't about to waste a single minute.

Judging by the recognition that flashed in her eyes, it didn't take Tessa long to realize where they were headed. The road that snaked along the rocky mountain wall on one side and the coast on the other was one they frequented years ago. Though their special spot was tucked out of plain sight and hard to get to if one didn't know where to go.

"Here?" The word hardly escaped Tessa's lips, but he heard the whisper.

"Raven likes to lounge out in the sun." It was the truth. Never mind that the reason the dog loved it so much was because it was a normal part of their routine since he adopted her earlier that spring. "Plus, it's only a couple minutes from my shop."

"Your grandpa's shop?"

He put the truck in park and hopped out, ignoring that question. Could it be it was driving her crazy not knowing everything he'd been up to? Would it also cause her distress to learn that Grandpa Bill passed away two years earlier? It seemed kinder to let her think the man retired.

"C'mon, let's eat." He let Raven leap out the driver's side before he closed the door. The dog trotted to the faded blue picnic table they frequented, running a circle until she lay down in the grass.

From the table, their view included a breathtaking display of the bay and the mountains in the distance. The road to get even this far wasn't one most cars could travel safely anymore. Too many falling rocks had beaten up the asphalt, and the town hadn't deemed the repair expenses a priority.

As a result, benches were worn down. Others broken. Tree branches and rocks littered the once-smooth sand they lounged on as teenagers. But Liam loved this spot the same, if not more, for the quiet it now offered.

"Does Warren still run his restaurant?" Tessa asked as Liam spread out the contents of the bag. Jett packed enough napkins for a roomful of toddlers being introduced to spaghetti. He set the pile on the table and anchored them with his fountain drink.

"Yep."

"Hmm."

He recognized the skepticism in her eyes. She'd worn it often her first couple of weeks in Sunset Ridge, always expecting everything to be too good to be true. He understood it then, as Tessa'd lost her mother only months earlier. But over time, those hard edges had softened. He hoped they could again.

"You're not so New York City that you're too good for Warren's Taco Tuesday, now are you?" He gave her a playful smile, mostly because he'd pushed a button.

"Give me one of those tacos." She made quick work of unwrapping it and bit into it before he could get in another jab. The hesitation that lingered in her gaze a moment ago evaporated. Tessa let out a soft moan of delight, her eyes falling closed. These had been her favorite once, he remembered.

"Still good, huh?"

"Mmm-hmm."

"You know, Warren's Sea Shack wins Best in Alaska for plenty different restaurant categories every year." He said that too, to push another button. "The halibut tacos are legendary. Tourists in Anchorage and Fairbanks get told to make the drive for them."

"Really?"

"It's no five-star restaurant," he said, unwrapping one for himself, "but I challenge you to find one of those fancy places that can make halibut tacos like these. The fish come right out of this bay, you know."

"I forgot that." Her next nibble was smaller, slower. She savored the bite, rolling the flavor around in her mouth as though trying to identify ingredients. She'd always done that. That was how he knew she was destined to be a great chef, even before she applied to culinary school.

"Figure out Warren's secret sauce yet?"

She used her pinky to scoop up a dab of sauce seeping out of her partially eaten taco, tasting it delicately. "There's salt, cilantro, and lime. But there's something else . . ."

"All that special chef training and you *still* can't crack the secret?"

"Don't you worry. I'll get to the bottom of this."

She always had been cute when she was determined. He almost said so aloud, but caught himself before it slipped. "You could just ask Warren."

Tessa laughed then, the creases between her eyebrows loosening, the tension between them lifting a notch. "Yeah, right. Warren'll take that secret to the grave and you know it."

Raven let out a small grumble and stretched in the middle of lounging at their feet, apparently annoyed by the chatter she wasn't accustomed to during lunch breaks. But also completely indifferent to the feast on the table. She'd never been given table scraps, and Liam didn't want to start a bad habit. But it made him a little sad, as if the dog had somehow missed out on her childhood.

Tessa must've caught him staring. "When did you adopt her?"

"A few months ago." They'd always talked about getting a dog—an older one who needed a good home for its last few years. He'd been gone too much while in the Army to get one, and when he moved back home, there was always a reason the time wasn't right. But he found Raven by accident while scrolling for plane parts on Craigslist, and that was it. "Would you believe she has more than eight thousand miles on those paws?"

"No wonder she's so happy to nap." A dab of the special halibut taco sauce dribbled onto the corner of her lips. Tessa let out the faintest blush before patting it away with a napkin. The Tessa he knew would've swiped at it with a finger and licked it right off. This made Liam frown.

"What happened to the Army?" she asked as she lowered her napkin to her lap.

Liam readjusted himself on the bench, his appetite fading after the first couple of tacos were down. But it wasn't that his hunger was satisfied. It was the tiniest fear growing that Tessa might not be the same person he remembered. Seventeen wasn't thirty. Maybe there was less left of the old Tessa Whitmore than he imagined. "Did my time. Got out."

"Came back here, obviously."

"Yep." The dozens of questions he wanted to ask her lingered on the tip of his tongue. But Liam feared the longer they stayed out here, away from distractions, the more she'd pry about a time he wasn't eager to talk about. His curiosity would have to wait. "Probably better get you to the lodge. Your sisters'll be surprised to see you."

CHAPTER THREE

Tessa

When Tessa boarded the plane in Vegas, Liam was the last person she expected to run into in this tiny Alaskan town. *He wasn't supposed to be here*. Part of her longed to run as far as she could from Sunset Ridge—from *him*. Too many memories lingered, like a thick, stubborn fog. She tried not thinking of the man sitting in the driver's seat.

She fought back the reminiscent emotions, but now, the longer she stayed in town, the weaker those barriers would become. Liam had always had that effect on her.

"You miss this place?" Liam shifted the truck into park, finally waking the slumbering dog in her lap. Raven hopped to her feet and perched herself on the center console to scout out their location.

"I'll let you know." A mixture of emotions fizzled in her chest at the thought of seeing her sisters. The last time the three of them had been together was for their father's funeral, and none of the trio had been in overly social moods. She wasn't naïve; she knew Cadence and Sophie both thought of her as the most coldhearted of the Whitmore sisters. She could be direct, blunt, and sometimes unsympathetic. As a sous chef in New York City, she had to be.

"The door's unlocked you know," Liam said, hand on his door.

"Right."

Palms sweaty and heart rate escalated, Tessa forced herself out of the truck. Her sisters might not be so happy to see her. She was the first one to insist they sell the lodge, as though there was no other option. What if they thought that was all about the money? *It wasn't.*

For longer than Tessa cared to admit, she'd yearned for an evening with only the three of them, sipping wine, playing some silly board game, and catching up on life. It was what normal sisters did. Now, with the lodge, maybe they could, too.

A bubble of dread bounced in her stomach, knowing they would eventually ask about the show. She badly wanted *someone* to confide in. But as the oldest, Tessa felt the bar was set higher for her. Confiding in one or both of her sisters what happened would only put a burden on them they didn't deserve.

"I'll get your bags," Liam said. "Why don't you head inside?"

It was better, she supposed, to walk through that door alone. Sooner or later, Cadence and Sophie would piece together that she bummed a ride with Liam, and why. But for a few minutes, she wanted to pretend her entire life wasn't hanging in shreds. In limbo.

Tessa hooked her purse strap over her shoulder and braved the distance to the front door. It wasn't until she reached the first step that she really stopped to look at the place. Bright flowers lined the deck. The massive structure reached for the sky with its full-length front windows, the golden hue of its logs glistening in the sunlight. How many times had Great-Aunt Patty sat outside with the midnight sun, waiting for Tessa to come back past curfew?

The flicker of Raven trotting a lap around the truck reminded her that she didn't have long until Liam joined her reunion. She hurried across the deck and went inside before she could chicken out.

Because Tessa spent most of her summers here as a teenager sneaking in back doors and second-story windows, it felt odd to use the front door. The magic of the lodge swept over her as if she were a visitor, not an owner. The vaulted ceilings and wall of glass invited in the sunlight, casting a warm glow on the open room. How long had it been since she booked herself a weekend away in a place like this? *Have I ever?*

Everything was Alaskan—from the rug decorated with wildlife to the chandelier made from stacked caribou antlers. Even the coasters on the coffee table had silhouettes of bears on them.

The quiet stirred her from her trance, and Tessa frowned.

The lodge should be bustling with guests. Hadn't her sisters told her that it rarely had a vacancy in the summer, even in the middle of the week? They'd used that statistic as part of their sales pitch a month ago when they begged her to go in on keeping the place rather than selling. A quick peek out the front windows revealed an empty gravel lot—no cars. It also warned her Liam would be headed inside any minute with her bags.

"Hello?" she called out.

"Just a minute!" Cadence's voice echoed from somewhere in the back. The kitchen, Tessa guessed.

She followed the sound of her sister's footsteps against the tile floor, along the path from her distant memories. The kitchen, however, didn't fit the image in her mind. It looked completely different than she remembered. She'd worked in restaurants with lesser quality appliances. *Go, Aunt Patty*. It appeared . . . updated. Modern. New appliances, new countertops, new flooring.

Cadence stood at the sink, washing a baking dish by hand. Tessa waited for her sister to cut the running water. "Hey."

Cadence spun at the unexpected voice and nearly dropped the glass pan. She caught it inches before it crashed against the charcoal floor tile. "Tessa?" Cadence slowly rose to her feet and set the dish on the counter, her eyes never leaving Tessa's face. "What are you doing here?"

"Surprise!" She forced a smile that she couldn't find the gusto to feel. During her weeks filming *Order Up*, she'd become exceptionally good at feeling one way but wearing an expression that said the opposite.

The reality she'd been running from hit her like a freight train on a mission. She had planned to win, the possibility of losing a faint reality. But never had she expected to be kicked off for cheating. She didn't need to *cheat*. But the producers and head chef hadn't believed her. Luckily, Cadence wrapped her in a hug before her legs gave out and sent her crumbling to the floor.

"I didn't know you were coming," Cadence said.

Me, either. The faint jingling of a dog collar forced Tessa to let go. "Well, here I am."

"It's a good thing we don't have any more sisters," said Cadence. "I don't know how many surprise visits I can take in one summer!"

Tessa stretched her neck, looking around the kitchen and through the doorway as far as her sight-line would carry. "Where *is* Sophie?"

"She and Caroline went to the store. They'll be back soon."

The last time the three sisters had chatted on the phone, Sophie dropped a bomb. Her now ex-husband was no longer in the picture and she'd moved with her young daughter to Alaska. Tessa had quite a few questions about all that, but they'd have to wait for some privacy.

Raven arrived in the kitchen before Liam, ears perked in greeting as she sat calmly near the doorway. She was such a docile creature. Tessa could hardly imagine her ever having run twenty miles or more a day.

"Got a room for this one?" Liam asked Cadence, hooking a thumb toward Tessa. She waited for him to drop the bags, but the man couldn't be bothered to do anything practical that might relax those flexed muscles. Diverting her eyes shouldn't be such a chore when it came to a man she didn't want to be around.

"Depends how long you're planning to stay." Cadence's tone was kind yet curious.

"Does it really matter?" Tessa asked, unable to hold the tongue that often got her into trouble. "Doesn't look like we have any guests."

"Have you *been* outside today?" Liam teased, finally setting her suitcases down. That obnoxious twinkle danced in his eyes—the same one that had caused many heart flips when Tessa was a teenager. "It's the nicest day we've had all summer. No one's inside who doesn't have to be."

"Liam's right," said Cadence. "Everyone is in town

or on some outing this afternoon. We've got whaler watchers, hikers, a party of four that took an ATV adventure tour, and a couple visiting a dog musher."

"Sounds like you've got it all under control," Tessa said. When she thought back to how long ago that phone call happened—the one in which her sisters sabotaged her into agreeing to keep this place—she estimated that the lodge may have been open for a week. Maybe two. "I'm impressed."

"We're going to make this place a success." Confidence radiated from Cadence. They may have been reopened for a short period of time, but her sister had invested time into getting to know their guests. It reminded Tessa a lot of Great-Aunt Patty.

"So is there a room, or . . ." Tessa'd never considered the place might be full when she booked her one-way ticket. Maybe she'd be forced to bunk with one of her sisters.

"Yes, we still have a couple of rooms open until Friday."

"What happens Friday?" Tessa asked.

"The Blueberry Festival's this weekend," Liam answered, leaning against the door jamb in a cool magazine centerfold pose. The man was hot enough to melt a North Pole snowman at Christmas. After all these years, couldn't he have the decency to be fat and bald?

"I should be gone before then anyway," Tessa finally said.

Cadence's smile dropped into a frown. Maybe she thought Tessa had lost and was now here to help them run the lodge. But there was nothing for Tessa in this small town. Nothing but broken hearts and shattered dreams. Even if the show didn't end up giving her a call back, admitting they were wrong, she had open job offers in half a dozen New York restaurants. Well, she did right now. If any of them watched the future dramatized episode that convinced America she was a cheater, that might change.

"I thought you'd call us," Cadence said, drying the baking dish she rescued earlier and putting it away in the cupboard. "Tell us how the show went."

Tessa kept her eyes on her sister and off of Liam. Either he had no idea what they were talking about or he did a good job pretending he'd never heard of *Order Up*. She shouldn't care. He made his choice all those years ago, and it split them apart.

"There hasn't been a lot of time, really."

During her flight to Alaska, it struck Tessa how isolated she'd become in her pursuit of greatness. She didn't have anyone to talk to about what happened. She was too focused on accomplishing, and she let socializing fall to the wayside.

She'd set out to achieve specific goals, never allowing failure to stop her: move to New York, work and learn from the best chefs, and someday run her own kitchen. She'd spent the past five years with her head down, hardly coming up for air. There'd been no time for friends. There had hardly been time for

Derek. But he was a chef in pursuit of the same. They understood each other and the severe lack of free time in going after those things.

At least, Tessa thought so until he broke up with her the night before they left for Vegas. *I don't want emotions to come between us. Only one of us can win, Tessa.*

"Jerk," she mumbled beneath her breath.

"What's that?" Cadence asked.

"The show is fine," Tessa said, embarrassed that the last bit had been vocalized.

"What show are we talking about?" Liam asked. The lug was still leaning against the door jamb, this time running his fingers along the back of Raven's neck. The sunlight caught in his tousled hair, showcasing exactly how kind time had been to him. Tessa forced her eyes away.

"You haven't heard?" Cadence gave Liam a genuine, excited smile, one that said she was proud of her sister. It made Tessa ache a little inside. "*Order Up: Las Vegas* is the name of it. It's been airing for, like, the past three weeks. On three nights a week. There are only eight chefs left, and Tessa is one of them."

Leave it to Liam to size her up with those intimidating eyes, searching for the hidden truth. "So that's why you're worried about the paparazzi."

"Paparazzi?" "Cadence repeated, her eyes widening as they fell on Tessa. "Do we—"

"Ignore him."

"You didn't win, did you?" Liam pressed on.

"Excuse me?"

"The show. You obviously didn't win or you wouldn't be here."

Tessa steeled her emotions, the way she had to do not only during the demanding show but throughout her time in stressful New York kitchens, too. "Just because the show is still airing doesn't mean it's still *filming.*" Liam's taunt replayed in her mind, but there was no way he had insider information. Anyone who leaked that would face a hefty penalty, as she was reminded on her way out the door. "How do you even know what *kind* of show it is if you haven't heard of it? Might not be a competition at all."

Liam let out an unguarded laugh that caused Raven's tail to swish against the tile. "You never cared about the limelight, sweetheart. Only winning. I dare you to tell me it's *not* some sort of a competition."

Tessa crossed her arms over her chest. "Fine, so it is."

"Did you win?" he asked.

Despite how desperately she needed someone to talk to about the show, she didn't want to give Liam ammunition by admitting a thing. Besides, the contract offered a valid excuse she could hide behind: the fine for leaking spoilers was a quarter of a million dollars. "I can't say anything about the show until the last episode airs. It's in my contract."

"They made you sign a contract?" Cadence asked.

"Of course they did." Tessa marched up to Liam and hooked her hand around a suitcase strap. Raven looked up at her with wide, expectant eyes, distracting her. She contemplated yet again how difficult it would be to borrow his dog for a few days. She wondered what kind of treats Raven favored, because she was willing to buy a case if it bribed the dog to stay with her.

"You can't kidnap her," Liam said for the second time that day.

Tessa spun away after a quick glare, the lighter of the two bags in hand. The other one might make her stumble over her own feet, and she didn't need to add that embarrassment to her already bad streak of luck. "Doesn't mean I won't try."

"I can get that." Cadence reached for the bag, relieving Tessa of her load. But this close, Tessa didn't miss the flicker in her sister's eyes. Cadence was piecing things together. "Did you . . . rent a car?" she asked.

"Yeah."

Liam huffed out a laugh behind them, causing Tessa to twist sharply. Over her shoulder she shot daggers at him with her eyes. The look was intended as a warning to keep his trap shut, but Liam had never been intimidated by her.

"I better get back to the shop," Liam said, giving Tessa a wink that caused tingles to dance in her chest. "Got to run the tow truck out."

She hadn't expected to see him. That was why she kept reacting in such irrational ways. It had to be.

"I hope no one's hurt?" Cadence asked.

33

"Nope, the driver didn't have a scratch on her." Liam let his gaze linger a little too long on Tessa before he headed out to his truck, Raven at his heel.

The moment the front door closed, Cadence jumped. "Why did he carry your suitcases inside?"

"It's nothing." Tessa grabbed the heavier bag with both hands. "Can you show me to my room?"

"Tessa?"

"Fine!" She dropped the bag, already regretting letting Liam leave before she had him carry this one to her room. It certainly wouldn't strain him to lug it a little farther; he had muscles for days. "Liam's going to tow my rental car."

"Why?"

"Because I saw a moose in the road and—"

"You didn't hit Ed, did you?" Tessa was so caught off-guard that her sister knew the moose she was talking about, words failed to form. Cadence blinked. "Oh no, you did!"

"No, I most certainly did not." Tessa shook her head, as if this was a normal conversation about some Moose named *Ed*. "Cadence, if I had hit a moose in a Mustang, there's no way I would be standing here without a scratch."

"Oh, thank goodness!"

Tessa wasn't convinced the relief was on her account. More than likely on Ed's. "I swerved into a ditch and ended up with a flat tire." No need to mention the radiator or any other noises she heard during impact. Hopefully, Liam could patch the car up and the rental company would be satisfied.

"I'm glad you're okay."

"How about that room?"

"I'll grab a key." Cadence gave her another hearty hug. "Tessa, I'm so glad you're here."

CHAPTER FOUR

Liam

Back out on the private road, Liam whistled as he hooked the tow cables to the Mustang. Raven stood by his side, just to let him know she was there. "You're really something, girl, you know that?" He ran his hand along the back of her neck a couple of times and then got back to work. Never before had he met such a mellow dog. It was nearly impossible to imagine that she had at one time been an Iditarod champion.

Raven tilted her head, her eyes falling on the crushed front corner of the car.

"Could've been worse," he told her.

The only damage he could see was to the front end —busted radiator, broken tie rod, and one flat tire. He'd have to take a closer look when he got it to the shop, but the frame appeared okay. He hadn't wanted to alarm Tessa, but if she bent the frame in her attempt to miss Ed, there wasn't much he could do without involving the rental company. It wasn't as though he could switch out her car for another. It wasn't a goldfish.

Before he hauled the convertible out of the ditch, Liam took a look inside for anything Tessa might've left behind—especially breakables. She'd never let him hear the end of it if the bumpy road busted up something important to her.

Raven poked her head around his leg as he kneeled on the driver's seat. The interior appeared empty, except for a cell phone charger cord. He rolled it up and stuck it in his jeans pocket.

About to close the door, Raven took the rare opportunity to slink into the car like a cat. "Raven, what are you doing?" The dog didn't normally misbehave or cause mischief. "You can't ride in the convertible today, girl." He tried to coax her out, but she sat in the seat, tail swishing against the leather. She gave a faint whine.

Liam bent down, prepared to scoop her out. She was less than fifty pounds and wouldn't likely put up a fight. But before he could wrap his arms around her, he caught the glimmer of something silver on the passenger side floor.

"It can't be."

Raven moved now, hopping out of the car and

allowing him room to lean over and retrieve the necklace.

His heart stopped as time rewound.

The weekend of the Blueberry Festival, thirteen years ago. Tessa in a light yellow sundress, her long dark hair curled and dancing in the breeze. She was only in his life a mere six weeks, but Liam knew then in the depths of his heart there would never be another for him. Everyone thought he was crazy for how certain he was, but he didn't care. Tessa was it.

Liam, it's so beautiful!

She'd thrown her arms around his neck and squeezed so tight his airway was nearly cut off. But he wouldn't have loosened her hold for any amount of Alaskan acreage. Snaking the silver chain through her fingers, she let the heart dangle and studied it. In the center, where the two top loops met, a tiny jewel twinkled in the sunlight.

Aquamarine, he'd told her.

My birthstone.

That earned him one heart-pounding kiss and a few hoots and hollers from people around them.

Raven let out a bark, bringing him back to the present. Liam hurried out of the car and shut the door. It was best to get going before someone caught him. Old Man Franks, by popular vote, was the grumpiest man in Sunset Ridge. Every town had one. He was supposed to be gone all week on a fishing excursion, though. It was the only reason Liam had been using the private road as a shortcut to his plot of land.

Old Man Franks knew a handful of people used his road to get to other places faster, but pretended not to so when he caught someone, he could show off his shotgun. Liam heard rumors that he fired shots on occasion, but he'd never had that personal experience.

He slipped the necklace into his shirt pocket for safekeeping. He could give it back to her tonight at the lodge. "Or not," he told Raven.

She let out a grumble. He dismissed the possibility that she didn't approve of his plan and instead decided Raven was tired of being in the middle of nowhere. Back in his shop, she had a perfectly comfortable dog bed that beckoned her for naps.

The dog trotted back to the truck and waited for him to open the door. Though aging, she still had decent agility. Enough to hop into the lifted truck as though it was nothing. In the few months they'd been together, they had developed an easy routine. For an older husky, he was impressed with how easy Raven was to train. He'd grown up with dogs, but she was definitely the smartest one he'd ever met. He set to pulling the Mustang out of the ditch.

He decided to keep the necklace. *For a day or two.* It couldn't be only a coincidence that Tessa kept it all these years. Even less of a chance since she brought it with her to Sunset Ridge. If it meant something to her, she'd come looking for it.

"Maybe there's still hope, Raven. Maybe."

All those years away in the Army, he'd never given up on Tessa Whitmore. Liam dated off and on, but no one held a torch to the woman who plagued his dreams. In the depths of his soul, he knew fate would bring them back together.

Liam wasn't too proud to admit that the vision he'd kept in mind didn't quite match up to the woman he found stranded on the side of the road. But the necklace gave him hope. Fate, he had learned, had a funny way of setting you straight. If Old Man Franks wasn't out of town, Liam never would've risked taking the shortcut. Tessa would still be here waiting for help. Or worse, arrested for trespassing.

The tow back to town was slow, made slower by the sharp turns on the narrow road. Liam had time to wonder why fate thought *now* was the ideal time for Tessa to show back up in his life, months before he had a chance to get everything done.

His new house was hardly more than a hole in the ground with a pile of logs stacked nearby. The builder hadn't even poured concrete for the crawlspace yet—that would happen tomorrow. He knew because he'd been out there to check minutes before he found Tessa stranded. Liam had plans to have the dream house they always talked about finished before she finally made her way back to Sunset Ridge.

Despite his best attempts to slip through town unnoticed, three different people waved at him. Their raised eyebrows and tilted heads warned of their curiosity. No one in Sunset Ridge owned a cherry-red Mustang. "You couldn't get a gray one, Tessa?" he muttered.

But subtle wasn't a trait Tessa Whitmore possessed.

Back at the shop, he waited for the smaller of the two garage bay doors to open. The other held an old diesel truck with a drive shaft problem. Usually both bays contained projects, but he'd just returned an old John Deere tractor this morning and freed up the south bay. People brought Liam all sorts of things to tinker with. As long as it had a motor, he could usually figure out how to fix it.

"Guess we have company, girl." His sister's sea-green compact SUV sat on the east side of the shop, along the road. He wondered what it was he forgot. April didn't come by here often, as it made her too sad. She'd been closer to their grandpa than any other grandkid. If she had a mechanical bone in her body, Grandpa would surely have left the place to her. But April was better suited at being a nurse than a mechanic. "Better get out and face the music, huh?"

He had no more than released the Mustang from the tow hook when April appeared through the open door. "Where have you *been*?"

"Found someone stranded." He nodded toward the car.

"You've been gone for over three hours. And where's your phone?"

"Left it in the shop." Liam had better signal than

most, which was why he left his phone whenever he didn't feel like being bothered. "And a guy's gotta eat. Want a taco?"

"No." April folded her arms across her chest, resting them on her very round baby bump. "Maybe." She was due in less than a month. He thought about riling her up with a beachball comment. But the heavy glare in her narrowed eyes made him a little afraid she might shoot fire if he tried. So no teasing her right now.

"They're in the truck."

"What kind?"

"Halibut."

"Wait, can you eat halibut?"

"In moderation." April didn't take her eyes off him as she made her way to the cab.

"Can you please tell me what I did so we can move on?" April was a spitfire when hormones *weren't* involved, so his prodding was dangerous at best. Catastrophic at worst. Liam had faced less terrifying things in combat than April Averetts.

She returned around the side of the truck and unwrapped a taco. "You really don't know?"

Liam scanned through his week's memories, but everything was tied to someone needing something repaired either at the shop or the house. Add to that Tessa's unexpected arrival, and there wasn't room for much more. Had he skipped dinner at his parents' house? Owen turned five in January, so he definitely hadn't missed a birthday party.

April stopped mid-chew and demanded, "The *crib,* Liam."

With the force of a tidal wave, guilt twisted in Liam's chest as the slipup came crashing back into his mind. *Crap.* "I'm sorry, April. I completely forg—"

"Yeah, yeah. You're always so busy lately." She jabbed a finger at his chest. Though he towered over his older sister, April instilled fear in him with little effort. "I wish you and Dad would get over your little feud so you'd come around more. Owen misses his uncle."

He'd promised to assemble the crib since her husband, Miles, was working on the oil fields in the North Slope for the next couple of weeks. The baby wasn't due until after he came back, but that didn't guarantee anything. "It has nothing to do with Dad. I'm sorry, Apr—"

"And these tacos are *cold.*"

"I'll get the crib put together soon, I promise."

"When?"

He wished he could say tomorrow, but time was against him this week. Too many commitments, a necessary trip to Anchorage, and Tessa's inevitable departure if he didn't figure out how to make time to convince her to stay. But his sister didn't want excuses, not when it came to promises made. "Saturday morning?"

"*Saturday?*" Her scowl alone was a hazard to any nearby flammable object. Add in those fiery eyes, and spontaneous combustion was a high risk—to him included. "There's no guarantee this baby is waiting even *that* long."

He revised his answer. "Tomorrow. I'll come by tomorrow." Liam didn't have a clue how he would make that work, considering he was due to pick up an ATV at seven-thirty, fit in an oil change at nine, a couple more in the afternoon, and he still had to make a few calls to track down a radiator for Tessa's rental. But he'd figure it out.

"I don't care if there's a cockroach infestation. You're putting that crib together *tomorrow*." She jabbed Liam three times in a row with that pointy finger, and then a fourth to emphasize her seriousness.

Liam tried his best to keep a straight face. April sure was random during her pregnancy. He couldn't resist a little jab, though. "We don't have cockroaches in Alaska."

"You're *lucky*." She dropped the remainder of the cold taco in his aluminum trash can outside the south bay door, making Liam a little remorseful that he'd offered to share at all. He'd have eaten it cold even if it were three days old. Warren's halibut tacos were *that* good.

"I'll be there at eleven," Liam said.

"Eleven?" April was about to launch into some additional argument, but before the first few words spewed, she took a deep breath. He imagined her counting backward from ten. She did that more frequently since Miles started working on the North

Slope. He was gone two weeks at a time, and this time it'd been a month. "Fine."

He thought luck might be on his side when April took a couple of steps toward her car. Sunset Ridge was a small town by most standards, and it didn't take long for rumors to circulate. His sister seemed to have a direct line to the town's gossip vein. But even April couldn't possibly know that Tessa Whitmore was back.

"Whose car is that?"

"Does it matter?" He tried to sound indifferent. If April figured out Tessa was around, she'd tell Mom for sure. Mom had always been a little reserved when it came to their whirlwind romance. *You're both too strong-willed. Like adding gasoline to a forest fire.* Those words, like his love for Tessa, had never left him.

"Snot. Be by at eleven, or I'm hunting you down."

"Right."

Before she left, April helped herself to another taco. This time, she didn't seem at all bothered that it was cold. "Eleven, Liam. I don't care *what* happens."

CHAPTER FIVE

Tessa

Tessa riffled through the open suitcases on her bed, tearing through clothes and scattering them all over the black bear comforter. Giving her the bear-themed room had surely been a cruel joke. She *hated* bears.

But that wasn't her biggest concern right now.

Her necklace was *missing*.

She dumped the contents of her overloaded purse. Makeup, hand lotion, a dead cell phone, and a half-eaten package of Red Vines fell out. She never boarded a plane without the tasty licorice. But no necklace.

It was stupid to have kept it all these years. She never let herself forget that, every time she scrambled to make sure she had it with her. But each time she tried to get rid of it, it felt as if she were ripping out a chunk of her heart. Rather than examine the irrational feelings, it was easier to keep the dang thing.

She'd worn the heart-shaped pendant beneath her shirt every day she was in Vegas. Maybe it had something to do with Derek breaking off their relationship the day before they left New York to compete on the show. But if Tessa was being honest with herself, she'd worn it more than not in the past year. She rarely took it off. But this time, something about it triggered the metal detector at the airport—that was a first—and forced her to take it off. She tucked it into her purse for safekeeping.

The car.

When she swerved into the ditch to avoid *Ed* —"Seriously, who names a *moose*?"—her purse slid, and dumped out half its contents. The necklace probably spilled out. She only hoped it was still on the passenger side floor. If not, she would have to venture back onto Old Man Franks' private road.

A knock sounded at the door. "Come in."

"Hey." Sophie poked her head inside, offering a warm, welcome smile in greeting. "Can I come in?"

"Of course." Tessa pretended to ignore the wreckage spread across her bed, hoping her indifference kept Sophie from questioning the mess. She went to give her sister a hug in case indifference wasn't enough.

"I can't believe you're here." Sophie cupped her

hands around Tessa's shoulders, as if to get a good look at her sister. "When did you get in?"

"Flew into Anchorage this morning," Tessa answered, pulling free of Sophie, afraid if she looked too closely, she might figure out everything.

"It's such a pleasant surprise to have you here. We had no idea you were coming."

"Me, either."

"Hence the bears." Sophie gave her an apologetic shrug, and the two laughed. "The other room's worse, unless you prefer grizzlies to black bears. But that would be too cruel of a joke. You don't really like that nickname, do you?" Sophie was referring to what they called Tessa on *Order Up*: Tessa the grizzly bear.

"Never my idea." Tessa shook her head, pulling her sister to the opposite side of the bed that offered a window view. She shoved aside a pile of clothes so they could sit. "Where's Caroline?"

"Helping Cadence with dinner."

"Dinner . . ." Tessa realized there were so many things she didn't know about the lodge she was now part-owner of. From the moment she arrived at the filming studio for *Order Up*, her cell phone and any other electronic device that might give her an advantage were surrendered. The last conversation she had with her sisters was the one agreeing to keep the lodge. Everything that happened since was a mystery. "Do we serve meals to guests?"

"No. But we bake muffins and leave fruit and coffee out in the morning. Donuts got a little expensive. We'd like to offer more down the road, but we're still figuring out a lot."

On one hand, Tessa felt relieved she wouldn't have to interact with guests during an evening meal. But it also made her feel guilty, leaving her sisters to figure this out on their own. Tessa may not know much about running a business, but she did know her way around a kitchen, guest counts, and catering numbers. "Hmm."

"It's not the worst setup. We recommend local restaurants, and so far, guests have loved them. Moosecakes is a huge hit. So is Willamina's Big Dipper."

"Moosecakes is still open?"

"Oh, yes!"

Tessa smiled. Typical Sophie. Always adding a silver lining, even when things were tough. Maybe Tessa should wait to ask, but patience had never been one of her top qualities. "What happened with Blake?"

Sophie rose from the bed and took two strides to the window.

Giving her sister a minute to collect her thoughts, Tessa followed her gaze outside. Her room offered a view of the serene backyard and the thick woodline. Somewhere back there was a trail to a lookout point. Her view *was* serene, but she would have no warning if Liam decided for any reason to return. Knowing him, he would.

"He left me, Tessa," Sophie finally said, hugging

her arms against her chest. "The jerk knocked up one of his patients and divorced us to be with her and their new twins."

"Caroline?"

"He doesn't want anything to do with her. It doesn't even make sense."

"But she's his *daughter*."

"She's had a hard time understanding why Daddy isn't around anymore. Why he doesn't call or visit or take her to the beach on Saturday mornings." A tear trickled down Sophie's cheek, making Tessa feel guilty for springing the topic.

More than that, anger twisted inside her. Maybe it would have been better to pursue a law career. She'd take that poor excuse for a man to the cleaners. "Any man who doesn't appreciate how valuable you and your daughter are, Soph, isn't worth a second of your time."

"I only wish he wasn't so cold to Caroline." She gave a weak smile. "He's her father, for crying out loud. But I think his new wife's convinced him he's not."

Tessa had a whole lot of opinions of said *new wife*, but none of them were very nice or anywhere near appropriate, so she kept them to herself. "Men are just a load of trouble, aren't they?"

Finally, Sophie let out a laugh. "Guessing your hot chef boyfriend is old news?"

Tessa yearned to spill it all to Sophie. She could trust either of her sisters not to go running to the tabloids with spoilers. But another knock came at the door, this one more like an excitable woodpecker than the earlier gentle knock from her sister.

"Dinner's ready!" a small voice announced.

A layer of ice melted around Tessa's heart at the sound. The tiny thing was the most adorable child she had ever seen, in her curly pigtails, with those bright eyes she'd obviously gotten from Sophie, and her cartoon moose T-shirt.

"Hey, sweetie!" Tessa smiled so big her cheeks hurt.

"Hi." Caroline's small hand gripped the doorknob as she swung her petite body from side to side. A stuffed moose dangled from her other fist, thrashing about with her nervous movements.

"Do you remember Aunty Tessa?" Sophie asked.

"Yeah."

"Can you come give her a hug?"

In the last decade or more, Tessa had given very little thought to having children of her own. Derek— her latest mistake—had no desire to have kids. With both of them so career-driven, it made sense that kids didn't fit into their lifestyle. But Tessa would be lying if she said her breath didn't hitch, waiting to see whether this precious child would warm up to her or not.

"What about dinner?" Caroline asked with a delicate voice.

"She'll come around," Sophie said, patting Tessa on the shoulder. "She's just shy at first."

"Of course." Inside, though, Tessa felt like a failure. It was a strange feeling, one she never thought she'd experience. The idea of a family hadn't taken root since the last time she was in Sunset Ridge—when she was seventeen years old. Back then, she and Liam had talked about the future all the time. Three kids, that was the number they'd agreed on.

But then he joined the Army without telling her, and all the plans they made for the future crumbled away. Since the day she boarded a plane leaving Alaska behind, kids no longer crossed her mind.

Tessa shook free of the fantasy's hold. There wouldn't be time for dating, much less settling down and starting a family. When she returned to Vegas and won *Order Up*, she'd be too swamped running her own kitchen in a brand-new restaurant. One that already had a lot of hype and was guaranteed to have a packed dining room every night of the week.

"Coming?" Sophie asked from the doorway as she wrapped her hand with her daughter's.

"In a minute. I just want to . . . clean up."

"We'll wait to start eating," Sophie promised.

Tessa refolded her clothes and placed them back in her suitcases, refocusing her emotions on something she could control: finding that necklace. Tomorrow she'd stop by the shop to check on her rental. She needed to know she had a ride to the airport should she get the call. A call that would only come if she found a way to prove she never snuck a recipe card to her work station and cheated her way to a victory she rightfully earned.

Men really are the worst, she mused on the walk down the hallway toward the kitchen. They couldn't be trusted not to break your heart to forward their own agenda. That's why she needed to avoid Liam at all costs.

"I saved you a seat."

Her heart throttled in her chest. "Liam?"

"So, we don't serve *most* of the guests," Sophie said. "But we do serve this one."

"Guest?" *No, no, no.* Liam Davies was *not* staying at the Sunset Ridge Lodge. Impossible. If he owned a mechanic shop, surely he owned—or at least rented —a house. Or even stayed in his parents' basement. *Desperate times.* Why on earth would he pay for a lodge room?

"That's right," Cadence chimed in. "He was actually our first one."

"How long have we been open again?" Tessa asked, reluctantly circling the table to the one remaining spot. At least she'd be close to Raven, even if the husky was curled in a ball, napping behind Liam's chair.

"Eleven days," Cadence answered, passing a bowl of mashed potatoes. Normally, Tessa would turn her nose up at mashed potatoes she hadn't prepared herself—no one else ever put in enough sour cream, and most didn't use chives at all—but after the diet she'd suffered through during the filming of the show, everything on this table made her mouth water. At least for a couple of days she wouldn't be eating out of a vending machine.

"I'm sure meatloaf and potatoes aren't exactly what you're used to," Cadence apologized to her once Tessa took her seat. "But this is an extra special meal. Caroline helped me cook the potatoes and added her very own secret ingredient. Didn't you, honey?"

When the mashed potatoes reached Tessa, she peered into the bowl, expecting to find gummy bears or bacon bits—something worthy of a four-year-old's imagination. But there was nothing extra visible to the eye.

"It's a secret!" Caroline exclaimed from across the table, kicking her legs against her chair until Sophie scolded her to stop.

Desperate to win her niece's affections, Tessa spooned a generous pile of potatoes onto her plate. After passing the bowl to Liam, ignoring the slight graze of their fingers and electrical charge it shot up her hand, she scooped some onto her fork and savored it, making the bite last until she could identify the special ingredient. There were the usual suspects. The milk, butter, sour cream, a dash of salt. "These are really good," she said to Caroline and meant it. She took another bite to confirm her suspicions.

Melted gouda.

"I know what it is," Tessa said to Caroline.

"Don't tell!"

Slipping out of her chair, Tessa made her way to her niece. "Can I whisper it in your ear and you'll tell me if I'm right?"

"Okay!"

Tessa whispered *gouda cheese* in Caroline's ear, careful to cover her mouth with her hand so no one else would hear.

"How did you know?" The pouty tone, drawn eyebrows, and pursed lips weren't exactly the reaction Tessa expected. How was she to know that guessing the right answer would spoil Caroline's happiness?

Sophie offered her one of her famous sympathetic shrugs.

"I'm a chef," Tessa told Caroline, hoping to salvage her mistake. "I'm good at guessing flavors."

"A chef?" Caroline repeated, the pouting expression replaced with a curious one.

"Yep. Don't worry, I won't tell anyone what your secret ingredient is. I promise."

The girl studied her for a moment, then stuck out her hand. Balling it into a fist, she said, "Pinky swear."

Tessa's heart warmed at the small bond they'd formed. She didn't know how long she'd be around this visit, but she hoped to have enough time to become Caroline's favorite aunt. And if her niece was a future chef in the making, it would be a piece of cake.

Feeling victorious, Tessa returned to her seat and finished filling her plate with meatloaf and green beans. The meal looked phenomenal compared to the several nights of eating Cheetos in bed for supper. Tomorrow, Tessa decided, she'd cook for her family.

She tried her best to ignore Liam during the meal, but it didn't seem he was interested in ignoring *her*. "I would have saved you a taco," he said, leaning against her shoulder, an electrical current now constant between them, "but my sister raided my stash."

"How is April?" Polite conversation. Tessa could do that. Especially in front of an impressionable child.

"A couple of weeks from popping with kiddo number two."

"So, you're an uncle?" He'd always had an easy way with kids, able to make them burst out in a fit of giggles on a moment's notice. He was probably the *fun* uncle, too.

"Owen. He's a year older than Caroline." Liam emptied his glass of milk, his gaze falling back on Tessa. "Want to meet him?"

"How's your mom?" she asked to deflect that question, hoping her sisters would find other things to talk about rather than eavesdrop on this uncomfortable train wreck. But she couldn't deny the allure. "Still selling houses?" It was one thing to sit next to Liam at a dinner table. Quite another to spend time with his family. *This is temporary*, she reminded herself.

Liam lifted his water glass in toast. "You know Mom." Jolene Davies had never been Tessa's biggest fan. She'd thought Tessa and Liam were all wrong for each other—both too rash and reckless. Too much yin and no yang. That was *before* Liam joined the Army. "Can't sit still."

"And your dad?"

"Want to go with me to Moosecakes tomorrow for breakfast?" Liam asked.

Tessa swallowed, hoping to regain her composure in front of the table full of staring family. The blunt question threw her. Even Raven perked from her slumber and was now looking at her expectantly. "I can't."

"Why not?"

Because if I do, I'll be in trouble. It was bad enough Liam was staying at the lodge for an undetermined amount of time. She could handle him for a few hours in the evening but only if she avoided him during the day. "I'm making breakfast here tomorrow. For the guests."

"You are?" Cadence asked.

"Sure. Why not? I'm part owner, too. It's the least I can do to pitch in while I'm staying in town."

"That would be lovely," Sophie said.

"Can I help?" Caroline's eyes widened with excitement, and there was no way Tessa was going to burst her bubble twice in one night.

"Of course you can, sweetie."

She ignored the subtle frown Liam now wore. He was up to something; she'd bet her chef's knives on it. Though Tessa felt relieved for dodging this one bullet, there would be more.

CHAPTER SIX

Liam

The night had been a sleepless one, knowing the woman he'd pined for all these years was staying in the room across the hall. After more than a decade of separation by thousands of miles, a mere hallway now stood between them. Liam tossed and turned, and couldn't even blame the sun that never set for keeping him up.

Raven snuggled with him, sleep growling from time to time, and kicking at the invisible ground beneath her paws. He wished he could have joined her; drifted off for even an hour. But his alarm sounded too soon. Earlier that week, Liam promised to pick up a boat. Its motor wasn't running quite right. If he didn't get it this morning, he wasn't sure when he could fit it in his schedule.

"Time to get up, girl." He roused the dog from her slumber and led her outside through a back door. Unlike the dogs he grew up with, Raven didn't run off or chase after rabbits without a leash. She stayed within ten yards of him at all times, always curious but never straying.

Liam thought he caught a hint of Ed's brown hide in the trees, but the flash of it was gone too soon to be sure. "C'mon, Raven. My turn now."

After a shower, he stroked his beard, deciding against a trim. He'd caught Tessa staring more than once yesterday. With the blush that crept up that soft neck of hers, Liam suspected she approved. If the beard helped convince her to give them the second chance they deserved, who was he to shave it?

He slipped on a long-sleeved button-up shirt he would no doubt shed mid-morning. The forecast was calling for a high of seventy-eight, but the morning still had its usual cool, crispness to it.

Tessa's necklace spilled out of yesterday's shirt pocket when he moved it from the floor to the bench at the foot of the bed. *Almost forgot*. He should give it to her this morning—any excuse to talk to her was one Liam wouldn't mind taking—but it didn't feel like the right time.

During the duskiest hours that sleep had eluded him, Liam found himself thinking about his future. He'd been itching to settle down for a while now. It wasn't until Cadence Whitmore came to Sunset Ridge that he believed Tessa might come back, too.

That event had sparked everything—the sale of his house, the start of construction on a lot his grandpa left him, even the Alaskan Woodsman competition where he won the plane they'd always talked about owning.

But if Tessa decided to leave to run some fancy five-star restaurant, Liam would have to accept that they weren't meant to be.

"Better get to it, girl." He held the door open for Raven.

He was about as far down the hall and away from the kitchen as a guest could get on the main floor. The clattering of dishes reached him as he locked up his room. If all that banging and clanging was any indication, someone was irritable this morning. *Odd*.

Cautiously, Liam took quiet steps toward the kitchen, Raven leisurely strolling by his side. Liam kept his boots on the runner rug so his steps wouldn't echo off the hardwood floors and give away his presence. He wondered how anyone else slept through this racket. The entire place would be up before long.

"How did he *do* it?" he heard Tessa mutter between closing drawers. "There are freaking cameras *everywhere*."

When Liam stopped in the doorway, Raven sat. Her tail wagged against the tile at the sight of her new friend. Liam was half surprised Tessa hadn't broken into his room last night and stolen his dog. But right now, he was more intrigued by the things he heard her muttering and what they might mean.

He leaned against the door jamb, crossing his legs at the ankles, and waited until there was a break in the noise. "Good morning, sweetheart."

Tessa looked up briefly from her frantic cupboard search. "Breakfast isn't ready, so go on. Get."

"I'm not here for that."

She stopped her rummaging long enough to turn in Liam's direction, hands planted on her hips. A dishtowel dangled from her fingers. In her faded T-shirt, dark hair pulled into a loose ponytail, and face devoid of most of her makeup, she looked simply breathtaking. He liked her so much better this way, not all made up for the camera.

"What do you want, *Liam*?" She snapped his name with extra emphasis.

"It's not too late to take me up on my invitation." From the look of the mess spread along the counter, there'd been a whole lot of scrounging for ingredients but no actual success *cooking* anything. "Moosecakes is still as good as you remember." Liam didn't really have time anymore to sit down and eat breakfast, but if he could change Tessa's mind by doing so, he'd make time.

"If I want moose-shaped pancakes, I'll make them myself. From *scratch*."

Something had her extra irritated this morning, and he desperately wanted to know what. He'd bet his Super Cub that it had something to do with her mutterings. *Is it about the show?* But Tessa Whitmore was a complex woman. A lifetime wouldn't be enough time to figure her out. Liam sure wanted to try, though.

"What are you smiling about?" she demanded.

"Not everyone is on that East Coast time zone, you know."

"I've been in Vegas for the last month."

"So I've heard." If she only knew how badly he wanted to know every detail about the competition, she'd be shocked. Learning he'd watched every episode would probably give her a heart attack. There was another episode tonight, and he planned to barricade himself inside his room with some heavily buttered popcorn. But Liam couldn't let Tessa have all the cards. It was too dangerous admitting any of this. "What seems to be the trouble?" He nodded toward the mess on the counter.

"I want to make breakfast, but there's no *food* here."

Knowing it would rile her up, he strutted to the fridge and tossed open the door. "Looks pretty stocked to me."

She tossed her hands up, sending a towel flying in the process. It landed at Raven's feet. "I can't cook with this."

"I see eggs, milk, and bacon. Fresh blueberries even. I bet Tillie Grant brought those over. What more do you need?" Liam wasn't the greatest cook. And when it came to grilling, it was best to have the fire department on speed dial. But he could rustle up eggs and bacon with little trouble.

Tessa rolled her eyes, retrieving the towel. "You wouldn't get it."

He almost told her this wasn't some gourmet challenge, but he caught himself before that slipped out. Instead, he offered, "There're muffins and fruit already out for the guests." Just like there had been every morning since they opened. In half an hour, Sophie or Cadence would add orange juice and a pot of coffee to the spread. The routine had worked well, and as far as Liam knew, not a single guest complained. "Come to Moosecakes with me," he said once again.

Tessa narrowed her eyes, but softened when the husky trotted over to her and offered her head for a scratch. Raven leaned against her legs, but even her soft, pleading eyes didn't seem to do the trick. "I can't."

"What's all this racket?" Cadence asked with a yawn, rubbing her tired eyes in the process.

"Chef Tessa isn't impressed with your kitchen," Liam chimed in before Tessa had a chance to defend herself.

"Don't listen to him," Tessa said. "It's just not a setup I'm used to, that's all. And you don't have baking powder."

"You don't have to worry about breakfast, Tessa." With another yawn, Cadence crossed the kitchen to a tall cupboard near the fridge and pulled out a canister. "They like the muffins. Besides, most of the guests have plans, and some already left. A few of them booked a kayaking trip today, and the show time is five. Here's your baking powder."

"Where did you find that?"

"In the cupboard by the fridge. Where it always is."

"Then I have scones to make. I'm going to make breakfast while I'm here. Make myself useful."

With that declaration, Liam stopped pressing for a Moosecakes date he didn't have time for anyway. Denver Grant was expecting him to pick up his boat in twenty minutes. But he was curious about one thing. "How long *are* you here for?"

"I'm waiting for a call," Tessa said, stuffing the towel she'd been holding over the oven handle and hefting the canister of baking powder. "When they tell me to come back, I have to leave."

Liam didn't like the sound of that. It put everything he thought he'd figured out up in the air again. He'd been convinced Tessa lost or she wouldn't be here. She'd be lounging in Vegas, enjoying the spoils of her victory until the final episode aired and she could tell the world. But instead, she'd hopped—unannounced—on a plane to Alaska.

His eyes dropped to the rolled-up chef's knives on the counter. If she wasn't planning to stay more than a couple of days, why would she risk something happening to her most prized possession by putting it in a checked bag? The expensive knives could get lost or stolen, and were better left in a safe place.

Something still didn't add up.

The thoughts only whirled around in his head as Liam drove the short distance to the Grant residence. Tessa Whitmore was not an easy woman to wear down, and she'd only gotten tougher during their years apart. But Liam wasn't deterred. He'd give this his best shot, and if Tessa still decided to leave, well, Liam would move on.

He had to.

As he snaked his truck up the driveway, he spotted Denver standing beside his aluminum fishing boat, once a bright yellow, but now in desperate need of a paint job. It was definitely a little rougher around the edges than Denver described. But it had potential.

Denver—the oldest of Tillie Grant's sons—moved home a month ago after completing his military commitment. He had joined the Army a year after Liam got out. He was staying with his parents while waiting on the closing of a house he bought on Fireweed Lane. Liam knew because his mom was Denver's realtor. But even if that weren't the case, most of Sunset Ridge knew, too. Secrets never kept long in this town.

"Thanks for coming by," Denver greeted as Liam hopped out of his truck. "Ryder needed my truck this week for a fishing trip."

"He left you behind?" Liam said with a smirk.

Denver shook his head. "Said I could come when my boat was working." Denver was three or four years younger than Liam, so they hadn't spent much time together when they were kids. But from what Liam remembered of him, he was a good kid. "Motor doesn't sound too great. Was hoping you could take a look."

"Where'd you get this?" Liam asked.

"From a guy in Kenai. Said it needed some TLC, but the price was too good to pass up, even if it ends up being a yard ornament."

"I'm sure I can get it running one way or another." Liam loved a good puzzle when it came to motors. Even one as old as this one.

"That'd be great."

He could remove the motor and take that back to the shop, but he'd feel better taking the boat on the water when he was done. Liam preferred to follow all the way through on things like this. Maybe why he had more business than he could handle, but it was just his way.

"I should have some time this afternoon." Really, he wanted to close the shop for a week and spend all the time he could convincing Tessa to stay. But that was the plight of a desperate man, and Liam wasn't desperate. Yet. He refused to believe he was anyway.

Tessa aside, he still had to stop by his parents' place and help April with that crib.

"How's life at the lodge?" Denver asked.

"They spoil me." It was the truth. Though the

other guests hardly got more than complimentary muffins, fruit, and cookies, Liam had been invited to every meal. He usually didn't take them up on it. "Raven more." On cue, the husky poked her head out of the open window of his truck, ears perked and tail swishing in leisurely contentedness.

Denver helped Liam hook the boat up to his truck. "Any idea on the timeline of the house?" Denver asked.

Even with the favor owed to him by the builder, Liam's house wasn't due to be finished until late October. But he had a few tricks up his sleeve and favors left to redeem. "Not soon enough." Finishing it earlier had become a much bigger priority since he found Tessa stranded on the side of the road.

"I'll let you know when she's ready," Liam assured him about the boat.

Temptation to stop by the construction site was almost too much to fight. He'd been all over the world during his time in the military. He'd had his time of thrills and adventure. The only adventure Liam wanted now was the one in Sunset Ridge, Alaska. He was ready to settle down with a wife . . . in their new house.

CHAPTER SEVEN

Tessa

Tessa let out a breath she'd been holding since Liam showed up in the kitchen, leaning against the door jamb and looking like some smug movie star. If Raven hadn't been at his side, looking so dang happy to see her, Tessa would've shooed him away much sooner.

Turning down breakfast with him went against her instincts. She hated that after all this time, Liam could so easily wedge his way into her thoughts so she hardly had the ability to say no to anything he asked. The pull to go with him wherever he wanted was as strong today as it was when she was seventeen. It was as if no time had passed at all. Like he never joined the Army without telling her and left before she could do anything about it.

Except, he had. The broken fragments of her

heart that had yet to heal gave her the strength to turn him down.

"Whatcha making, Aunty Tessa?" Caroline let out a sleepy yawn that could bust a cuteness meter. Her faithful stuffed moose dangled from her tiny fist.

"Blueberry scones."

"What's a scone?"

Tessa tied her apron on. "Oh, sweetie, you've never had a scone?"

Caroline shook her head.

"Then you're in for a real treat."

"Can I help?"

Tessa poked her head out the doorway in search of Sophie. Her sister might still be asleep, though most of the guests were up. She wouldn't make that phone call again anywhere near a kitchen. The answer hadn't changed anyway. *Sorry, they still think you cheated, Tessa*.

"Of course you can." She fished an apron out of a drawer—it too was Alaskan themed with moose and blue flowers. Forget-me-nots if Tessa recalled the state flower correctly. "You need to wear this."

Caroline's curly hair crimped in a couple of different places, probably from her pillow. Tessa removed a hair tie from her wrist and combed her fingers through the girl's tangles as gently as she could. "The first rule of being in my kitchen is your hair goes up. We don't want it to get in the scones, now, do we?"

"No," Caroline replied with a delightful giggle

that made Tessa want to squeeze her in a hug. The innocence of it resonated a feeling of freedom. Could she even remember the last time she had a good laugh?

The show had been one stressful day after another. Little sleep. Vending-machine meals. Contestants constantly suspicious of each other—especially the women. Tessa had hoped to make a friend or two, or at least an ally. But it turned out she couldn't even trust Derek not to stab her in the back, much less the strangers she met. The only thing she had close to an ally was Janet, one of the minor producers. Without her, there wouldn't even be someone *to* call.

"I need help getting the rest of the ingredients together," Tessa told Caroline, happy to give her a task. Usually she wasn't willing to let anyone touch her station. But the yearning to win Caroline's affections pushed all of that aside.

"Where do you suppose the eggs are?" Tessa pretended to think, giving Caroline a chance to answer.

"In the fridge!"

"Oh, I bet you're right." Together, they retrieved the eggs, Caroline handling the carton. It amazed Tessa how easily she could relinquish control to someone with the ability to make the biggest mess. Caroline stumbled a step before the counter, but she cradled the eggs like a running back with a football and kept herself upright.

"Thanks, sweetie." Tessa took the carton, opening it for Caroline to see. "We have to first check that none of the eggs are cracked."

Caroline scanned and pointed to each one. "All good!"

"Let's set them on the counter so they can warm up. We want them at room temperature."

"Why?"

"Because eggs mix better with batter if they're warmed up a little."

"Really?" Caroline's eyes widened in fascination.

"They rise better, too." Tessa couldn't hide her smile, growing by the second. She wasn't sure how much of today's lesson Caroline would retain, but maybe her niece would grow up to be a baker or chef.

"What's next?" Caroline asked.

Tessa scanned the cupboard, already filled with most of the ingredients. Only a couple were missing. "We need salt. Why don't you go check that cupboard by the fridge?" She watched Caroline search the cupboard for the canister. "It's blue," she told her from the counter.

The little girl had an aura of serenity about her. In her own kitchen, Tessa would be pushing someone else out of the way to get it herself. She swallowed, ashamed of that realization. Even the show portrayed her as a bear not afraid to take anyone down who got in her way. *A freaking grizzly bear*.

She hated bears.

"Is this it?" Caroline held up a small spice bottle with a blue and white label.

"No, sweetie. It's bigger than that."

As Caroline kept searching, Tessa carried a bowl of fresh blueberries to the sink to rinse them. She'd hardly turned on the faucet before she let out a scream. The bowl dropped into the sink, but her eyes were transfixed on the massive moose in the window staring back at her.

"Ed!" Caroline announced with way too much excitement as she abandoned her salt search and skipped across the kitchen to Tessa. The moose didn't seem startled or even to mind. He just stared and blinked.

"Ed, huh?" *This must be normal?* Tessa narrowed her eyes at the creature, feeling bolder since a pane of glass separated them. Ed's rack spanned wider than the window, so the chances of him breaking in were slim. "You owe me a new radiator, buster!"

Caroline scurried, grabbing her step stool. She bumped Tessa out of the way as she hopped up and unlatched the window too quickly for Tessa to object before Ed's massive snout poked through.

Tessa yanked Caroline back from the sink, holding her tight with both arms as her heart raced. She didn't think Ed could break in, but that long nose of his could travel a pretty fair distance before his antlers stopped him. She wasn't about to let Ed harm her niece. "What are you doing, sweetie?"

"He wants blueberries." Caroline squirmed in her

arms, apparently unimpressed with her restraint. But Sophie would never forgive her if Ed scooped her up with those antlers and carried her away into the woods.

"Well, he can't have any. Mr. Moose here is the reason my car is all banged up, aren't you, *Ed*?"

"Don't blame the moose." Shivers raced through Tessa at the unexpected sound of Liam's voice. Without any warning to prepare, he could do that to her. It annoyed her to no end.

Ed didn't seem interested in car repairs. He lowered his nose toward the sink and licked up the stray blueberries, pushing the bowl around the stainless-steel sink in the process. "What are you doing back here?" Tessa asked Liam since no one seemed concerned about the moose sucking up blueberries through the window.

"Forgot my shop keys."

"Right." That reminded Tessa she needed to stop by later to see whether her necklace was in the car, because it definitely wasn't at the lodge. She'd gone through her things twice more last night before finally relenting and letting sleep take her. Either her necklace was in the car or it was on the private road.

"Ed'll go when he decides there's nothing left," Sophie said from the doorway. The moose continued to sniff the sink, occasionally licking the side. But the blueberries—from what Tessa could see—were gone. "What are you two girls up to?"

"We're making scones!" Caroline announced,

squirming her way right out of Tessa's arms to run to her mom.

"Are you now?" Sophie gave her sister an approving smile.

"Yeah!"

"I better grab my keys and get to work." Liam gave Tessa a wink—at least she thought it was for her. But it could have easily been for Caroline or Ed. No matter, Tessa still found breathing more laborious. *It's not fair.*

"That's very thoughtful of you," Sophie told Tessa. "I don't know how to make much more than muffins from a boxed mix. We thought about donuts and pastries from downtown, but the daily expense was too much to justify this early."

"I don't mind." Tessa gave a shrug. "Least I can do while I'm here. I can leave the recipe. Caroline will be a pro at this by the time we're done, won't you?"

"Yeah!"

"You know," said Sophie, "if you're staying through the weekend, there's a clam chowder contest for the Blueberry Festival. Cadence and I are going to try out Aunt Patty's recipe. You should do it with us. We're even digging our own clams Friday afternoon."

"Yeah, maybe," Tessa answered, wishing she could just say yes and mean it. But any day the producers might figure out how Derek framed her and call her back. She hated to commit to more than one day at a time on the chance she needed to board a plane. Even if Tessa wanted to stay—should her presence be requested—well, the contract she signed wouldn't allow her.

"The winning chowder gets five thousand dollars. We thought we could invest it in the lodge if we won."

"Sounds like a great idea." Liam poked his head into the doorway, likely headed back out and unable *not* to eavesdrop. "You should do it, Tessa."

"You should do it, Aunty Tessa!" Caroline seconded. "Do it!" Tessa wondered if the child even knew what she was asking or if she was simply repeating everyone else.

"We'll see," she said again. Tessa hated to break a promise and tried hard not to make any she couldn't keep. Maybe that was why she was still single at thirty. Her gaze flickered to Liam lingering in the doorway. *Or maybe it has to do with a little bit more.* "Aren't you late for work?"

"Leaving."

"Bye, Uncle Liam!" Caroline called out.

"Bye, Care Bear."

The adorable nickname both touched and irritated Tessa. Liam shouldn't be closer with her niece than she was. But how could she be jealous of that relationship when she had no plans to stay in Alaska?

"Let's get these scones started," Tessa said to Caroline, turning her back to the doorway Liam had vacated.

Both Tessa's sisters had sold their cars where they lived before. Since Sophie used the money to buy plane tickets, a detail that still made Tessa's heart ache—*Why didn't she call me?* Tessa would've bought the tickets in a heartbeat—Cadence bought an SUV they could share. Tessa tried borrowing it, but Sophie needed it to take Caroline to tee-ball practice. That left Tessa without a vehicle, and Liam's shop was at least a mile hike from the lodge.

"I'm size eight," Cadence said from the doorway of Tessa's room, dangling a pair of sneakers by the laces. "A little birdy told me you might not have a pair of sensible walking shoes."

"Thank you!"

"Where're you headed?"

"Just want to pick up a few groceries from the store."

"It's a warm day. Maybe you should wait until Sophie gets back with the car for that."

"Good idea." But Tessa couldn't just sit here. She needed to find her necklace. "But . . . I think I'll take a walk into town. For old times' sake, you know?"

"Of course." Cadence set the shoes on the chair near the door. "If you ever want to talk . . ."

"Thanks." Though the urge to talk tugged at her constantly, Tessa's priority was finding her necklace. Tomorrow the forecast called for an eighty-five percent chance of rain. She didn't want to dig through muddy puddles if it wasn't necessary. "Maybe later?"

"Sure." Before Cadence left, she added, "I have a bottle of wine that needs to be opened."

Before hopping off the porch and heading down the driveway, Tessa surveyed the yard for Ed. The moose seemed to have it out for her, but she couldn't understand why. From now on, she'd watch for him everywhere.

Though her intention had been to rush to Liam's shop as quickly as her feet would take her, she found herself slowing her step. Tessa'd spent a lot of that teenaged summer on foot because Aunt Patty wasn't a fan of sharing her car. Tessa laughed out loud remembering her words, *You might hit a moose*. "Good call, Aunt Patty."

The blocks of houses transitioned into the post-card-worthy downtown strip. Even the streets had charming names. "Mooseberry Lane." She shook her head. "Of course it would have a name like that."

Waiting on the only crosswalk sign in town, the years rewound. Tessa could see her younger self standing on the sidewalk outside the ice cream shop, sharing a cone with Liam. It was always a game between them to see who could get the other on the nose first with ice cream.

The old Phillips 66 station she remembered from years ago now had a fresh paint job. When Liam's grandpa owned it, the place always looked as though it needed a good power washing. It still showcased the same name—*Davies Auto Repair*—but the sign was different. Liam had always talked about taking over the station one day. He loved tinkering with motors and old cars. It was either that or his dad's hardware store. *Guess I know which he chose.*

In the parking lot to the side of the smaller garage bay door, she spotted a worn yellow fishing boat. "What are you doing with a boat, Liam?"

Tessa was shaken from her trance by the roar of a motor. Liam's brake lights illuminated as he backed out of the cramped parking area on the other side of the station. She hurried across the street to catch him because the shop appeared locked up tight. If he left, she wouldn't be able to get in.

The truck shifted into park and Liam's window rolled down. He leaned out, and so did Raven. The sunlight only made him more handsome. *That darn beard.*

"Need a ride?" he called.

"I need to check my car."

"I promise it's in the same condition it was yesterday."

"No, *inside* the car. I lost my . . . my watch." Tessa never wore a watch, but hopefully Liam wouldn't figure that out. "Can I run inside and check really quick?"

"Sorry, I'm in a bit of a hurry."

"Give me the key?"

"Can't do that, sorry." Liam leaned out the window, a mischievous twinkle in his eye. "If you come with me, though, I'll get back quicker."

"Where?"

"I have to go. You coming or not?"

Tessa muttered under her breath about what a terrible idea this was. But she wasn't in the mood to walk back to the lodge emptyhanded. Knowing it was wiser to say no, she decided, "Let's go."

CHAPTER EIGHT

Liam

Fate smiled on Liam when he spotted Tessa across the street from the shop. He hadn't expected to see her until later that evening, when he'd be dodging her to watch *Order Up: Las Vegas*. But there she stood on the corner of Mooseberry Lane and Fourth Street, wearing practical shoes and a confused expression.

"Where are we going?" Tessa asked again three blocks away from the shop. She leisurely stroked Raven who was content to sit in her lap and watch the world go by out the window.

"How are your construction skills?" Liam asked, keeping his eyes on the road ahead. But he didn't need to see Tessa's face to know what expression she wore. It made him chuckle. She could dice an entire onion in under thirty seconds—he'd it seen on TV—but he wasn't sure she could wield a screwdriver.

"I'm not building a house or something like that. Liam, I don't have time—"

"Relax." At a stop sign he let his head drop over his shoulder. Their gazes fused together, so many memories buried deep within them both. What they had that summer was *real* no matter how many people tried to convince him it was a kid's summer romance. "My sister needs help with a crib."

"April?"

He gave her a wink before he rolled forward. "Only sister I got."

"What is she up to these days?"

Liam didn't hide his smile. Tessa had only met his older sister briefly that summer, but he was touched she asked. "She's a nurse, though she cut back on her shifts here lately. Eight-plus months pregnant and crankier than a badger caught in a hornet's nest. Husband is up working on the North Slope, so my parents get the pleasure of her company until he's back sometime next week."

"Boy or girl?"

"Girl." Liam didn't have time to take the road along the water—the long way—and instead turned directly into his parents' neighborhood. Seemed time was his biggest enemy this week. He yearned to ask Tessa what call she was waiting for, but instead he talked about Owen. "Owen, my nephew, is sharp as a tack. The things he says are so far beyond a five-year-old, it's like there's an old man trapped inside a tiny body. He'll be a great big brother."

"He sounds wonderful."

"I think my mom has him today, so you might not get to meet him."

Tessa's easy expression tensed, her lips dropping into a straight line. To say that Tessa and his mom were enemies was a stretch. But Jolene Davies was certainly not Tessa's biggest fan. When Liam made the decision to join the Army the day after his eighteenth birthday, his mom was devastated at him leaving.

You could be killed, Liam.

Never mind that Alaska could be far less forgiving than many battlefields. But his mom blamed Tessa.

"Is your mom . . ?"

"Still the top realtor in town," said Liam, avoiding the real question.

"Still the *only* realtor in town?"

"There's some other part-timer, but otherwise she's pretty much it." He almost told Tessa he sold his house a month ago. But it didn't really matter. She had to guess there was a reason he was staying at the lodge. If one of her sisters hadn't told her yet, they would eventually. "Dad's good, too. Had a scare a couple of years ago. Minor heart attack. But he's back in the hardware store full time again."

"I wondered which one you would choose," said Tessa.

"Much to my dad's disapproval, I was always better with motors than people."

"I don't know if that's true."

Unable to delay the inevitable any longer, Liam put the truck in park outside his parents' home. He hoped his mom was still out. She wouldn't be thrilled to learn Tessa was back in town. If she wasn't expecting to see her and Tessa appeared in her house, it could get very uncomfortable for everyone.

Liam's parents had upgraded to a larger log home on a hill while he was serving his second tour in Iraq. "New house," he said, because talking about the deployments he was happy to leave behind was not at the top of his list today.

"I see that. Nice view."

From the front deck, a small part of the bay peeked through a cluster of trees on one side and a hill on the other. "Great view of the sunset from here, too." Of course, this town had several spots that offered amazing sunset views. That one summer, Liam and Tessa had tried to find them all.

"You made it. I'll forgive that you're three minutes late." April's voice held an edge of sarcasm, reminding him of his failure yesterday. It appeared she wasn't going to let him forget it anytime soon. Raven wedged her way around April's legs to explore inside. His mom was a sucker for Raven and kept special treats just for her. The husky would be devastated to find her treat supplier out.

"April, you remember Tessa Whitmore?"

April's gaze bounced between Liam and Tessa a few times. "You're on that show! *Order Up: Las Vegas*!"

"I am." Tessa wasn't normally so coy around anyone, especially someone showering her with positive attention. But right now, she seemed shy with her hands shoved in her front pockets. "Good to see you, April."

"Did you win?" April's eyes and smile grew to twice their size as her hands flew to her cheeks. "Oh wait, don't tell me! The last eight are competing tonight. I don't want any spoilers."

"Where's the crib?" Liam asked, pretending impatience. But really, he had no idea that his sister was a super fan of the show. It made sense she never mentioned that detail to him considering his history with one of the contestants. But April sure wasn't holding back now.

"Guest room downstairs, down at the end of the hall." April pointed, but she wasn't even looking at him. Her eyes were glued to Tessa. "You're my favorite on the show. And not just because I know you. You're so *fierce*. It's so empowering. I love how you don't put up with any crap from anyone."

"Thanks," Tessa said as she followed Liam downstairs.

"I bet they make you sign a contract or something to prevent spoilers, don't they?" April was much too excited about this. Liam hoped she'd switch gears when he pulled the crib pieces out of the cardboard box. Maybe she'd get all excited about the baby, but no luck.

"Yeah. There's a pretty big penalty if you talk about the show before the last episode airs." Tessa knelt on the floor to sort wood pieces by the letter indicated on their stickers.

"How big?"

"You'll have to excuse my nosy sister. She has pregnancy brain."

"That's *not* what pregnancy brain is."

"Two-hundred and fifty thousand dollars," Tessa said, her tone nonchalant. She seemed more interested in arranging the crib pieces than the stiff fine that could bankrupt a person. Though Liam suspected she was hiding behind that contractual detail, it made sense why she'd been so tight-lipped about the show. Nothing kept secret in this town, no matter how good the intention.

"Holy guacamole, that's a lot."

"Yeah, that's for sure," said Tessa.

April perched on a wooden toy chest, but her rounded belly prevented her from leaning over at all. Instead, she braced her hands on the back edge of the chest and leaned back. "I hope once it's over you'll tell me all about some of the people on there. Like Victoria. She has to be a nightmare to be around!"

Tessa offered April a smile, but no insider information. Liam had to hide his chuckle at his sister's annoyance. Maybe her infatuation with the show wasn't a bad thing. It seemed to keep April off the topic of more serious things. Like why he brought Tessa with him and whether or not she was staying in Sunset Ridge. "Hand me that piece over there," Tessa said to Liam. "The one marked with the letter F."

They worked in sync assembling the crib all while April rambled on and on about the characters of the show. She had plenty of opinions. He wondered what his sister would think if she knew how many of them he agreed with. "What about that awful guy Derek? I can't stand him! Please tell me he doesn't win. I think I'd never watch another season if he did."

Liam had wondered whether there was something between Tessa and the dreadful Derek character his sister mentioned. The camera had caught small moments that may or may not have been anything. He knew better than to give reality TV too much credit for authenticity, but it still caused a flare of jealousy when he thought about it.

"Are you going to watch it tonight?" April continued. "Or is that too weird for you?"

"It's not really my thing."

"Being on TV?" April pressed on. Liam hid his face in embarrassment, wanting to apologize to Tessa for the ten thousand questions.

"Cooking's my true passion. The rest is really just a means to an end."

"*That* I believe. You're one of the only ones there who seems to have any heart behind it. Even though they call you a grizzly bear."

As Tessa handed him the next pieces, Liam

assembled the crib through April's commentary. She paid more attention to the instruction manual than he did, which surprised him. It was not at all how she approached her cooking. Even as a teenager, she added things by taste. Recipes were only starting points.

When the crib was assembled, Tessa offered to grab a wet rag to wipe it down. That left Liam alone with his overbearing sister. "Miles will be home next week?" He tried to head her off with a diverting question before she realized she hadn't pried enough.

"This baby isn't waiting for her daddy to get home." April tried to push herself up from the chest, but she gave up and reached out her hand. Liam pulled her to her feet. "What's with Tessa? Didn't think you two kept in touch."

Oh, well. "We didn't."

"I have two dozen questions about all this, but lucky for you, I *do* have pregnancy brain and can't remember most of them." April opened the closet and brought out a set of sheets. "You know you'll have to help Miles move this to our house when he gets back."

"I planned on it."

"That means no disappearing in that plane of yours."

Liam's head snapped toward the door, worried Tessa might've overheard. The Super Cub was supposed to be a surprise. It was easier to break through her fortified barriers if he caught her a little off guard. The last thing he needed was her asking about it.

"I'll be here, April. I promise."

She opened her mouth to say something, but her eyes filled with tears. The sudden onset of emotion left Liam clueless. "Aren't these the cutest sheets you've ever seen? Look at those tiny little bunnies." She swiped at her eyes. "Stupid hormones." She laughed through the tears. "I'm so ready to have this kid out of me."

Tessa reappeared in the doorway. "I'm gone for two minutes and you already made her cry?" she teased.

April sniffled. "I like her."

Tessa helped April with the tiny mattress, covering it with a sheet splattered with pink and yellow bunnies.

"Aren't you afraid she'll be *too* girly?" Liam teased.

"I already have one very boyish boy." April looked at Tessa, and added, "Owen is five. He would play in the dirt all day every day if we didn't make him come inside. He already loves fishing more than his mama."

Liam gave April a side hug. "That's not true."

"It's all he's talked about since the moment Miles went back up to the North Slope for a month."

"North Slope?" Tessa questioned.

"Prudhoe Bay," Liam answered. "Miles works on the oil fields. He's an electrician."

"I'm ready for him to come home," April mumbled.

Liam could read between those lines with little difficulty. "I know you guys'll have your hands full. I'll take him fishing, get it out of his system." He looked over at Tessa, wanting badly to invite her, but not knowing if she'd even still be here. The girl he used to know would try anything . . . but would the woman?

"It's not fishing, but my sisters and I are digging up clams on Friday. I have a four-year-old niece. Maybe Owen would like to come, too?"

It took all of Liam's restraint not to scoop Tessa into his arms and kiss her until they were both dizzy. He was so relieved to see the girl he'd fallen in love with was still there. She wasn't merely some fierce, cold shell they portrayed on TV. She was inclusive and thoughtful.

"He'd love that!" April teared up again, and Tessa took over finishing with the bedding. "Any chance that kid has to get his hands dirty, he's all in. He's never gone clamming before. You might have to carry him away from the sand kicking and screaming."

"I'm sure we can show him the ropes." Tessa's gaze lingered on Liam, and she didn't look away when he met her eyes. In fact, she offered him a warm smile. Hope bubbled in his chest that maybe—just maybe—she was thinking of staying.

CHAPTER NINE

Tessa

"If I get eaten by a bear, Ed, I swear I'll haunt you as a ghost," Tessa muttered as she and Sophie trekked up Old Man Franks' private dirt road. The accident site was nearly two miles from town, and Tessa hadn't been to the gym since she left New York. Her Cheetos and Skittles diet hadn't really done her any favors either. *Just a little four-mile hike. That's not so bad, right?*

"Tell me again why we're hiking right past a no-trespassing sign?" Sophie looked as daunted as Tessa felt. From here, the road offered a steep grade. Easy enough for a truck, but not for someone with weak calf muscles.

"I lost a necklace." Tessa didn't see any reason to lie to Sophie. If she told her sister she was searching for a watch, it would just waste time they didn't have. As it was, she had promised to help with laundry later.

"Let's get a move on it, then. We still have four loads of towels and linens to get through tonight." The winding road *would* be mostly uphill.

Earlier, Tessa had scoured every inch of the Mustang's interior, but there was no trace of her necklace. Liam was being extra nosy, too. She doubted he bought the watch lie. Tessa had never worn one, and wasn't about to start now. They got in the way when she was cooking. But she refused to tell him she kept that necklace, much less how upset she was about losing it now.

Tessa kept an open ear for the sound of an engine. Though years had gone by, she hadn't forgotten the risk of traveling uninvited on the private road. Old Man Franks' house was more than four miles from town; the dirt road offered a shortcut to a handful of other properties and to the highway she used yesterday. But he didn't care much for sharing.

Though Tessa was prepared to jump behind a tree, she hoped it didn't come to that. Sophie couldn't realize how risky this little venture was. But for Tessa, hiking alone with her thoughts was riskier. There were too many, and they gave her a heavy case of anxiety. It was as if she was trying to be two different people.

"You ready to tell me what happened?" Sophie asked after several minutes of silence, filled only by huffing and puffing. After the first steep leg of their hike, the incline smoothed to an almost flat stretch. Tessa's calves burned just the same.

"Ed happened."

"I don't mean about the car," Sophie said.

Out in the woods, it was safe to talk. Not that any paparazzi had followed her to Alaska, but they wouldn't find them in the wilderness even if they had. "I made it to the final four."

"But?"

Sophie, the sweetheart, was so intuitive. Unlike Liam, who automatically assumed she lost. She wasn't a loser until the winner was broadcast on TVs across America. After that, it was too late to change anything. An entire country would have a predetermined perception of who she was, and she might never again find decent work in a respectable kitchen. "Derek framed me for cheating."

"What?" Sophie gasped, though it might have been from the hike. They had one meager bottle of water to share between them, only because her sister was wise enough to bring any at all. Sophie took a small sip, then handed the bottle to Tessa.

"Remember my coq au vin with the risotto?" Tessa had made it for her sister during her rare—and only—vacation to Hawaii. She tried not to think too much about that trip, because it only reminded her of what Sophie's ex-husband had pulled. It was a good thing Liam was the Army veteran and not her. Otherwise Tessa would fly south and try out some hand-to-hand combat. *For starters*.

"Oh, that was so good! Can you pretty please make that before you leave?"

"Sure."

"Go on, sorry. I was lost in a food trance thinking about how much I *loved* that."

Tessa stopped at what she hoped was three quarters of the way. The break was risky, but if they didn't catch their breath, they'd be in no shape to run should they have company—whether it be Old Man Franks or a black bear. *Ed should know to keep his distance*. "Derek stole my recipe card and smuggled it to Vegas. I don't know how he did it. I mean, they checked our bags. Went through *everything* to make sure no one brought anything in that might give them an unfair advantage."

"I see."

"The card they found at my station wasn't even *folded*." Tessa hated to think how Derek might've gotten away with it, though she remembered well how cozy he'd gotten with one of the minor producers. He always was an impossible, arrogant flirt. Some women ate that up.

Tessa used to be one of them.

"I made that dish for one of our challenges. I know that recipe blindfolded and in my sleep. I don't need written instructions. But he somehow managed to plant the card at my station. And it was my card from my recipe box. It was my handwriting and had the same coffee stain on the lower left corner."

"They can't prove it." Sophie didn't ask a question. She understood. "And no one believes you?"

"Well, one of the producers was always nice to me. Janet rooted for me from the beginning. I've called her every day, just to see if anything has come to light. But I don't have any other allies outside of her. She, at least, believes me. Everyone else is so freaking giddy at the gut punch this will give America that they don't care what the truth is."

"Why would you want to win, then?"

Sophie's question was one that had been whispering in the back of Tessa's mind since she boarded the plane to Alaska. But the desire to run a highly sought-after restaurant with instant success based on the owner was too much to pass up. Tessa could make a name for herself running that kitchen. "I want to be somebody."

Sophie nudged her with her shoulder gently. "You *are* somebody, Tess. You don't need some fancy restaurant to prove that."

"Someone people will remember. But not for some cheating scandal I had *nothing* to do with." Tessa nodded for them to keep walking. "I feel stupid. I'm the one who encouraged Derek to apply for the show. I invited my demise to tag along, and the rat dumped me the night before we left for the airport."

"What if they set you up?" Sophie said. "The

show, I mean. Derek brought that recipe from New York, but think about it, Tess. They might've taken it from him, and then decided it would make a good bit of drama should you get far enough."

Tessa swallowed, refusing to believe that. "No, this was definitely Derek's idea. He knew I'd beat him."

"Don't we just have the best taste in men?" Sophie joked.

Except Liam. But Tessa didn't dare say that out loud. "There, it's up ahead." She pointed to the fresh divot in the mountainside and picked up her pace, relieved to finally return to the crash site so they could get back sooner. They might be able to play the 'we didn't know' card once. But with Old Man Franks, there was never a guarantee.

"What does it look like?" Sophie asked.

"It's a heart on a silver chain. Has a little blue gem on the heart where the top hoops meet." Tessa had given herself a lot of excuses over the years as to why she kept the gift. Mostly, she thought, it was so she never stopped believing that love existed. Because no matter how things ended that summer, what she and Liam had was real.

Tessa crept along the edge of the dirt road, careful to avoid the soft muck that had sucked in her tire. She didn't want to clean Cadence's shoes tonight if she didn't have to. Laundry would take long enough.

"The necklace Liam gave you."

Tessa's breath hitched. "How'd you know about that?"

"Because I saw you two at the festival."

"You were eleven."

"With eyeballs. Crazy concept, huh?" Sophie's smile, even in jest, was kind. Like a much-needed hug after a long day. Her gentle spirit had been passed down to her daughter, as well. The world needed more Sophies.

"I don't know why I've kept it."

"So, what about you and Liam, then?" Sophie asked.

"There is no me and Liam." But even Tessa had a hard time believing those words. It was so easy to be sucked into his orbit. She'd only been back in Sunset Ridge for two days, and already it felt like home. Of course, it had felt that way all those years ago, so Tessa was extra cautious of her feelings now. *So easy to get swept away*.

"Are you sure?" Sophie asked.

"Yes."

"He's quicksand, Tess."

"I know." How Liam laid his trap less than forty-eight hours after her return was something she couldn't wrap her head around. It should be impossible, yet her memories of New York and the show were fading, replaced by the possibilities of a future with Liam. He was more dangerous than any contractual penalty the show could impose.

"How'd you lose the necklace out here?"

"I don't know." They searched for at least twenty minutes, Tessa's borrowed shoes no longer void of mud and pasted-on leaves. Her fingers needed a rinse, too. But she didn't want to waste the last of their water, even if the hike back was mostly downhill.

"I don't think it's here, Tess."

About to admit defeat and suggest they head back, the faint roar of an engine echoed in the distance. Tessa's breath froze. It was too loud to be on some other road. If they didn't get off this one, they'd be caught. "We need to hide."

"What?"

"Hide!" She yanked Sophie's arm and pushed her up the dirt embankment toward the tree line. "We're not supposed to be out here."

"Did the no-trespassing sign not give that away?" Sophie called over her shoulder just before Tessa gave her a final push upward. Sophie rocked at the top of the soft, eroding dirt but managed to grab on to a birch tree trunk.

Once stable, Sophie extended her hand and yanked Tessa up with seconds to spare before a truck blazed by. They crouched behind too-skinny tree trunks, holding their breath. At the last second, Tessa poked her head out from her hiding spot to see who was barreling down the road as if being pursued. "Liam?"

She hopped to her feet, very curious now.

"What would Liam be doing out here?" Sophie asked.

She followed his truck with her eyes until it slowed at a curve. The brake lights lit up, possibly indicating a turn . . . or another Ed encounter. Either way, if they cut through the woods quickly, they could find out. "C'mon."

"Are you no longer worried about bears?" Sophie called out to her.

Tessa didn't have time to worry about getting eaten by wildlife. She picked up her pace, turning her head over her shoulder every so often to make sure Sophie was still within sight, until she reached a rutted road. "He turned." The side road snaked off the private one. One of the shortcuts this road offered, though judging by how overgrown it was, not well-traveled.

Why Old Man Franks hoarded his road from others, she might never know.

Tessa stopped when she spotted Liam's truck, parked near a pile of logs. A little stretch of her neck revealed three more log piles. They were notched, reminding her of Lincoln Logs.

"Even if you're not worried about bears, I still am." Sophie huffed alongside her now, taking another sip of water. Tessa felt a twinge of guilt, remembering how low their supply was. But she was too transfixed on the construction site in front of her to say so. "What is he doing out here? No way he needs a part-time job."

"Didn't you hear?" Sophie said between slower pants. "He's building a house."

"What?"

"Why do you think he's been staying at the lodge?"

Tessa shrugged. "I guess I hadn't really thought about it."

Sophie stared at Tessa in obvious disbelief. "Really?"

From their higher vantage, Tessa saw the rectangular hole dug into the ground for a crawlspace or walkout basement—she wasn't quite sure which. Several stacks of precut logs sat in various piles, all with notches. A cement truck was backed up to the dirt hole, ready to pour. Liam hopped out of his truck and met another man. They shook hands.

Raven poked her head out of the driver's side, sniffing the air with high interest. It took her less than ten seconds to spot Tessa. "Crap!" The gentle breeze must've carried their scent down to the too-smart-for-her-own-good dog. Raven let out a couple of rare happy barks in their direction. "Time to go."

CHAPTER TEN

Liam

"You sure you don't want dessert?" Sophie asked after the dinner dishes were washed. Liam had offered to dry, but Sophie shooed him away from the dishrack before he could grab a towel. "We have scones coming out our ears thanks to our overzealous chefs."

Caroline erupted in a fit of giggles at the accusation. Tessa gave an innocent shrug before she opened the refrigerator and set a pan of leftovers inside.

"Thanks, I'm good. I've had a long day." Liam wasn't lying. On top of fixing a boat motor, assembling a crib, and changing oil for three different folks, he also assisted in the pouring of the concrete at his future home. Add to all that he barely slept the night before, and Liam would be lucky to keep his eyes open through half an episode of *Order Up: Las*

Vegas. Too bad the lodge didn't offer DVRs for guests.

"Take one to go?" Tessa dropped one onto an oversized napkin, then held it out to him.

He never had been great at telling her no. "Thanks."

"I heard Owen's coming with us to dig clams," Cadence said to him from the table before he reached the hallway. She'd pulled out some archaic book from Patty's office and was scribbling things in it. Liam thought reservations, but he was too tired to ask.

"He is." Liam's gaze lingered on Tessa, a silent thank you from his lips. "My sister says he's pretty excited for the invitation."

"We'll be happy to have him along," said Sophie.

"C'mon, Raven. You've gotten enough neck rubs to last you a week."

After he took the husky outside one last time, he sat on the edge of his bed, cell in hand so he could set his alarm. He could text April, ask her to record tonight's episode, but that one favor would out him for watching at all. No one needed to know. Sometimes they played reruns on the weekends.

Placing his phone on the nightstand, he settled into the full-sized bed. Raven nudged her way under an arm, snuggling against him and resting her head on his chest. Her eyes fell closed before the opening credits could finish. Three weeks ago, when the show started airing, the highly dramatized reality felt like his only lifeline to Tessa. But now that she was here, it was easy to pick apart its ridiculousness.

Tonight's episode featured the remaining eight chefs pairing up to prepare a mystery entree together. The announcer made the contest sound as if it were life or death. The winning duo would each run a kitchen for a dinner service later that evening. Liam wondered if the challenges and the dinner service happened in the same day, but he wasn't willing to ask Tessa.

Footsteps echoed on the other side of his door, causing his heart to race. He tried not to wake Raven as he patted the mattress in search of the remote to cut the volume. He muted the TV and waited for the door across the hall to close. Tessa was the only other person this far down the hallway, unless a guest wandered down here in curiosity.

A soft knock sounded at the door, and Liam muttered under his breath. Whoever it was probably had good intentions. But he didn't have the ability to pause live TV in here, and he couldn't exactly ask the knocker to come back during a commercial break.

"Just a second," he called, happy he'd remembered to bolt the door. He shimmied off the bed without disturbing Raven's slumber. She curled herself into a ball and continued sleeping as he answered the door.

"Sorry to disturb you," said Sophie, lifting up a stack of green towels. "We got a late start on the laundry."

"Thanks, Sophie." Liam fought a yawn and lost.

The warm towels in his hands only made his urge to sleep stronger. He hoped tonight would bring him a solid night of rest, because tomorrow he had a full day of important plans. "Hope I wasn't too rude after dinner."

She offered him a kind smile. Sophie was good at those. "Not at all."

"Will you need my room this weekend?" he asked, hoping not. He had offered to stay with his parents any weekend that the lodge needed the space. But that was before everything changed.

"No, you can stay. Tessa'll be getting the boot."

"She can have—"

"You're a paying guest. She'll sleep in Cadence's room." She winked at him. "Don't spoil the surprise, though."

Liam let out a gentle laugh at that, because it was his only defense for giving in to his fears. The unspoken question lingered in the space between them. *Will Tessa even stay the weekend?* "Wouldn't dream of ruining your fun."

"Need anything?" Sophie asked.

"All set, thanks."

Sophie pulled the door closed partway, then paused with her fingers still curled around the knob. "You're not the only one who wants her to stay, Liam. We do, too." With that, she left him standing on the other side of his door, holding the small stack of warm towels.

Tessa

"You really do laundry *every* night?" Tessa asked Sophie as she shoveled a second load of bath towels out of the dryer and dropped them into a laundry basket to fold.

Though they'd spent a portion of their time in Vegas cleaning and prepping kitchens—and dorm rooms—Tessa and the other contestants never had to do their own laundry. It was one perk to make up for the floor scrubbing, oven cleaning, and *so* many dishes. She thought she'd hate the chore tonight, but oddly, she found it therapeutic.

"We don't have to worry about running out that way." Sophie rolled a basket on wheels toward the washing machine. "I don't mind. Gives me something to keep my mind occupied."

Tessa almost asked Sophie if she missed her comfortable life in Hawaii, but that question might be more complicated to answer than either could handle. With her sister so content to move linens around the laundry room, it was hard to imagine her married to a ridiculously rich man who hired not one but three housecleaners. At least during Tessa's visit to Hawaii, Sophie didn't have to lift a finger if she didn't want to. Her ex-husband usually stopped her if she tried.

"How do we only have one washer and one dryer?" Tessa wondered aloud. "It'll only get worse when the place is packed."

"I know. But Aunt Patty made it work. We can, too."

Tessa'd been avoiding most thoughts that centered around her late great-aunt. She and Patty had butted heads quite a bit that summer, and she never truly apologized for being a bratty teenager. Add to that she was the first to insist they sell the lodge instead of giving it a shot, and Tessa had a solid dose of guilt churning her stomach.

"Are you happy here?" Tessa asked, eager to rid the unwanted thoughts from her head. She asked a question she was pretty sure she knew the answer to. Gone were the worry lines Sophie had during their video conferences last month. She seemed content here, in her element.

Sophie reached for a dry towel and started folding. "I'm happier here scrubbing toilets and doing laundry than I ever was with Blake. Sometimes you just don't realize how lonely you've been until you have some distance."

Tessa's relationship with Derek didn't have substance or depth, something she'd been blind to in New York. The truth had seeped out over time in Vegas. But being in Sunset Ridge—around her sisters —it was crystal clear that she never loved Derek. She'd been lying to herself if she ever thought she did.

"You can see yourself creating a life here?" Tessa pressed on.

Sophie stopped in the middle of folding and looked Tessa right in the eye. "I already have."

"Are you worried Blake might change his mind? About Caroline?"

"We've talked an awful lot about me tonight," Sophie deflected. "What about you? If the show doesn't pan out, do you think you could see yourself staying with us?"

Part of her longed to stay, but Tessa still hadn't discerned whether that was nostalgia from a simpler time tricking her.

The lodge didn't need a chef, and it seemed Cadence and Sophie had split the other duties equally. "Maybe," she finally answered. "But what would I *do* here?" Tessa didn't want to add another salary to the payroll if she wasn't doing a thing to bring in income, and she could only live off her savings for so long.

"Offer room service?" Sophie suggested.

"We'll see how the rest of the scones go over tomorrow."

Stay in Sunset Ridge? It sounded like a dream, but Tessa couldn't stay if it only meant running away from reality. She had no idea what *Order Up* would decide to do, but right now it didn't look as though it would work in her favor. But hiding in a small Alaska town after such public humiliation seemed a sure way to kill her career. Wouldn't it be more heroic of her to beat the odds and prove to the show—and the viewers—that she could overcome any obstacle?

"What's going through that head of yours, Tess?"

"What if—"

"Mommy?" Caroline's faint voice called over the machines. She appeared in the doorway, moose nightgown down to her ankles, stuffed animal in tow, rubbing her eyes. "I had a bad dream."

Sophie gave Tessa an apologetic shrug as she scooped her daughter into her arms. "It's all right, sweetie. Let's go read a story."

"About Mister Moose?"

"Yes, we can read about Mister Moose."

"I'll finish the towels." Tessa's gaze followed them out of the room and down the hall until they turned a corner. Caroline clung to her mom like a life raft, such open trust. Though Sophie had that effect on people, Tessa wondered what it might be like for her own daughter—or son—to cling to her like that.

She quickly folded the remaining towels to drown out her thoughts. She placed them on the rack by the door, wishing the dryer would run quicker so she could keep the momentum going. Another basket of laundry sat on the floor, waiting its turn. *Why don't we have two washers and dryers?*

Restless, Tessa strolled down the hall to her room where she last left her phone. Before *Order Up*, Tessa wouldn't have gone five feet from it. But since the show mandated they surrender all cell phones and other electronic devices with internet access or information stored on them, within days, she no longer thought about her phone at all.

Even now, with her desperate hope for a call to come back, Tessa hardly remembered to carry it with her.

"Still nothing." She tossed her cell back on her mattress. No point in taking it with her. She didn't have girlfriends in New York anymore—no one to ask how things were going. The friends she had, she lost when she took on her last job. They got tired of her canceling on them, never able to understand why she spent most of her life in a kitchen.

She wished she had a book or something else that might occupy her mind while she waited on the dryer. Tessa considered investigating the office but the faint hum of a TV drew her attention to Liam's door before she could follow through. "That can't be . . ." The music sounded familiar. *Too familiar*. A tune that'd been stuck in her head for weeks.

She knocked softly on Liam's door, then waited. No footsteps. No answer.

Fingers curled around the knob as she turned it, Tessa knocked again. "Liam?" she called out quietly.

She found him lying on his back, chest rising and falling, eyes closed. In a simple T-shirt, all those muscles were much too distinct, even relaxed as they were. They'd do nothing but get her into trouble. But the biggest threat to her heart was the sight of the sleeping husky, resting her head on his chest, Liam's arm snaked over her back. If that couldn't melt a heart right into a puddle of goo, nothing could.

If the music hadn't reclaimed her attention, Tessa might have remained too distracted by the Instagram-worthy moment to notice what played on the TV.

She tried to figure out a way to dismiss it. It was possible he was asleep before it ever started. Or maybe curiosity finally got the best of him. His sister had talked about it nonstop this morning.

But what if he's been watching it all along?

The thought stirred her into motion. Closing the door, Tessa hurried back to the laundry room. She dropped into a corner chair and waited for the dryer to finish a load of linens.

If Liam had watched any of that episode on purpose—or any previous episodes—Tessa wouldn't know whether to feel touched or mortified. The woman on the screen—*Tessa the Grizzly Bear*—wasn't someone she was proud of anymore. In New York, that take-charge, take-no-prisoners mentality made her sought-after. Here, in the charming town surrounded by family and good people, it made her feel ashamed.

Maybe I don't want to go back.

CHAPTER ELEVEN

Liam

Bob Barker was calling someone to *come on down!* when Liam awoke the next morning. He suspected Raven stepped on the remote in the middle of the night, because the channel he'd been watching didn't play old game show reruns. *Isn't Bob Barker dead?* Raven had moved from her spot nestled under his arm to her dog bed beneath the window. She blinked up at him, as if to ask if they *had* to get up yet.

"It's time, girl."

He stretched out all the kinks. Sleeping the full night on his back never left him without a few aches. Not to mention he slept on top of the comforter instead of under it. But he didn't care. Liam was simply happy to have been out like a light. He didn't even remember dreaming. Well, maybe there had been a couple with Tessa. In the new house. *A family*.

"Let's get outside, Raven." He led the husky out the back door, inhaling the cool, crisp air that promised rain. Sunset Ridge had been blessed with a beautiful summer. Just enough rain to keep nature happy. No forest fires nearby to cover the town in a cloud of yellow smoke or to dust cars in ashes. Even the mosquitos seemed to be traveling in thinner droves.

The clouds didn't linger too low in the sky, so Liam figured visibility should be good enough for a flight. He'd double-check once they were back inside.

Raven let out a gentle whine, drawing his attention. Ed stood at the trailhead and stared back, ears mostly raised. But the wild look in the moose's eyes warned Liam he wasn't crazy about a dog nearby. "C'mon, Raven."

The husky stood ten feet away, heavy debate hanging in her eyes. She recognized the antlered beast from the other day, no doubt. Probably by the scent more than Ed's unusual antlers. Though he was adored by the majority of Sunset Ridge, a provoked moose was a dangerous moose, no matter how cherished. Ed was still a bull who wouldn't hesitate to charge if threatened—and he had more than once.

"I sure wish you could be bribed by blueberry scones," Liam muttered at Raven, slowly stepping toward his dog. He was prepared to dive for her if she decided to chase Ed. "Let's get inside."

Two feet away, Raven looked back at Liam and finally seemed to register what he was saying. She trotted toward the back door, leaving Ed to his mischievous ways.

"Something smells like heaven," Liam said as he entered the kitchen. He'd gone a little heavier than usual on the aftershave; figured it couldn't hurt in persuading Tessa to come with him today if she needed the extra nudge.

"Eggs Benedict," Tessa told him, an easy smile on those lips he had a hard time not staring at. *Guess I did dream about kissing her.* "Want me to fix you a plate?"

"Please."

Liam slipped into a chair at the table he'd become very comfortable around lately. Though he ate a lot of to-go meals on the fly, he spent more time at this kitchen table than his mom's, a detail she frequently reminded him of since he took up residence at the lodge. Jolene wanted him to be home with the rest of the family, but the tension between Liam and his dad made meals uncomfortable lately.

Tessa carried a plate over to him. "Any chance you'll get to work on my car today?"

It wasn't the question Liam hoped she'd ask, but it served his plan just the same.

"Maybe."

She stopped halfway to him, plate clutched in both hands. Her expression steeled, then loosened again. "I might have to leave any day, Liam," she said gently. "Is there any chance you can work on it today?"

His gaze lingered on the woman standing before him. They'd both grown up so much since they were kids. It only made Tessa prettier with his breakfast, especially without all that stage makeup. "I'll make you a deal."

"Here we go," mumbled Tessa, setting the plate in front of him and crossing her arms. "What do you want?"

Liam smirked, cutting into his Eggs Benedict and savoring a slow bite just to make her wait. When she tapped her foot and huffed out a couple of breaths, he finally said, "I need to go to Anchorage to get a new radiator."

"What?"

"I don't know if you noticed, but no one else in town has a Mustang. I don't keep those radiators in stock." He could get one from Seward—closer by a hundred miles—but that wouldn't work in his favor the way Anchorage would. "So I have to make a trip to get it."

"Can you go today?"

"Possibly."

The half-dozen emotions flashing across her face amused him before she settled on a response. Tessa was obviously trying hard not to get worked up, but she knew him well enough to know he was up to something. "Just spit it out, Liam. What's this going to cost me?"

"Come with me."

"What?"

"You heard me."

She turned away, busying herself at the sink rinsing off dishes. "I can't."

"Can't? Or won't?"

Her shoulders rose and fell with her heavy breath. "Both?"

"I want to show you something, Tessa. But you have to come with me." He'd give anything to freeze time. The clock was ticking too fast these days. Since that wasn't an option, he had to play a little dirty. "Either you come with me, or I don't go until Monday."

She cut the running water. "Monday?"

"What's it going to be?"

"Liam—"

"Aunty Tessa, Aunty Tessa!" Caroline burst into the room, her volume turned as high as her excitement. "Ed's in the front yard. Come see!" The girl, still in her moose pajamas, yanked Tessa by the hand until she relented. "*Come see!*"

Liam ate his breakfast—so incredibly tasty—until the girls returned. Tessa had been an amazing cook years ago, before any formal training. But now, she was incredible. A seed of doubt wedged its way into his heart. How could a refined chef ever find happiness in a remote town like this one? Even if she didn't win *Order Up*, she could still work in any number of elite restaurants across the country. Sunset Ridge didn't have any of those.

"His antlers are *this* big!" Caroline stretched one arm as wide as it would go as they returned to the kitchen. The girl was still wide-eyed, her hair sticking up in three different directions, her hand latched on to Tessa's wrist. *A glimpse of our future?*

"Caroline," Sophie called from down the hall. "You need to brush your teeth."

The girl's eyes widened, as if she'd been caught with her hand in the cookie jar.

"Better go." Tessa gently nudged her toward the doorway. Caroline scurried away, her footsteps padding down the hall.

"I have to leave in twenty minutes," Liam said, carrying his empty plate to the sink. "Otherwise the trip will have to wait." Standing mere inches apart, he fought the urge to scoop her into his arms. But this way—the tease—would be much more effective in the long run. He hoped.

He tucked the loose strand of hair behind her ear, barely grazing his fingertips against her skin. His gaze swept her lips, making the game almost impossible for him to win. Her hooded eyes betrayed her feelings, and before he couldn't anymore, Liam abruptly dropped his hand. "What's it going to be, Tess?"

Her heavy breathing stilled as she narrowed her gaze at him, her lips pursed. But there was no mistaking that twinkle in her eyes. Even if she was annoyed at not being kissed, she wasn't as upset about this adventure as she wanted to pretend. "How long will we be gone?"

"Few hours."

"Let me grab my jacket."

———

"Who let you borrow this?" Tessa rolled her eyes at him when they pulled up to the marina. Normally Liam kept his Super Cub docked by his future home —maybe *their* future home—but he wasn't ready for Tessa to see the build yet. Not until he was almost out of time. Every added touch—no matter how slow or seemingly unimportant—made visualizing the finished product that much easier.

Liam could spin her a tale, but what was the point? Today he had plans to reveal some things he'd been working on. They'd always talked about a future together, and he wanted to show her he hadn't forgotten the dreams they cooked up years ago. "It's mine."

"Stop it. Whose plane is this really?"

"I won it."

Tessa pushed open the door, meeting him at the front of the truck. "What are you talking about?"

"At the Fireweed Festival. Ask Cadence. She was there."

"You *won* a plane?"

They walked side by side, close enough for Liam to reach out and take her hand. But he feared the gesture would make Tessa turn tail and run back to the lodge. *Better to wait.* "Yeah. Cool, huh?" He tried to sound nonchalant, but inside he was still excited to the bone. He and his buddy Ford had won the Alaska Woodsman competition fair and square, and since Ford didn't want a plane, Liam got to keep the grand prize.

"Why do we need to *fly* to Anchorage?"

"We'll get there in a third of the time." But really, that had nothing to do with it. Liam wouldn't mind the extra hours in his truck with Tessa as his passenger. It would give them a chance to catch up on life. An opportunity to remind her how much she once loved it here. But the plane was special. Soon, she'd remember.

"Why is it in the water?" Tessa asked as she followed him down a wood-planked ramp.

"You'll see."

"I hope you know how to fly this thing," Tessa said as he helped her in first, instructing her to scoot over to the copilot seat so he could get in as well. "I'm not the copilot you want stuck saving us if you forget how it's operated."

Liam nodded to his pilot's license, strapped to the sun visor. "You're in good hands, Tess. Trust me." He'd never admit he was nervous, but it had nothing to do with flying the plane. "Relax, and enjoy the view." He almost made a quip about the helicopter ride she got to take in Vegas when her team won a challenge on the show, but he caught himself before the words tripped off his tongue. "It's not every day you get to fly in your own personal plane in *Alaska*."

Once they were in the air and leveled out, Tessa's tense shoulders finally seemed to loosen. Her eyes were glued to the scenery. Liam had grown up in Alaska, and outside of his eight years in the Army, had lived here the whole time. He'd never get tired of the mountain backdrop or vastness of wilderness that stretched for hundreds of miles the farther north one traveled. Tessa appeared just as fascinated.

He let her soak in the beauty during their forty-three-minute flight, instead inviting the comfortable silence. The overcast sky in the distance promised rain soon, but for now, it gave the mountains an eerie foggy look that Liam loved. Drizzly raindrops splattered the windshield, but not enough to be of concern.

"It's amazing up here," Tessa said, never peeling her eyes away.

Liam wondered if she remembered that day, at their special spot just beyond the beach, where the waterfall was hidden a stretch after the path ended. They found refuge and privacy behind the wall of water. On the rocks looking out, they talked about the future. About one day having a small plane of their own so they could go off on Alaskan adventures anytime they wanted.

Closer to Anchorage, Liam radioed in, ensuring he was cleared in the airspace near the float plane pond. It was as much a small airport for bush planes as any place in town. But this one offered more than just a place to park a plane for a few hours.

"You're going to land in the pond?" Tessa asked, hearing his concise request.

He gave her his mischievous smirk. "We have skis, remember?"

"Right." A flash of the old, thrill-seeking Tessa returned in that fearless smile. It made him feel seventeen again. "What is that?" She pointed toward a brown two-story building with an abundance of windows. A patio of tables was filled with people.

"Restaurant and lodge."

"Really?"

"We can grab lunch there before we head back." He wished it were dinner, but there was just too much in his schedule to swing that this week. *Next week though . . .*

"Trying to give me ideas, are you?"

Liam never did anything without intent, and it seemed he'd been caught this time. "Can't hurt, right? You're one of the owners, too."

Sunset Ridge had too many eating establishments to support a new standalone restaurant, but if the lodge opened one, the chance of success would be higher. And it would give Tessa a purpose—a reason to stay without sacrificing her dreams. Years ago, that type of option hadn't existed. He knew she wouldn't have become the chef she did without culinary school and years in New York learning from the best.

Liam wondered for years what life would have

been like had he not joined the Army. No one was thrilled to learn he signed the papers the day after his eighteenth birthday—especially Tessa. She'd been hurt and angry, much as he expected. But he enlisted because Tessa would've sacrificed everything she wanted out of life to stay in Sunset Ridge with him. Liam hadn't needed a crystal ball to know how that would eventually work out.

He landed on the water nice and smooth; the perfect landing to impress a perfect girl.

"That was fun!" Tessa's eyes sparkled with a light he hadn't seen in years. Liam wanted to lean across the console and kiss her, and almost did with the way her gaze kept dropping to his lips. Instead, he focused on floating to the dock and shutting down the engine.

"Not a bad way to travel, huh?"

"When did you get your pilot's license?"

"Couple years ago." His evasive answer didn't go unnoticed, if Tessa's raised eyebrow said anything. But he wasn't about to launch into detail about an idea that sparked during his time in the service. Talking about the Army today—as proud as he was of his time in—might unravel all the progress they'd made. It could bring Tessa back to that awful day, her cheeks soaked in tears. Liam shook away the memory he didn't want to relive. "Bucket list thing, you know?"

She allowed him to help her out of the plane, rocking against him when her unstable boots caught on the dock at an odd angle. Liam held her against him a few moments longer than necessary, enjoying the familiar vanilla scent from a shampoo she apparently still used. "What else is on this bucket list of yours?" she asked, low and near.

"Oh, a few things," he finally answered, his lips close to her ear. She shivered in his arms seconds before she shrugged her way free. They'd always had that electrical current strung between them. Some thought they made a dangerous combination. *Maybe they're right.* "Still have skydiving on my list."

"Everybody says that."

"Okay. I want a family," he said with such raw honesty Liam surprised himself. It was no secret to anyone in town he was ready to settle down. And Tessa knew years ago he wanted that. But speaking the words so plainly now, he felt vulnerable.

"Is that why you got out of the Army? Moved home?"

"Something like that." But Liam wasn't in the mood to discuss any of that today. Someday he'd tell her all about his time in the military, when it was no longer a sore spot between them. Though he'd joined to push Tessa to pursue her own dreams, Liam had a lot of incredible experiences. *Bad ones, too.*

He led the way down a sidewalk that traveled past diners enjoying a late breakfast on the patio. When he noticed Tessa several steps behind him, her eyes on the people, he retreated the few paces and took her hand. "Getting ideas, are you?"

"Can't hurt, right?"

"C'mon, we need to go get your radiator. You can gawk later."

"We're not walking, are we?" she asked glancing down at her shoes. They were the same impractical little boot things she had on the day he found her half-dangling from her car window.

"We have a truck. A buddy owes me a favor, so I cashed in today."

She let out a laugh at that. "Why am I not surprised? You and those favors."

Hope. That was what Liam felt swelling in his chest, growing by the hour, as Tessa flashed her illuminating smile. The way her eyes dazzled in the sunlight made him feel anything was possible. And today, maybe it was.

CHAPTER TWELVE

Tessa

Tessa fiddled with the sleeve of her jacket as they waited for a table. A bush plane coming in for a landing buzzed overhead. In the couple of hours they spent chasing down the radiator and a few other spare parts, the lakeside restaurant had exploded with a lunch crowd.

She wasn't nervous around Liam anymore, and that seemed to be the problem. It had taken less than three days to feel comfortable, as though he was a regular part of her life. *I'm in trouble.* Their brief time running errands left her yearning to return to Anchorage to explore and enjoy—with him.

Outside of airport trips, Tessa had only been to Anchorage once before. She'd taken a rare trip with Aunt Patty to pick out new linens for some of the guest rooms. Only the finest bedding and towels would do for her guests. *Give them the best night of sleep they've ever had, and they'll always come back*. But now Tessa yearned for date nights and walks downtown.

She dug in her purse to check her phone, hoping the gesture would ground her back in reality. But no word from anyone. Not even her sisters, much less the show.

"When's the last time you cooked with fresh Alaskan salmon?" Liam asked her, brushing away a stray hair from her neck, forcing her to abandon her purse rummaging. Would she always shiver at his featherlight touch?

"Never," Tessa admitted. She'd cooked with fresh salmon, but not the Alaskan variety. She added it to her list of things to try before she left. *Because I am leaving*. She'd been reminding herself of that little detail all day.

"They have the best here. You should try it." Liam's smirk warned her he was set on riling her up.

She saw right through that trap. He remembered what appealing to her competitive side did, it seemed. "You just want me to cook for you."

"If I had Alaskan salmon twice in the same week, I wouldn't complain."

"I'm sure you wouldn't." He stood much too close, but Tessa couldn't seem to take even a single step back. The magnetic pull between them was impossible to fight. Her gaze dropped to his lips, remembering the first time he kissed her that summer, beneath the waterfall. He was her very first kiss. Back then, Tessa was certain he'd also be her last.

"I *do* have some salmon in my parents' chest freezer."

"Why at your—"

"Davies, party of two?" the host called before Tessa could pry. She wanted to know why it was at his parents' house, and more importantly, why he'd give up a place to live—and his own freezer—before the next one was ready. It would cost him a small fortune living at the lodge for several months.

"We're up." He reached for her hand, probably hoping to rattle her nerves and make her forget her questions. But Tessa wriggled free and walked forward.

His parents had upsized. Tessa had caught two more guest rooms in that basement besides the one with the crib, and April could only be using one of them. Liam never did anything without a purpose. She just hadn't figured out what this was about.

He followed close enough behind her that a wave of heat danced between them. It might be the sun; someone at the auto parts store told them Anchorage hadn't seen a bit of rain since early morning.

Are we on a date? Tessa wondered as she took a seat. The tables and chairs were cast iron, but thick maroon cushions made her comfortable with little effort.

"Your server will be with you shortly to grab your drink order," the host said once they were both situated and goblets were filled with ice water. "I recommend the salmon today. It's extra good."

"See," Liam said.

Tessa felt the urge to stick her tongue out at him, just to be silly. But with so many other diners around them, she refrained. It seemed strange to be on the other side of the kitchen. She could appreciate a good meal as much as the next person, but Tessa couldn't recall the last time she'd dined at any restaurant.

Had it been lack of time or pickiness? She wasn't sure.

"Relax," Liam told her after they ordered beverages. "All you have to do is enjoy yourself."

"I'm trying," admitted Tessa, feeling more vulnerable than usual. Her guard was dropping, her feet sinking into that quicksand, and there was nothing she could do about it. The gentle breeze brought the scent of Liam's aftershave to her, and she nearly melted in her chair.

"Have you thought about—" Whatever Liam had been about to say was interrupted by a buzzing in his pocket. He pulled out his phone, and his expression changed to apologetic. "Sorry, I have to take this. It'll be quick."

"Sure."

"Order me the salmon." He winked at her as he stood and headed toward a gate. "We're not ready to talk about tile yet," she heard him say before he walked too far out of hearing range.

Tile?

"Do you want me to come back?" the server asked, nodding toward Liam.

"No, it's okay. I know what he wants." She ordered them both the salmon—her curiosity really was piqued even if all he did was cause her to cook it later—and she fiddled with her phone. Still no word. No texts or missed calls. *I really have no one, don't I?*

Except here in Alaska she had a family. Her gaze flickered to Liam, still pacing in the grass. *I have a future.*

Liam had brought her here for a reason. Did he want her to note the details? Pick up ideas to add a restaurant to the lodge so she would want to stay? She really did like the patio dining idea, even if it would only be appropriate a few months of the year —fewer here than anywhere else.

She tried to recall what type of deck furniture they had at the lodge, and how much they'd need to add to serve a few tables. But Tessa hadn't even sat down with her sisters to talk about financials of the lodge. All she knew was that they had enough funds to run the place for a year, even if the occupancy was low. Any extra money should probably first go toward a second washer and dryer.

Breaking apart a chunk of bread and buttering it, Tessa's eyes fell on Liam like a compass returning to true north.

How many evenings had they spent years back, cuddled up on the hammock in his backyard, or the bed of his old truck with a pile of blankets, talking about the future? They made plans together—the house on the water with the enormous kitchen, the elderly dog in need of a good home, three kids, fishing trips. Liam could catch and clean the fish, she'd cook it. *The plane.* The plane that could take them anywhere they desired to go on a moment's notice.

"Sorry about that," Liam said, returning to his seat. "Business call." Tessa was much too distracted by his chiseled features and the dazzling look in his eyes to push for more information. She'd gone too far back down memory lane, and she wasn't sure there was any returning.

"I ordered you the salmon," she said, and instantly felt silly. Like the shy teenager on her first date with the most attractive, popular guy in town.

"It really is delicious." He broke himself off some of the bread, and poked his butter knife her way. "Bet you can outdo it though."

All through dinner, and during the wondrous plane ride home, Tessa thought of nothing else but kissing Liam. She wanted to know if the brush of his lips against hers felt as breathtaking as she remembered. The kisses they shared had left the ground rumbling beneath their feet, and Tessa had never experienced another like those since.

Back at the marina, Liam said, "I'll get working on your radiator right away. Tire is already fixed. And other than a tie rod and some body damage I can fix easily enough, everything else looks good."

Had anyone else found her on that road, Tessa wouldn't have been so lucky. "Thank you." She wanted to tell him what a great time she had today, even if half the trip had been about a parts run. It felt . . . normal. As though this could be their life together if only she let it be.

She waited on the ramp while Liam carried the radiator to the truck.

Tessa had always loved to cook, and even at a young age, could lose an entire weekend in the kitchen if the ingredients were plentiful. But she'd also yearned for the freedom to drop everything and go on a whim. It was a part of her that Liam brought out. A part that had been dormant for years while she worked ten, twelve, sometimes fourteen-hour days to learn as much as she could to prove her worth. When she accomplished everything she could at one restaurant, she moved on to another. Always chasing more; never satisfied.

She wouldn't take any of it back; she'd learned from some of the top chefs in New York City. But she felt ready for . . . more. For something that didn't include working herself to the bone for a paycheck that was never enough and an ego that was never content.

"What's going on in that pretty little head of yours?" he asked, returning to his plane for the rest of the parts he'd procured.

Tessa looked back at the bay, desperate for a few more minutes. "Just thoughts."

"That doesn't sound mysterious at all," Liam teased, standing much closer to her now than he had been a few minutes ago. If she took a single step forward, she could reach out and touch his cheek. Comb her fingers over his beard. Draw his lips to her own.

But if Liam's presence was quicksand, his kiss would be her ultimate demise.

"Thank you for lunch," she said, because she had to say something. "And the plane ride."

If Vegas called her back—the *if* felt bigger than ever now—she'd always have the view of the mountains and water from Liam's plane to keep her company on the loneliest days. If she could only capture that feeling of freedom in a jar and take it with her, maybe her life would feel more complete than empty.

"I don't want you to leave, Tess."

Her heart squeezed. She wished she could be two different people. One who could run a kitchen like the bear they portrayed her as on *Order Up*; the other, the woman who settled down with the man in front of her and started a whole new life.

Lately, she yearned for the latter just a little bit more.

Finally, she said, "I can't."

"Even if you don't win?"

She studied his expression, searched deep into

those mesmerizing eyes that had the ability to penetrate clear into her soul, and wondered at Liam's choice of words. *Especially then.* "It's complicated."

Liam took the step that closed the gap between them, his fingertips brushing a featherlight touch along her cheek. "Doesn't have to be."

How she wished his words were as true as they promised. She could walk away from all her hard work—all the hours she'd worked herself to the point of exhaustion—but to what? Open a small restaurant inside the lodge? Offer room service? She'd be the laughingstock of the viewers. They'd think she admitted defeat, curled up into a ball and threw in the towel when things got tough.

"Liam—"

Distance didn't exist between them anymore. He set the sack of parts down. His chest brushed against her, and his arms cradled her in his embrace. Tessa didn't know when it happened, but she could no more tear herself away than she could stop the rain from coming.

A drizzle tickled her cheek, warning them that the forecasted precipitation had finally reached Sunset Ridge. But neither made a move toward his truck for shelter.

"Stay, Tess."

Any sensibility she had left vanished when Liam leaned down. Her gaze locked on his lips, and the only thing she could think about was whether his beard would tickle when she kissed him. Because she was most definitely going to kiss him.

The drizzle turned to raindrops, and still they didn't move from the dock. Shelter was a faraway concern.

Unable to handle the suspense, Tessa reached both her hands to his cheeks and pulled him the rest of the way to her lips.

Every cell in her body tingled to life. Memories of kissing Liam had nothing on reality. Their lips fused as if nothing else was promised but this very moment. The world spun around them, rain fell in droves, and still they kissed.

CHAPTER THIRTEEN

Tessa

Tessa's lips still buzzed long after Liam dropped her off at the lodge. They'd both been drenched by the rain, but he didn't come in to change. "I have a dry set of clothes at the shop. I better get your car fixed."

She almost told him to forget it. Wait until Monday. Any excuse to kiss him again before her senses kicked in and warned her to keep her distance. But the small chance she might need the car sooner —and the fear of what that first kiss, let alone any others, might mean—made Tessa choose silence. "I'll see you tonight?"

"We'll see how late it gets."

It was better this way, she decided as she slipped inside and watched his taillights disappear into the foggy rain. Had they waited even another thirty minutes to leave Anchorage, they might've been stranded. She didn't need a pilot's license to know flying in low visibility was a terrible idea.

The click-clack of claws sounded. Raven greeted her with a happy tail, leaning against Tessa's damp pant leg until she got her neck rub. "You're going to get all wet."

Though the main room was lit by the glow of the antler chandelier, it was empty. Tessa had hardly caught more than a glimpse of any of their guests, which was not the way she remembered it when Aunt Patty ran things. On rainy days, guests usually congregated in the main room. Of course, if she'd been around more maybe that would have made a difference in her perception.

But no guests loitering meant no guests to feed. She frowned.

"Guess it is early afternoon, isn't it, girl?" Tessa gave Raven a second good rub on the back of her neck after she removed her wet shoes and left them in the coat nook off the front entry.

She couldn't do much about her wet clothes without changing, but at least she wasn't dripping water. If she did that to Aunt Patty's wood floors, the woman might make a trip back from the dead to haunt her. Tessa had enough on her plate to worry about without a ghost too.

"Hope you've been a good girl today." Tessa knelt down on her knees, petting the husky with both hands. Had her clothes not been sticking to her skin, she would've hugged the dog. She needed to hug *someone*.

She tiptoed across the empty room, maneuvering around the sofas so she could steal a chocolate on the way. The bowl sat next to the now-empty scone pan. Only crumbs remained. *At least I got something right.*

Intending to sneak straight off to her room and change into dry clothes before she had to face either of her sisters, voices in the kitchen caused her to pause just out of sight. Raven stopped right at her heel and sat. *What a great dog.*

"You didn't have to do this, Tillie!" Sophie's gracious voice echoed. "You spoil us so much already."

"You know me, I can't help but bake, bake, bake!" The woman's laugh reverberated from the kitchen. "Plus, how else was I going to introduce my son, Denver? Too bad Cadence and Tessa are out, but you're who I wanted him to meet anyway. She used to live in Hawaii, Denver. Isn't that something?"

Curiosity at its height, Tessa poked her head in the far doorway.

She hadn't seen Tillie Grant in years. Outside of the graying hair and new shade of rimmed glasses, the woman looked the same. The nights Tessa had been caught sneaking out—or sneaking back in—Tillie had been sitting on the deck, sharing a glass of wine with Patty.

Tessa shook her head now, wondering what lack of sense she had at that age. The sun never set in the summer here; how she thought she could sneak around in the cover of darkness that didn't exist amused her. Add to her misguided teenaged logic that Tillie had better hearing than most dogs, and it was a wonder Tessa didn't spend her entire summer grounded.

"He just got out of the Army last month," Tillie continued to brag.

A further stretch of her neck revealed that aside from Tillie and her son, the only other person in the kitchen was Sophie, who was sporting quite the blushing cheeks. Tessa's gaze bounced between her sister and Denver. Was there . . . *a spark*?

"Thank you for your service," Sophie finally said, more choked for words than Tessa had ever seen her. In fact, Sophie didn't *get* choked for words. She always knew the right thing to say no matter the situation.

Raven nudged her leg, leaning against her calf. Tessa absently ran her fingers on the husky's head, staying out of sight and watching what might unfold. Sophie's heartbreak seemed too recent—too raw—for her to move on again so quickly. She might need to keep an eye on this Denver character and Tillie's incessant matchmaking efforts.

"Will you ladies be at the Blueberry Festival this weekend?" Tillie asked.

"We plan on it."

"Oh, good! Good, good, good!"

"Are you entering the clam chowder contest, too?"

Sophie asked. Tessa's ear perked at that. Tillie Grant was legend in this town for her cooking skills, and Tessa feared even a refined chef such as herself might have a hard time beating her.

"Oh, yes! That and I'm making my famous blueberry crumble for the baking contest."

Baking contest? Tessa's competitive side warmed to life. Maybe if she helped lead her sisters to victory with the clam chowder, and possibly take home a victory of her own in a baking contest, she'd win over some of the people in Sunset Ridge. The small town seemed a lot more likely to accept her than the rest of the country, should that episode air.

"C'mon, Raven," she whispered to the dog. "We have plans to make."

It was entirely possible that Tillie saw her fleeing, but if she did, the woman didn't say anything. *Too busy playing matchmaker.*

Tessa was much chillier than when Liam was with her. She rinsed off in a warm shower, all the while pondering what she might enter in the baking contest. The scones were a hit, if the empty plate in the main room was any indication. But would they *win*? "I need to try a few different things," she murmured. When Cadence returned, she'd ask to borrow her car to stock up on blueberries and baking ingredients.

Wondering about baking contests, as if attending town festivals was a regular part of Tessa's life, only left her pining for Liam. *This* was the life she could've had if only he hadn't joined the Army without consulting anyone.

But would she have been happy before now? Tessa couldn't answer that.

"What's he up to, Raven?" she asked the dog, about the construction site. "You were there. Have any insider knowledge to share?" The husky looked up from her cozy spot on the bed, refusing to lift more than her eyes.

She'd tried a couple of different times during lunch to ask Liam about the house—it couldn't be a secret after all—but they'd always been interrupted. "Does he have blueprints in his room, girl?" she asked the husky. "Maybe just a sketch?" Despite how much time had passed, Tessa remembered in detail the conversation she and Liam had one evening after the Blueberry Festival about the house they wanted to build together. Tessa had to know if he was building *that* house.

Leaving Raven asleep on her bed, she tiptoed across the hall. Making sure the coast was clear, she twisted the door knob. But unlike last night, it was locked. "Dang it." Anyone else might've taken the locked door as a sign to leave well enough. But not Tessa. *Where do we keep the keys?*

Tessa checked the laundry room first, thinking she might find a skeleton key hanging beside the door since Sophie had to change linens and towels. Doubtful she had a spare key to *every* room; that didn't sound efficient.

"Nothing, huh?" she mumbled.

The office was the next room down the hall, and she slipped inside, closing the door behind her. Considering she was part owner, this shouldn't have been her first visit to this room. Tomorrow, after the clams were collected, it was time for a family business meeting. Tessa found she had several more questions than she ever expected.

Even if she needed to go back to Vegas, she cared what happened to the lodge. Tessa wanted it to be successful without both her sisters running themselves into the ground making it happen. She wanted them all to thrive together.

Tessa discovered a ring of keys in the desk drawer, all marked with numbers that corresponded to the rooms. She wrapped the ring tightly in her palm to prevent the jingle of metal giving her away, and snuck back.

It shouldn't matter to her that Liam was building a house. He was thirty, going on thirty-one. Who waited to get married anymore before building a house? Not Liam Davies. But if he was building the house they dreamed up together, they were supposed to get married first. Marriage, then the house. That had always been the plan. And if he was getting married to someone else, she'd know by now.

To build the house first was like adding ingredients out of order. "What made you move up your plan?" she mumbled, reentering her own room.

She waved Raven over to her as an alibi, to be

safe. Surely the husky had a treat stash or something in Liam's room.

Cautiously, she unlocked the door and slipped inside. Tessa expected to have more trouble coaxing Raven out than in, but instead of curling up on the bed as Tessa expected, the dog sniffed around the room as if they were in cahoots together. She felt a sliver of guilt for snooping, but she *had* to know.

Liam appeared well settled in his room. *How long has he been here already?*

"Let me know if you find anything good."

Tessa made quick work of her own snooping. It was possible anything to do with the house was electronic, including a blueprint. Her search might be pointless. But knowing she might not get another chance kept her riffling. She opened drawers, went through the closet and the wardrobe, and even searched under the pillows.

"I don't know, Raven. Maybe I'm crazy to think I'll find anything. Unless you have any insider information?"

About to abandon her search and return the keys before she was caught with them, the chest at the foot of the bed caught her eye. A couple of shirts sat crumpled on top of it. "What do you suppose he's hiding in there?"

Tessa tried to push open the lid, but the latch caught. *He locked it.* She wiggled the chest hoping it would give, unsure how she would lock it back up, and knocked off a shirt in the process. She hadn't spotted a key in any of her searching. But no matter how she rocked the chest, the lid wouldn't give.

"I guess we're not breaking into that," she said to Raven, who stood beside her, head tilted. The husky, too, seemed to expect to find some hidden treasure inside. Tessa lifted the shirt off the floor. Instinct caused her to start folding it, but Tessa stopped midway. Liam would notice since it hadn't been folded to begin with. Rolling it into a wad, she left it on the chest.

"Time to go." At the door, she noticed Raven hadn't moved. "What is it, girl?"

The glimmer of something shiny caught her eye near Raven's front paw. *It can't be.*

The heart-shaped necklace Tessa had desperately been searching for lay on the floor, as if placed there for her to discover all along. It must've fallen out of the shirt's pocket. Tessa threaded the silver chain through her fingers and clutched it against her chest, such relief washing over her. She had thought it lost, and that shattered her heart.

Raven let out a whine, and it quickly brought Tessa back to reality. Hating to part with the treasure at all, she stuffed the necklace back in the pocket from whence it came. "What are you doing with my necklace, Liam?" she muttered. Just because she claimed to be looking for a watch didn't mean he believed her. He had to know.

So why had Liam let her suffer?

Raven nudged her arm with her wet nose. "You're

right. We better get out of here before we get caught."

Tessa poked her head out into the hallway, finding it deserted. With a sigh of relief, she motioned Raven out of the room. Just as she was relocking the door, a voice startled her.

"What are you doing, Aunty Tessa?" Caroline stepped out from the window nook she'd been hiding in. How had she not heard the girl's feet pad down the hallway?

"Hey, sweetie. Just forgot something."

"Isn't that Uncle Liam's room?"

Well, dang. The four-year-old was smarter than she gave her credit for. She had Whitmore in her blood for sure. "Yes, it is." No sense in lying to the girl about that. "We were looking for Raven's treats."

"They're in the kitchen."

Of course they are. "Oh, I didn't know that. Do you want to show me?" The sooner they got away from the scene of the crime, the better. Tessa just had to figure out how to drop the ring of room keys off before someone heard them jingle in her pocket. "Raven really wants a treat, don't you, girl?"

Tessa followed the duo to the kitchen. She'd dropped the *T* word so much that Raven's tail was wagging more than usual. Hopefully, the diversion would keep Caroline from spilling the beans to anyone else. Either of her sisters—or worse, Liam— would never buy the treat excuse.

CHAPTER FOURTEEN

Liam

"What happened in here?" Liam stood in the kitchen doorway, his eyes widened by the chaos that lined every counter. Half a dozen mixing bowls, several sets of measuring cups, and more ingredients than one found in the baking aisle of Freeman's Grocery filled every surface.

Tessa turned at his voice, a smear of flour on one cheek. Resisting the urge to wipe that smudge away was futile. He didn't care who saw him kiss her. He would because he wanted to. Their kisses were like dynamite—unstable and incredibly explosive. There was no way Tessa could deny her feelings after a second one.

"Baking contest."

"I thought we were digging clams." He pulled

her toward him by the sides of her apron, forcing her to slow down for a moment and look him in the eye. He'd worked late last night catching up on all the promises he'd fallen behind on since Tessa arrived back in town, and tried to get a little ahead so they had more time to spend together.

"We are. In an hour."

"Sweetheart, I don't think an hour is enough time to tidy up this kitchen. How many things are you making?" He finally wiped away the smear of flour with his thumb, unable to keep his eyes off her lips. She wore a light layer of lipstick today, but he didn't care if he wore the dark pink shade, too. Another night of tossing and turning had led him to the only logical conclusion—he was as much in love with Tessa Whitmore today as he had been thirteen years ago. Maybe more.

"Well . . ." Her gaze swept the busy counter. "There's blueberry cream cheese cookies, blueberry-lemon pie bars, blueberry cheesecake egg rolls—though I'm not crazy about those—and blueberry bread pudding. I thought about a good old-fashioned blueberry pie, but that's never really fared well for me. Pies hate me."

He gave a chuckle, remembering that an early challenge on the show involving pies had nearly got her booted off. The only thing that saved her was a blindfolded palate test. She'd been the only one to get all of the flavors correct.

His hand dropped to her shoulder, his breaths ever so heavier. "You can only enter one, Tess."

"That's why I'm experimenting. I'll enter the best one."

"And do what with the rest?"

She shrugged, her eyes flickering at the counter behind him, but her feet firmly planted in place. "We have plenty of guests. I'm sure they'd be happy with complimentary goodies. The rest . . ." She gave it a moment of thought, then returned her eyes to his. "We can give them away at the festival with business cards for the lodge!"

"Always thinking. I love that about you." He longed to free the long hair trapped in a precise bun, but quick little footsteps echoed down the hall. He stole the kiss he'd been wanting all morning before it was too late. Her lips tasted of blueberries and sugar.

"Clams, clams, clams, clams, clams!" Caroline's youthful voice rang down the hall.

Liam released his grip on Tessa's apron and took a step back. "You gonna be ready?" He nodded at the cluttered counter, wanting to volunteer to help, but running late himself to pick up Owen.

"Maybe?"

"Oh, no," said Cadence, popping into the kitchen. From where, he wasn't sure. She might've been there during that kiss for all he knew. It didn't matter. Liam was never shy about kissing Tessa in front of anyone. "Low tide's in an hour, and you're going with us, Tess. We need your clam expertise."

"We'll help her clean up," Sophie said to Caroline. "Won't we?"

"Can I wear my apron?" the little girl pleaded.

Liam squeezed Tessa's hand until she met his eyes. "I'm going to grab Owen. I'll be back."

"Owen, get your rain boots," April ordered. "You are *not* wearing sandals to dig clams."

Liam heard his nephew's gripes as he stomped down the hall. Something about *I hate my boots* and *stupid clams*. But the kid would change his tune when he had a chance to stick his hands in the sand and pull out the clams himself. He'd forget all about the boots he now protested.

"Don't worry," April reassured him. "He slept in until seven. Shouldn't be too cranky for you today."

"Thanks?"

"You *should* be thanking me. Owen's tantrums can stop traffic. You don't ever want to see meltdown level five when he's sleep-deprived. And naps? At his age, those things are a distant memory."

Liam had witnessed pieces of Owen's tantrums, but he'd never been stuck with one himself. The very idea should make him want to prolong having his own kids, but instead, it made him excited. Together, he and Tessa could overcome any challenge. Even cranky kids throwing themselves on grocery store floors, acting as though the world was ending because they weren't allowed the breakfast cereal they wanted but might never eat.

"Make sure you return the favor and wear that kid out." April rubbed her belly and winced. "I don't need him staying up until midnight."

"You okay?"

"Yep, just peachy." She winced again. "It's normal."

When Owen was born, Liam had still been a month out from moving home. He missed every stage of April's first pregnancy and had no idea whether or not what she told him was enough to go on. "Sure you don't want to run to the hospital? Check in with your doctor?"

"I'll be much happier when you get Owen out of my hair for a couple of hours. I want to eat every cupcake and piece of bacon in sight. My back hurts and I'm crabby. I just want some peace and quiet so I can binge-watch Harry Potter with my fuzzy purple blanket that's for once free of whatever that kid spilled."

Liam lost the fight to hide his smile.

"Just you wait until your wife is pregnant and random. God help you if you cross her, Liam. Praying might be the only thing that saves you then."

Owen's heavy feet padded down the hallway, boots dangling from each hand. "I want to dig clams!"

"We're going, buddy. Get your boots on."

"You're really ready, aren't you?" April assessed him a little too long for comfort, so Liam knelt and helped Owen with his boots. The beach was likely to be extra mushy from yesterday's rain. He wondered if Caroline had a pair of boots, too. "Okay, pretend to ignore me, Liam Michael Davies. But I know the look. Miles had it, too."

"Where's Mom?"

"Writing another offer."

Liam straightened. "There aren't *that* many houses in Sunset Ridge." He wondered if his mom was avoiding him. The possibility was high, considering April had turned out to be a super fan of Tessa the Grizzly Bear. April probably talked nonstop about her unexpected visit last night. If he couldn't track Mom down today, he'd find her at the festival. No way Jolene Davies missed entering the baking contest. She and Tillie were old rivals.

"You never ask where *Dad* is." April helped Owen into his jacket, best she could without the ability to bend over.

"That's because I *know* where Dad is. At the store, where he always is. Hardware never rests."

Their dad, Harold, hadn't exactly disowned Liam. But he'd certainly worn his disappointment on his sleeve when Liam announced plans to take over his grandpa's shop rather than follow in his dad's footsteps. Never mind how much more Liam knew about a motor or the components under the hood of a car than half the items in the hardware store. Or that he'd been an Army mechanic.

"Maybe you should try stopping by there every

once in a while. Dad's got a sweet spot for a caramel espresso from Black Bear Coffee."

If Owen's large eyes hadn't been so intently fixated on them both, the kid no doubt hanging on their every word, Liam might've continued this argument. He might be in the minority of Sunset Ridge residents, but he didn't drink coffee or believe in spending seven bucks on one his dad would possibly pour down the drain out of spite. "Owen, you ready to go?"

"Don't forget his booster seat."

Liam winked at his sister, mostly because he knew how much it annoyed her. "Already in there."

He ushered Owen out the door to his truck, but not before April got in one more nugget of wisdom.

"Be careful, Liam."

"I'm watching this kid like a hawk." The claw-like gesture he made with his fingers made Owen laugh uncontrollably, but it didn't soften April's concerned expression. Seemed he wouldn't get away without things turning heavier.

"She might win."

Liam's entire body went rigid over the possibility he knew existed but happily denied. He didn't want to think about this now. "I know."

"She has what it takes. I know you don't watch the show, but maybe you should start. She ran a kitchen last night like a pro. Like she'd been doing it all her life."

If only you knew. "I'll make him run laps," he joked

about Owen once the kid was secured in his booster seat. "You want me to keep him for a while? I can take him back to the lodge for a few hours."

"I like her, Liam. But I don't want to see you hurt again." April might be the only one who knew why he joined the Army when he did, and why it had been so hard on him. She was gone a lot that summer, but they'd stayed in touch. In many ways, his sister was his best friend.

"I know the risks." He hopped up the couple of stairs on the deck and gave his sister a gentle squeeze. "You call me if you need a ride to the hospital."

Despite the sunshine on the shore, a crisp breeze kept everyone bundled in light layers. The wind could be chilliest on the beach. Tessa hadn't brought practical clothes for clam digging. Though her sisters helped with some of the essentials—old jeans and a pair of rain boots—Liam loaned her a waterproof jacket at least two sizes too big. But it looked perfect.

It looked like the future.

"Uncle Liam, Uncle Liam!" A clam cradled in his sand-covered hands, Owen ran to Liam who carried the last spade to the beach. "Look, it's a clam!"

"Sure is, buddy. Drop it in the bucket. We have to keep every clam we dig up, remember. Those are the rules." He didn't have the heart to tell the kid that the clam would later be chopped up and cooked in a chowder. Even though the clams didn't wiggle around quite the same way a fish did, it still might traumatize the youngsters to know what fate awaited their catches once they were dropped into that bucket.

"Do you remember doing this with Aunt Patty?" he heard Sophie ask Tessa. "How cold it was that day? And raining?"

"I was so mad at her. I had *other* plans," Tessa said with a laugh. Her gaze flickered to Liam, then back to the hole she was digging. Liam smirked, suspecting those plans had been with him. "But that chowder was worth it."

"I hope we can do Aunt Patty's recipe justice," Cadence chimed in. "I still dream about how good it was. I remember thinking how much I hated clams, too, until I had that chowder. Boy, was I wrong."

"Nothing beats fresh clams," Tessa said.

Liam wedged the spade near a round dimple in the sand, enjoying the Whitmore sisters acting like, well, sisters. Sophie had let on more than once during his stay at the lodge how far apart they'd grown. Hope existed now when weeks ago it was only a faint possibility. Liam suspected it was exactly what Patty Whitmore had wanted for her nieces.

If Tessa stayed in Sunset Ridge, they could form that bond once again. He hoped Tessa saw how much her staying would mean to everyone.

"Can I help you, Uncle Liam?" Owen asked when he spotted Liam lifting a pile of sand with his spade.

"Sure, buddy. Dig gently now."

The warm look in Tessa's eyes made his chest swell. Someday this could be the two of them, digging up clams with their own children. The same thought had to be circling in her mind, too.

April's words whispered through his thoughts, trying their best to plant fear. *Tessa might win. She might leave.*

"I got it!" Owen shouted, drawing Caroline's attention. The girl came running across the beach, her hands sandy but empty.

"How did you do that?" Caroline asked.

Owen launched into a theatrical retelling of his most recent clam discovery, then waited for Liam to dig up another pile of sand so he could talk Caroline through her own successful clam retrieval.

"You're really good with them," Cadence said.

"What can I say?" Liam shrugged. "I like kids."

"I sure hope so," Cadence continued. "Ford says you're building a house big enough to fit ten of them."

"How's he like Boston?" Liam flipped the subject before Tessa had a chance to launch into questions about the house he wasn't ready to show her yet. She'd no doubt demand to see it now that the cat was out of the bag.

"Rilee *loves* it. Ford's ready to come home." Cadence looked at Tessa and explained, "Rilee's Ford's younger sister. She's going to college this fall at Boston University." Cadence looked back to Liam, a raised eyebrow letting him know she was allowing him off the hook, but not lowering her suspicious. "They fly back tonight, just in time for the Blueberry Festival tomorrow."

"And Ford's your . . ." Tessa's question dropped off into silence.

"My boyfriend."

"I *have* missed a lot." She looked back at Liam, lumping the house in her comment, no doubt.

The sun dipped behind a patch of clouds, and Tessa shivered despite the layers. Staking his spade in the ground, Liam ran his hands up and down her arms. "Vegas was a little warmer, huh?" No one else seemed to be fazed by the cool breeze, but they were all acclimated.

"Little bit."

"Decide what you're baking?" he asked.

"Not yet." Tessa turned toward him. "Liam, what are you building—"

"Uncle Liam, dig another hole!" Caroline begged this time.

"Please," Owen joined in.

Liam left Tessa with a wink and unanswered questions. "Let's try over there," he told the kids. He was no fool; Tessa wouldn't let this go for long. "We need to look for little dimples in the sand. See any?" Owen and Caroline rushed ahead, such innocent excitement in everything they did.

The sisters continued digging up razor clams in one area, and Liam helped the youngsters in another. He wished he hadn't waited to break ground on the new house. But how was he to know Tessa would come back to Sunset Ridge ahead of schedule? If she could only see the finished product, it might be enough. But with nothing more than a poured foundation and piles of logs, Liam feared Tessa could too easily let go of their possible future.

Before she showed up in that banged-up Mustang, the idea that he might have to let her go was easier to swallow. If she left this time, Liam wasn't sure he'd recover from that kind of heartbreak. He yearned to settle down, but he didn't want that with anyone else.

Only Tessa.

CHAPTER FIFTEEN

Tessa

When they all returned to the lodge that afternoon, Sophie took the kids to wash up and promised them a movie as a reward for their hard work. Apparently, the idea of slicing the clams out of their shells was too much for them to grasp, and Sophie worried a couple of meltdowns might ensue in the process.

"We'll help," Cadence promised Tessa, referring to herself and Liam. "I have a couple of hours before Ford and Rilee are due home anyway."

The trio spread newspaper along the counter and got to work as Raven curled up in her dog bed Liam had set up in the corner by the window.

Part of Tessa wanted Liam all to herself. Another part felt thankful her sister was there. Being alone with him was proving far more dangerous than she bargained. Even now, with a barrier, Liam stood too close. A man shouldn't smell that good after handling clams.

"Is your mom entering the baking contest?" Cadence asked Liam, and Tessa was glad. Otherwise, they worked in awkward silence. Tessa had too many questions she didn't want to ask in front of Cadence.

"You know it," Liam said. "She can't stand it when Tillie beats her."

"She might have some competition," Cadence said, nodding at Tessa. "If she can decide which *one* to enter tomorrow."

"I've narrowed it down to the blueberry cream cheese cookies or blueberry-lemon pie bars," Tessa broke into the conversation the two seemed to be having *about* her without including her. "I'm going to make them both again tonight and decide."

"Isn't the clam chowder contest enough?" Liam said, that irritating smirk spread on his lips. Tessa squeezed the shell in her hand, frustrated that she wanted both to wipe that expression right off his lips, but also wanted to kiss it away. She still wanted to know why he had her necklace, but asking would admit to snooping in his room.

Too many emotions buzzed through her, which was always a danger in Liam's presence. It was exhilarating yet *so* confusing. *Why did I let that kiss happen?* It made every decision that much harder when it came to Liam Davies.

"You would think," said Cadence. "But you know

Tessa. When her competitive side is unleashed, there's no stopping her from anything."

"Guess there's a reason they call her a grizzly bear."

The clam shell slipped right out of Tessa's hand and bounced off the tile backsplash. In a quick ninja-like maneuver that could only be attributed to sheer luck, Tessa blocked the ricocheting shell with her hands before it could shoot across the room and crash to the floor. "You *do* watch the show." Her words came out as an accusation.

"Does that surprise you?" Cadence asked. "Almost everyone in town has seen some of it."

Tessa's gaze narrowed at Liam, but her heart thundered in her chest. She wanted to be mad at him for lying. For misleading her about all he actually knew. But mostly, she was embarrassed. She had a chance to stream a few episodes during a layover, and Tessa wasn't proud of the woman the show portrayed. She wasn't ready to admit that to herself a few days ago, but Sunset Ridge reminded her of the person she wanted to be. Tessa the Grizzly Bear wasn't it.

"You lied to me."

"It was on some commercial preview," Liam said with a nonchalant shrug.

"Right." Tessa didn't believe that. Not since she caught *Order Up* playing on his TV screen last night. Sure, he was asleep. But with the show hardly half over when she found him, she was certain the intent had been there.

"Those previews make it all out to be pretty dramatic," Liam continued. Tessa kept her gaze on his hands, watching him drop an empty shell in the bowl and start on another clam, because looking him in the eye might make her do something crazy. "I guess the prize must be worth putting up with all that. What do you win? A restaurant, a boat load of money, or both? Or is telling us in violation of the contract?"

"I'm going to run to the restroom," said Cadence, quickly washing her hands and fleeing the kitchen. Tessa couldn't blame her sister for evading what might quickly turn into a war zone.

"Why do you care, Liam?" Tessa snapped. "You're already convinced I lost."

"Did you?"

Tessa thought about her phone, sitting on her nightstand. This was the only day she hadn't called her producer friend Janet first thing in the morning since she was told to leave. She had finally accepted that they weren't going to make things right. They would exploit her for cheating because that would increase ratings more than the truth.

"I have to dice the celery," said Tessa, going to the sink to wash her hands. "I suggest you keep your distance." Chopping vegetables with her extra-sharp utility knife always made her feel better, and it would give her some distance. Especially if Liam saw the episode that included a vegetable dicing contest. Tessa won by a landslide.

"What does it matter if I watched the show, Tess?"

Because you made me feel like a fool. But Tessa was too proud to say those words out loud. She hacked through three times the celery they actually needed and moved on to onions. There had been a running joke with the cast on the show that Tessa was made of stone, because even the most odorous onions didn't make her cry. They were convinced nothing would. It was one of the factors that attributed to her unwanted nickname.

"Tess, put the knife down," said Liam, approaching boldly. "Please."

She was running out of vegetables that needed dicing. If she let herself loose on the potatoes, they might be so small they'd dissolve in the chowder. "I'm not doing this right now, Liam."

"What's next?" Cadence returned to the kitchen, retying her apron. Tessa had to give her sister points for braving the battle.

"Bacon needs to be fried. Potatoes peeled. Please tell me we were able to get the Colby-jack cheese and red pepper flakes?"

"Yes, we have everything on Aunt Patty's list."

"Tessa," pleaded Liam.

She slammed her knife down on the cutting board. "I need to make a call. I'll be back." She made it two steps into the hallway before the cloud of Liam's aftershave drifted to her. "*Don't* follow me."

Halfway through marching down the hall, the first

guest Tessa had seen since her arrival popped her head out her door. Flushed, Tessa lightened her footsteps and offered a smile. "I hope you're having a lovely stay." Though she wouldn't be pursuing an acting career anytime soon, Tessa had mastered the skill well enough on the show to serve her now.

"We love the Sunset Ridge Lodge," the elderly woman said, a cautious smile on her lips. "We used to come here every summer and were devastated to hear it closed down. I'm sorry about your great-aunt. She'd be proud you girls reopened it."

"Thank you." Tessa tried her best to be polite—to act like a professional business owner—but all she wanted to do was run away. "I'm sorry if I was making too much noise out here."

"It's no bother," said the woman. "Just wanted to make sure everything is all right."

"Just peachy." Tessa spoke the words so suavely that she almost had herself convinced they were true. "Have a wonderful rest of your stay." She hurried down the hall to her room. If there was an inkling of a chance that she was going to stay in Alaska, the living arrangements would have to change. Tessa would not live out her days in a lodge room decorated with black bears.

"Hey," said Sophie, popping out from the window nook, a phone cradled in her hand.

"You okay?"

"Lawyers," Sophie muttered. "Nothing I can't handle."

Tessa wasn't so sure about that, but right now she couldn't process the whirling thoughts in her own head, much less add another layer. Later, she would sit Sophie down and make sure her ex wasn't giving her any grief. She'd made a couple of powerful friends in New York, and those connections might come in handy.

"I need to make a phone call," Tessa said, as if explaining her invasion.

"Oh, I have some unfortunate news."

Tessa lifted the key to her lock. "What?"

"We needed your room."

"So I need to move out?"

"You already did."

Tessa blinked at Sophie, experiencing trouble processing her words. "Where's my stuff?"

"You're bunking with Cadence. Everything is upstairs. Aunt Patty's old room. Sorry we didn't tell you earlier. We forgot until the guest called to verify their reservation and requested an early check-in."

Tessa swallowed, wondering if Sophie had found the spare ring of keys buried in her suitcase. Considering her sister was able to get into her room, there had to be another set, or at least a skeleton key. "It's no problem. Really."

"You okay?"

"Nope. Not really." Tessa gave a shrug. "But I have something to do. Talk later?"

Sophie's expression was riddled with concern. "Sure." It only made Tessa more eager to flee.

Tessa flew up the stairs to the second floor. Since arriving in Sunset Ridge, she'd been so caught up in her own agenda that she hadn't even bothered to go upstairs in the lodge she owned. Besides Aunt Patty's master suite, there were also guest rooms and a couple of private nooks she used to frequent when guests weren't using them. One offered a way onto the eave of the roof—an easy way to sneak out.

Her suitcases were neatly stacked in a corner, her cell phone resting on top.

It was stupid to call Janet now, especially since there'd been no activity on her phone whatsoever since she last checked it. But Tessa had to try.

"No service?" She held her phone up toward the window, as high as she could, and still nothing. "I thought Cadence said this was one of the only spots in town . . ." Tessa searched her memories of other nearby high points. "Of course."

She could be a sensible person—an adult—and use the back door. But the risk of running into Liam on the way there felt too high. Summoning her inner teenager, Tessa tiptoed to the end of the hall and snaked a right into a nook heavily decorated in bears. "Always *bears*." She glanced around, ensuring the coast was clear, then undid the window latch.

Tessa lowered herself to the steepled eave until her foot caught on a small landing. From here, the ground was a short hop down. Though she wasn't quite as agile as she'd once been, she landed without a stumble.

Raising her phone one more time, Tessa sighed. She wasn't crazy about running off into the woods to the lookout point—not with the chance she might encounter a bear—but for some reason, her signal wasn't returning. "I'm making that call," she muttered, convinced that her lack of notifications might have something to do with the no service warning.

Still in Cadence's loaned sneakers, Tessa began to jog. Then run. Her feet kept her going until she reached the lookout point. "Aha! Three bars." Before notifications stood a chance to flood in, she dialed Janet from her call history—the only number she'd called in the last several weeks—and waited.

"Tessa, hi."

"Hey, Janet. Just my daily check-in call."

"Yeah." Uneasiness dripped from Janet's tone, warning Tessa something was wrong. More than Tessa not getting called back. She wondered if Janet would—or *could*—tell her.

"What is it?"

"You're not going to like it."

Tessa had already envisioned all the worst-case scenarios. Outside of America thinking she really had cheated and Derek winning the whole show, she couldn't come up with anything that might be worse. Janet had agreed with her, too. This had to be something else. "Just spit it out. If you can."

"You know I can't *tell* you." So Tessa would have to guess.

"Derek won."

"They still have to film the finale."

"Derek made it into the final two." She briefly wondered who his competition might be, but it had to Francine. From day one, Tessa was certain Francine would be her only true competition, and it made sense now if she had made it to the final round. Francine was an incredibly talented chef, worthy of a taking first place. "There's obviously going to be a big over-the-top drama of me being caught cheating."

"*Mmmm.*"

Tessa was getting warmer, but she was still missing something. "Did they move up airing that?'

"No."

"They're not going to call me back to compete?"

"No." But the way Janet drug out the *o* this time warned Tessa a curveball was coming. "Janet, those are literally the worst things I can think up. Can you give me a hint? Just a tiny one?"

"Sorry, you know the rules." The producers had signed a contract similar to Tessa's but with stiffer penalties. Janet talking to a former contestant at all skated a very fine line around a gray area that if contested might or might not hold up in court. "But it's worse. Definitely worse."

Tessa gasped, afraid she'd figured out exactly what they wanted of her now. "They want me to be on the next season, don't they?"

"Mmm, well . . ."

The only thing worse than being accused of

cheating on air for every viewer to see was having to return for another round of the same, labeled a cheater. With her nickname, the producers no doubt wanted her to fight for redemption. Which meant she would have to go along with the angle and pretend to redeem herself. "When does it start?"

"They're not messing around."

"Two months?"

Janet laughed. "You're not that lucky, doll. Change that two months out for two weeks."

Tessa's stomach plummeted somewhere near her toes. It was one thing to go back and win what was rightfully hers. But quite another to go along with such a humiliating lie. "They can't do this."

"I'm sorry, Tessa. Read your contract. I'm afraid they can."

"I have to go." Tessa's voice cracked, but when she started to cry, she didn't want anyone to know. She ended the call and dropped to the ground. She couldn't breathe through her tears. Half an hour ago, her biggest problem was Liam admitting he'd watched her show.

She heard the scuffle of feet on dirt and looked up, expecting to see Liam. He was good at appearing in her time of need, as if they were telepathically connected. But it wasn't Liam, or even her sisters.

"Ed." Tessa wiped at the moisture on her cheeks and slowly forced herself to her feet. She didn't have anywhere to run that didn't involve a steep drop-off, but she was more vulnerable to broken ribs on the ground than standing. "Why? Why do you always find me at the *worst* times?"

The moose stood at the trail opening, tilting his head much like a dog. He was still a good twenty feet away, but he blocked her only escape.

Still facing Ed, Tessa leaned back against the wooden railing, testing it for sturdiness before she dropped her full weight against it. "The least you could do is offer some advice. I mean, what am I supposed to do about this mess?" She didn't have a plan if the moose charged, but hopefully he'd find her stance nonthreatening.

"They *own* me, Ed. How could I have been so stupid? I never should've signed that piece of paper. Well, that's not true. I never should've dated that rotten turd. If it weren't for Derek and his greedy insecurity, *I'd* be competing in the final two right now. Not labeled some cheater and at the mercy of a stupid contract. I might be *winning*."

Ed reached his enormous snout up and pulled down a few leaves from a nearby branch for a snack. He kept his eyes on Tessa, so she stayed put and continued to unload her worries to the bull.

"I love Liam, Ed. I do. I mean, I always have really. And even though he drives me crazy—and I mean absolutely, totally, and completely bonkers—I want the choice to go or stay to be *mine*. It's not fair that they can steal five more weeks of my life." Because if Tessa had to compete, she wouldn't allow herself to lose a second time. The producers were probably betting on it, too.

Between bites, Ed tilted his head again. The way his unique antlers sat crooked with his angled head made Tessa smile. He looked downright goofy for a two-thousand pound creature with the ability to break most of the bones in her body.

"What do I do, Ed? Tell me."

But the moose turned and sauntered back down the trail, leaving Tessa without answers.

CHAPTER SIXTEEN

Tessa

The sun made intermittent appearances during the Blueberry Festival, causing most of the crowd to wear a sweatshirt or light jacket. But Tessa was sweating over the last full stockpot of clam chowder they had left, stirring it too frequently. If she didn't keep herself occupied, she spent too much time scanning the crowd for Liam. No doubt he was upset with her for disappearing last night. They'd always had that kind of hot-and-cold relationship.

"I'm sorry you didn't win the baking contest," Sophie said gently. "I thought your cookies were amazing."

Tessa offered a forced smile, but couldn't manage much else. If Janet hadn't burst her bubble the night before, maybe she'd be upset that Tillie Grant took the first-place ribbon for her blueberry crumble, with Tessa one of eight honorable mentions. But the contest that had her so spooled up no longer seemed to matter. Seemed lately she had a way of putting too much energy into the wrong things. "Baking isn't my strong suit anyway," she admitted.

"I need more samples," Cadence called over her shoulder to Tessa. "They're cleaning us out!"

The sisters were set up under an open tent, one of dozens of tables strewn together. Tessa kept an eye on the reserve of chowder in the tall stockpot while Cadence and Sophie manned the crowd hungry for samples. "Do we have enough cups left?" Tessa asked, happy for the distraction. Even if only for a few minutes, it was nice to pretend her life was her own. *I'm an idiot for not reading that contract thoroughly enough.*

"I'll get more," Sophie said. "Be back in a minute."

"Try smiling a little. This is a good problem to have." Cadence nudged Tessa's shoulder as she stole the last dozen sample bowls from the back table. "Means you did a good job."

Tessa set the ladle in the biggest stockpot and topped it with a lid. "*We* did a good job."

"Then what's wrong?"

"Nothing." She busied herself searching under the table for cups she knew weren't there. Since their mom passed, Tessa had always taken charge. She never put her own problems on her sisters' shoulders. She figured out how to manage them herself. It was part of what had steeled her in so many aspects of life. Probably the truest reason why they nicknamed her the grizzly bear.

"I don't believe you."

"This is the last of what they have," said Sophie, holding up a stack of small sample bowls she'd tracked down on her search. "I guess they've already cleaned out Freeman's Grocery. We'll have to make do. Unless Ford knows anyone who might have a stash?"

"I'll text him," said Cadence. "Take over."

Though she had yet to meet Cadence's new man, Tessa envied her sister. Tessa wasn't very good at relationships. Anyone she dated left because she never let them in to begin with. Liam was the only man who had ever busted past her fortified walls, crumbling them away as if they were nothing more than dust.

"No luck," reported Cadence.

"We'll manage," said Sophie, her tone optimistic as always. Tessa wished she could be a little more like either of her sisters. *I'd be better off for it.*

"You can talk to us, you know." Cadence ladled chowder into the sample bowls as a new line formed. Great-Aunt Patty's recipe was a hit, it seemed. The festival goers' votes would reveal *how* great later that afternoon. "We're only your *sisters*."

"Really, it's nothing." Tessa focused on stirring the chowder from their last full stockpot so she didn't have to look either of them in the eye.

"Liar." It wasn't often that Sophie called her out,

much less in front of Cadence. "Tell her the truth, Tessa. We're family. She deserves to know."

Last night, when Ed disappeared into the woods and Tessa managed to stop shaking from shock, she snuck back inside the lodge through the back door because someone had closed the upstairs window. Raven followed her back to her room and snuggled against her in bed as she cried beneath the covers. Tessa'd feigned sleep when Cadence finally turned in.

"I can't," said Tessa, glancing around at all the people. Some of them had recognized her from the show, and several wished her good luck as if she still might have a shot at winning. She entertained a few pictures and even a couple of autographs. But the joy that might've brought her even a month ago was nonexistent now.

"You tell her, or I will," Sophie threatened.

"The contract—"

"Stop hiding behind that stupid thing." If Caroline had been in the tent with them, Tessa doubted Sophie would've used that word. But Tillie had offered to take the girl to get her face painted half an hour ago. "We're your family, not some tabloid."

"Fine." With folded arms, more to hold herself together than anything, Tessa told Cadence everything she'd already shared with Sophie. How Derek broke up with her and somehow managed to sneak her recipe card to Vegas. "I still don't know how he planted it. I told them to check the cameras, but they claimed there was nothing to see." She confessed her pitiful hope that the producers would call her and beg her to come back once they realized she was innocent. It all sounded so empty and foolish now. How she thought some reality show could ever give her more than her own family made her feel ashamed.

"That rotten, weaselly—"

"I wish that was the worst part," Tessa said, cutting Cadence off before a word slipped from her lips that might alarm a few chowder samplers and sway their vote to another team.

"Wait, there's more?" Sophie said between serving customers.

"I talked to one of the producers last night. She's my only ally—the only one who believes I didn't cheat." Tessa had a suspicion a handful of others knew the truth and were sitting on it for the benefit of their ratings. They probably deleted the camera footage. *But why?* "They want me to be on the next season. In *two* weeks."

"I hope you're kidding," said Sophie. "They can't expect you to drop everything like that."

"You're not going," Cadence said, hands on her hips. "Right?"

Tessa gave a helpless shrug. "It's not exactly up to me. I signed a contact."

Cadence shook her head. "No. No way they can do that. Guest appearances and stuff like that, sure. But this? They can't mandate you give up five more weeks of your life. You didn't join the military, Tessa." She untied her apron and tossed it on the back table.

"Where are you going?" Tessa asked.

"To talk to our lawyer, Mr. Jenkins. Email him a copy of the contract." When Tessa didn't make an immediate move to fish her phone out of her purse, Cadence added, "Like yesterday."

"It's pointless," said Tessa, remembering what Janet told her last night. If there were a way around it, her only ally—the only one truly rooting for her—would have let her in on that secret. "I know what I signed. I remember the clause, I just didn't think it mattered." She glanced around and lowered her voice. "I expected to win."

Cadence rolled her eyes as dramatically as she used to when they were younger. "When are you going to stop trying to fix everything yourself and trust us? We're not kids that you have to protect."

"We want you to stay, Tessa," added Sophie. "But if you're going to be a part of this, you have to be honest with us. Trust that we can handle things *together*. You're not alone."

"Sophie's right. Either you're a silent partner or you're all in," said Cadence from the other side of the table. They'd been blessed with a small break of eager tasters, but even if that weren't the case, Tessa suspected any line of people would have to wait. "What's it going to be?"

Liam

. . .

Liam was in a sour mood. One that started the afternoon before when Tessa marched out of the kitchen, and continued through to the next day. She'd been avoiding him, but to be fair, he'd been avoiding her, too. He hadn't missed a Blueberry Festival except while he was away during his years in the Army, but today he was hiding out in his shop.

"April," Liam growled. Everything had been going great until his sister had to remind him that Tessa might leave again. Sure, it was a legit risk. But Liam was quite happy living in denial. He wanted desperately to believe that little moments they shared this week would be enough to convince her to stay for good.

But the seed of doubt had been planted when his sister warned him Tessa might *win*. And with how much Tessa talked about needing to go back on a moment's notice, maybe she still would. Liam wanted to see her accomplish all of her dreams, but he also wanted her to stay and build a life with him—the life they dreamed up years ago.

Why did the two scenarios have to repel each other like oil and water?

"You hammer on that Jeep bumper any harder and you're going to bust it, not work out that dent."

Liam wiped away a line of sweat on his forehead with a shop towel, dropping the mallet. He turned to find his buddy Ford standing behind him with folded arms and a raised eyebrow. "How was Boston?"

"Too many people. Glad to be home."

"Good."

"Festival already started."

"Not going."

"Sure, you are." Ford picked up a socket wrench and got to work tightening the bolts on the new radiator.

It was the last thing Liam needed to do for the Mustang before it was good as new. But he wasn't ready to install it and put everything back together, which was why he'd switched to a different task. Banging on a steel bumper felt more satisfying than turning a socket wrench anyway. "No point."

Liam had offered his friend a job multiple times, but Ford kept too busy doing handyman work for most of the town. But the two of them worked well together with a synchronization that accomplished a lot. With Liam's luck, that radiator repair job would be finished in half an hour tops and leave him without an excuse to stall. "Cadence won't let me go if I don't bring you with me."

"I've got too much to do."

Ford stopped ratcheting. "You're not giving up, are you?"

Liam took a long, deep breath. "Maybe I am." If he threw in the towel now, at least he'd know his fate. He wouldn't have to wait on some stupid phone call to make up Tessa's mind.

"You've been waiting years for Tessa Whitmore to come strolling back into town." Ford shook his head. "And now you're just going to let her go without a fight?"

As much as he wanted to continue pounding on the bumper, Liam relented and helped Ford attach the upper hose for the radiator. "I'm tired of not knowing." There. He'd said it. "This way, I know what I'm in for."

"Sure, maybe she gets a call." Ford handed Liam one of the upper brackets and worked on the other himself. "But can you go the rest of your life wondering what would've happened if you'd just gone all in?"

It was easier to stay mad. Liam knew he was hiding behind that emotion so he didn't have to deal with any of the others. "Maybe this is the way it's always been meant to be. This town isn't big enough for her." With her skills and her ambition, how could she ever be happy in Sunset Ridge? "We're a little short on five-star restaurants, in case you haven't noticed."

"Is that what *she* thinks?"

Liam dropped a nut, and it rolled under the Mustang. He leaned down to reach for it and Tessa's necklace spilled out of his pocket, missing a fresh grease puddle by inches. *Odd*. He was certain he left it in another shirt. No way he'd risk dropping it in a puddle of oil.

"What's that?" Ford nodded toward the necklace.

Liam used a clean shop towel to pick it up. "Nothing."

But Ford's smirk said what he thought of Liam's answer.

"I don't want to hold her back," Liam admitted.

"I get why you did it the first time. Maybe this time you should let *her* decide?" Ford wiped his hands with a shop towel, but they'd be stained with grease for at least a couple of days. The Mustang was back in one piece though, and unless the rental company checked serial numbers, they'd never know the difference. There was nothing left for him to do.

Liam dropped the necklace back in his shirt pocket. "I don't want Tessa resenting me for staying." That fear had pushed him to sign his name on the dotted line thirteen years ago. The only thing worse than being without Tessa would be living with her knowing she was unhappy from a sacrifice she made for him.

"What if she resents you because you didn't ask her to stay?" Ford asked. "Can you live with yourself then?"

He hated that Ford was right. Wadding up the shop towel, Liam shot it across the garage bay into an empty bucket. "Guess we better get to this festival before I get you in trouble."

CHAPTER SEVENTEEN

Liam

By the time Liam and Ford arrived at the festival, the Whitmore sisters were standing on stage, holding a giant check. Caroline's tiny head poked out the side, right next to *pay to the order of.* Their combined smiles were radiant enough to illuminate the town on the darkest day of the year.

"Guess they won," Ford said.

Regret tugged at Liam for his stubbornness. He should have been *here* supporting Tessa and her family. Sneaking samples and kisses. Instead, he wasted half the day brooding inside his shop.

One look at the woman he loved washed all the sour feelings away. It'd always been that way with Tessa. He could only stay mad if he kept his distance, because her presence cast a powerful spell over him that made it impossible to remain upset.

"Let's give these ladies another round of applause!" No surprise that his dad was on stage announcing the winners. Outside of the hardware store, Harold lived for the festivals. Maybe April was right. He should bring a coffee by and try to mend their relationship. If he didn't take the first step, it might never happen. He came from a long enough line of stubborn Davies men to know that was how things worked.

"What are you waiting for?" Ford clapped him hard on the back, rocking him a couple of steps forward as the women stepped down from the stage. "Clock's ticking."

"Oddly familiar words," said Liam over his shoulder.

"Stop stalling."

Liam wove his way through the crowd, spotting his mom off in the distance. He'd have to talk to her, too. The woman who had so eagerly invited him to multiple family dinners each week had sent less than a handful of texts this week. But right now, Liam had to maintain his focus. Time wasn't on his side. Something about having that Mustang repaired made the feeling more prominent than ever.

"Liam." Tessa's feet tangled to a stop, probably the fault of those stupid boot things. A cautious smile fought its way through her confused expression.

Sophie gave her a side hug. "We'll see you later,

Tess."

"But we still have to clean up—" The words evaporated into the space Sophie and Cadence left between them and Tessa. Within seconds, they were impossible to spot in the crowd.

"That scared to be alone with me?" Liam asked with a coolness he definitely didn't feel. Nerves rattled his entire body, and he felt like that seventeen-year-old boy again, working up the courage to talk to the beautiful girl sitting all by herself in the corner booth at Moosecakes.

"We need to talk."

Liam kept his facial expression from betraying his worst fears. "Good, I need to talk to you, too." He took her hand as though it was the most natural thing in the world—in many ways it was—and led her through the crowd toward the exit.

"Wait, where are we going? Liam, I can't take another plane ride right now—"

A few feet from the gate, Liam stopped and turned to Tessa. Droves of people wound around them, but he didn't care if they were in the way. "Do you trust me?"

"Yes."

Her answer was quick and confident. A testament to their relationship. Together, they were a bit wild and reckless. Two stubborn but free spirits, mingled together. But the unyielding trust they'd always held for one another was what made it all work.

In the truck, Liam turned onto the private road,

ignoring the no-trespassing sign so many others were wiser to obey. The long way would have been smarter, as Old Man Franks was rumored to have returned early from his trip. But they didn't have the luxury of time.

"I know about the house," Tessa said as the truck bounced over a rut.

"You do?" It shouldn't have come as a surprise. Sophie almost let it slip a handful of times, and who knew if Cadence told her. Even if her sisters hadn't revealed his secret, any number of people in town could have.

"I saw you out there the other day."

"Oh."

"I was looking for my necklace."

The silver pendant burned a hole in his pocket. He'd been saving the precious piece of jewelry for the day he showed her the house. Maybe he thought it was more symbolic than she did. But now, he just felt guilty.

"I know you have it."

Liam swallowed, wondering how she figured that out. Other than Ford, no one else knew. But then it dawned on him. Tessa'd been snooping. "Guess that's why it ended up in the wrong shirt."

"Maybe I—"

But Tessa wasn't given a chance to finish her sentence because Liam floored the gas pedal. "Behind us." The other truck grew larger in his rearview mirror. They had seconds to climb the hill and dip down a side road. Many of those paths were overgrown and hard to find, but Liam had spent more than a few hours poking around out here before Tessa came back.

Tessa gripped the back of the seat as she stared out the back window. "You were serious about him."

"I was hoping to reason with Franks at some point," said Liam as he took a sharp turn onto a heavily wooded path that was better suited for moose and ATVs than his large truck. But Old Man Franks liked his power, it seemed. The only thing that spoke to him was obscene amounts of money. "His road has shorter routes to so many different properties."

"Yours included."

"Yep."

Liam tried to lose him on this path, but he caught the faint red of Old Man Franks' bumper. "Hold on."

Tessa braced herself with the dashboard and the grab handle over the door. Somewhere in this chaos, she'd found her seatbelt. *Smart girl.* The rutted path grew bumpier and narrower, and Liam worried he'd mixed up this trail with another.

"Why did you have my necklace?" Tessa had to yell over the noisy engine and the thunking of tree branches that were no doubt scratching the paint. "You knew I was looking for it."

"We're doing this now?"

Liam sped up when he spotted the clearing, relieved they were exactly where he thought. Three options lay ahead, and if he was quick enough, he could be out of sight before Old Man Franks had a clear view of which one he'd taken.

"Why'd you keep it?" Liam asked, another glance over his shoulder because he didn't trust his mirrors to give him the full picture.

"Because."

A shotgun fired. Tessa screamed. Liam's heart pumped double time.

"I think he got *crazier*," Tessa hollered. "He never shot at us before!"

Accepting that they would be a little late to tour the unfinished house, Liam aimed for the most direct route to a public road. It might not stop the old man, but it would slow him down if they encountered traffic. Franks was careful not to tangle with the law if he didn't have to.

"Probably just a warning shot," Liam guessed with feigned confidence.

After what felt like hours but had likely only been a couple of minutes, Liam's tires hit pavement. He sped down the road, passing a couple of cars and a slow-moving fifth wheel. Any hint of the old red truck faded away.

"I'll take my necklace now," said Tessa, her breaths as heavy as his.

He fished the heart-shaped pendant out of his pocket and placed it in her hand. This wasn't at all how he imagined tonight going. Days ago, he planned something more romantic. Meaningful. He almost told her.

"I'm still going to show you the house," he said. "We just have to take the longest way to get there now." He cut across on a road that snaked behind Sunset Ridge. Trying to cut through town while it was overpopulated would only slow them even more.

He yearned to hold her hand, but his were still shaking from the pursuit. He didn't want Tessa to know how rattled that encounter made him. He used the drive to even his breathing and soon enough, he turned down the main drive to the plot of land that would soon be home.

The sun fought its way through heavy cloud cover, almost a positive omen that they were in the exact place they needed to be. Amazing how they could still feel that way about each other after all this time. It conjured such powerful emotions just being in each other's presence.

"C'mon."

"It looks a little muddy." Tessa glanced down at her boots.

"You and those boots." If Liam could convince her to stay, the first thing they were doing was flying to Anchorage to find her practical shoes. Ones that meshed well with the Alaskan environment. He'd buy her five pairs.

"I'm afraid they're just going to get dirty, sweetheart." He hopped out of the truck, happy he left Raven with his sister today. She didn't much care for sitting in the truck when they were out here, and he didn't need a muddy dog to hose down later.

"When did you—"

Liam took her hand, silencing her with a gentle kiss that stirred his soul. "Let me show you what the future could hold." He led her to the front of the house, where the entry door would be installed in a few weeks. "Ready for a tour?"

"Liam—"

He scooped her into his arms, and she let out a squeal. "I know it's not a threshold yet, but use your imagination." Setting her back on her feet, he led her from room to imaginary room, even though they were standing on the floor of the crawlspace. "The living room will have all windows in the front, over-looking the bay." He pointed.

"Your plane. And the view!" Tessa's hands clapped over her mouth as her eyes widened. He followed her gaze out to the water, the feeling never fading no matter how many times he took in the sight of the blue water and mountains. It was like looking at a photograph in a travel magazine.

"We always talked about building a house on the water, remember?" he asked.

Tears sprang to the corners of her eyes. "This is *our* house, isn't it?"

"Yes."

"You remembered. After all this time?"

"C'mon. Let me show you the rest. We still have to go upstairs—wait until you see the master bedroom."

"Liam, wait."

Fear prickled his chest at her tone. He didn't expect to like what she was going to say. "Let me go first." If the house wasn't enough, maybe his words would change her mind.

She fiddled with the necklace in her palm. "Okay."

"Here, let me put that back where it belongs." He fished the jewelry out of her tightly clenched palm and strung it around her neck. The hair he brushed out of the way was longer than it had been those years ago, but still had that vanilla scent. She shivered at the graze of his fingers. "Tessa, I don't want you to leave. Not this time."

He waited as she faced him. "I didn't win."

"Then why—"

"My ex framed me for cheating, and I haven't been able to prove I didn't do it."

Liam let the pieces fall together, though they didn't land in a complete picture. Just glimpses. *An ex. Cheating. Didn't win*. If they booted her for cheating, how could she possibly expect to go back? He searched her dim eyes for the answer, and then it came to him. "You've been waiting for them to make it right."

"They're not going to." Despite her pasted-on smile, tears threatened the corners of Tessa's eyes. "You'd think living in New York would've toughened me up, but I guess not." She laughed and gave the tiniest of shrugs. "The reality is that a lot of people don't play fair."

Liam was a mixture of relieved and infuriated. He closed the distance between them and drew her into his arms. She fit so comfortably in his embrace. He couldn't imagine a life where this wasn't something he could experience every day. "You don't deserve this, Tess. I'm so sorry."

"Me, too."

He wanted to know more about this ex. He'd like to wring the guy's neck. He'd bet his new house that it was the weasel Derek from the show. If that snake won the whole thing—

"Well, it gets better."

Liam tensed at the apprehension in her tone. He took a small step back so they could look each other in the eye, leaving his hands resting on her arms. "What do you mean?"

"They're supposed to call me any day and tell me I have to show up for season two."

Words didn't form, because Liam was waiting for Tessa to correct herself. No way she said that right. But when she didn't, he said, "They don't *own* you, Tess." No reality show could own people the way the military did once that contract was signed.

"Their contract apparently claims that they do." She shook her head, but the worry lines faded from her forehead and around her eyes. She tried to curl those lips into half a smile, and it almost stuck. "Coming here was the best thing I ever did. If I'd stayed in Vegas, waited it out . . ." She ran a finger along the necklace, moving the heart back and forth.

Something she used to do a lot after he first gave it to her. "Cadence found Mr. Jenkins at the festival. I'm going full grizzly."

Liam finally felt it was okay to laugh. Safe, even. "So, you're staying?"

"That's the plan." She reached for his hands, wrapping her fingers tightly around his. She waited until he locked their gazes. "Liam, I don't know how that call will go. I might have to go along with what they want. I met with Mr. Jenkins after Cadence hunted him down. He still has to review the document, but he thinks I have a pretty solid defense."

"That sounds promising."

"These producers only care about ratings. They'll play dirty to win. The lodge is one of my assets now. I won't put it at risk if I have to make that choice."

Liam could read between the lines. They could try to use the lodge as ammunition against her. And if she lost in court, they might lose the lodge. The *Whitmore family* would lose the lodge. "Wow."

"Yeah, so there's that. Liam—"

"I did watch the show, you know. Every episode." The words blurted before he could rein them in, but it felt good to have that off his chest. He'd hate it if Tessa was forced to go back, but he wasn't going to leave anything unsaid. "I've never stopped loving you, Tessa. All these years, you're the only one I've wanted in my life." He brushed back a lock of hair, tucking it behind her ear. "I want you to win, but I also want you to lose. I want you to come home. To *our* home."

CHAPTER EIGHTEEN

Tessa

Rather than return to the Blueberry Festival, Tessa and Liam opted to hide away at the lodge. They needed to check on Raven anyway—the excuse they gave everyone else. "Plus there's a rerun on tonight," Liam said to Tessa, wiggling his eyebrows until she laughed. If time was against them, Tessa would rather spend it alone than with a crowd of people who no doubt wanted a picture or for her to let them in on secrets she couldn't—and wouldn't—share.

Tessa dug a crocheted blanket out of the den closet and carried it to the couch. Raven's tail wagged at the prospect of snuggling with them. "I can think of more exciting things to do than watch my own show."

"But look at it from my point of view; I get exclusive bonus commentary." Liam snuck in a quick kiss on her cheek, pulling her toward him by her hands. "You can tell me all the little secrets. I want to know the things the cameras don't show."

Tessa rolled her eyes at him. "I'm not supposed to talk about the show. At all. Blame Mr. Jenkins. He thinks they could use that against me."

"Oh, come on. I have to know about some of these people. I'm invested."

"Fine."

They snuggled up together on the couch, wrapped in a blanket. Raven dozed, content to lay on Tessa's feet and keep them warm. "I can't believe you talked me into this," Tessa said.

The episode was from the other night—the one she caught Liam sleeping through.

"Start dishing, sweetheart."

It felt freeing to talk about the show as if it wasn't some quarter-of-a-million-dollar threat. Tessa told Liam about the different contestants—their real cooking skills, bad habits, and true personalities. "Barry—that guy is the *worst* whiner. I know sometimes they make things dramatic for TV, but I think they underplayed his true potential. He kept blaming the scallops, like they were the ones cooking wrong."

"How did he make it into the top eight?"

"I think it was sheer dumb luck." Tessa didn't tell him that Barry wouldn't progress beyond this week. The final eight would get a pass at elimination this episode, but Barry would get the boot on the next one. She didn't want to spoil all the surprises. "I suspect they might've rigged a couple of the contests. Not for certain people to win or anything like that. But staged things to go wrong."

"I'll never watch another challenge the same," Liam said overdramatically.

"Barry never seemed to encounter any of those, and I think it saved him." Tessa found she quite enjoyed talking about the show, as if it was something she'd already put behind her. Two weeks ago, running that restaurant in Vegas was her chief aspiration—it was the only thing that mattered. Now, she didn't even want it. Under this blanket with Liam, and Raven on her feet, that was what she wanted.

She wanted to stay.

The dining addition to the lodge wouldn't be a quick or easy transition. But Tessa was excited to have a new challenge. She'd banked enough savings to start something small without touching the reserved funds. And she had no doubt her sisters would back her idea. Best of all, it was something they could work on together, as a team.

"I've always thought Derek was a weasel." Liam pointed to the TV. "He's always watching what everyone else is doing. Hardly knows how to pay attention to his own tasks."

"Yeah, he's a real piece of work."

"The ex?"

"Not my brightest moment," admitted Tessa. "But

that's in the past. I don't even care how he did it anymore. I just want this to be over." She hoped freedom was simply one tough phone call away.

"I want that, too," said Liam. "I only wish it wasn't this way. You deserved your shot."

Liam's phone buzzed in his jeans, which was just as well. Tessa was done talking about Derek and all the things she wanted to leave behind. They could joke about the show, and she could tell Liam about the few *good* memories she did have. Like the helicopter ride over the city. Or the spa day. If there was one thing *Order Up* got right, it was their rewards.

"We have to go." Liam rocketed up on the couch, bringing Tessa with him. "April's in labor."

Tessa'd only visited the single-story Sunset Ridge General Hospital once before, after a nasty cut on her arm required stitches; her first attempt at sneaking out a second-story window had been unsuccessful. It was smaller than Tessa remembered, but it had a room dedicated to labor and delivery.

"Thanks for staying," Liam told Tessa in the waiting room. The chairs were comfortable three hours ago, but the cushions had long since lost their appeal. "I know she told us to go home, but since Miles can't be here . . ."

Tessa reached her hand over and grabbed his. "We should be here. Just in case."

Liam stared at her so long Tessa felt herself blush. But the second she turned her gaze away, he asked, "You know why I joined the Army, right?"

"I didn't at first," admitted Tessa. "But I figured it out." The younger she was back then, the easier it was to stay mad at Liam and act like he took the choice from her. But as she grew up, the truth was too clear to argue. "You knew I wouldn't go to culinary school—or New York, or anywhere else—if I stayed."

"I didn't want you to resent me five, ten, or twenty years later, for holding you back."

She wished she could tell Liam he was wrong, but he wasn't. Tessa would've been over the moon for the first few years, but over time she would have wondered what opportunities she had missed out on. "I wish you didn't have to give up eight years of your life."

Liam shrugged. "It started out as two, actually. Ended up kind of liking it."

Liam's mom, Jolene, appeared in the waiting area, ending their conversation. "Well, she's resting best as she can right now. It probably won't be long." If there was anyone still resentful about Liam's time away in the service, it was his mom. Until tonight, Tessa had managed to avoid running into Jolene.

"Any word on Miles?"

"They can't spare him. There's no one to cover if he leaves early," Jolene said with a heavy sigh as she fell into a chair beside Liam. "He'll be back next Wednesday, as scheduled."

"We're here to help," said Tessa. "If you need anything."

"Thanks." Jolene's smile was forced, but it had already been a long evening.

"Why don't you go home and get some rest?" Liam suggested. "I'll call you if things start moving."

Jolene shook her head. "Your father just got Owen to bed. I'm not going to chance waking that kid up."

"His lack-of-sleep tantrums are legendary in Sunset Ridge," Liam said to Tessa.

"I wish he was kidding," Jolene added. "I'll stay for a while yet. I feel better being here."

Maybe past transgressions could be forgiven. Tessa loved Liam, completely. And starting a life with him meant starting one with his family, too. This easy conversation with a woman who used to glare at her every chance she had gave Tessa hope she could be accepted by the Davies clan.

About to offer to retrieve coffee, Tessa's phone buzzed on the seat next to her. She showed the screen to Liam, as shocked as him at the Las Vegas area code at ten-thirty on a Saturday night. "Reality TV never sleeps, I guess. I'll be right back."

Despite how exhausted she felt, Tessa found an empty private waiting room, steeled herself, and answered.

"Tessa Whitmore?"

"Yes."

Great. Ron. This particular producer had rubbed her the wrong way since day one. Obnoxious, telling jokes in poor taste only people who wanted to suck up to him found funny. Always interjecting ideas to stir up drama. *The viewers are gonna love this!* was Ron's favorite phrase.

"Ron Pearson. How you doing?"

"Have you called to tell me you're going to clear my name?" Grizzly bears didn't waste time with pleasantries when a threat lingered. Tessa wouldn't either.

Ron gave that obnoxious laugh. "You know we can't look the other way about that matter."

"You mean the truth—*that I didn't cheat*—isn't good for ratings."

His laugh turned uneasy, and Ron cleared his throat. When he spoke again, he used his authoritative tone everyone hated. "Tessa, it's your handwriting. You even admitted it was your recipe card."

Tessa bit her tongue before she said one of many things Mr. Jenkins warned her against. "What do you want?"

"To give you a chance at redemption. Join us for season two, Tessa."

"No."

"I was hoping you would be excited for the opportunity."

Tessa paced the small space, but she wouldn't let any shred of doubt cause her to back down. If they wanted to call her a grizzly bear, then she would be one to the fullest extent. "I'd be excited if you cleared my name. On season *one*."

"That's not possible. And I'm afraid you signed a contract that doesn't give you the option to turn down a follow-up season. Unless you've contracted a highly contagious disease or have since passed away, you'll need to be in Vegas in two weeks."

"I read it."

"Good, good. Then you know——"

"So did my lawyer."

Silence lingered from the other end, causing Tessa to smile victoriously. It wasn't easy to render Ron Pearson speechless, but if she'd managed it, that contract was as flimsy as Mr. Jenkins suggested.

"I'm not coming back. If you have a problem with that, you can contact my lawyer."

"I didn't want to take this to court . . ."

Mr. Jenkins also warned her they would use scare tactics to avoid legal fees and potential messy press. "If that episode airs—and you know the one I'm talking about—I'm going to take your show to court, Mr. Pearson, for slandering my name. You haven't been able to show me one shred of *actual* evidence."

"Let's not be rash, Ms. Whitmore."

"Rash?" Tessa let out an incredulous laugh. Had Mr. Jenkins been present, he might have advised her not to comment, but Tessa couldn't help herself. "You're going to play me off as some cheater to boost your ratings. I don't know if you read your contract, Mr. Pearson, but you kicked me off the show under those false pretenses. You didn't have proof that I planted the recipe." She almost launched into her theory about Derek, but she'd been advised that speculation would likely be turned against her.

"Maybe we can work out an arrangement."

CHAPTER NINETEEN

Tessa

Tessa stayed at the hospital with Liam until the last possible minute. "Am I making the wrong decision?" she asked at the front door. April was expected to be ready any time, but Tessa had a plane to catch. They'd already talked about this at length, how the producers offered to let her come back and compete in the final challenge and clear her name if she agreed not to sue them. But leaving still felt . . . wrong. "I can call them back—"

Liam drew her into his arms and kissed her forehead. "You'll always wonder, Tessa. That's why you have to go."

Ron Pearson had offered a compromise—one texted with a legally binding document that had Mr. Jenkins' stamp of approval. Tessa'd return to compete for the finale, replacing Derek. Seemed the producers realized their viewers weren't rooting for him anyway, and they were more than thrilled for him to get booted right before he expected to take the victory. Ron had a whole plan to maximize the drama.

"I hate this reality TV drama," Tessa mumbled into Liam's chest. She didn't want to win, but she was too competitive to throw the final challenge on purpose. "I won't be able to call for a while."

"I know."

Mr. Jenkins had countered that after this final challenge and a few days for interviews and press releases, Tessa was released of any and all future obligations for *Order Up*, whether she won or lost. They could ask her to make a guest appearance if they covered all of her travel expenses, but they couldn't mandate it.

Cadence honked her horn outside. In almost any other place, idling outside the hospital's main entrance might've gotten her sister ticketed or towed. Certainly in New York or Vegas. But in Sunset Ridge, no one seemed to notice. "I guess it's time."

Liam dug into his jeans pocket, and pulled out a set of keys. "She's like new. No one will ever know."

Tessa tried so hard to steel her emotions, just as she'd managed for years through all kinds of frustration, heartbreak, and stress. But a tiny fear pricked her heart that she might never see Liam again, and it was too much to hold back. "I can call them back," she said again.

"You have to go. We both know that."

He swept his hand along her cheek, drawing her in for a deep kiss. Her entire body responded, tingling clear into her toes and fingertips. *Home*. Liam felt like home. *I'll come back*. She didn't dare speak the promise out loud. "I love you."

"I love you, Tess. Now, go."

She hurried out the door and into the waiting car before she lost her nerve.

After too many hugs, tears, well wishes, and pleas to come back from both her sisters, her niece, and Raven, Tessa hurried out the door before she lost her nerve. Her suitcases were loaded in the trunk, and Sophie had packed her a snack for the road. But Tessa still hesitated on the front deck of the lodge. If she didn't get on the road she'd miss her flight for sure. As it was, she'd have to use the Mustang's V8 engine to navigate around leisurely tourists on the Seward Highway.

If someone had told her several weeks ago when Mr. Jenkins first read Great-Aunt Patty's will that she would want to make the lodge a permanent part of her life, she would've laughed it off.

"Ed?" Tessa called out, wishing the moose would make one last appearance. It felt like unfinished business to leave Sunset Ridge and not see him once more. "I hear you're pretty good at stopping people from leaving."

She waited until one minute turned into three.

But Ed didn't come.

Tessa stood behind a kitchen counter in the open warehouse that had served all the show's main challenges, outside of dinner services and off-site competitions. Her opponent—the well-deserving Francine —stood beside her, behind her own counter. They waited on the cameras to find their preferred angles and the lighting to be adjusted.

The moment Tessa had arrived at the baggage claim, her phone was confiscated. Luckily, she'd managed a text to Liam and her sisters when the plane landed to let them know she arrived safety. And she received a message during her flight, announcing April had a healthy baby girl—Patricia Jo Averetts.

"Almost ready, ladies."

Tessa'd been rushed by limo to the studio, a microphone attached to her shirt the second Janet greeted her inside. On the short drive, Janet gave Tessa a rundown of the day's packed events. Everything happened so fast she didn't even have time to talk to Francine or wish her luck.

After the cue, both women stood with their hands behind their backs and looked toward the stage in front of their workstations. The star chef stepped onto the platform, but Tessa tuned out most of what he rambled on about. Her mind was still in Sunset Ridge, wishing she had a chance to hold Patricia before she left.

"Our final challenge is simple," said the celebrity chef. Tessa's attention tuned back in. Nothing was ever *simple*. There was always a catch. "You have to prepare two things: clam chowder and apple pie. You have one hour."

The clam chowder—in the bag. But the dessert . . . *A stupid pie*.

CHAPTER TWENTY

Liam

The days dragged out longer since Tessa left. After thirteen years apart without contact, Liam thought he could handle a couple of weeks of radio silence. But the truth was, he hated every minute of it.

Bells jingled overhead as Liam entered Davies Hardware and Electrical Supply, cup of recommended coffee in hand. "Hey, Dad." It was time to take the first step in repairing their once close relationship. He'd been putting this off for far longer than April called him out on.

"Come in here to buy something?"

Liam left the coffee on the front counter, scanning a nearby shelf. He could never have enough wood screws, he figured. He grabbed a bucket of a thousand and set it next to the coffee. "You know why I did it, don't you? Why I kept Grandpa's shop?"

Harold scanned the bucket of screws. "Twenty-two eighty-nine."

Liam fished cash out of his wallet and handed it over. "I'm good with cars. Good with motors." Never mind that Grandpa left the shop to him in his will. Liam couldn't sleep at night if he sold it.

"Plenty of that knowledge would be useful in here."

"Some." But Liam didn't know a lot about building things or running electrical wire. He could figure out his way around a power drill or nail gun if someone showed him. But not the same way he could take apart a motor and put it back together. He almost said all this to his dad, but Liam didn't have a lot of fight left in him. Tonight was the finale episode. The one they all expected to see Tessa reappear on. "Coming to the lodge later?" he asked.

"We'll see."

"Be good to support the Whitmore sisters," he added. Liam lifted the bucket of screws off the counter and turned toward the door. He wouldn't sort all this out with his dad in one conversation. It would take time. "See you later, Dad. Enjoy the coffee."

"You love her, don't you?"

The words came as a surprise. Harold had always liked Tessa, and Liam was mostly dumbfounded his dad hadn't set aside his grudge toward Liam to see her while she was in town. "Very much."

"I hope she comes back, son."

"Me, too."

———

Liam carried the flatscreen TV from the den out into the lodge's main open area to accommodate the turnout of Tessa supporters. Half a dozen people were sitting on the floor as it was. He stood, too nervous to sit. Raven sensed it, too. She kept right on his heel each time he shifted and found a new spot.

"What do you think the final challenge is?" Sophie asked, coming to stand beside him. Her daughter had burrowed a spot on the floor up front with Owen.

"I don't know, but I hope there's a pie."

"I think we all do."

When *Order Up: Las Vegas* began, the room fell quiet. No one knew how they would introduce this big, dramatic change because the last episode that aired only two days ago named Francine and Derek as the final two contestants. There'd been a small hint at a huge twist, but nothing more.

"Have you heard from her at all?" Liam asked Sophie.

"No."

"I didn't think it would be this long," he admitted.

"Me, either. But they might've asked her to wait until the last episode aired. I think she rattled more than a few cages when she consulted Mr. Jenkins." Sophie gave him a wink, and they both laughed.

The first part of the episode revealed never-before-seen camera footage of Derek planting a recipe card on Tessa's station. Liam balled his fists at his sides, certain they had that all along and didn't care about doing the right thing—or what with-holding it put their best contestant through. When the star chef of the show asked Derek to leave, the weaselly man had a full, embarrassing meltdown that had the group rolling in laughter.

"Never liked that guy," muttered Liam. "One bit."

"It's Aunty Tessa! It's Aunty Tessa!" Caroline pointed from her spot right up front. A few people clapped; one even whistled.

It touched Liam how many people were here—not only the usual suspects like Ford and his sister Rilee, but other locals who'd no doubt tasted that chowder.

Liam couldn't tear his eyes away. The two weeks they'd been apart felt far longer than the thirteen uncertain years they went separate ways. She had all that stage makeup on again, but it was the twinkle in her eyes that reassured him she was still the same person; he hadn't lost her yet.

"Clam chowder?" Sophie said, stirring him from his thoughts.

"You've got to be kidding me." *She'll never be back.* Liam's heart sank, certain Tessa would ace this chal-lenge. He'd sampled Tessa's chowder the night before the festival. The voters weren't wrong. It was the best chowder he ever had. He'd heard that sentiment from dozens of people since.

"Aha!" said Sophie. "She has to bake an apple pie. There's no way she pulls that off."

"All within an hour." Liam hated that he wanted her to both win and lose. If she won, she'd promised to turn down the job offer that was her prize: head chef in an elite restaurant. But he didn't want Tessa to give that up just for him.

The crowded room remained enraptured by the competition. The two very talented chefs worked meticulously as the clock ticked down. Their viewers were unable to tear their gazes away until commercial breaks. Speculation rumbled throughout the group; both contestants appeared to have a solid plan. Neither woman seemed rattled, though the producers did their best to add little moments of drama. When Francine dropped her bowl of cubed potatoes and was forced to start over, Liam wondered whether it was real or staged.

"Did she put in red pepper flakes?" Sophie asked.

"Not sure," said Liam. "But I bet she did. She doesn't forget stuff like that."

"You're right."

After more than an hour of agonizing suspense—the final episode was ninety minutes long instead of the usual sixty—the timer buzzed. The head chef had mostly positive comments for Francine's dishes. *Flaky crust on the pie. Perfect blend of flavors. Apples could be cooked a hair longer. Chowder superbly seasoned. Clams cooked to perfection.*

As Tessa carried her tray up to the stage, Liam noticed that she didn't look quite the grizzly bear they portrayed her to be on the rest of the season. She seemed . . . nervous. Not once had they ever captured her as anything but confident and collected. "Superb chowder. Decent blend of flavors. The clams are cooked perfectly. But there's something missing. The wow-factor. Shame, too. Your pie is baked beautifully. One of the best apple pies I've ever tasted."

Liam and Sophie exchanged confused expressions.

"Did Tessa really just pull off the pie but *not* the chowder?" Sophie asked.

Liam walked off toward the kitchen, thirstier than he'd been all day. Or was that just nerves? "Red pepper flakes, Tessa?" he mumbled at the sink.

"You're right. I forgot the red pepper flakes." Tessa's voice, so close to him, didn't feel real. He'd been so focused on the woman on the TV screen, listening to her give interviews of things that would boost ratings but didn't really matter, that hearing her voice beside him gave him chills.

Liam hardly managed words at her unexpected presence. He thought there would at least be a phone call or a text before she returned. "Tessa, you're here?"

"Spoiler alert," she whispered, taking his hand in her own. "I don't win."

"Did you forget—" Liam wanted to ask if she'd

skipped the red pepper flakes on purpose, but the Tessa Whitmore he knew would never intentionally lose a competition, no matter what the stakes.

"It was a careless oversight. I couldn't seem to focus. All I could think about was . . . here." She met his eyes. "And you."

"You're back," he said.

"And I'm staying. For good."

"Staying."

"Yes, and I'm not going anywhere else. Being without you isn't a fate I can live with, Liam. I want to start a life together. I really like that living room view of the bay." Seemed she realized he was still too stunned to form words, and she went on. "When you have time, I was hoping you'd meet me in Anchorage with the plane so I can drop off the rental car."

Liam let out a gentle laugh at that. Relishing the last few moments before rumor that she was back traveled like a wildfire through the other room. He drew Tessa into his embrace, memorizing the way she fit perfectly in his arms. "Why didn't you call me to come get you this time?"

"And miss making an entrance?"

"I shouldn't have expected anything less." Liam caught a glimpse of eyes through the kitchen window and nodded toward the sink. "Looks like someone else is glad you're back, too."

"*Now* he shows up." Tessa turned her head over her shoulder at the moose. "You'll just have to wait for the goods, mister." She drew her hand to Liam's cheek, combing her fingers over the beard she'd come to love—and miss—so much. Such love lingered in the gaze between them. It reassured Tessa that she was right where she was meant me to be. "Ed's waiting on me. You going to kiss me now or what?"

EPILOGUE

DENVER

"Hold on tight to that cake," Tillie Grant said to her son. "Can't be dropping the crown jewel of the party, now."

Denver steadied his arms stretched beneath the decorated sheet cake—baked into the shape of a moose—as they trekked cautiously down the sloped gravel drive toward the Sunset Ridge Lodge. He'd take a bullet before he let anything happen to Sophie's daughter's birthday cake. "I've got it, Mom."

"I know you do." She gave him a smile, but it didn't reach her sullen eyes. He closed on his house less than a week ago, but as far as Mom seemed to be concerned, he'd abandoned her and moved to another state. Never mind the *three* family dinners she hosted this week alone.

"You know I'm only five minutes away."

She patted his forearm gently as they stepped onto the hardpacked dirt trail that snaked its way to the kitchen entrance of the lodge. "It was just nice having you home after all this time."

If he didn't have his hands full with precious cargo, Denver would've wrapped her in another hug. He'd given them out in surplus this week. "I'm *still* home." He loved his mom dearly, but where she was social, Denver was introverted. He preferred working quietly on his mystery novels to endless conversation about the goings-on in town.

His new house was quiet, and he loved it.

"Four *years*, Denver."

He swallowed, certain nothing he could say would help. Yes, he enlisted in the Army right after college graduation, only weeks after losing his dad. At first, his commitment was intended to honor the Desert Storm veteran; he wanted to do something to make his dad proud. But in the midst of that goal, Denver forgot to come home for visits. "I bought a house. I'm not going anywhere."

On the top step, Mom stood at eye level and kissed his cheek. "Good. Let's get the cake inside."

Stepping inside, Denver's heart jackhammered in his chest. The sheet cake shook slightly in his hold, and he tightened his grip. He barely knew Sophie Whitmore, but there was something about her presence, her warm smile, and her kind eyes that rocked him to the core.

During his enlistment period, Denver had searched for the right woman to settle down and start a life with. But all he found was disappointment. He'd moved home a few weeks prior, content to settle into a quiet solo routine and finally accomplish his dream of becoming a published mystery author.

Until he met Sophie.

"I can't wait to see the cake." Tessa hurried over to him. "Tillie, it's perfect! Caroline is going to flip. Thank you so much for baking this."

Denver couldn't help stretch his neck around Tessa in search of Sophie. Not staying at his mom's house meant fewer excuses to see Sophie, and he wasn't sure what to do about it. He thought asking her to dinner might be a good place to start . . . or maybe to the Moose Days Festival.

"Set it over here," Tessa directed.

After the cake was safely on the counter, Denver meant to slip out of the kitchen, but Tessa shackled his arm with tight fingers. "I need to have a word with you." Her stern tone caused him to swallow.

He waited until Mom disappeared down the hall toward the party zone. "What about?"

"Sophie."

His heart pounded so loudly in his chest it was a wonder Tessa couldn't hear it. Or maybe she could.

"Look, I've seen the way you look at her. I think you're a nice guy, Denver, I really do. But my sister is still recovering from a nasty divorce. Caroline, too.

She needs time. She needs a *friend*. Do you get what I'm saying?"

He caught a glimpse of Sophie passing in the hall, completely unaware of him in the kitchen. His pulse raced. "A friend?" he repeated, digesting what this meant. No dinner dates, no romantic gestures, no stolen kisses. Any feelings he might have needed to be shoved down.

"*Just* friends. For now."

"Okay."

"I mean it." Tessa glanced over her shoulder at the doorway, likely ensuring they were still alone. "Be her friend, be kind, be someone she can trust. You try anything too soon, and you'll have to answer to me."

Maybe this way was better, for both of them. They could get to know each other and build a foundation. And being Sophie's friend was certainly better than not having her in his life at all. "Got it."

"Good. Now let's get to this party."

OTHER BOOKS BY JACQUELINE WINTERS

SWEET ROMANCE

Sunset Ridge Series
    1 - Moose Be Love
    2 - My Favorite Moosetake
    3 - Annoymoosely Yours

Starlight Cowboys Series
    1 - Cowboys & Starlight
    2 - Cowboys & Firelight
    3 - Cowboys & Sunrises
    4 - Cowboys & Moonlight
    5 - Cowboys & Mistletoe

Stand-Alone
    *Hooked on You

STEAMY ROMANTIC SUSPENSE

Willow Creek Series
    1 - Sweetly Scandalous
    2 - Secretly Scandalous
    3 - Simply Scandalous

Sign up for Jacqueline Winter's newsletter to receive alerts about current projects and new releases!

http://eepurl.com/du18iz

ABOUT THE AUTHOR

Jacqueline Winters has been writing since she was nine when she'd sneak stacks of paper from her grandma's closet and fill them with adventure. She grew up in small-town Nebraska and spent a decade living in beautiful Alaska. She writes sweet contemporary romance and contemporary romantic suspense.

She's a sucker for happily ever after's, has a sweet tooth that can be sated with cupcakes. On a relaxing evening, you can find her at her computer writing her next novel with her faithful dog poking his adorable nose over her keyboard.